SECRETS OF HEAVEN

SECRETS OF HEAVEN

The Portable New Century Edition

EMANUEL SWEDENBORG

Volume II

Translated from the Latin by Lisa Hyatt Cooper

SWEDENBORG FOUNDATION
Royersford, Pennsylvania

Originally published in Latin as *Arcana Coelestia,* London, 1749–1756. The volume contents of this and the original Latin edition, along with ISBNs of the annotated version, are as follows:

Volume number in this edition	Text treated	Volume number in the Latin first edition	Section numbers	ISBN (hardcover)
1	Genesis 1–8	1	§§1–946	978-0-87785-486-9
2	Genesis 9–15	1	§§947–1885	978-0-87785-487-6
3	Genesis 16–21	2 (in 6 fascicles)	§§1886–2759	978-0-87785-488-3
4	Genesis 22–26	3	§§2760–3485	978-0-87785-489-0
5	Genesis 27–30	3	§§3486–4055	978-0-87785-490-6
6	Genesis 31–35	4	§§4056–4634	978-0-87785-491-3
7	Genesis 36–40	4	§§4635–5190	978-0-87785-492-0
8	Genesis 41–44	5	§§5191–5866	978-0-87785-493-7
9	Genesis 45–50	5	§§5867–6626	978-0-87785-494-4
10	Exodus 1–8	6	§§6627–7487	978-0-87785-495-1
11	Exodus 9–15	6	§§7488–8386	978-0-87785-496-8
12	Exodus 16–21	7	§§8387–9111	978-0-87785-497-5
13	Exodus 22–24	7	§§9112–9442	978-0-87785-498-2
14	Exodus 25–29	8	§§9443–10166	978-0-87785-499-9
15	Exodus 30–40	8	§§10167–10837	978-0-87785-500-2

ISBN of e-book of library edition, vol. 11: 978-0-87785-743-3
ISBN of Portable Edition, vol. 11, containing translation only: 978-0-87785-438-8
ISBN of e-book of Portable Edition, vol. 11: 978-0-87785-742-6

(The ISBN in the Library of Congress data shown below is that of volume 1.)

Library of Congress Cataloging-in-Publication Data

Swedenborg, Emanuel, 1688–1772.
[Arcana coelestia. English]
Secrets of heaven / Emanuel Swedenborg ; translated from the Latin by Lisa Hyatt Cooper. — Portable New Century ed.
p. cm.
Includes bibliographical references and indexes.
ISBN 978-0-87785-408-1 (alk. paper)
1. New Jerusalem Church—Doctrines. 2. Bible. O.T. Genesis—Commentaries—Early works to 1800. 3. Bible. O.T. Exodus—Commentaries—Early works to 1800. I. Title.
BX8712.A8 2010
230'.94—dc22

2009054171

Ornaments from the first Latin edition, 1749–1756
Text designed by Joanna V. Hill
Senior copy editor, Alicia L. Dole
Typesetting by Mary M. Wachsmann and Sarah Dole
Cover design by Karen Connor
Cover photograph by Magda Indigo

Further information about the New Century Edition of the Works of Emanuel Swedenborg can be obtained directly from the Swedenborg Foundation, 70 Buckwalter Road, Suite 900 PMB 405, Royersford, PA 19468 U.S.A.
Telephone: (610) 430-3222 • Web: www.swedenborg.com • E-mail: info@swedenborg.com

Contents

Volume 11

Exodus Chapter 12

Exodus Chapter 13

Exodus Chapter 14

Exodus Chapter 15

Conventions Used in This Work

MOST of the following conventions apply generally to the translations in the New Century Edition Portable series. For introductory material on the content and history of *Secrets of Heaven,* and for annotations on the subject matter, including obscure or problematic content, and extensive indexes, the reader is referred to the Deluxe New Century Edition volumes.

Volume designation *Secrets of Heaven* was originally published in eight volumes; in this edition all but the second original volume have been divided into two. Thus Swedenborg's eight volumes now fill fifteen volumes, of which this is the eleventh. It corresponds to approximately the second half of Swedenborg's volume 6.

Section numbers Following a practice common in his time, Swedenborg divided his published theological works into sections numbered in sequence from beginning to end. His original section numbers have been preserved in this edition; they appear in boxes in the outside margins. Traditionally, these sections have been referred to as "numbers" and designated by the abbreviation "n." In this edition, however, the more common section symbol (§) is used to designate the section numbers, and the sections are referred to as such.

Subsection numbers Because many sections throughout Swedenborg's works are too long for precise cross-referencing, Swedenborgian scholar John Faulkner Potts (1838–1923) further divided them into subsections; these have since become standard, though minor variations occur from one edition to another. These subsections are indicated by bracketed numbers that appear in the text itself: [2], [3], and so on. Because the beginning of the first *subsection* always coincides with the beginning of the *section* proper, it is not labeled in the text.

Citations of Swedenborg's text As is common in Swedenborgian studies, text citations of Swedenborg's works refer not to page numbers but to section numbers, which unlike page numbers are uniform in most editions.

In citations the section symbol (§) is generally omitted after the title of a work by Swedenborg. Thus "*Secrets of Heaven* 29" refers to section 29 (§29) of Swedenborg's *Secrets of Heaven,* not to page 29 of any edition. Subsection numbers are given after a colon; a reference such as "29:2" indicates subsection 2 of section 29. The reference "29:1" would indicate the first subsection of section 29, though that subsection is not in fact labeled in the text. Where section numbers stand alone without titles, their function is indicated by the prefixed section symbol; for example, "§29:2".

Citations of Swedenborg's unnumbered sections Some material in *Secrets of Heaven* was not given a section number. Swedenborg assigns no section numbers to his quoting of a biblical chapter before he takes up each verse in turn. He also gives no section numbers to occasional prefatory material, such as his author's table of contents in *Secrets of Heaven* (before §1), his prefaces to Genesis 16 and 18 (before §§1886 and 2135, respectively), and his preface to Genesis 22 (before §2760). The biblical material needs no section number, as it is referred to simply by chapter and verse. In this edition, references to the author's unnumbered prefaces follow these models: "(preface to Genesis 22)"; "see the preface to Genesis 18."

Citations of the Bible Biblical citations in this edition follow the accepted standard: a semicolon is used between book references and between chapter references, and a comma between verse references. Therefore "Matthew 5:11, 12; 6:1; 10:41, 42; Luke 6:23, 35" would refer to Matthew chapter 5, verses 11 and 12; Matthew chapter 6, verse 1; Matthew chapter 10, verses 41 and 42; and Luke chapter 6, verses 23 and 35. Swedenborg often incorporated the numbers of verses not actually represented in his text when listing verse numbers for a passage he quoted; these apparently constitute a kind of "see also" reference to other material he felt was relevant. This edition includes these extra verses and also follows Swedenborg where he cites contiguous verses individually (for example, John 14:8, 9, 10, 11), rather than as a range (John 14:8–11). Occasionally this edition supplies a full, conventional Bible reference where Swedenborg omits one after a quotation.

Quotations in Swedenborg's works Some features of the original Latin text of *Secrets of Heaven* have been modernized in this edition. For example, Swedenborg's first edition generally relies on context or italics rather than on quotation marks to indicate passages taken from the Bible or from other works. The manner in which these conventions are used in the original suggests that Swedenborg did not belabor the distinction between direct quotation and paraphrase; but in this edition, directly quoted material is indicated by either block quotations or quotation marks, and paraphrased material is usually presented without such indicators. In passages of dialog as well, quotation marks have been introduced that were not present as such in the original. Furthermore, Swedenborg did not mark his omissions from or changes to material he quoted, a practice in which this edition generally follows him. One exception consists of those instances in which Swedenborg did not include a complete sentence at the beginning or end of a Bible quotation. The omission in such cases has been marked in this edition with added points of ellipsis.

Special use of singular verbs Swedenborg sometimes uses a singular verb with certain dual subjects such as love and wisdom, goodness and truth, and love and charity. The wider context of his works indicates that his reason for doing so is that he understands the two given subjects as forming a unity. This translation generally preserves such singular verbs.

Special use of singular nouns In the Bible we often find references to a plural number of persons to which is ascribed a single personal feature, such as a *heart, soul, mind, face, body, head,* or *life;* indeed, we might well term this usage the *biblical singular.* Swedenborg generally adopted this usage, and not only in his Bible translations. It has often been retained in this edition. For an example, see *Secrets of Heaven* 5573:2: "They engaged in commerce only for the sake of their job in the world, and beyond that they did not set their heart on [riches]."

Italicized terms Any words in indented scriptural extracts that are here set in italics reflect a similar emphasis in the first edition.

Special use of vertical rule The opening passages of the early chapters of *Secrets of Heaven,* as well as the ends of all chapters, contain material that derives in some way from Swedenborg's experiences in the spiritual world. Swedenborg specified that the text of these and similar passages be set in continuous italics to distinguish it from exegetical and other material. For this edition, the heavy use of italic text was felt to be antithetical to modern tastes, as well as difficult to read, and so such passages are instead marked by a vertical rule in the margin.

Changes to and insertions in the text This translation is based on the first Latin edition, published by Swedenborg himself (1749–1756); it also reflects emendations in the third Latin edition, edited by P. H. Johnson, John E. Elliott, and others, and published by the Swedenborg Society

(1949–1973). It incorporates the silent correction of minor errors, not only in the text proper but in Bible verse references and in section references to this and other volumes of *Secrets of Heaven*. The text has usually been changed without notice where the verse numbering of the Latin Bible cited by Swedenborg differs from that of modern English Bibles. Throughout the translation, references or cross-references that were implied but not stated have been inserted in brackets; for example, [John 3:27]. In many cases, it is very difficult to determine what Swedenborg had in mind when he referred to other passages giving evidence for a statement or providing further discussion on a topic. Because of this difficulty, the missing references that are occasionally supplied in this edition should not be considered definitive or exhaustive. In contrast to such references in square brackets, references that occur in parentheses are those that appear in the first edition; for example, (1 Samuel 30:16), (see §42 above). Occasionally square brackets signal an insertion of other material that was not present in the first edition. These insertions fall into two classes: words likely to have been deleted through a copying or typesetting error, and words supplied by the translator as necessary for the understanding of the English text, though they have no direct parallel in the Latin. The latter device has been used sparingly, however, even at the risk of some inconsistency in its application. Unfortunately, no annotations concerning these insertions can be supplied in this Portable edition.

Biblical titles Swedenborg refers to Hebrew Scripture as the Old Testament and to Greek Scripture as the New Testament; his terminology has been adopted in this edition. As was the custom in his day, he refers to the Pentateuch (Genesis, Exodus, Leviticus, Numbers, and Deuteronomy) simply as "Moses"; for example, in §8017 he writes, "as can be seen in Moses," and then quotes a passage from Numbers. Similarly, in sentences or phrases introducing quotations he sometimes refers to the Psalms as "David," to Lamentations as "Jeremiah," and to the Gospel of John, the Epistles of John, and the Book of Revelation as simply "John." Conventional references supplied in parentheses after such quotations specify their sources more precisely.

Problematic content Occasionally Swedenborg makes statements that, although mild by the standards of eighteenth-century theological discourse, now read as harsh, dismissive, or insensitive. The most problematic are assertions about or criticisms of various religious traditions and their adherents—including Judaism, ancient or contemporary; Roman

Catholicism; Islam; and the Protestantism in which Swedenborg himself grew up. These statements are far outweighed in size and importance by other passages in Swedenborg's works earnestly maintaining the value of every individual and of all religions. This wider context is discussed in the introductions and annotations of the Deluxe edition mentioned above. In the present format, however, problematic statements must be retained without comment. The other option—to omit them—would obscure some aspects of Swedenborg's presentation and in any case compromise its historicity.

Allusive References in Expositional Material

Swedenborg's use of pronouns that refer back to vague or distant antecedents may cause confusion for readers. Such allusive references occur in two situations in his expositions:

In mentions of Jesus If the pronoun *he* without a nearby antecedent appears in a proposition, the reader can assume that it refers to Jesus, the main topic of the exegesis as a whole.

In preview material Swedenborg's preview sections (see the Deluxe edition of *Secrets of Heaven,* vol. 1, pages 30–35) feature a series of propositions, each of which consists of a phrase of biblical text followed by a brief assertion of its inner meaning. These glimpses of the inner meaning quite often use pronouns that point back to other inner meanings mentioned earlier in the preview section. For instance, in *Secrets of Heaven* volume 7, §4962, a preview section, we read this:

> *And Joseph* symbolizes spiritual heavenliness drawing on rationality. *Was taken down to Egypt* means to religious learning. *And Potiphar, Pharaoh's chamberlain, bought him* means that **it** had a place among items of inner knowledge. *The chief of the bodyguards* means **that** were of primary importance in interpretation. *An Egyptian man* symbolizes earthly truth.

The words "it" and "that" (shown here in boldface) are confusing: *What* had a place among items of inner knowledge? *What things* were of primary importance in interpretation? The answers lie in the fragments of inner meaning given in propositions earlier in the preview section: The "it" refers back to the "spiritual heavenliness" mentioned in the first proposition.

The referent of "that" is the "items of inner knowledge" mentioned at the end of the immediately preceding proposition. Thus Swedenborg has laid the propositions out in such a way that if put together, the five statements might read as follows:

> *And Joseph was taken down to Egypt, and Potiphar, Pharaoh's chamberlain, the chief of the bodyguards, an Egyptian man, bought him* means that spiritual heavenliness drawing on rationality was brought to religious learning and given a place among items of inner knowledge and earthly truth that were of primary importance in interpretation.

Secrets of Heaven

Exodus 9

Teachings on Neighborly Love

WHAT I have said about self-love and love of worldly advantages [§§7366–7377] makes it plain that they are the source of all evil; and since they are the source of all evil, they are the source of all falsity. By the same token, love for the Lord and love for one's neighbor are the source of everything good, and since they are the source of everything good, they are the source of all truth. 7488

This being so, it is clear that the more we love ourselves and our worldly advantages, the more we do not love our neighbor, let alone the Lord. These kinds of love are opposites. 7489

It is also clear that the more we love ourselves and our worldly advantages, the less we know what neighborly love is, until eventually we cease to know it exists. Likewise, we know less and less what faith is, until eventually we cease to know it is anything. Again, we know less and less what conscience is, until eventually we cease to know it exists. We even know less and less what the spiritual dimension is or what the life of heaven is. In the end we cease to believe that heaven exists or that hell exists, so we cease to believe that there is life after death. This is plainly the effect self-love and materialism produce when they are in charge. 7490

The goodness of heavenly love and the truth of a faith inspired by such love constantly flow in from the Lord, but they are not accepted where love for oneself and love for one's worldly advantages predominate. When these two kinds of love control us—when they live constantly in our thoughts, purposes, and intentions and make up our life—we reject, snuff out, or corrupt the goodness and truth flowing in from the Lord. 7491

Anyone who *rejects* a loving goodness and religious truth looks on them with contempt and loathing. Anyone who *snuffs out* a loving goodness and religious truth denies them and endorses evil and falsity, their opposites. Anyone who *corrupts* a loving goodness and religious truth misrepresents them and uses them to support evil and consequent falsity. 7492

Self-love and materialism begin to take over in us when we come into our own judgment and independence. After all, that is when we start to 7493 think for ourselves, and that is when we start to adopt such things as our own—which we do more and more as we increasingly commit ourselves to evil by the way we live.

The more we make evil our own, the more the Lord separates out innocent, charitable goodness and hides it away in our inner depths. (This goodness is something we received as babies and children and continue to receive from time to time later on.) He hides it away because a goodness marked by innocence or by neighborly love cannot possibly coexist with self-loving or materialistic evil, and the Lord does not want such goodness to be destroyed.

7494 People who corrupt, snuff out, or reject a loving goodness and religious truth in themselves, then, do not have life within them. Life, which comes from the Divine, is to will what is good and believe what is true, but people who will evil rather than goodness and believe falsity rather than truth have the opposite of life. The opposite of life is hell and is called death, and these people are described as dead.

Many passages in the Word demonstrate that a life of love and faith is called life and eternal life and that the people who have this kind of life in them are the living, while the opposite of life is called death and eternal death, and those people are the dead. Examples are Matthew 4:16; 8:21, 22; 18:8, 9; 19:16, 17, 29; John 3:15, 16, 36; 5:24, 25; 6:33, 35, 47, 48, 50, 51, 53, 57, 58, 63; 8:21, 24, 51; 10:10; 11:25, 26; 14:6, 19; 17:2, 3; 20:31; and other passages.

Exodus 9

1. And Jehovah said to Moses, "Come to Pharaoh, and you are to speak to him: 'This is what Jehovah, God of the Hebrews, has said: "Send my people away and let them serve me.

2. Because if you refuse to send them away and you still detain them,

3. watch: the hand of Jehovah will be on your livestock that is in the field, on horses, on donkeys, on camels, on the herd, and on the flock, a very heavy contagion.

4. And Jehovah will distinguish between the livestock of Israel and the livestock of the Egyptians, and out of all that belongs to the children of Israel none will die.'""

5. And Jehovah set a fixed time, saying, "Tomorrow Jehovah will do this thing in the land."

6. And Jehovah did this thing the next day. And all the Egyptians' livestock died. And out of the children of Israel's livestock not one died.

7. And Pharaoh sent, and here, not even one of Israel's livestock had died. And Pharaoh's heart turned leaden, and he did not send the people away.

8. And Jehovah said to Moses and to Aaron, "Take cinders from a furnace for yourselves by fistfuls. And have Moses scatter them toward the sky before Pharaoh's eyes.

9. And they will become dust on all the land of Egypt; and on humans and on animals they will become sores blooming with pimples in all the land of Egypt."

10. And they took the cinders from the furnace and stood before Pharaoh, and Moses scattered them toward the sky, and they became pimply sores blooming on humans and on animals.

11. And the magicians could not stand before Moses on account of the sores, because the sores were on the magicians and on all Egyptians.

12. And Jehovah hardened Pharaoh's heart, and he did not listen to them, as Jehovah had spoken to Moses.

13. And Jehovah said to Moses, "Get up early in the morning and stand before Pharaoh, and you are to say to him, 'This is what Jehovah, God of the Hebrews, has said: "Send my people away and let them serve me.

14. Because this time I am sending all my plagues onto your heart and onto your servants and onto your people, so that you may know that there is no one like me in the whole land.

15. Because now I would put out my hand and strike you and your people with the contagion and you would be cut off from the land.

16. However, for the sake of this I have let you remain: for the sake of your seeing my strength and in order that my name may be told in all the land.

17. You are still exalting yourself against my people by not sending them away.

18. Watch: at this time tomorrow I am raining down a very heavy hail such as has not existed in Egypt from the day it was founded until now.

19. And now send, gather your livestock and everything that is yours in the field. Every human and animal that is found in the field and is not gathered home—the hail will come down on them and they will die.'"'

20. And those of Pharaoh's servants who feared Jehovah's word made their servants and their livestock run to their homes.

21. And those who did not take Jehovah's word to heart left their servants and their livestock in the field.

22. And Jehovah said to Moses, "Stretch your hand out toward the sky, and there will be hail in all the land of Egypt, on humans and on animals and on all the grass of the field in the land of Egypt."

23. And Moses stretched his staff out to the sky, and Jehovah sent voices [of thunder] and hail, and fire went to the earth, and Jehovah rained hail on the land of Egypt.

24. And there was hail, and fire going with it in the middle of the hail, very heavy [hail], such as had not existed in all the land of Egypt from the time it turned into a nation.

25. And in all the land of Egypt the hail struck everything that was in the field, from humans even to animals; and the hail struck all the grass of the field and shattered every tree of the field.

26. Only in the land of Goshen, where the children of Israel were, was there no hail.

27. And Pharaoh sent and called Moses and Aaron and said to them, "I have sinned this time; Jehovah is in the right, and I and my people are in the wrong.

28. Plead to Jehovah, and let this be enough of God's voices [of thunder] and hail! And I will send you away, and you will no longer remain."

29. And Moses said to him, "When I leave the city, I will stretch my palms out to Jehovah, the voices [of thunder] will stop, and the hail will no longer come, so that you may know that the land is Jehovah's.

30. As for you and your servants, I know that you do not yet fear the face of Jehovah God."

31. And the flax and the barley were struck, because the barley was a ripening ear and the flax was a stalk.

32. But the wheat and the spelt were not struck, because they were hidden.

33. And Moses went out from Pharaoh, from the city, and stretched his palms out to Jehovah, and the voices [of thunder] and the hail stopped and rain did not pour on the earth.

34. And Pharaoh saw that the rain and the hail and the voices [of thunder] stopped, and he continued to sin, and he made his heart leaden, as did his servants.

35. And Pharaoh's heart hardened, and he did not send the children of Israel away, as Jehovah had spoken by the hand of Moses.

Summary

THIS chapter continues to focus on the devastation undergone by spirits who harass people of the spiritual church. The inner meaning 7495
of the chapter deals with the sixth, seventh, and eighth stages or steps in their devastation, which are depicted as *contagion, sores* blooming with pimples, and a *rain of hail.* These symbolize the devastation of any traces of religion they had had.

Inner Meaning

EXODUS 9:1–7. *And Jehovah said to Moses, "Come to Pharaoh, and you are to speak to him: 'This is what Jehovah, God of the Hebrews, has said: "Send my people away and let them serve me. Because if you refuse to send them away and you still detain them, watch: the hand of Jehovah will be on your livestock that is in the field, on horses, on donkeys, on camels, on the herd, and on the flock, a very heavy contagion. And Jehovah will distinguish between the livestock of Israel and the livestock of the Egyptians, and out of all that belongs to the children of Israel none will die."'" And Jehovah set a fixed time, saying, "Tomorrow Jehovah will do this thing in the land." And Jehovah did this thing the next day. And all the Egyptians' livestock died. And out of the children of Israel's livestock not one died. And Pharaoh sent, and here, not even one of Israel's livestock had died. And Pharaoh's heart turned leaden, and he did not send the people away.* 7496

And Jehovah said to Moses symbolizes being taught anew. *Come to Pharaoh, and you are to speak to him* symbolizes the manifestation of truth from the Divine among spirits who inflict harassment. *This is what Jehovah, God of the Hebrews, has said,* symbolizes a command from the Lord, the God of the church. *Send my people away and let them serve me* means to leave people of the spiritual church alone to worship the Lord. *Because if you refuse to send them away and you still detain them* means if the spirits still insisted obstinately on inflicting persecution. *Watch: the hand of Jehovah will be on your livestock that is in the field* means that they would be stripped of any religious truth and goodness they had from the church they had been part of. *On horses, on donkeys, on camels* symbolizes matters of the intellect and a knowledge of religious truth. *On the herd, and on the flock* symbolizes matters of the will. *A very heavy contagion* symbolizes widespread obliteration. *And Jehovah will distinguish between the livestock of Israel and the livestock of the Egyptians* symbolizes the difference between the religious truth and goodness of people in the spiritual church and religious truth and goodness as received from the church by the persecutors. *And out of all that belongs to the children of Israel none will die* means that they will not be obliterated. *And Jehovah set a fixed time* symbolizes a determination made ahead of time. *Saying, "Tomorrow Jehovah will do this thing in the land,"* means that this will be the spirits' permanent lot in regard to the true ideas and good desires characterizing the church's faith. *And Jehovah did this thing the next day* symbolizes bringing about what had been determined ahead of time. *And all the Egyptians' livestock died* symbolizes obliteration of religious truth and goodness among the persecutors. *And out of the children of Israel's livestock not one died* means that nothing of religion was obliterated among people of the spiritual church. *And Pharaoh sent, and here, not even one of Israel's livestock had died* means that this became known to the persecutors. *And Pharaoh's heart turned leaden* symbolizes obstinacy. *And he did not send the people away* means that they did not leave them alone.

7497 *And Jehovah said to Moses* symbolizes being taught anew, as before in §§6879, 6881, 6883, 6891, 7226, 7304, 7380.

7498 *Come to Pharaoh, and you are to speak to him* symbolizes the manifestation of truth from the Divine among spirits who inflict harassment, as the following shows: *Coming to* or approaching someone symbolizes presence, or visible manifestation, as discussed below. *Speaking* symbolizes communication. *Pharaoh* represents spirits who harass people of the spiritual church in the other life, as dealt with in §§7107, 7110, 7126, 7142, 7220, 7228, 7317. And Moses, who was to go in to Pharaoh and speak to him, represents truth imparted by the Divine, as dealt with in §§6771, 6827, 7014, 7382.

Coming to and approaching is presence, or visible manifestation, because in a spiritual sense it symbolizes a mental process. So it symbolizes something involving thought, and when thought is said to come to or approach someone, it means presenting that person to oneself; when we think about someone, we mentally set that person in our presence. In the other life, strange to say, anyone we think about from a wish to speak with her or him is actually presented to us. It is plain, then, that there is a similarity between our thoughts in this world and our in-person interactions in the other world. From this it can now be seen that coming to or approaching someone symbolizes presence, or visible manifestation.

This is what Jehovah, God of the Hebrews, has said, symbolizes a command from the Lord, who is the God of the church. This can be seen from the symbolism of *saying* as a command (noted in §§7036, 7107, 7310) and from that of *Hebrews* as people in the church and therefore as the church itself (discussed in §§5136, 5236, 6675, 6684, 6738). For the idea that where *Jehovah* is mentioned in the Word, it means the Lord, see §§1343, 1736, 2921, 3023, 3035, 5041, 5663, 6280, 6281, 6303, 6905, 6945, 6956. **7499**

In the Word, the Lord is called Jehovah in regard to divine goodness, because divine goodness is divinity itself. In regard to divine truth he is called the Son of God, because divine truth comes from divine goodness—just as the Son comes from the Father—and is likewise said to be born of it. I need to explain this further. When the Lord was in the world, he turned his human side into divine truth, and at that time he referred to divine goodness (Jehovah) as his Father, because as just mentioned, divine truth comes from divine goodness and is born of it. However, once the Lord had fully glorified himself (which happened when he had endured the final trial on the cross), he turned his human side into divine goodness as well, or Jehovah. Ever since, genuine divine truth has come from his divine humanity. This divine truth is what is called the Holy Spirit, and it is the holy influence of the divine humanity. This shows what is meant by the Lord's words in John:

> The Holy Spirit did not yet exist, because Jesus was not yet glorified. (John 7:39)

Concerning the idea that divine goodness is what is called the Father and divine truth is what is called the Son, see §3704.

7500 *Send my people away and let them serve me* means to leave people of the spiritual church alone to worship the Lord. This can be seen from the symbolism of *sending away* as leaving alone (mentioned many times before), from the representation of the children of Israel—*my people*—as members of the spiritual church (discussed in §§4286, 6426, 6637, 6862, 6868, 7035, 7062, 7198, 7201, 7215, 7223), and from the meaning of *let them serve me* as letting them worship the Lord. Serving obviously means worshiping, and Jehovah—the one they were to serve—is the Lord, as may be seen directly above at §7499.

7501 *Because if you refuse to send them away and you still detain them* means if the spirits still insisted obstinately on inflicting persecution, as the following shows: *Refusing* means obstinately insisting, so refusing *to send them away* means obstinately insisting on not leaving them alone. And *detaining them* means continuing to inflict persecution. People who are being persecuted, you see, are detained by the evil spirits persecuting them.

Let me explain how it is that victims of the persecution are detained by evil spirits. When evil spirits attack someone, they know how to worm their way into the pleasures that come of the person's urges and into the interests that develop out of the person's principles. So they know how to introduce themselves into anything the person loves. As long as they keep this up, they essentially hold the person they are persecuting hostage. No matter how hard the person struggles, he or she cannot escape without the Lord's divine help, because love [on the part of the victim] and infiltration into a beloved pleasure [by the persecutors] unite [the two parties]. This is a device used by evil spirits and demons in the other life.

The same thing is illustrated in the world when one person finds a way into another's pleasures and passions, holds that other captive, and leads the other around at will.

7502 *Watch: the hand of Jehovah will be on your livestock that is in the field* means that they would be stripped of any religious truth and goodness they had from the church they had been part of, as the following shows: *Jehovah's hand* on someone symbolizes a punishing blow. After all, a hand symbolizes power (§§4931–4937, 6292, 6947, 7188, 7189), and Jehovah's hand symbolizes omnipotence (§§878, 3387). It appears as though all blows of punishment come from Jehovah, and people who are superficially religious believe in this appearance, since they ascribe everything to his power. So Jehovah's hand on someone symbolizes a punishment. Here it symbolizes the process of devastation, because the different steps of devastation undergone by the persecutors were punishments. *Livestock* symbolizes religious truth and goodness, as discussed in §§6016, 6045, 6049. And a *field* symbolizes the church, as discussed in §§2971, 3310. A field means the church for two reasons. One is that the seed put into a field symbolizes the true ideas composing faith. The other is that the crops produced by a field—wheat, barley, spelt, and so on—are neighborly love with its good desires and faith with its true ideas, and are therefore attributes of the church.

[2] Why is it that hellish spirits who trouble the upright in the next life are purged of the religious truth taught by the church? Remember that spirits who harass the upright in the next life are individuals who were part of the church while they lived in the world. People who were not in the church cannot harass others who *were* in the church, because the means of persecution are falsities that go against the church's religious truth. People who were outside the church cannot harass anyone with this kind of falsity because they were unacquainted with it. In the other world, people who claimed to have faith and yet lived an evil life resort to falsity and harass the upright (see §§7097, 7127, 7317). The religious truth they gleaned from the teachings of their church when they lived in the world is capable of lending them a bit of heavenly light. (Everything they knew during bodily life they take with them to the next life. Nothing is missing.) And they are capable of using what they see by this light to justify falsity and evil, which belong to hell. To guard against such a danger, then, all resources of this kind are taken from them, until in the end they are left to the evils of the life they lived and to the resulting falsities. This divestment is the current theme.

[3] The reason people in the church who lived an evil life undergo this gradual devastation before being cast into hell is that they knew religious truth, which put them in touch with heaven. The heavenly communities with which they were in contact—and with which they remain in contact in the other world—can be detached from them only step by step. The Lord structures heaven in such a way that nothing is done violently; everything happens in a free and apparently spontaneous way. As a result, the heavenly communities are not wrenched away from those spirits but are gradually separated, so that the spirits appear to depart voluntarily.

These remarks now show what the process of devastation is like for people who know the religious truth espoused by the church but led an evil life.

[4] No one can know that this is how matters stand except from revelation. After all, except from revelation we have no idea what exists and

happens in the other world. Humankind is not very concerned about searching the Word for religious truth and goodness, because people do not desire truth for its own sake, let alone for the sake of living by it. Consequently no information on the current subject is revealed to them either. Nonetheless it is present in the Word, and the whole sequence and process is laid out in the Word's inner meaning.

People in the church have no desire, then, to learn truth from the Word, only to confirm the teachings of their church from worldly motives, regardless of whether those teachings are actually true or false. In consequence they know nothing at all about conditions after death, about heaven, or about hell. They do not even know what makes heaven or hell in us. In fact, they are so uninformed that they teach and believe that we can all be let into heaven—some on the basis of a power they arrogate to themselves, some on grounds of the Lord's mercy—no matter how we had lived. Hardly anyone knows that a life of neighborly love and faith grants heaven to us while we are living in the world and that this life lasts.

The purpose of these comments is to expose the nature of religious people who champion faith alone and have no interest in a *life* of faith. They are the people represented by the Egyptians here and in what follows.

7503 *On horses, on donkeys, on camels* symbolizes matters of the intellect and a knowledge of religious truth. This is established by the symbolism of *horses* as matters of the intellect (discussed in §§2761, 2762, 3217, 5321, 6125, 6534), of *donkeys* as information that serves the intellect and therefore also as knowledge (mentioned in §§5492, 7024), and of *camels* as knowledge in general (discussed in §§3048, 3071, 3143, 3145). These three animals symbolize the contents of the mind's intellectual side. The other animals, herd and flock animals, symbolize the contents of the mind's volitional side.

The intellectual side is the side that takes in the truth that leads to faith. The intellect is the inner power of sight, which is illuminated by heaven's light, and the more light it receives, the more it discerns, sees, and acknowledges religious truth when we are reading the Word. That is why people with a perception of such truth are called understanding and wise and also enlightened.

For the idea that the intellect is a container for the truth that leads to faith, see §§5114, 6125, 6222.

7504 *On the herd, and on the flock* symbolizes matters of the will. This is established by the symbolism of a *herd* as goodness on the outer earthly plane and of a *flock* as goodness on the inner earthly plane, discussed at

§5913. Since they symbolize goodness, they symbolize the will, because all goodness relates to the will, and all truth to the intellect.

7505 *A very heavy contagion* symbolizes widespread obliteration. This can be seen from the symbolism of *contagion* as a stripping away of truth. Since the contagion is described as *very heavy,* it symbolizes obliteration of truth.

The symbolism of contagion as the stripping away of truth is evident from the following Scripture passages. In Ezekiel:

> When I send my four evil judgments—the sword and famine and the evil wild animal and *contagion*—on Jerusalem, *to cut humans and animals off from it,* . . . (Ezekiel 14:21)

Cutting off humans and animals stands for stripping away inner and outer goodness. In the same author:

> The sword outside, and *contagion* and famine inside! Those who are in the field will die by the sword, but those who are in the city—*famine and contagion will consume them.* (Ezekiel 7:15)

The contagion stands for the stripping away of goodness. In the same author:

> Because you have defiled my sanctuary with all your abominations, *a third of you will die of contagion* and be *obliterated* in your midst. (Ezekiel 5:11, 12)

The contagion stands for obliteration of goodness. In Amos:

> *I sent contagion among you as in Egypt;* with the sword I killed your young men, along with your captured horses. (Amos 4:10)

The contagion as in Egypt stands for the stripping away of goodness and truth through falsity—the use of falsity being what "as in Egypt" refers to. "With the sword I killed the young men, along with the captured horses" stands for the stripping away of truth. Young men stand for truth, and horses for matters of the intellect (as above at §7503). In David:

> You will not be afraid of the horror at night, of the arrow [that] flies by day, *of contagion that creeps in the dark,* of death [that] ravages at midday. (Psalms 91:5, 6)

The contagion that creeps in the dark stands for evil that devastates secretly. Death that ravages at midday stands for evil that devastates openly. There are other passages as well.

7506 *And Jehovah will distinguish between the livestock of Israel and the livestock of the Egyptians* symbolizes the difference between the religious truth and goodness of people in the spiritual church and religious truth and goodness as received by the persecutors. This can be seen from the symbolism of *distinguishing* as a difference, from the symbolism of *livestock* as religious truth and goodness (as above at §7502), from the representation of the children of *Israel* as people of the spiritual church (also mentioned above, at §7500), and from the symbolism of the *livestock of the Egyptians* as goodness and truth in the church as they are received by the persecutors. On the point that the Egyptians mean people who were once part of the church and therefore knew about religious truth and goodness but led a life of evil, and who inflict harassment in the other life, see §§7097, 7127, 7317, 7502.

[2] I should say a little about the difference between the religious truth and goodness of people in the church who are being saved and the religious truth and goodness of people in the church who are being damned. With people in the church who are being saved, religious truth and goodness grow out of neighborly kindness. To be affected by neighborly love is spirituality itself, so this kind of truth and goodness are spiritual. They come as an inflow from the Lord through heaven, because in these people, the inner depths that receive the inflow are open to heaven. With people in the church who are being damned, though, truth and goodness do not grow out of neighborly kindness and are therefore not spiritual. They do come as an inflow through heaven but meet with a cold, dark reception—cold because neighborly kindness is absent; dark because the light in which they are received is a wintry light, which is darkness in comparison with heaven's light. Moreover, the inner depths of these people are open not to heaven but to the world. That is where they bring to rest the inflow of truth and goodness from heaven. The concepts they have of religious goodness and truth are therefore merely earthly or even matter-based. In the spiritual world these concepts are represented as ugly and bear no resemblance to a human being. The concepts of religious truth and goodness held by people in the church who are being saved, on the other hand, are spiritual. Although they rest on a worldly, material base, they are separate from it, because they can transcend it. The concepts of these people are represented in the spiritual world as beautiful and bear a resemblance to a human being. Such is the difference between the two kinds of religious truth and goodness, no

matter how similar they look on the outside—that is, in people's discussion of them and preaching about them.

[3] The difference is due to the way people live. When the good they do in life, which grows out of neighborly love, flows into the intellect (which is a container for truth), it forms an idea of religious goodness and truth that is beautiful. When the evil they do in life, which is opposed to neighborly love, flows into the intellect, it creates an idea of religious goodness and truth that is ugly, and that kind of idea is not acknowledged in heaven.

And out of all that belongs to the children of Israel none will die means 7507
that they will not be obliterated, as the following shows: *None dying* means not being obliterated. And livestock, when the text says none will die, symbolizes religious truth and goodness, as mentioned above at §7502. And the *children of Israel* represent people of the spiritual church. The reason religious goodness and truth belonging to people of the church cannot die is that neighborly love unites that goodness and truth with divinity. Divinity is life itself, and is eternal. Anything united to life itself and the eternal cannot die or be obliterated. It remains forever and is constantly being improved.

With people in the church who are being damned, though, religious qualities are not united with divinity and therefore have no life in them, so they die. These qualities are like lifeless statues. Because they are not alive, they are obliterated in the other world, which is to say that they are taken away.

And Jehovah set a fixed time symbolizes a determination made ahead 7508
of time, as needs no explanation.

Saying, "Tomorrow Jehovah will do this thing in the land," means that 7509
this will be the spirits' permanent lot in regard to the true ideas and good desires characterizing the church. This can be seen from the meaning of *tomorrow,* or the next day, as permanently, which is treated of in §3998. The last few verses make it plain that the clause has to do with true ideas and good desires characterizing the church. After all, such truth and goodness are the subject there, the message being that they will be obliterated among the people meant by the Egyptians and will last among the people represented by the children of Israel.

And Jehovah did this thing the next day symbolizes bringing about 7510
what had been determined ahead of time, as the following shows: *Doing this thing* means bringing it about. And a set time—the *next day,* in this

case—symbolizes something determined ahead of time, as above at §7508. When a predetermination by the Divine relates to something permanent, it is expressed as "the next day."

7511 *And all the Egyptians' livestock died* symbolizes obliteration of religious truth and goodness among the persecutors. This is evident from the symbolism of *dying* by contagion as obliteration (as above in §§7505, 7507) and from that of the *Egyptians' livestock* as the church's truth and goodness among the persecutors (as also above, at §7506).

7512 *And out of the children of Israel's livestock not one died* means that nothing of religion was obliterated among people of the spiritual church. This is evident from explanations just above in §§7506, 7507.

7513 *And Pharaoh sent, and here, not even one of Israel's livestock had died* means that this became known to the persecutors. This is established by the representation of *Pharaoh* as the persecutors, as mentioned above at §7498. Their learning that no religious goodness or truth perished among people of the spiritual church is clearly what is symbolized by Pharaoh's *sending* and finding that *none of Israel's livestock had died.*

7514 *And Pharaoh's heart turned leaden* symbolizes obstinacy, as earlier in §§7272, 7300, 7305.

7515 *And he did not send the people away* means that they did not leave them alone; that is, they did not leave alone the people in the spiritual church whom they were harassing. See §7474, where the same words occur.

7516 Exodus 9:8–12. *And Jehovah said to Moses and to Aaron, "Take cinders from a furnace for yourselves by fistfuls. And have Moses scatter them toward the sky before Pharaoh's eyes. And they will become dust on all the land of Egypt; and on humans and on animals they will become sores blooming with pimples in all the land of Egypt." And they took the cinders from the furnace and stood before Pharaoh, and Moses scattered them toward the sky, and they became pimply sores blooming on humans and on animals. And the magicians could not stand before Moses on account of the sores, because the sores were on the magicians and on all Egyptians. And Jehovah hardened Pharaoh's heart, and he did not listen to them, as Jehovah had spoken to Moses.*

And Jehovah said to Moses and to Aaron symbolizes being taught anew. *Take for yourselves by fistfuls* means that as much power would be given as could be received. *Cinders from a furnace* symbolize [power] to stir up the false thinking that goes with corrupt desires by being present among the harassers. *And have Moses scatter them toward the sky* means exposing this falsity to the inhabitants of heaven. *Before Pharaoh's eyes* means in the presence [of the harassers]. *And they will become dust on all the land of Egypt* symbolizes the damning of that falsity in the earthly mind. *And on humans and on animals* symbolizes what grows out of inner and outer evil. *They will become sores blooming with pimples* symbolizes unclean thoughts and the blasphemies that result from them. *In all the land of Egypt* means throughout the earthly mind. *And they took the cinders from the furnace* symbolizes the false thinking that goes with corrupt desires. *And stood before Pharaoh* means in the presence of the harassers. *And Moses scattered them toward the sky* means that it was exposed to heaven's inhabitants. *And they became pimply sores blooming on humans and on animals* symbolizes unclean thoughts along with blasphemies growing out of both inner and outer evil. *And the magicians could not stand before Moses on account of the sores* means that being present was impossible for spirits who misused the divine plan in order to produce an effect that would look the same on the outside. *Because the sores were on the magicians* means that the same unclean thoughts came from them. *And on all Egyptians* means as lay in the minds of the persecutors. *And Jehovah hardened Pharaoh's heart* means that they were obstinate. *And he did not listen to them* means that they did not obey. *As Jehovah had spoken to Moses* means as predicted.

And Jehovah said to Moses and to Aaron symbolizes being taught anew. 7517
This is established by the symbolism of *Jehovah said* as being taught, as above at §7497. It means being taught anew because the text is treating of a new state, now that the previous one has ended. Jehovah teaches by means of truth that radiates from him. Truth coming from Jehovah is being represented by *Moses* and *Aaron*—inner truth by Moses and outer truth by Aaron (§7382).

Take for yourselves by fistfuls means that as much power would be given 7518
as could be received. This can be seen from the symbolism of *fists,* or hands, as power. Fists, or hands, symbolize power because that is what the lower part of the arm symbolizes, as discussed below. "As much as can be received" is symbolized by the *full* part of "fistfuls."

In respect to the symbolism of fists, or hands, it needs to be known that in the universal human, the arms correspond to power. Not only the arms themselves symbolize power, then, but also the upper and lower parts of them, down to the fingers. On the point that arms mean power, see §§878, 4932, 4934, 4935, 7205; that shoulders do, 1085, 4937; that hands do, 878, 3387, 5327, 5328, 5544, 6292, 6947, 7011, 7188, 7189; and that fingers do, 7430. For the general correspondence of these, see §§4931–4937.

The reason all parts of the arm correspond to power is that the body exercises its power through them.

This discussion now makes it possible to see what *sitting on the right [hand]* means in Matthew:

> Jesus said, "From now on you will see the Son of Humankind *sitting on the right [hand] of power.*" (Matthew 26:64)

And in Luke:

> From this time now, the Son of Humankind will be *sitting on the right [hand] of God's strength.* (Luke 22:69)

To be specific, it means the omnipotence of the Lord; that is why these verses speak of the right [hand] of power and the right [hand] of strength. The same applies in David:

> You have *an arm with strength; mighty is* your *hand; your right [hand]* will be lifted high. (Psalms 89:13)

All this shows what light the inner meaning sheds on the Word. If it were not known that the right hand symbolizes power, the statement that the Lord would sit on Jehovah's right would be taken literally.

7519 *Cinders from a furnace* symbolize [power] to stir up the false thinking that goes with corrupt desires by being present among the harassers. This can be seen from the symbolism of *cinders from a furnace* as the false thinking that goes with corrupt desires, which is discussed below. The reason it means stirring this up by being present among the harassers is clear from the rest of the verse, which says that Moses was to scatter them toward the sky before Pharaoh's eyes. "Before the eyes" symbolizes being present, and Pharaoh symbolizes the harassers, as shown many times.

[2] Without revelation it is impossible to know how this works, because it is the kind of thing that happens in the other life and is unknown in this world. Evil, hellish spirits are unaware they are immersed in evil and falsity as long as they are remote and separate from heaven, or from the loving goodness and religious truth there. While distant, they believe falsity to be true and evil to be good. However, as soon as they are approached by heaven—that is, by some community in heaven—they perceive their own falsity and evil. The religious truth that then acts on them enables them to sense the falsity, and the loving goodness that acts on them enables them to sense the evil. In addition, the closer heaven draws, or the more present the inflow of a loving goodness and religious truth from heaven, the more heavily they are gripped by their evil and by their falsity, since they cannot bear that presence and inflow.

[3] This information now explains why Moses was commanded to take cinders from a furnace and scatter them toward the sky, and to do so before Pharaoh's eyes. It also explains why Moses rather than Aaron was commanded to scatter the cinders toward the sky. The fact that the cinders were scattered toward the sky symbolizes an inflow from heaven. The fact that it was done before Pharaoh's eyes means in the presence of the persecutors. It was Moses (not Aaron) who did so, because truth coming directly from the Divine is what has this effect on evil spirits, and Moses is truth coming directly from the Divine, whereas Aaron is truth coming indirectly (see §7009).

This shows what the contents of this verse and the next few mean in an inner sense: that foul, unclean thoughts would be stirred up out of corrupt cravings, and blasphemies along with them—these being symbolized by the sores blooming with pimples. Sordid thoughts and blasphemy are stirred up when divine truth flows in and heaven draws closer.

[4] Anyone can see that these measures—taking cinders from a furnace and scattering them toward the sky—would never have been demanded of Moses by Jehovah if something heavenly had not lain hidden inside them. Jehovah would never have ordered such a means of producing the effect unless it held heavenly content, to which it corresponds. You can see, then, what the Word is like—that it is packed full of secrets, but secrets that do not come into view in the literal meaning.

[5] Cinders from a furnace symbolize the false thinking that accompanies corrupt desires because cinders result when something is burned. In the Word, the fuel burned and the fire itself symbolize the goodness associated with heavenly desires, in a good sense, while in the opposite sense they symbolize the evil associated with hellish cravings. For this symbolism of fire, see §§934, 1861, 2446, 4906, 5071, 5215, 6314, 6832, 6834, 6849, 7324, and for the meaning of burning as the evil associated with corrupt passions, §§1297, 5215. It is as a consequence of this that cinders symbolize falsity, because falsity results from craved-for evil.

Since fire symbolizes evil that is craved, a furnace does too. (An object that holds something inside it—as a furnace does—often carries the same meaning as what it holds.) [6] This symbolism of a furnace is evident from the following passages. In Malachi:

> Look: the day is coming, *blazing like a furnace!* And all the proud and everyone doing evil will be stubble, and the coming day will *light them on fire;* it will not leave them root or branch. (Malachi 4:1)

Blazing like a furnace stands for craving evil. Lighting them on fire stands for kindling those cravings. [7] In Genesis:

> Abraham looked out opposite the face of Sodom and Gomorrah and opposite the whole face of the land of the plain, and he saw, and the smoke rose like the *smoke of a furnace.* (Genesis 19:28)

The smoke of a furnace stands for falsities rising out of cravings for evil, Sodom being the cravings for evil produced by self-love, and Gomorrah being the falsity that results (§§2220, 2246, 2322). In John:

> From the pit of the abyss went up smoke, like the *smoke of a furnace.* (Revelation 9:2)

Once again the smoke of a furnace stands for falsities that come from cravings for evil. The pit of the abyss stands for hell. [8] In Matthew:

> The Son of Humankind will send his angels, who will gather together out of his kingdom all the stumbling blocks and those who do wickedness, and he will *send them into a fiery forge.* (Matthew 13:41, 42)

The fiery forge stands for evil cravings, because the fire of our cravings is what the Word means by the fires of hell. Besides, love in all its forms is nothing but the fire of life, and cravings are an extension of love. [9] In Nahum:

> Draw water for the siege for yourselves; shore up your strongholds; go into the clay and tread mortar; *repair the brick kiln.* There fire will consume you and the sword will cut you off. (Nahum 3:14, 15)

Going into the clay stands for going into falsity. Treading mortar stands for treading evil (§6669). The brick kiln stands for falsities that the evil invent and introduce (1296, 6669, 7113). The fire stands for evil cravings (1861, 2446, 5071, 5215, 6832, 7324) and the sword for falsity (4499). [10] In Jeremiah:

> Take big stones into your hand and hide them in the clay *in the brick kiln* that is at the doorway of Pharaoh's house in Tahpanhes, before the eyes of the men of Judah, and say to them, "Watch: I am sending and will take Nebuchadnezzar, king of Babylon, and put his throne on these stones that I have hidden, so that he may stretch his tent out on them. He will come and strike the land of Egypt." (Jeremiah 43:9, 10, 11)

Here too the meaning cannot be seen without the inner sense. Big stones are falsities. The brick kiln is corrupt desire sparked by falsity from evil.

Nebuchadnezzar, king of Babylon, is one who destroys truth and goodness. The placement of his throne and tent on these stones means that this destroyer will make falsity reign supreme. The land of Egypt that Nebuchadnezzar will strike is the earthly mind.

And have Moses scatter them toward the sky means exposing this falsity to the inhabitants of heaven. This can be seen from the symbolism of cinders as falsity (discussed below) and from that of *scattering them toward the sky* as exposing them to the inhabitants of heaven. Scattering something obviously means exposing it, because scattering it makes it visible. 7520

In an inner sense, the sky means heaven.

The symbolism here is plain from the comments directly above at §7519: that truth from the Divine (represented by Moses) exposes and reveals to heaven the falsity adopted by the persecutors as a result of their cravings. This exposure leads to heaven's presence; and among the evil, heaven's presence brings about the results symbolized by sores blooming with pimples.

The meaning of cinders as falsity can be confirmed from passages mentioning ash, because ash has the same origin as cinders and therefore the same symbolism, as in Isaiah 44:15, 20; 58:5; Jeremiah 6:26; Ezekiel 27:30; 28:18; Jonah 3:6; Psalms 102:9, 10; Job 2:8; 30:19.

Before Pharaoh's eyes means in the presence [of the harassers], as can be seen without explanation. 7521

And they will become dust on all the land of Egypt symbolizes the damning of that falsity in the earthly mind. This can be seen from the symbolism of *dust* as something damnable (discussed above at §7418), from that of the cinders in a furnace (the substance to be turned into dust) as falsity that comes of cravings (discussed just above at §§7519, 7520), and from that of the *land of Egypt* as the earthly mind (discussed at §§5276, 5278, 5280, 5288, 5301). 7522

Evidence for the meaning of *dust* as something damnable, in addition to the Scripture passages quoted in §7418, can also be seen in Moses:

> If you do not obey the voice of Jehovah your God, a curse on you in the city, a curse on you in the field! Jehovah will turn your land's rain to *fine dust* and *coarse dust;* from the sky it will come down on you until you are destroyed. (Deuteronomy 28:15, 16, 24)

And on humans and on animals symbolizes what grows out of inner and outer evil. This is evident from the symbolism of a *human* as a good desire, and in a negative sense as an evil craving. An *animal* has the same symbolism, but when the text mentions both human and animal, the 7523 human symbolizes an inner desire or craving, while the animal symbolizes an outer one. For these meanings, see §7424.

The inner goodness and the inner evil symbolized by humans have to do with intention or aim, because the intention or aim is a person's inmost core. The outer goodness and outer evil symbolized by animals have to do with thought and accordingly (if nothing stands in the way) with action.

The reason an animal symbolizes something outward is that in regard to our outer, earthly self we are nothing but animals; we have the same passions, sensual pleasures, appetites, and senses. The reason a human symbolizes something inward is that in regard to our inner, spiritual self we are human; our inner self has the same desire for goodness and truth as the angels in heaven. Another reason is that our inner self is the means by which we control our earthly, creaturelike self, which is an animal.

For the meaning of an animal as good desires, and in a negative sense as evil cravings, see §§45, 46, 142, 143, 246, 714, 715, 719, 776, 2179, 2180, 3218, 3519, 5198.

[2] That is also what "humans and animals" symbolizes in the following passages. In Jeremiah:

> My anger and my wrath have been poured out on this place, *on humans and on animals.* (Jeremiah 7:20)

In the same author:

> I will strike the residents of this city, *both humans and animals;* by great contagion they will die. (Jeremiah 21:6)

In the same author:

> It will make their land a desolation so that nothing can live in it; *from humans to animals* they have moved off, they have left. (Jeremiah 50:3)

In Ezekiel:

> When the earth sins against me, committing a transgression, I will cut *humans and animals* off from it. (Ezekiel 14:13, 19, 21)

In the same author:

> I will stretch my hand out over Edom and cut *humans and animals* off from it and make it a wasteland. (Ezekiel 25:13)

In Zephaniah:

> I will consume *humans and animals,* I will consume the bird in the heavens and the fish in the sea and stumbling blocks in the godless, and I will cut *humanity* off from the surface of the earth. (Zephaniah 1:3)

[3] "Humans and animals" stands for inner and outer goodness in the following passages. In Jeremiah:

> I myself made the earth, the *humans, and the animals* by my great power. (Jeremiah 27:5)

In the same author:

> "Look! The days are coming," says Jehovah, "on which I will sow the house of Israel and the house of Judah with the *seed of humans* and the *seed of animals."* (Jeremiah 31:27)

In the same author:

> The land will be a desolation, so that there is no *human or animal.* (Jeremiah 32:43)

In the same author:

> In the cities of Judah and in the streets of Jerusalem, devastation; *no human* and no resident *and no animal.* (Jeremiah 33:10; 51:62)

In David:

> Your justice is like the mountains of God, your justice is a great abyss; *humans and animals* you preserve, Jehovah. (Psalms 36:6)

This being what "humans and animals" symbolized, the firstborn of the Egyptians, both *humans* and *animals,* died (Exodus 12:29). For the same reason the firstborn both of *humans* and of *animals* were consecrated (Numbers 18:15). Again for the same reason, in keeping with a sacred ritual, the monarch of Nineveh commanded both *humans* and *animals* to fast and also to be covered in sackcloth garments (Jonah 3:7, 8).

They will become sores blooming with pimples symbolizes unclean thoughts and the blasphemies that result from them. This can be seen from the symbolism of *sores* as unclean thoughts stirred up by evil and from the symbolism of *pimples* as the blasphemies that result. 7524

Sores on the human body correspond to filth inspired by evil, and pimples correspond to blasphemies. You would find them on all wicked people, too, if their state while living in the world were not one in which they receive religious goodness and truth. For the sake of that state, the Lord prevents their wickedness from breaking out in such lesions.

[2] The symbolism of sores as unclean thoughts accompanied by blasphemies is also evident in John:

> The first angel poured out his bowl on the earth, and it became a *bad and damaging sore* on people who had the mark of the beast. The fifth angel poured out his bowl on the beast's throne, and they *blasphemed the God of heaven* because of their troubles and *because of their sores.* (Revelation 16:2, [10,] 11)

And in Moses:

> *Jehovah will strike you with the sores of Egypt* and with hemorrhoids and with rash and with itching, so that you cannot be healed, wherefore you will go mad from the sight of your eyes by which you see. Jehovah will strike you with *bad sores* on your knees and on your thighs from which you cannot be healed. Jehovah will lead you, and the monarch that you will set over you, away to a nation that you do not know. (Deuteronomy 28:27, 34, 35, 36)

The sores of Egypt stand for unclean thoughts along with blasphemies. Since blasphemies too are symbolized, the passage says the people will go mad from the sight of their eyes, because anyone who blasphemes God is mad. [3] The different kinds of sores are hemorrhoids, rash, and itching, which symbolize as many varieties of falsity from evil. The sores on the knees and thighs have almost the same symbolism. Because they symbolize falsity, the passage immediately goes on to say that the monarch they will set up will be led away. A monarch symbolizes truth, and in a negative sense falsity (§§1672, 2015, 2069, 3009, 4581, 4966, 5044, 6148). The leprous sores mentioned in Leviticus 13:1–end—swelling, abscess, blister, burn, scaly leprosy, white spot—also have this meaning, because leprosy in a spiritual sense is profanation of truth (§6963).

[4] *Wounds* have this symbolism as well, as is plain in Isaiah:

> From the sole of the foot right to the head, there is no soundness in it; *wound* and bruise and recent injury have not been pressed out and have not been bandaged and have not been softened with oil. (Isaiah 1:6)

And in David:

> My iniquities have passed over my head. *My wounds have turned foul-smelling, have festered,* because of my stupidity. (Psalms 38:4, 5)

For the fact that *in all the land of Egypt* means the earthly mind, see just above at §7522. 7525

And they took the cinders from the furnace symbolizes the false thinking that goes with corrupt desires. This can be seen from the discussion above in §7519 of the symbolism of *cinders from a furnace* as the false thinking that goes with corrupt desires. 7526

And stood before Pharaoh means in the presence of the harassers. This can be seen from the symbolism of *standing before someone* as standing in that person's presence and from the representation of *Pharaoh* as the harassers (noted in §§7107, 7110, 7126, 7142, 7220, 7228). 7527

And Moses scattered them toward the sky means that this kind of false thinking was exposed to heaven's inhabitants. This is clear from the remarks above at §7520, where similar words appear. 7528

And they became pimply sores blooming on humans and on animals symbolizes unclean thoughts along with blasphemies growing out of both inner and outer evil. This is evident from the symbolism of *pimply sores* as falsity together with blasphemies (discussed above at §7524) and from that of *humans and animals* as inner and outer evil (also discussed above, at §7523). 7529

And the magicians could not stand before Moses on account of the sores means that being present was impossible for spirits who misused the divine plan in order to produce an effect that would look the same on the outside. This can be seen from the symbolism of *not being able to stand before someone* as not being able to be present, from that of *magicians* as spirits who misuse the divine plan in order to produce an effect that looks the same on the outside (discussed in §§7296, 7337), and from that of *sores* as unclean thoughts accompanied by blasphemies (discussed above at §7524). 7530

Because the sores were on the magicians means that the same unclean thoughts came from them. This can be seen from the discussion directly above at §7530. 7531

And on all Egyptians means as lay in the minds of the persecutors. This can be seen from the symbolism of *Egyptians* as the persecutors, as discussed in §§7097, 7317. 7532

7533 *And Jehovah hardened Pharaoh's heart* means that they were obstinate. This is established by the symbolism of a *heart* that *hardens,* or turns leaden, as obstinacy, which is mentioned in §§7272, 7300, 7305.

In an inner sense, the statement that Jehovah hardened [Pharaoh's] heart means that they themselves, not Jehovah, hardened their own heart—in other words, made themselves obstinate. It is the evil in people that hardens them obstinately against anything divine, and the evil comes from them, flowing in from hell, not heaven. From the Lord through heaven flows only what is good. Evil cannot issue from anything good, let alone from Goodness itself. Evil proceeds from its own origins, which are the opposites of love for God and love for one's neighbor. These origins exist in humankind, certainly not in God. Where the Word says that God brings about something bad, then, it is obviously speaking according to appearances. But on this subject, see §§2447, 6991, 6997.

7534 *And he did not listen to them* means that they did not obey. This can be seen from the symbolism of *not listening to someone* as not obeying, as also in §§7224, 7275, 7301, 7339, 7413.

7535 *As Jehovah had spoken [to Moses]* means as predicted, as before in §§7302, 7340, 7414, 7432.

7536 Exodus 9:13–18. *And Jehovah said to Moses, "Get up early in the morning and stand before Pharaoh, and you are to say to him, 'This is what Jehovah, God of the Hebrews, has said: "Send my people away [and] let them serve me. Because this time I am sending all my plagues onto your heart and onto your servants and onto your people, so that you may know that there is no one like me in the whole land. Because now I would put out my hand and strike you and your people with the contagion and you would be cut off from the land. However, for the sake of this I have let you remain: for the sake of your seeing my strength and in order that my name may be told in all the land. You are still exalting yourself against my people by not sending them away. Watch: at this time tomorrow I am raining down a very heavy hail such as has not existed in Egypt from the day it was founded until now."'"*

And Jehovah said to Moses symbolizes further instruction on what to do. *Get up early in the morning and stand before Pharaoh* means elevating the awareness of the persecutors by being present. *And you are to say to him, "This is what Jehovah, God of the Hebrews, has said,"* symbolizes a command from the Lord as God of the church. *Send my people away and let them serve me* means to leave people of the spiritual church alone to worship the Lord their God. *Because this time I am sending all my plagues* means that all impending evils could have rushed in on them at the same time. *Onto your heart* means into their inmost core. *Onto your servants and onto your people* means into each and every element. *So that you may know that there is no one like me in the whole land* means that they would learn from this that the Lord alone is God. *Because now I would put out my hand* means that all communication could have been abolished. *And strike you and your people with the contagion* symbolizes thoroughgoing devastation as a result. *And you would be cut off from the land* means that under those circumstances religious qualities would no longer provide a channel of communication. *However, for the sake of this I have let you remain* means that communication would continue after all and they would run through the stages in order. *For the sake of your seeing my strength* means in order to recognize how strong divine power is. *And in order that my name may be told in all the land* means that the Lord is therefore acknowledged as the only God wherever the church exists. *You are still exalting yourself against my people* means because he is not yet ceasing to harass individuals who possess truth and goodness. *By not sending them away* means and is not yet leaving them alone. *Watch: at this time tomorrow I am raining down a very heavy hail* symbolizes falsity that is totally destroying the church among them. *Such as has not existed in Egypt from the day it was founded until now* means that others' earthly minds are not destroyed to this extent.

And Jehovah said to Moses symbolizes further instruction on what to 7537
do. See above at §7517.

Get up early in the morning and stand before Pharaoh means elevating 7538
the awareness of the persecutors by being present. This can be seen from the symbolism of *getting up early in the morning* [as elevated awareness] (discussed at §7435), from that of *standing before someone* as being present (mentioned at §7527), and from the representation of *Pharaoh* as the harassers (noted in §§7107, 7110, 7126, 7142, 7220, 7228).

And you are to say to him, "This is what Jehovah, God of the Hebrews, 7539
has said," symbolizes a command from the Lord as God of the church. This is clear from the symbolism of *saying* (when Jehovah—the Lord—is speaking to spirits devoted to evil who inflict harassment) as a command (as in §§7036, 7310) and from that of *Hebrews* as [people] in the spiritual church and therefore as the church itself (noted in §§6675, 6684, 6738). When the Word mentions Jehovah, it means the Lord; see §§1343, 1736, 2921, 3023, 3035, 5041, 5663, 6280, 6281, 6303, 6905, 6945, 6956. So *Jehovah God of the Hebrews* is the Lord as God of the church.

7540 *Send my people away and let them serve me* means to leave people of the spiritual church alone to worship the Lord their God; see above at §7500, where the same words occur.

7541 *Because this time I am sending all my plagues* means that all impending evils could have rushed in on them at the same time, as the following shows: *Plagues* symbolize evils, and here they are evils these spirits were going to suffer until being thrown entirely into hell, which is why the text speaks of *all* the plagues. And *sending* means rushing in. Jehovah, or the Lord, does not send plagues, or evils. Rather, they rush in from evil itself. In the other world, you see, evil carries its own punishment with it and harbors that punishment within itself, so to speak (§§696, 967, 1857, 6559). That is why *I am sending all my plagues* means that all the evils would rush in on them.

[2] The orderly plan is for one plague to follow another and thus for the wicked to be cast down into hell gradually. That is the reason for saying they *could have* rushed in at the same time.

Because people in the church know nothing about the conditions of life after death, they believe we are either raised into heaven or thrown into hell immediately after life in the body. The reality is that it happens gradually, although with wide variety in timing and in the states we go through. The good, who are to be taken up into heaven, gradually have evil detached from them and are filled with goodness, so far as they developed a receptivity to what is good while they were in the world. The evil, who are to be thrown into hell, gradually have goodness detached from them and are gradually filled with evil, so far as they developed a receptivity to what is evil while they were in the world.

[3] Furthermore, people come into new states in the other life and undergo changes. Those who go to heaven are perfected and continue to be perfected after they go there, forever. Those who go to hell suffer constantly worsening evils after they go there, until they no longer dare to hurt anyone. After that they remain in hell forever. They cannot be released, because it is impossible for them to wish anyone well, only to refrain under threat of punishment from actually wronging anyone without ever giving up the desire.

7542 *Onto your heart* means into their inmost core. This is established by the symbolism of the *heart* as something willed and therefore something loved, as discussed in §§2930, 3313, 3888, 3889. The heart consequently symbolizes something truly living, since love, being connected with the will, constitutes life itself. That is why the heart symbolizes the inmost core.

In good people the inmost core is love for the Lord and love for their neighbor, but in evil people it is self-love and love for worldly advantages. That is the core meant here. What surrounds the core and makes up the periphery, so to speak, is the evils and accompanying falsities that favor such love, and the degree to which they favor it determines the way they are arranged.

[2] In the other world, these evils and falsities unfold in order according to their arrangement. The ones on the outer bounds come to light first, then those deeper within, and finally the inmost core is revealed. This explains why we run through many states in the other life and why the evil bring plagues down on themselves by gradual steps in the period before they are thrown into hell, as was said just above. The core at which they finally arrive is hell itself in them, because it is the very evil that had marked their love and accordingly their goal in everything they did—a goal they had kept hidden deep inside while they were in the world.

Onto your servants and onto your people means into each and every element. This is established by the discussion in §7396 of the symbolism of *servants and people* as each and every person and therefore each and every element. 7543

So that you may know that there is no one like me in the whole land means that they would learn from this that the Lord alone is God. This can be seen from the discussion above at §7401. 7544

Because now I would put out my hand means that [all] communication could have been abolished. This can be seen from the symbolism of a *hand* as power (dealt with in §§4931–4937, 6292, 6947, 7188, 7189, 7518) and of Jehovah's hand as omnipotence (§§878, 3387, 7518). *Putting out his hand,* then, means displaying power and omnipotently doing what he was saying he would do. This omnipotence is described as the ability to send all the plagues onto Pharaoh's heart, onto his servants, and onto his people, meaning that all the evils would rush in at the same time and that communication with anything heavenly would consequently be abolished. That is the power symbolized by the current clause. 7545

I have already explained about this kind of communication before [§§7137, 7498, 7502]: The individuals who harass the upright in the other life were part of the church when they were in the world, read the Word, knew and confessed the religious teachings of their church, but lived a life of evil. In the other life, as long as they retain their religious knowledge, they have communication with heaven and cannot be cast into hell. So that is what is gradually taken away from them. Once it is taken away they no longer have anything to hold them aloft. Like weights without support, like birds shorn of their wings, they plummet into the depths.

This shows what is meant by the statement that [all] communication could have been abolished for them.

7546 *And strike you and your people with the contagion* symbolizes thoroughgoing devastation as a result. This is clear from the symbolism of *contagion* as the stripping away of goodness and truth, as discussed at §7505. Here it symbolizes thoroughgoing devastation, because the statement is that Pharaoh and his people would be struck with it. Earlier, in the third verse, it said that the livestock would be struck, so the contagion mentioned there does not symbolize thoroughgoing devastation but a widespread stripping away of the church's true ideas and good desires—the outer ones.

7547 *And you would be cut off from the land* means that under those circumstances religious qualities would no longer provide a channel of communication, as the following shows: In relation to religious qualities, *being cut off* means being separated. When religious qualities are separated, or when they no longer provide a channel of communication with heaven, the person concerned falls into hell, which is what being cut off means. See above at §7545. And the *land* symbolizes the religion, as discussed in §§662, 1066, 1262, 1733, 1850, 2117, 2118 at the end, 2571, 2928, 3355, 4447, 4535, 5577.

7548 *However, for the sake of this I have let you remain* means that communication would continue after all and they would run through the stages in order. This can be seen from the symbolism of *letting someone remain.* In relation to the plagues, or evils, it means that these would not rush in at the same time (§7541). In relation to communication with heaven, it means that the people concerned would not be deprived of it (§7545), which means that it would continue after all. As a result they would run through the stages in order, which is to say that they would undergo a gradual, step-by-step devastation (§7541).

7549 *For the sake of your seeing my strength* means in order to recognize how strong divine power is, as is self-evident.

7550 *And in order that my name may be told in all the land* means that the Lord is therefore acknowledged as the only God wherever the church exists, as the following shows: A *name* symbolizes every means of worshiping the Lord, collectively, as discussed in §§2724, 3006, 6674. The most essential ingredient of worship is the acknowledgment that the Lord is the only God, that his human nature is divine, and that all faith and love emanate from his divine humanity, so the *telling* of Jehovah's name means that the Lord must be acknowledged as the only God. (For the idea that the Lord's divine humanity is the name of Jehovah, see §§2628, 6887.) And the *land* symbolizes the church, as mentioned just above at §7547.

Here and in many other passages Jehovah (or the Lord) wants his strength and power to be seen and his name to be told, and elsewhere he asks to be worshiped and adored in humility. This makes it look as though he wants to show off his glory and loves adoration on his own account, but the case is actually quite different. He seeks these not for his own sake but for the sake of the human race, not with an eye to glory for himself but out of love. He longs to unite with the human race and to give us life and happiness that are eternal, which he cannot do unless we worship him humbly. Humble worship is impossible unless we acknowledge and believe that we are dust and ashes—nothing but evil—and that Jehovah (the Lord) is the greatest and holiest and that we do not dare presume to approach him. When we engage in humble worship of this kind, the Lord can flow into us with the vitality of his love and give us heaven and eternal happiness. That is the reason Jehovah (the Lord) extols his power and glory so highly in the Word.

You are still exalting yourself against my people means because he is 7551
not yet ceasing to harass individuals who possess truth and goodness, as the following shows: *Still exalting himself* means not yet ceasing to harass people. Harassers believe they are lording it over the people they attack when they see their victims suffering and not yet freed, and when they see themselves warned. And the children of Israel—*my people*—represent members of the spiritual church, or to put the same thing another way, individuals possessing truth and goodness, as treated of in §§4286, 6426, 6637, 6862, 6868, 7035, 7062, 7198, 7201, 7215, 7223.

By not sending them away means and is not yet leaving them alone. 7552
This can be seen from the symbolism of *sending away,* which means leaving alone, as it has a number of times before.

[Watch:] at this time tomorrow I am raining down a very heavy hail 7553
symbolizes falsity that is totally destroying the church among them. This can be seen from the symbolism of a *rain of hail* as falsity-from-evil that wreaks destruction on religious truth and goodness and therefore on attributes of the church. That is the symbolism of a rain of hail because hail is like stones, destroys people and animals and crops, and is cold.

Rain in general symbolizes a blessing, and in a negative sense symbolizes a curse (§2445). When it symbolizes a blessing, it symbolizes an inflow of faith with its truth and of neighborly love with its goodness, and the acceptance of that inflow, because these are a blessing. When it symbolizes a curse, it symbolizes falsity that opposes the truth taught by faith, and evil that opposes the goodness urged by neighborly love, because this falsity and evil are a curse. A rain of *hail* in general symbolizes a curse that consists of falsity growing out of evil and in fact of falsity-from-evil that opposes the church's true ideas and good desires. [2] That is what a rain of hail symbolizes in the following passages. In Ezekiel:

> I will argue my case with Gog by contagion and by blood. And a flooding rain and *hailstones,* fire and sulfur I will rain down on him and on his wings and on many peoples who are with him. (Ezekiel 38:22)

Gog stands for outer worship detached from inner, so it stands for people who blot out neighborly love and then reduce all divine worship to superficialities. The hailstones stand for falsities stemming from evil. [3] In the same author:

> Let my hand be against the prophets who see empty visions and practice lying divination. Say to the people applying foolish plaster that it will fall. A flooding rain will occur in which they will fall, you *hailstones,* and a stormy wind will break out. (Ezekiel 13:9, 11)

The prophets who see empty visions and practice lying divination stand for teachers of false and evil teachings. "Applying foolish plaster" means that they invent falsities and make them plausible. They are addressed as hailstones because of these falsities. The word used in the original language for hail here and in the previous quotation, though, is a different one meaning large hail. [4] In Isaiah:

> Then Jehovah will make the glory of his voice heard, and his arm will see repose, in wrathful anger and the flame of a consuming fire, in dispersal and flood and *hailstone.* (Isaiah 30:30, 31)

The hailstone stands for the wiping out of truth by falsity. In the same author:

> Indeed the Lord is strong and mighty, like a *flood of hail,* a storm of carnage; like a flood of strong, overflowing water he will throw them down to the earth with his hand. *Hail will overturn the refuge of falsehood,* and water will flood its hiding place. (Isaiah 28:2, 17)

The flooding stands for immersion in falsity and consequently for the wiping out of truth (§§705, 739, 790, 5725, 6853). A flood of hail stands for the destruction of truth by falsity. In David:

> He *struck their grapevine with hail* and *their sycamore figs with heavy hail.* And he *closed up their animals in hail* and their livestock in flaming embers; he sent against them the wrath of his anger. (Psalms 78:47, 48, 49)

[5] In the same author:

> *He has sent them hail for their rains,* flaming fire on their land, and has struck their grapevine and their fig tree and shattered the tree within their border. (Psalms 105:32, 33)

The hail and rain stand for the wiping out of truth and goodness by falsity that rises out of evil. A grapevine stands for truth and goodness in the inner part of the church, and sycamore figs and the fig tree for truth and goodness in the outer part of the church. In the same author:

> The one who gives snow like wool scatters frost like powder; the *one who casts out his hail like crumbs*—who will stand up to his chill? (Psalms 147:16, 17)

The hail stands for falsity from evil. In the same author:

> He turned the dark into his hiding place, his environs into his tent—watery darkness, the clouds of the heavens. From the radiance before him clouds passed over with *hail* and *coals of fire.* Jehovah thundered in the heavens, and the Highest One uttered his voice—*hail* and *coals of fire*—so that he sent his arrows and scattered them. (Psalms 18:11, 12, 13, 14)

The hail stands for falsity-from-evil that devastates truth and goodness. [6] In John:

> The first angel trumpeted, and *hail appeared,* and *fire mixed with blood,* and it fell onto the earth, so that a third of the trees were burned and all the green grass was burned up. (Revelation 8:7)

The hail stands for falsity resulting from evil. The fire mixed with blood stands for cravings for evil mixed with falsified truth. The burned trees stand for concepts of truth destroyed by cravings for evil. The burned-up green grass stands for a knowledge of truth destroyed in the same way. For the meaning of fire as cravings for evil, see §§1297, 1861, 2446, 5071, 5215, 6314, 6832, 7324 [at the end]. For the meaning of blood as truth rendered false, §§4735, 6978, 7317, 7326. For the meaning of trees as concepts, §§2722 at the end, 2972. [7] In Joshua:

> It happened as they fled before Israel while on the descent to Beth-horon, when Jehovah cast *large stones from the heavens* on them, all the way to Azekah, that they died. *There were more who died in the hailstones* than whom the children of Israel killed with the sword. (Joshua 10:11)

This is about five monarchs who attacked Gibeon. The monarchs and their citizenry represented people dedicated to falsity from evil, so they were killed by hailstones. The lumps of hail are being called stones because stones too symbolize falsity.

This discussion clarifies the fact that hail, and a rain of hail, symbolizes falsity grounded in evil, and since it symbolizes this, it also symbolizes the stripping away of truth and goodness, because falsity from evil is what strips them away.

7554 *Such as has not existed in Egypt from the day it was founded until now* means that others' earthly minds are not destroyed to this extent. This can be seen from the symbolism of a rain of hail (which this clause describes) as the destruction of truth by falsity (discussed directly above at §7553) and from that of the land of *Egypt* as the earthly mind (discussed in §§5276, 5278, 5280, 5288, 5301). *From the day it was founded until now* means not to this extent in others because a day symbolizes a state, founding symbolizes the nature of the state, and Egypt symbolizes the earthly mind in general.

The reason there is not the same extent of destruction in others as in those who harass the upright in the other life is that in the world these harassers were part of the church (§§7317, 7502). Their memory (which is part of the earthly mind) they filled with information about faith taken from the Word and from the teachings of their religion, but they lived contrary to it. So when they are undergoing the process of devastation, any knowledge of faith they have is rooted out, along with much else that clings to it. This leaves holes and gaps that are deep and disgusting. Obsessive evil inevitably attaches itself in some fashion too, and so does falsity. These cannot coexist with the religious knowledge, so if they cannot be separated from it, they are of course relegated to the outer bounds, leaving empty spaces at the center, which reek. (All stench comes from evil mixed with goodness, and falsity mixed with truth.) This cannot happen with people outside the church, because they learned nothing about faith and its truth from the Word.

This is what it means to say that others' earthly minds are not destroyed.

Exodus 9:19, 20, 21. *"And now send, gather your livestock and everything that is yours in the field. Every human and animal that is found in the field and is not gathered home—the hail will come down on them and they will die." And those of Pharaoh's servants who feared Jehovah's word made their servants and their livestock run to their homes. And those who did not take Jehovah's word to heart left their servants and their livestock in the field.* 7555

And now send, gather your livestock symbolizes the necessity of collecting truth-from-goodness. *And everything that is yours in the field* means which characterizes the church. *Every human and animal* symbolizes inner and outer goodness. *That is found in the field* means which characterizes the church. *And is not gathered home* means which is not preserved. *The hail will come down on them and they will die* means that falsity will completely destroy it. *And those of Pharaoh's servants who feared Jehovah's word* symbolizes those elements in the earthly mind that were the Lord's. *Made their servants and their livestock run to their homes* means that they were hidden away and preserved deep within. *And those who did not take Jehovah's word to heart* symbolizes what did not come from the Lord. *Left their servants and their livestock in the field* means that it was not hidden away or preserved.

And now send, gather your livestock symbolizes the necessity of collecting truth-from-goodness. This can be seen from the symbolism of *gathering* as collecting and from that of *livestock* as goodness from truth and truth from goodness, as dealt with in §§6016, 6045. For a definition of truth from goodness and goodness from truth, see §§2063, 3295, 3332, 3669, 3688, 3882, 4337, 4353, 4390, 5526, 5733. 7556

This verse and the next two are about goodness and truth that the Lord preserves even in the evil. Any goodness or truth that is not joined to evil or falsity is hidden away deep within by the Lord rather than being devastated. Later he brings it out of storage to put it to use. The Lord's preservation of goodness and truth in us is symbolized in the Word by survivors. For a discussion of them, see §§468, 530, 560, 561, 576, 661, 798, 1738, 1906, 2284, 5135, 5342, 5344, 5897, 5898, 5899, 6156.

And everything that is yours in the field means which characterizes the church. This can be seen from the symbolism of a *field* as the church, which is discussed in §§2971, 3317, 3766, 4440, 4443, 7502. 7557

7558 *Every human and animal* symbolizes inner and outer goodness. This can be seen from the discussion above in §§7424, 7523 of the symbolism of *humans and animals* as inner and outer goodness.

7559 *That is found in the field* means which characterizes the church. This can be seen from the symbolism of a *field* as the church, which is mentioned just above at §7557.

7560 *And is not gathered home* means which is not preserved. This can be seen from the symbolism of *not being gathered home* as not being preserved. A home means the inner part of the earthly mind (where goodness resides, along with truth), and it also means the rational mind, so it means the person herself or himself, as discussed in §§3538, 4973, 5023, 7353. Being gathered home accordingly means being gathered within a person and hidden away there.

The reason goodness and truth are hidden away within and preserved there by the Lord, even in the evil, is to make sure we still have some remaining trace of humanity. Without them we are not human, because what is hidden away and preserved is goodness and truth, which are our channel of communication with heaven. The more contact we have with heaven, the more human we are.

[2] It is true that the evil—even those in hell—have contact with heaven, but they form no bond with it through goodness and truth. As soon as goodness and truth pour down from heaven and arrive in hell, they turn into evil and falsity, which immediately breaks any bond. Such is the contact. The goodness and truth that are stored away and saved deep within a person do create a bond, but in the evil, the truth and goodness there do no more than enable them to reason, to think and speak from their senses, and to confirm falsity and defend evil. The good desires and true ideas hidden away and preserved within them can yield no more than this, because if they did yield more, the true ideas and good desires would perish, and nothing human would remain to them.

7561 *The hail will come down on them and they will die* means that falsity will completely destroy it—that is, will destroy what belongs to the church—as the following shows: *Hail* symbolizes falsity that comes of evil, so it symbolizes the wiping out of goodness and truth by falsity, as discussed at §7553. And *dying* means ceasing to exist, as discussed in §§494, 6587, 6593, and since it is being connected with the wiping out of goodness and truth, it means being destroyed.

7562 *And those of Pharaoh's servants who feared Jehovah's word* symbolizes those elements in the earthly mind that were the Lord's, as the following shows: *Those who feared Jehovah's word* symbolizes elements that are the Lord's. In an inner sense, one who fears means a quality rather than a person who is feeling fearful. (For the idea that in heaven the concept of a person turns into the concept of some attribute, see §§5225, 5287, 5434.) "Those who feared Jehovah's name" therefore means goodness and truth from the Lord. And *Pharaoh's servants* symbolize the contents of the earthly mind. Pharaoh is the earthly plane in general (see §§5160, 5799), so his servants are the contents of that plane. In other words, they are the contents of the earthly mind, since the earthly-level attributes that form the basis of our thoughts and conclusions are the components of our mind.

There are contents of the earthly mind that are the Lord's and contents that are not the Lord's; see below at §7564.

Made their servants and their livestock run to their homes means that 7563
they were hidden away and preserved deep within. This is clear from the symbolism of *servants* as the contents of the earthly mind (as directly above at §7562), from that of *livestock* as truth and goodness (also mentioned above, at §7556), and from that of *homes* as something deep within a person, where goodness and truth from the Lord are hidden away and preserved (discussed at §7560). Clearly, then, *made their servants and their livestock run to their homes* means that such truth and goodness in the earthly mind as are the Lord's were collected and were hidden away and preserved deep within.

And those who did not take Jehovah's word to heart symbolizes what 7564
did not come from the Lord. This is plain from the explanation above at §7562, where "those who feared Jehovah's word" symbolizes elements that were the Lord's. *Those who did not take Jehovah's word to heart* in turn, then, symbolizes elements that were not from the Lord.

Good desires and true thoughts are either the Lord's or not the Lord's. Those that are the Lord's are those we carry out for the sake of our neighbor, our country, the church, and the Lord's kingdom. So they are those we carry out for the sake of truth and goodness itself and for the Lord's sake most of all. These are the goodness and truth that are the Lord's. The good desires and true thoughts that are not the Lord's are those we carry out for the sake of ourselves or for the sake of worldly advantages as the ultimate goal. This goodness and this truth sometimes resemble the first kind in outward appearance, but inwardly they are completely different. These latter lead back to oneself, but the former lead away from oneself. For the most part the truth and goodness we act on in a state of misfortune, sickness, pain, or fear and not in a state of freedom are also not the Lord's, because these too are for our own sake.

All truth and goodness do indeed flow from the Lord, but when we turn the Lord's goodness and truth in our own direction, they become ours; they become the personal property of the person in whose direction they have been turned. This is because they become the "goodness" sought by self-love and materialism. That is the "good" the evil all do to each other.

The discussion above shows what I mean by goodness and truth belonging to the Lord and by goodness and truth not belonging to the Lord.

7565 *Left their servants and their livestock in the field* means that it was not hidden away or preserved. This is evident from the symbolism of being *left in the field* as being destroyed by falsity from evil (symbolized by the hail by which they would die); see §§7559, 7560, 7561. That which would be destroyed by falsity from evil is what was not hidden away or preserved, and it consists of truth and goodness that are not the Lord's, as discussed directly above at §7564. *Servants* symbolize the contents of the earthly mind (§§7562, 7563), and *livestock* symbolize truth and goodness that are not the Lord's and therefore cannot be hidden away deep within.

7566 Exodus 9:22–26. *And Jehovah said to Moses, "Stretch your hand out toward the sky, and there will be hail in all the land of Egypt, on humans and on animals and on all the grass of the field in the land of Egypt." And Moses stretched his staff out to the sky, and Jehovah sent voices [of thunder] and hail, and fire went to the earth, and Jehovah rained hail on the land of Egypt. And there was hail, and fire going with it in the middle of the hail, very heavy [hail], such as had not existed in all the land of Egypt from the time it turned into a nation. And in all the land of Egypt the hail struck everything that was in the field, from humans even to animals; and the hail struck all the grass of the field and shattered every tree of the field. Only in the land of Goshen, where the children of Israel were, was there no hail.*

And Jehovah said to Moses symbolizes a command. *Stretch your hand out toward the sky* means drawing attention to heaven, and its closer approach. *And there will be hail in all the land of Egypt* symbolizes falsity in the earthly mind that wreaks destruction. *On humans and on animals* symbolizes both inner and outer goodness. *And on all the grass of the field in the land of Egypt* symbolizes all truth in the earthly mind that comes from the church. *And Moses stretched his staff out to the sky* symbolizes communication with heaven. *And Jehovah sent voices [of thunder]* symbolizes a withdrawal and severing of communication with people who possess goodness and truth. *And hail* symbolizes falsity that destroys goodness and truth. *And fire went to the earth* symbolizes cravings for evil. *And [Jehovah] rained hail on the land of Egypt* symbolizes an earthly mind taken over by falsity from evil. *And there was hail, and fire going with it in the middle of the hail, very heavy [hail],* symbolizes a convinced belief in falsity, together with cravings for evil. *Such as had not existed in all the land of Egypt* means that this state was not seen in the earthly mind of others. *From the time it turned into a nation* means from the day on which it became capable of letting in goodness and therefore truth. *And in all the land of Egypt the hail struck* means that this falsity destroyed the contents of the earthly mind. *Everything that was in the field* symbolizes any contents that had to do with the church. *From humans even to animals* symbolizes both inner and outer goodness in the church. *And the hail struck all the grass of the field* means that this falsity destroyed all the truth learned from the church. *And shattered every tree of the field* symbolizes all the concepts of truth and goodness received from the church as well. *Only in the land of Goshen, where the children of Israel were, was there no hail* means not where the people of the spiritual church were.

And Jehovah said to Moses symbolizes a command. This is established by the symbolism of *saying* as a command, which is mentioned in §§7036, 7107, 7310. **7567**

Stretch your hand out toward the sky means drawing attention to heaven, and its closer approach, as the following shows: *Stretching out a hand* means drawing attention, because to stretch out a hand is to draw attention to something and point it out. And the *sky* symbolizes heaven. When the heavens are brought to our awareness and are pointed out to us, we turn our eyes and our thoughts toward them. That is why a closer approach is also being symbolized; all nearness in the spiritual world comes about through the directing of one's thoughts. In fact, at §7519 I already explained how this works, but since nothing like it is known in the world, let me throw a little more light on it. **7568**

When a change of state looms for wicked people who are in need of being purged (such as those on whom the current chapters focus), what brings the change about is a more immediate inflow of goodness and truth from heaven. The closer to them heaven draws, the deeper the level on which the evil and falsity in them are stirred up. Goodness and truth from heaven penetrate to their inner reaches, and the closer heaven comes, the deeper these penetrate. That is why hellish spirits do not dare go near any heavenly community but rather back as far away as they can; see §§4225, 4226, 4299, 4533, 4674, 5057, 5058, 7519.

[2] This discussion now shows what is meant by drawing attention to heaven, and its closer approach, as symbolized by Moses' stretching his hand out toward the sky. The text is depicting a new state, in which falsity from evil will destroy all religious goodness and truth in the persecutors. This state is brought on by a more immediate inflow of truth from the Divine and also by the closer advance of heaven, and that is why Moses is told to stretch his hand out toward the sky.

7569 *And there will be hail in all the land of Egypt* symbolizes falsity in the earthly mind that wreaks destruction, as the following shows: *Hail* symbolizes falsity-from-evil that wreaks destruction—the destruction of everything good and true in the church—as discussed at §7553. And the *land of Egypt* symbolizes the earthly mind, as discussed in §§5276, 5278, 5280, 5288, 5301.

7570 *On humans and on animals* means both inner and outer goodness. This is evident from the discussion in §§7424, 7523 of the symbolism of *humans and animals* as inner and outer goodness.

7571 *And on all the grass of the field in the land of Egypt* symbolizes all truth in the earthly mind that comes from the church. This is clear from the symbolism of *grass* as truth (discussed below), from that of a *field* as the church (mentioned above at §7557), and from that of the *land of Egypt* as the earthly mind (also mentioned above, at §7569).

Grass symbolizes truth because the land symbolizes the church, as does a field. Any produce they yield symbolizes either the truth that leads to faith or the goodness that comes from neighborly love, because these are what the church produces.

The grass in a field means any product of a field in general, as is plain from a parable of the Lord's in Matthew:

> The kingdom of the heavens became like a person sowing good seed in a field; *when the grass sprouted* and bore fruit, then appeared the tares. (Matthew 13:24, 26)

The grass stands for the produce of the field. Plainly it symbolizes truth known to the church, and the tares symbolize falsity. Yes, it is a simile, but all similes in the Word are based on symbolism (§3579). In David:

> [You are] the one who causes grain to sprout for the beast and *grass for the service of humankind,* to bring bread from the earth. (Psalms 104:14)

Here too the grass stands for the produce of the field and symbolizes truth, on an inner level. [2] In the same author:

> *He will make me lie down in grassy pastures;* he will lead me to quiet waters. He will revive my soul. (Psalms 23:2, 3)

Grassy pastures stand for spiritual nourishment, or nourishment for the soul. That is why the passage says, "He will revive my soul." In Isaiah:

> The waters of Nimrim will be wastelands, because *the grain has dried out, the grass has been consumed,* there is no greenery. (Isaiah 15:6)

In the same author:

> I will devastate mountains and hills and *wither all their grass* and make rivers into islands. And I will lead the blind on a way that they have not known. (Isaiah 42:15, 16)

In Jeremiah:

> How long will the land mourn and the *grass of every field wither?* Because of the wickedness of those living in it, the animals and the bird will be consumed. (Jeremiah 12:4)

In the same author:

> The doe in the field gave birth, but [did so while] abandoning [the fawn], *because there was no grass.* And wild donkeys stood on the hills; they inhaled the wind like great sea creatures *since there was no grass.* (Jeremiah 14:5, 6)

In Joel:

> Do not be afraid, animals of my fields; *because the living-places of the desert have become grassy,* because the tree will bear its fruit, the fig tree and the grapevine will yield their strength. (Joel 2:22)

In Amos:

> When the locust finished *eating the grass of the land,* I said, "Lord Jehovih, pardon, please; how will Jacob stand, when he is so small?" (Amos 7:2)

[3] In Zechariah:

> Seek from Jehovah the rain that is late in time. Jehovah will make rain clouds and give them rain in a shower, [will give] *a man grass in his field.* (Zechariah 10:1)

In John:

> The fifth angel trumpeted, and it was said that *they should not harm the grain of the earth* nor any *greenery* nor any tree. (Revelation 9:4)

Anyone can see that neither grain nor grass is meant in these passages but rather something characteristic of the church. Clearly the grass of earth, land, and field means religious truth.

Without a spiritual meaning of this kind, no one could make sense of the statement in John that when the fifth angel trumpeted they were told not to harm the grain of the earth or any greenery. No one could make sense of the statement in Jeremiah that the doe in the field gave birth, and [did so while] abandoning [the fawn], because there was no grass; or that wild donkeys snuffed the wind like great sea creatures since there was no grass. Neither could they make sense of many other passages elsewhere.

This shows how meager people's understanding of the Word is and how mundane an idea they must have of most of its contents unless they know its symbolic meaning or at least know there is something holy infusing every word.

7572 *And Moses stretched his staff out to the sky* symbolizes communication with heaven. This can be seen from the symbolism of *stretching out a staff* as drawing attention and therefore as communicating, in keeping with the explanation above at §7568. The *sky* symbolizes heaven.

7573 *And Jehovah sent voices [of thunder]* symbolizes a withdrawal and severing of communication with people who possess goodness and truth. This is evident from the symbolism of *voices* of thunder as divine truth that enlightens and perfects the inhabitants of heaven and terrifies and devastates the inhabitants of hell. Since it devastates the latter, it symbolizes a withdrawal and severing of communication with people who possess goodness and truth, because that is the means of devastation.

Previous discussions at §§7502, 7541, 7542, 7545, 7554 show what the facts of the matter are here. That is, there are spirits who were formerly part of the church and consequently imbibed knowledge about truth and goodness from the Word but lived an evil life. These individuals have contact with heaven through the truth and goodness they brought with them from the world, when they were in the church. (We take with us to the other life whatever we knew in the world; in fact, we take whatever we saw, heard, thought, said, intended, and did. See §§2474, 2475, 2481–2486, 7398.) This contact is what is taken away when they undergo devastation. And once contact has been taken away, then truth and goodness, together with all knowledge of them, are also removed. That is because everything a spirit or even an angel knows flows in from the Lord through heaven and accordingly through channels of communication. See §§6053–6058, 6189–6215, 6307–6327, 6466–6496, 6598–6626. From this you can see what is meant by a withdrawal and severing of communication with people who possess truth and goodness.

Voices [of thunder] symbolize divine truth in heaven and in hell, and this truth resembles earthly thunder. Thunder high up in the mountains is heard as only a gentle, quiet sound, but thunder down at ground level is heard as a terrifying crash. Likewise, divine truth is gentle and mild in heaven but frightening in hell.

[2] The following passages make it plain that voices of thunder symbolize divine truth enlightening and perfecting the inhabitants of heaven and terrifying and devastating the inhabitants of hell. In Isaiah:

> There will be joy of heart like that of one who walks along with a panpipe to come onto Jehovah's mountain, toward Israel's rock. *Then Jehovah will make the glory of his voice heard* and cause his arm to see repose, in wrathful anger and in the flame of a consuming fire, in dispersal and flood and hailstone, *since at Jehovah's voice* Assyria will panic. (Isaiah 30:29, 30, 31)

In this passage the voice of Jehovah stands for divine truth enlightening and perfecting people devoted to what is good but terrifying and devastating people devoted to what is evil. In Joel:

> Before him the earth quaked, the sun and moon turned black, and the stars withdrew their rays. And *Jehovah utters his voice before his army;* his camp is very large, because those who do his word are countless. Because great is the day of Jehovah and very fearsome. (Joel 2:10, 11)

The same holds true here. [3] In the same author:

> From Zion Jehovah will roar, and *from Jerusalem he will utter his voice,* and the heavens and the earth will tremble. But Jehovah is a refuge for his people and a stronghold for the children of Israel. (Joel 3:16)

Again the voice of Jehovah stands for divine truth. He utters it from Jerusalem because Jerusalem symbolizes the Lord's spiritual kingdom, whose inhabitants have adopted goodness-from-truth and truth-from-goodness. [4] In David:

> *Jehovah thundered in the heavens,* and *the Highest One uttered his voice*—hail and coals of fire—so that he sent his arrows and scattered them, and [sent] many lightning bolts and troubled them. (Psalms 18:13, 14)

Uttering his voice and sending hail and coals of fire stands for the way falsity and evil that result from corrupt desires strip away truth and goodness. In the same author:

> The clouds showered water; *the heights of the sky uttered their voice.* Your arrows also went; the *voice of your thunder, into the world.* Thunderbolts lit up the world. (Psalms 77:16, 17, 18)

The voice stands for divine truth, which lights up the church and the people in it. [5] In the same author:

> *Jehovah's voice* is upon the waters; the God of glory *makes thunderings;* Jehovah is upon vast waters. *Jehovah's voice* has strength. *Jehovah's voice* has honor. *Jehovah's voice* is breaking cedars; Jehovah has shattered the cedars of Lebanon. *Jehovah's voice* is cutting through the fiery flame. *Jehovah's voice* makes the wilderness tremble. *Jehovah's voice* sends the does into labor and strips the forests bare. (Psalms 29:3–11)

Jehovah's voice here stands for divine truth and its power. So it also stands for the Word, since the Word is divine truth. [6] In John:

> A mighty angel coming down shouted with a loud voice. And when he shouted, *the seven thunders uttered their voices.* I was about to write, but I heard a voice from heaven telling me, "Seal up *what the seven thunders uttered* and do not write it." (Revelation 10:3, 4)

The voices stand for divine truth, and the thunders for carriers that bear divine truth from heaven to earth.

No one can help seeing that thunder and voices do not mean thunder and sounds but something divine. Since they mean something divine and are called Jehovah's voices, they obviously mean divine truth. That was why there were *voices, lightning bolts,* and *thunderclaps* when Jehovah came down on Mount Sinai and proclaimed divine truth (Exodus 19:16;

20:18), and that was also why he spoke from the middle of a fire (Deuteronomy 4:11, 12; 5:22, 23, 24, 25).

And hail symbolizes falsity that destroys goodness and truth. This is evident from the discussion in §7553 of the symbolism of *hail* as falsity-from-evil that destroys the church's goodness and truth. 7574

Hail symbolizes a kind of falsity that destroys the church's truth and goodness—the same thing symbolized by the contagion mentioned earlier in the chapter [verses 3, 15]. There are many, many categories and subcategories of falsity, as there are of the evil from which it rises. The falsity that hail symbolizes is a kind that destroys what belongs to the church. It can exist only in people who were born into the church but who lived contrary to the religious truth and goodness encountered there.

Further evidence that falsity, like evil, comes in many categories and subcategories is the fact that hell is divided up by category and type of evil and therefore of falsity and that the hells are countless.

This shows how matters stand with the fact that falsity and evil are symbolized by the miracles or plagues in Egypt—the blood, frogs, lice, winged pest, contagion, pimply sores, hail, and locusts. Each of these symbolizes a different kind of falsity and evil.

And fire went to the earth symbolizes cravings for evil, as the following shows: *Fire* symbolizes cravings for evil, as discussed in §§1297, 1861, 2446, 5071, 5215, 6314, 6832, 7324. And *going to the earth* means taking over the earthly mind, right to its lowest levels. For the meaning of the land of Egypt as the earthly mind, see §§5276, 5278, 5280, 5288, 5301. 7575

Since hail symbolizes falsity, and fire symbolizes the evil from which falsity rises, fire is mentioned along with hail in Isaiah 30:30, 31; Psalms 18:11, 12, 13, 14; Psalms 78:47, 48, 49; Revelation 8:7; and in the next verse here: "And there was hail, *and fire going with it in the middle of the hail,* very heavy [hail]."

And [Jehovah] rained hail on the land of Egypt symbolizes an earthly mind thus taken over by falsity from evil, as the following shows: *Raining* something down means pouring it on, and here it means being taken over. Raining down is used to describe what truth and goodness do, and in a negative sense, what falsity and evil do, because rain means both a blessing and a curse (§2445). *Hail* symbolizes falsity that comes of evil, as discussed in §§7553, 7574. And the *land of Egypt* symbolizes the earthly mind, as above at §7575. 7576

And there was hail, and fire going with it in the middle of the hail, very heavy [hail], symbolizes a convinced belief in falsity, together with cravings 7577 for evil, as the following shows: *Hail* symbolizes falsity that comes of evil, as noted above at §7574, and here it symbolizes a convinced belief in falsity, because the hail is described as *very heavy. Fire* symbolizes cravings for evil, as noted just above at §7575. And *going in the middle of something* means being combined with it. In fact, going in the middle of the hail means having cravings for evil right at the heart of that false thinking, since the false thinking grows out of the cravings.

[2] The text here is depicting people in the church who harass the upright in the other life, during a state in which the former have been purged of their religious heritage—that is, of the goodness and truth they once claimed to believe in. At that point, distorted convictions together with cravings for evil reign supreme in them. That is what their inner state is like.

A convinced belief in falsity is inseparable from cravings for evil, because people who lead an evil life adopt a distorted philosophy. To evil-living people themselves it can indeed seem otherwise, because when they pay lip service to truth gleaned from the Word or from the teachings of their religion, they imagine they believe in it. It even appears to them as though they do, but if their life is evil, they do not. Either they proclaim one thing with their lips and think another, or they do actually think that way, but only as a result of a dogmatic belief. Faith is dogmatic when it is adopted for the sake of financial gain or high position, so when the struggle for position and the pursuit of wealth end, their belief fails. They then seize on false ideas that harmonize with their cravings for evil. Falsity that harmonizes with cravings for evil exists deep inside people who live an evil life, despite their belief that it does not.

[3] It becomes quite clear that this is the case when outward appearances are taken away in the other life and people like this are left to their inner reality. The false thoughts they had in the world—both those they indulged and those they did not openly indulge—then erupt into view. It is from the evil in their life that this thinking erupts, because falsity is actually evil rationalizing and justifying itself. This shows what their state in the other life is: a state of immersion in distorted convictions combined with cravings for evil.

7578 *Such as had not existed in all the land of Egypt* means that this state was not seen in the earthly mind of others. This is evident from the explanation above at §7554, where similar words appear.

7579 *From the time it turned into a nation* means from the day on which it (the earthly mind) became capable of letting in goodness and therefore truth, as the following shows: A *nation* symbolizes goodness, as discussed in §§1159, 1259, 1260, 1416, 1849, 4574, 6005. Since the term is being applied to the land of Egypt, which symbolizes truth in the form of knowledge in the earthly mind, it also means truth growing out of goodness. And *from the time it turned into [a nation]* means from the day on which it became capable of this.

And in all the land of Egypt the hail struck means that this falsity destroyed the contents of the earthly mind. This can be seen from the symbolism of *striking* as destroying, from that of *hail* as falsity from evil (§7553), and from that of the *land of Egypt* as the earthly mind (mentioned at §7569). 7580

Everything that was in the field symbolizes any contents that had to do with the church. This is established by the symbolism of a *field* as the church (§7557). 7581

From humans even to animals symbolizes both inner and outer goodness in the church. This is established by the discussion in §§7424, 7523 of the symbolism of *humans and animals* as inner and outer goodness. 7582

And the hail struck all the grass of the field means that this falsity destroyed all the truth learned from the church. This is established by the symbolism of the *grass of the field* as truth known to the church (discussed above at §7571), from that of *striking* as destroying, and from that of *hail* as falsity (discussed at §7553). 7583

And shattered every tree of the field symbolizes all the concepts of goodness and truth received from the church as well. This is established by the symbolism of a *tree* as perceptions of what is good and true (mentioned in §§103, 2163, 2682) and also as concepts of what is good and true (§§2722 at the end, 2972). 7584

Only in the land of Goshen, where the children of Israel were, was there no hail means not where the people of the spiritual church were. This can be seen from the symbolism of the *land of Goshen* as the inmost part of the earthly mind (discussed in §§5910, 6028, 6031, 6068) and as the church (§6649), and from the representation of the *children of Israel* as people of the spiritual church (dealt with in §§6426, 6637, 6862, 6868, 7035, 7062, 7198, 7201, 7215, 7223). 7585

Exodus 9:27, 28, 29, 30. *And Pharaoh sent and called Moses and Aaron and said to them, "I have sinned this time; Jehovah is in the right, and I and my people are in the wrong. Plead to Jehovah, and let this be enough of God's voices [of thunder] and hail! And I will send you away, and you will no longer remain." And Moses said to him, "When I leave the city, I will stretch* 7586 *my palms out to Jehovah, the voices [of thunder] will stop, and the hail will no longer come, so that you may know that the land is Jehovah's. As for you and your servants, I know that you do not [yet] fear the face of Jehovah God."*

And Pharaoh sent and called Moses and Aaron symbolizes the presence of divine law. *And said to them* symbolizes humility. *I have sinned this time* symbolizes alienation from truth and goodness. *Jehovah is in the right, and I and my people are in the wrong* means that divine goodness could not bear the wickedness of the persecutors and that this was the consequence. *Plead to Jehovah* symbolizes a wish that they intervene. *And let this be enough of [God's] voices [of thunder] and hail!* means if the falsities cease. *And I will send you away, and you will no longer remain* means that they would leave them alone and not detain them anymore. *And Moses said to him* symbolizes the answer. *When I leave the city* symbolizes separation. *I will stretch my palms out to Jehovah* symbolizes intervention. *The voices [of thunder] will stop, and the hail will no longer come* symbolizes the end of that stage. *So that you may know that the land is Jehovah's* means this reveals that the Lord is the only God in the church. *As for you and your servants, I know that you do not yet fear the face of Jehovah God* means that the persecutors are not yet in awe of the Lord.

7587 *And Pharaoh sent and called Moses and Aaron* symbolizes the presence of divine law, as in §§7390, 7451, where similar words appear.

7588 *And said to them* symbolizes humility. This can be seen from the next words, "I have sinned this time; Jehovah is in the right, and I and my people are in the wrong." This is an expression of humility and is included in "he said."

7589 *I have sinned this time* symbolizes alienation from truth and goodness. This can be seen from the symbolism of *sinning* as a rift with and aversion to anything divine and therefore a rift with and aversion to truth and goodness, as discussed in §§5229, 5474, 5841. Sin also symbolizes alienation, then, since people averse to truth and goodness alienate themselves from it.

7590 *Jehovah is in the right, and I and my people are in the wrong* means that divine goodness could not bear the wickedness of the persecutors and that this was the consequence. This can be seen from the fact that Jehovah is divine goodness. Jehovah means the divine reality, which is divine goodness, and God means the divine presence, which is divine truth, as discussed in §6905.

Jehovah is being described as *in the right* because he cannot bear the wickedness of the persecutors. *Pharaoh and his people* symbolize the persecutors, and their being *in the wrong* symbolizes their wickedness.

Plead to Jehovah symbolizes a wish that they intervene. This can be seen from the symbolism of *pleading* for another as intervention, as in §§7396, 7462. 7591

And let this be enough of [God's] voices [of thunder] and hail! means if the falsities cease, as the following shows: *Enough* means if they cease. The *voices* of thunder symbolize divine truth terrifying and devastating the evil, and through its inflow and presence, stirring up the falsity-from-evil symbolized by the hail, as discussed at §7573. For the meaning of *hail* as falsity that destroys truth, see §§7553, 7574. 7592

And I will send you away, and you will no longer remain means that they would leave them alone and not detain them anymore. This can be seen from the representation of Pharaoh, who is talking about himself, as the persecutors (mentioned often), from the symbolism of *sending away* as leaving alone, and from the symbolism of *no longer remaining* as not being detained anymore. 7593

And Moses said to him symbolizes the answer, as is self-evident. 7594

When I leave the city symbolizes separation, as the following shows: *Leaving* symbolizes separation, as mentioned §§6100, 7404, 7463. And a *city* inhabited by Pharaoh symbolizes falsity adopted by people who inflict harassment. After all, a city symbolizes a doctrinal position, and since it symbolizes a doctrinal position, it also symbolizes truth and in a negative sense falsity (§§402, 2268, 2451, 2712, 2943, 3216, 4492, 4493). 7595

I will stretch my palms out to Jehovah symbolizes intervention. This can be seen from the symbolism of *stretching one's palms out to Jehovah,* or pleading, as intervention. About pleading, see §§7396, 7462, 7591. Pleading is oral, or spoken; spreading out one's palms is a gesture, or action, that corresponds to the pleading of the heart. There are physical gestures or motions corresponding to every frame of mind. What corresponds to humility is kneeling; what corresponds to deeper humility is full prostration; what corresponds to pleading is the stretching out of one's hands to heaven; and so on. The emotions these gestures or actions symbolize in the Word are the same ones they correspond to, because those are the ones they represent—which shows what representation is. 7596

The voices [of thunder] will stop, and the hail will no longer come symbolizes the end of that stage, as the following shows: *Voices* of thunder symbolize divine truth bringing devastation on the evil, as described in §7573. *Hail* symbolizes falsity destroying truth, as explained in §§7553, 7574. And *stopping* and *no longer coming* symbolize an end to those things and therefore an end to that stage. Each plague symbolizes one stage in the devastation of spirits who persecute the upright in the other life. 7597

7598 *So that you may know that the land is Jehovah's* means this reveals that the Lord is the only God in the church, as the following shows: *Knowing* symbolizes being revealed. The *land* symbolizes the church, as dealt with in §§662, 1066, 1068, 1262, 1413, 1607, 1733, 1850, 2117, 2118 at the end, 2928, 3355, 4447, 4535, 5577. And *Jehovah* means the Lord; see §§1343, 1736, 2921, 3023, 3035, 5663, 6303, 6905, 6945, 6956. This makes it plain that *the land is Jehovah's* means that the church is the Lord's and accordingly that the Lord is the only God in the church, as in §§7401, 7444, 7544.

7599 *As for you and your servants, I know that you do not yet fear the face of Jehovah God* means that the persecutors are not yet in awe of the Lord. This can be seen from the representation of *Pharaoh and his servants* as the persecutors (explained before) and from the symbolism of *[not yet] fearing the face of Jehovah* as a lack of awe for the Lord. For the idea that the Lord is meant by *Jehovah* in the Word, see the sections cited directly above at §7598.

The verse speaks of fearing the face of Jehovah because Jehovah's face symbolizes mercy and therefore peace and everything good (§§222, 223, 5585), and in a negative sense, the absence of mercy, peace, and anything good (§§5585, 5592, 5816, 5823). The reason Jehovah's face symbolizes the absence of mercy, peace, and anything good is that the evil turn away from Jehovah, or the Lord. They turn away from neighborly love with its goodness and from faith with its truth, which hold the Lord within them. What belongs to the Lord then lies behind their back and what belongs to themselves lies before their face, and they do not see what lies behind their back or care about it. This is the source of all evil and consequently of all unhappiness and hell for a person.

7600 Exodus 9:31–35. *And the flax and the barley were struck, because the barley was a ripening ear and the flax was a stalk. But the wheat and the spelt were not struck, because they were hidden. And Moses went out from Pharaoh, from the city, and stretched his palms out to Jehovah, and the voices [of thunder] and the hail stopped and rain did not pour on the earth. And Pharaoh saw that the rain and the hail and the voices [of thunder] stopped, and he continued to sin, and he made his heart leaden, as did his servants. And Pharaoh's heart hardened, and he did not send the children of Israel away, as Jehovah had spoken by the hand of Moses.*

And the flax symbolizes truth on the outer earthly plane. *And the barley* symbolizes the goodness that goes with it. *Were struck* means that they were destroyed. *Because the barley was a ripening ear and the flax was a stalk* means that this goodness and truth were conspicuous and faced downward. *But the wheat and the spelt* symbolizes goodness on the inner earthly plane and the truth that goes with it. *Were not struck* means that they were not destroyed. *Because they were hidden* means because they were not conspicuous and because they turned further inward. *And Moses went out from Pharaoh, from the city* symbolizes separation from all this. *And stretched his palms out to Jehovah* symbolizes intervention. *And the voices [of thunder] and the hail stopped* means that it was the end of that stage. *And rain did not pour on the earth* means that this kind of falsity was no longer visible. *And Pharaoh saw* symbolizes a perception. *That the rain and the hail and the voices [of thunder] stopped* means that the stage had ended. *And he continued to sin* symbolizes withdrawing still further. *And he made his heart leaden, as did his servants* symbolizes obstinacy. *And Pharaoh's heart hardened* means that their own evil made them obstinate. *And he did not send the children of Israel away* means against leaving them alone. *As Jehovah had spoken* means as predicted. *By the hand of Moses* means by way of the law from the Divine.

And the flax symbolizes truth on the outer earthly plane. This can be 7601
seen from the symbolism of *flax* as truth, but truth on the outer earthly plane, as discussed below. The earthly plane has an outer and an inner aspect (see §§4570, 5118, 5497, 5649), so truth and goodness on that plane can be inward or outward (§§3293, 3294). Truth and goodness on the outer earthly level are symbolized by flax and barley; goodness and truth on the inner earthly level are symbolized by wheat and spelt.

[2] This verse and the next are about truth and goodness that are destroyed and stripped away and about goodness and truth that are not destroyed or stripped away. The verses are therefore about truth and goodness that are hidden away and preserved for future use and truth and goodness that are not hidden away or preserved. When the evil are undergoing devastation—when they are being separated from truth and goodness and are being left to their evil and falsity—they are stripped of the truth and goodness in their outer earthly part that are connected with the falsity and evil there. This truth and goodness face downward, so they cannot be preserved (see below at §§7604, 7607), but truth and goodness in the inner earthly part are not stripped away. Instead they are taken further within, where they are preserved for future use. Then contact between the inner and outer aspects of the earthly level is shut down so thoroughly that no goodness or truth is able to flow from the inner to the outer earthly level. All that is allowed through is a general inflow of a

kind that enables a person to rationalize things and to string arguments together in support of falsity and evil.

The goodness and truth that are preserved are symbolized in the Word by a remnant, concerning which, see §§468, 530, 560, 561, 576, 661, 798, 1738, 1906, 2284, 5135, 5342, 5344, 5897, 5898, 5899, 6156, 7564.

This now is the message of the two current verses and is symbolized by the words "the flax and the barley were struck, because the barley was a ripening ear and the flax was a stalk;" and "the wheat and the spelt were not struck, because they were hidden."

[3] Flax symbolizes truth because of representations in heaven. In heaven, people absorbed in the truth that characterizes the earthly level are seen wearing a white that looks linen-white. Such truth itself is also represented there, as cloth woven of delicate linen thread. If the truth being represented is based on goodness, the thread looks like silk thread—lustrous, exquisitely translucent, and soft—and the clothing made of it looks the same. If on the other hand the truth being represented is not based on goodness, the thread, which resembles linen thread, does not look translucent, lustrous, or soft but rough and brittle, although it is still white.

[4] These comments now reveal the significance of the fact that angels seen by people on earth have appeared in linen. An example is some angels described in John:

> The seven angels having the seven plagues went out from the temple, *dressed in white and shining linen* and encircled at their chests with golden sashes. (Revelation 15:6)

In Daniel:

> I raised my eyes and looked, *and here, now, a lone man dressed in linen,* whose hips were girded with the gold of Uphaz. (Daniel 10:5)

In Ezekiel:

> Here, six men were coming by way of the upper gate, and each had a weapon for dispersing [people] in his hand. *But there was one man in the middle of them dressed in linen,* and the inkhorn of a scribe was on his hip. (Ezekiel 9:2)

More is said about this angel in verses 3, 4 of the same chapter and in Ezekiel 10:2–7. The same author describes an angel measuring the new temple with a *linen string* and a measuring reed in hand (Ezekiel 40 and following chapters). The angels seen in the Lord's tomb also appeared *dressed in white that shone like lightning* (Matthew 28:3; Mark 16:5; Luke 24:4; John 20:11, 12).

[5] Since linen symbolized truth on the outer earthly plane, and the outer earthly plane is what clothes the inner levels, that truth is what was represented by the linen the angels wore. It was also what was represented by the linen garments Aaron wore when he ministered in the Holy Place, as described in Moses:

> When Aaron enters the Holy Place, *he shall wear a holy linen tunic* and gird himself with a *linen belt* and put on a *linen turban;* these are the garments of holiness. (Leviticus 16:4)

Likewise in Ezekiel:

> The Levitical priests [who are] sons of Zadok, when they enter the gates of the inner courtyard, *shall wear linen garments,* and wool shall not go up onto them. When they minister in the gates of the inner courtyard and deeper within, *linen turbans shall be on their head, linen shorts* shall be on their hips. (Ezekiel 44:17, 18)

This is about the new temple and the new Jerusalem, which stand for the Lord's kingdom. For the same reason, priests bore *linen ephods* (1 Samuel 22:11, 18); Samuel ministered before Jehovah, a boy *girded with a linen ephod* (1 Samuel 2:18); and when David moved the ark into his city, *he was girded with a linen ephod* (2 Samuel 6:14).

[6] These considerations also show why the Lord, when he washed the disciples' feet, *girded his waist with a piece of linen* and wiped their feet with the *piece of linen* with which he was girded (John 13:4, 5). Foot washing symbolized purification from sin, purification being accomplished through religious truth, because this teaches us how to live.

[7] In the following passages as well linen symbolizes truth. In Jeremiah:

> Jehovah said to the prophet, "Go buy yourself a *linen sash* and put it on your hips, but you must not dip it in water. Take the *sash,* and get up, go to the Euphrates and hide it in a hole in the rock." At the end of many days, when he took the *sash* [from the place] where he had hidden it, look! The *sash* was ruined; it was not good for anything. (Jeremiah 13:1–7)

The linen sash on the prophet's hips represented truth-from-goodness as it exists at first in a religion being founded by the Lord and as it exists later, near the end, when it has been ruined for the people in the religion and is not good for anything. In Isaiah:

> *Those producing silk linen* and those who weave curtains will blush. (Isaiah 19:9)

This is about Egypt. Making silk linen stands for fabricating truths. [8] In Moses:

> You shall not plow with an ox and a donkey together. *You shall not wear a mixed garment of wool and linen together.* (Deuteronomy 22:10, 11)

An ox symbolizes goodness on the earthly level; a donkey, truth on the earthly level. The same applies to wool and linen. The prohibition against plowing with an ox and a donkey together and against wearing a mixed garment of wool and linen together meant that people were not to be in two states simultaneously. They were not to look toward truth from a standpoint of goodness and at the same time look toward goodness from the standpoint of truth. These words enfold the same meaning as the Lord's words in Matthew:

> Those on the roof of the house should not go down to take anything from their house. And those in the field should not turn back behind to take their garment. (Matthew 24:17, 18)

For an explanation of this passage, see §3652 at the end. People who view truth from goodness are in an inner heaven, while people who view goodness from truth are in an outer heaven. The latter gaze at heaven from the world; the former gaze at the world from heaven, so they are in an opposite mode. Each viewpoint would destroy the other, then, if they were put together.

7602 *And the barley* symbolizes the goodness that goes with it. This can be seen from the symbolism of *barley* as goodness on the outer earthly plane. Barley has this symbolism because it is produce of the field and is a grain that serves as food. The goodness that results from truth is symbolized by grain in general (§§3580, 5295, 5410, 5959) and by barley and wheat in particular, barley symbolizing goodness on the outer earthly plane, and wheat goodness on the inner earthly plane.

That is what barley symbolizes in Joel:

> Minha and libation have been cut off from the House of Jehovah. The priests, ministers of Jehovah, mourned. The field was devastated, the earth mourned, *because the grain was devastated,* the new wine dried up,

> the oil droops. The farmers were put to shame, the vinedressers wailed, *over the wheat and over the barley,* because the harvest of the field was destroyed. (Joel 1:9, 10, 11)

The prophet is dealing here with the devastation of goodness and truth, as the next verses in that chapter show. So the grain, new wine, wheat, and barley do not mean those products but rather symbolize something spiritual. The wheat, then, symbolizes an inner kind of goodness and the barley an outer kind. Barley has the same symbolism in Ezekiel 4:9 and Deuteronomy 8:8. [2] In Judges:

> When Gideon reached the camp, a man was recounting a dream to his companion and said, "Here, I had a vivid dream, and *here, a toasted round of barley bread rolled to the camp of Midian* and came right to the tent and struck it so that it fell, and turned it upside down, and that is how the tent fell." (Judges 7:13)

Midian symbolizes people in possession of the truth that goes with simple goodness, and in a negative sense, people who do not display goodness in their lives (§§3242, 4756, 4788, 6773). This goodness is the goodness of the outer earthly level and is symbolized by barley bread. However, the delight of sensual pleasure sometimes replaces this goodness as a person's ultimate goal, and a toasted round of barley bread symbolizes that pleasure under those circumstances. This is the state the passage depicts and the state the Midianites then represented.

Were struck means that they were destroyed, as is plain without explanation. 7603

Because the barley was a ripening ear and the flax was a stalk means that this goodness and truth were conspicuous and faced downward, as the following shows: *Barley* and *flax* symbolize goodness and truth on the outer earthly plane, as discussed just above at §§7601, 7602. And a *ripening ear* and a *stalk* symbolize something conspicuous, because the next verse says that the wheat and spelt were hidden, or were not conspicuous. After all, ripe grain stands visible in its ear and on its stalk, ready to fall. In a spiritual sense, which has to do with the goodness sought by faith and neighborly love, this means that it faced downward. 7604

The discussion above at §7601 goes into more detail on the subject.

[2] Goodness and truth on the outer earthly plane in an evil person face downward because they exist side by side there with evil and falsity and are connected to them. All evil and falsity face downward, that is, out toward the earth and the world, so any goodness and truth attached to

them do the same. This is because evil and falsity take goodness and truth along with them, by misapplying them.

This goodness and truth are what are stripped away from an evil person. If they were not stripped away, the goodness and truth that the Lord stores away and preserves on the inner earthly level would flow in and unite with the goodness and truth on the outer level and act in unison with them. As a consequence the goodness and truth on the inner level would also be bent downward and would therefore be destroyed.

What distinguishes us from brute animals is our ability to face up toward the Divine. Without this ability, a person would be like an animal, since an animal looks only downward.

This now shows why the downward-facing goodness and truth in the evil are taken from them. It also shows why this results in the shutting down of contact with inner levels, where goodness and truth are stored away by the Lord and preserved for future use.

7605 *But the wheat and the spelt* symbolizes goodness on the inner earthly plane and the truth that goes with it, as the following shows: *Wheat* symbolizes a loving, charitable goodness, as discussed at §3941, and since it is a higher-quality grain than barley, it symbolizes goodness on the inner earthly plane. And *spelt* symbolizes truth on the inner earthly plane corresponding to the goodness symbolized by wheat. The symbolism of spelt as this kind of truth is evident from the fact that where the Word speaks of goodness it also speaks of truth. This is due to the heavenly marriage, which is the marriage of goodness and truth at every point in the Word. In the highest sense it is due to the union of the divinity itself and the divine humanity in the Lord, to which the marriage of goodness and truth in heaven corresponds. The Lord himself in his divinity itself and his divine humanity is therefore present at the core of the Word; see §§683, 793, 801, 2173, 2516, 2618, 2712, 2803, 3132, 4137 at the end, 5502, 6179, 6343.

This shows that spelt symbolizes truth corresponding to the goodness symbolized by wheat.

7606 *Were not struck* means that they were not destroyed, as is plain without explanation.

7607 *Because they were hidden* means because they were not conspicuous and because they turned further inward. This can be seen from the symbolism of *they were hidden* as not being conspicuous. In a spiritual sense it means because they were on the inner earthly plane, where they turned further inward. The reason they could not be destroyed is that they faced toward heaven and the Lord (which is to face in an inward direction) rather than out toward the earth and the world (which is to face in an outward direction).

I need to say briefly what it means to face in an inward or an outward direction. We were created in such a way that we can look above ourselves toward heaven, all the way to the Divine, or below ourselves toward the world and the earth. This distinguishes us from brute animals. When we have as our goal our neighbor, our country, the church, heaven, or especially the Lord, we are looking above ourselves toward heaven, all the way to the Divine. When we have ourselves and the world as our goal, we are looking below ourselves. (To have something for a goal is to love it, because what we love is what we have as our goal; and what we love dominates everything—that is, every thought and intention.)

When we face one way, we do not face the other; when we look toward the world and ourselves, we do not look toward heaven or the Lord, and the reverse. The two directions are opposite.

[2] The ability we have to look above ourselves, or to think about the Divine and to be united to the Divine by love, makes it obvious that it is the Divine that raises our mind. We cannot possibly look above ourselves unless our mind is lifted up by the one above. This also shows that everything good and true in us is the Lord's.

It shows too that when we look below ourselves, we separate ourselves from the Divine and turn our inner levels toward ourselves and the world—the same direction in which the inner levels of brute animals turn. And of course to that extent we then divest ourselves of our humanity.

All this now makes plain what is meant by facing in an inward direction, above ourselves, and what is meant by facing in an outward direction, below ourselves.

And Moses went out from Pharaoh, from the city symbolizes separation 7608
from all this, as can be seen from the explanation above at §7595, where similar words appear.

And stretched his palms out to Jehovah symbolizes intervention, as above 7609
at §7596.

And the voices [of thunder] and the hail stopped symbolizes the end of 7610
that stage, as above at §7597.

And rain did not pour on the earth means that this kind of falsity was 7611
no longer visible, as the following shows: The *rain,* which in this case is

a rain of hail, symbolizes falsity, as dealt with in §§7553, 7574. And *not pouring on the earth* means that it ended and therefore also that it was not visible; that is, the falsity symbolized by the rain of hail was not visible.

7612 *And Pharaoh saw* symbolizes a perception. This can be seen from the symbolism of *seeing* as a perception, as discussed in §§2150, 3764, 4723, 5400.

7613 *That the rain [and] the hail and the voices [of thunder] stopped* symbolizes the end of that stage, as above in §§7597, 7610.

7614 *And he continued to sin* symbolizes withdrawing still further. This can be seen from the symbolism of *continuing* as still further, or more, and from that of *sinning* as disconnection, withdrawal, and separation from goodness and truth (discussed in §§5229, 5474, 5841, 7589).

7615 *And he made his heart leaden, as did his servants* symbolizes obstinacy. This is established by the symbolism of *making one's heart leaden,* or hardening it, as being obstinate, as mentioned in §§7272, 7300, 7305.

7616 *And Pharaoh's heart hardened* means that their own evil made them obstinate. This is established by the symbolism of a *heart's hardening* as being obstinate, as mentioned directly above at §7615, which says that he made his heart leaden. The difference is that falsity makes the heart leaden, but evil hardens it.

7617 *And he did not send the children of Israel away* means against leaving them alone. This is evident from the symbolism of *sending away* as leaving alone (a meaning given many times before) and from the representation of the children of Israel as people of the spiritual church—the people being persecuted—as dealt with in §§6426, 6637, 6862, 6868, 7035, 7062, 7198, 7201, 7215, 7223.

7618 *As Jehovah had spoken* means as predicted, as before in §§7302, 7340, 7414, 7432, 7535.

7619 *By the hand of Moses* means by way of the law from the Divine. This can be seen from the symbolism of *by the hand of someone,* which means indirectly (discussed below), and from the representation of *Moses* as the law from the Divine (treated of in §§6771, 6827).

The reason speaking by the hand of someone means by way of that person, or indirectly, is that a hand symbolizes power. "By the hand of someone" therefore means by the power of a surrogate, which is the same as indirectly. What happens to anyone indirectly happens through a third party's power. That is why Scripture uses this figure of speech, as for instance in Kings, which speaks a number of times of the word that Jehovah spoke by the hand of someone. For instance, *he spoke by the hand* of the prophet Ahijah (1 Kings 14:18), *by the hand* of Ahijah the

Shilonite (1 Kings 15:29), *by the hand* of the prophet Jehu (1 Kings 16:7, 12), *by the hand* of Joshua (1 Kings 16:34), *by the hand* of Elijah (1 Kings 17:16), and *by the hand* of the prophet Jonah (2 Kings 14:25).

The Spirits and Inhabitants of Mars (Continued)

ONCE I saw a gorgeous flame. It varied in color from dark red to a 7620
lighter, brighter red. The colors were also beautifully shimmering with the flame. I saw a kind of hand as well. The hand did not hold the flame, but the flame clung to it, first on the back, then on the palm, licking the hand all around. This went on for some time.

The hand with the flame then moved far off, and where it stopped, there was a glow. The hand faded into the glow, and when it did, the flame changed into a bird. In the beginning the bird had the same colors as the flame, and the colors sparkled the same way, but gradually they changed, and with them, the bird's vital energy.

It flew around, first circling my head and then moving out front into a narrow space that resembled a small room. The farther out it flew, the more the life drained from it, until finally it turned to stone. It then started out pearl-colored but later turned dark. Even when it was lifeless, though, it kept flying.

While the bird was flying around my head and still had its vital energy, 7621
there appeared a spirit who rose up from below through my pelvic region to the area of my chest. He wanted to take the bird away, but since it was so beautiful, all the spirits around me stopped him by keeping their eye on the bird. The spirit from below then launched a forceful argument that the Lord was with him and consequently that he was acting as he was on behalf of the Lord. Most of the spirits did not believe it, because he had come up from below, but the ones around me no longer prevented him from taking the bird. However, heaven then flowed in, so he could not hold on to the bird but soon opened his hand and let it go free.

After this episode, the spirits around me who had been so intently 7622
watching the bird and the series of transformations it was undergoing spent considerable time discussing it with each other. They perceived that a vision like this necessarily symbolized something heavenly.

A flame, they knew, symbolizes heavenly love and the desires that go with it; the hand with the flame clinging to it symbolizes one's life force and its strength; the changing colors symbolize differences in the vitality of one's wisdom and understanding. A bird has the same symbolism, except that a flame symbolizes heavenly love with its various aspects, while a bird symbolizes spiritual love with its various aspects. (Heavenly love is love for the Lord; spiritual love is mutual love and charity for one's neighbor.) The changing colors and different levels of life in the bird, to the point of petrification, symbolize a series of changes in the spiritual vitality of one's mind.

[2] They also knew that spirits who come up from below through the pelvic region to the area of the chest are firmly convinced they live in the Lord. Consequently these spirits believe that everything they do is done by the Lord's will, even if it is evil and wicked.

Nonetheless, the spirits around me could not tell from this just who it was that the vision stood for. Eventually they were informed from heaven that it stood for the inhabitants of Mars. The heavenly love of those inhabitants—a love many of the inhabitants [today] still possess—was symbolized by the flame that adhered to the hand. Their wisdom and understanding was symbolized by the sequence of changes in color. The bird as it first appeared, when its colors were still pretty and it had a lot of vital energy, symbolized their spiritual love. The fact that the bird became stonelike and lifeless and then turned dark symbolized inhabitants who have walked away from a loving goodness and are engaged in evil but yet believe that they live in the Lord. All this the spirits around me learned from heaven.

As there is more to reveal and illustrate about the inhabitants who are like this and about the state of their life, let me relate it at the end of the next chapter [§§7742–7751].

Exodus 10

Teachings on Neighborly Love

THERE are two things that radiate from the Lord and are therefore divine in their origin, one being goodness, the other truth. These two are therefore the qualities that predominate in heaven and in fact constitute heaven itself. 7623

In the church they are called neighborly love and faith.

As they go out from the Lord, goodness and truth are completely united, and united in such a way that they are not two but one. They are also one in heaven, as a result, and since they are one in heaven, heaven is an image of the Lord. 7624

The church would also be an image of the Lord if neighborly love and faith were one there.

The sun and its light enable us to form an idea of the goodness that marks neighborly love and of the truth that marks faith. When light coming from the sun joins with warmth, as it does in spring and summer, then everything on the planet sprouts and flourishes. When sunlight lacks warmth, though, as it does in winter, then everything on the planet droops and dies off. 7625

What is more, the Word compares the Lord to the sun and compares truth that joins with goodness and radiates from him to light. The Word also refers directly to faith and its truth as light and to love and its goodness as fire. Besides which, love really is the fire of life, and faith is the light of life.

The same example enables us to picture what religious people are like when faith joins with neighborly love in them, and what they are like when it does not. When the two join, a religious person is like a garden or a park, and when they do not join, the person is like a wilderness or earth completely covered in snow. 7626

It takes only the limited light of the earthly mind to see that truth and goodness agree and are capable of being joined together but that 7627 truth and evil clash and cannot be joined together. Likewise with faith and neighborly love.

Even common experience offers the same testimony: people who display evil in their lives adopt falsity as their faith, or lack faith altogether, or totally oppose faith.

Something not widely known is that people who live evil lives adopt whatever falsity accompanies their evil, even if they believe they have the truth. The reason they believe they have the truth is the dogmatic faith they possess, which will be discussed later.

Exodus 10

1. And Jehovah said to Moses, "Come to Pharaoh, because I myself have made his heart leaden, and the heart of his servants, in order that I may set these signs of mine in his midst

2. and in order that you may tell in the ears of your son and of your son's son what I have been about in Egypt, and my signs that I have set among them, and in order that you may know that I am Jehovah."

3. And Moses came to Pharaoh, as did Aaron, and they said to him, "This is what Jehovah, God of the Hebrews, says: 'How long will you refuse to be humble before me? Send my people away and let them serve me.

4. Because if you refuse to send my people away, here now, tomorrow I am bringing the locust into your border.

5. And it will cover the surface of the land, and no one will be able to see the land, and it will eat the rescued remainder left to you by the hail. And it will eat every tree sprouting from the field for you.

6. And your houses will be filled, and the houses of all your servants, and the houses of all Egyptians, [with locusts] that your parents have not seen, nor your parents' parents, from the day they were on the ground till this day.'" And he looked away and went out from Pharaoh.

7. And Pharaoh's servants said to him, "How long will this be a snare for us? Send the men away and let them serve Jehovah their God. Do you not yet know that Egypt is perishing?"

8. And Moses was brought back—as was Aaron—to Pharaoh, and he said to them, "Go serve Jehovah your God. Who exactly is going?"

9. And Moses said, "With our young and with our old we will go, with our sons and with our daughters, with our flock and with our herd we will go, because it is a feast to Jehovah for us."

10. And he said to them, "Right, Jehovah will be with you when I send you and your little children away! See? There is evil in your faces.

11. No! Go, please, you young men, and serve Jehovah, because that is what you seek." And he sent them away from the face of Pharaoh.

12. And Jehovah said to Moses, "Stretch your hand out over the land of Egypt to bring the locust, and it will go up over the land of Egypt and will eat all the grass of the land, everything that the hail has left."

13. And Moses stretched his staff out over the land of Egypt, and Jehovah brought an east wind into the land that whole day and whole night. Morning came, and the east wind brought the locust.

14. And the locust went up onto all the land of Egypt and came to rest on the whole border of Egypt very heavily. There was no locust like it before that, and there will be none after it.

15. And it covered the surface of the whole land, and the land was overshadowed, and it ate all the grass of the land and all the tree fruit that the hail had left remaining. And there was nothing green remaining on the trees or in the grass of the field in all the land of Egypt.

16. And Pharaoh hurried to call Moses and Aaron and said, "I have sinned against Jehovah your God and against you.

17. And now please forgive my sin just this time and plead to Jehovah your God and have him remove from me such great death as this."

18. And [Moses] went out from Pharaoh and pleaded to Jehovah.

19. And Jehovah turned a very strong sea wind and took away the locust and hurled it into the Suph Sea; not one locust was left within the whole border of Egypt.

20. And Jehovah hardened Pharaoh's heart, and he did not send the children of Israel away.

21. And Jehovah said to Moses, "Stretch your hand out to the sky, and there will be darkness on the land of Egypt, and people will feel about in the dark."

22. And Moses stretched his hand out to the sky, and there was thick darkness in all the land of Egypt for three days.

23. A man could not see his brother and none got up out of place for three days. But all the children of Israel had light in their dwellings.

24. And Pharaoh called to Moses and said, "Go serve Jehovah. Only your flock and your herd must stay. Even your little children will go with you."

25. And Moses said, "You yourself will put sacrifices and burnt offerings into our hand, and we will perform them to Jehovah our God.

26. And our livestock must also go with us; not a hoof will be left behind, because we must take from [our livestock] to serve Jehovah our God, and we won't know what we must use to serve Jehovah till we come there."

27. And Jehovah hardened Pharaoh's heart, and he did not want to send them away.

28. And Pharaoh said to him, "Go away from me; be careful not to see my face again, because on the day of your seeing my face you will die."

29. And Moses said, "You have spoken rightly; I will no longer see your face."

Summary

7628 THE inner meaning of this chapter treats further of the devastation of spirits persecuting people of the spiritual church. The subject here is the ninth and tenth stages or steps in the process, which are depicted as the locust and the darkness, symbolizing falsity-from-evil that strips away every trace of religion in these spirits.

Inner Meaning

7629 EXODUS 10:1–6. *And Jehovah said to Moses, "Come to Pharaoh, because I myself have made his heart leaden, and the heart of his servants, in order that I may set these signs of mine in his midst and in order that you may tell in the ears of your son and of your son's son what I have been about in Egypt, and my signs that I have set among them, and in order that you may know that I am Jehovah." And Moses came to Pharaoh, as did Aaron, and they said to him, "This is what Jehovah, God of the Hebrews, says: 'How long will you refuse to be humble before me? Send my people away and let them serve me. Because if you refuse to send my people away, here now, tomorrow I am bringing the locust into your border. And it will cover the surface of the land, and no one will be able to see the land, and it will eat the rescued remainder left to you by the hail. And it will eat every tree sprouting from the field for you. And your houses will be filled, and the houses of all your servants, and the houses of all Egyptians, [with locusts] that your parents have not seen, nor your parents' parents, from the day they were on the ground till this day.'" And he looked away and went out from Pharaoh.*

And Jehovah said to Moses symbolizes a command. *Come to Pharaoh* symbolizes truth imparted by the Divine present among the persecutors. *Because I myself have made his heart leaden, and the heart of his servants* means that all of them in general were obstinate. *In order that I may set these signs of mine in his midst* means for the evil to recognize that they are immersed in evil and for the good to be enlightened about the state of people within the church who live evil lives. *And in order that you may tell in the ears of your son and of your son's son what I have been about in Egypt* means for people committed to truth and goodness to realize what happens to people in the church who persecute the upright. *And my signs that I have set among them* means for them to be enlightened about the state of people in the church who live evil lives. *And in order that you may know that I am Jehovah* means for them to see from this that the Lord is the only God. *And Moses came to Pharaoh, as did Aaron* symbolizes the presence of divine truth. *And they said to him* symbolizes a perception. *This is what Jehovah, God of the Hebrews, says,* symbolizes a command from the Lord, who is the God of the church. *How long will you refuse to be humble before me?* symbolizes disobedience. *Send my people away [and] let them serve me* means to leave people of the spiritual church alone to worship the Lord. *Because if you refuse to send them away* means if they did not leave them alone. *Here now, I am bringing the locust into your border* means that falsity would occupy their most remote parts. *And it will cover the surface of the land* means consequently the outermost levels of their earthly mind. *And no one will be able to see the land* symbolizes the obscuring of the entire earthly mind as a result. *And it will eat the rescued remainder left to you by the hail* symbolizes the obliteration of everything that has any truth to it. *And it will eat every tree sprouting from the field for you* symbolizes the consequent obliteration of any concepts they had received from the church. *And your houses will be filled, and the houses of all your servants, and the houses of all Egyptians, [with locusts]* means that falsity will prevail in each and every part of the earthly plane, from its inner depths to its outermost surface. *That your parents have not seen, nor your parents' parents, from the day they were on the ground till this day* means that the kind of falsity found among them had not existed in the church from ancient times on.

And he looked away and went out from Pharaoh symbolizes being deprived of perception and cut off.

7630 *And Jehovah said to Moses* symbolizes a command—a command that was to be conveyed to Pharaoh. This is established by the symbolism of *saying,* when Jehovah is addressing the persecutors, as a command, which is discussed in §§7036, 7107, 7310.

7631 *Come to Pharaoh* symbolizes truth imparted by the Divine present among the persecutors. This can be seen from the symbolism of *coming to* or approaching someone as being present (as in §§5934, 6063, 6089, 7498), from the representation of Moses as truth imparted by the Divine (discussed in §§6771, 6827), and from the representation of *Pharaoh* as spirits who persecute members of the spiritual church in the other life (dealt with in §§6651, 6679, 6683, 7107, 7110, 7126, 7142, 7220, 7228).

7632 *Because I myself have made his heart leaden, and the heart of his servants* means that all of them in general were obstinate. This can be seen from the symbolism of *making someone's heart leaden,* or hardening it, as making oneself obstinate (mentioned in §§7272, 7300, 7305) and from the representation of Pharaoh, whose heart was being turned to lead, as the persecutors. When the text mentions *him and his servants,* it symbolizes all the persecutors in general, because the servants together with Pharaoh make up a household.

Where the text says that Jehovah made Pharaoh's heart leaden, the inner-level symbolism is that Pharaoh did it himself. In ancient times, on account of the uneducated, all evil was attributed to Jehovah, and that was because the uneducated could not see and mostly could not comprehend how events could come from any other source. They also could not see how to understand the concept that Jehovah allows the Devil's horde to inflict evil, without interfering, when he has all power. It was because this was beyond the grasp of the simple-thinking, and barely within the grasp of the more sophisticated, that even evil was said (and believed by many) to spring from Jehovah. This is a common occurrence in the Word, whose literal meaning agrees with the beliefs of the uneducated.

For the idea that the evil ascribed to Jehovah in the Word comes from humankind, see §§2447, 6071, 6991.

7633 *[In order that] I may set these signs of mine in his midst* means for the evil to recognize that they are immersed in evil and for the good to be enlightened about the state of people within the church who live evil lives. This can be seen from the symbolism of *signs* as proof—and therefore recognition—that a thing is true, as noted at §6870. A sign also symbolizes enlightenment (§7012). *Setting signs in his midst,* then, means for the evil to recognize that they are immersed in evil. The fact that it also means for the good to be enlightened about the state of people within the church who live evil lives is plain from the next words: "And in order that you may tell in the ears of your son and of your son's son what I have been about in Egypt, and my signs that I have set among them." What is symbolized here is an intention for people committed to truth and goodness to realize what happens to people in the church who persecute the upright.

On the point that the harassers of the upright in the other world are people who had been part of the church and knew the precepts of faith but lived a life contrary to them, see §§7317, 7502, 7545, 7554.

And in order that you may tell in the ears of your son and of your son's son **7634**
what I have been about in Egypt means for people committed to truth and goodness to realize what happens to people in the church who persecute the upright, as the following shows: *Telling in their ears* means for them to realize and perceive. A *son* and a *son's son* symbolize people committed to truth and goodness. For the meaning of a son as truth, see §§489, 491, 1147, 2623, 3373, and for that of sons' sons as further developments in truth, §6583. The sons here mean people devoted to truth and also to goodness because people in the church are being symbolized. That is why "your son's son" is addressed to Moses, who represents divine law. Divine law is divine truth radiating from the Lord's divine goodness, so it is divine truth united with divine goodness (§§7623, 7624), which together give rise to the church. And *what I have been about in Egypt* means what happens to spirits who persecute the upright in the other life. The symbolism of signs as what happens, and of Pharaoh and the Egyptians as those who inflict harassment in the other world, is evident from discussions above. For the idea that the harassers are people who were part of the church, see directly above at the end of §7633.

And my signs that I have set among them means for them to be enlight- **7635**
ened about the state of people in the church who live evil lives. This is evident from the discussion just above at §7633, where similar words appear.

[And] in order that you may know that I am Jehovah means for them **7636**
to see from this that the Lord is the only God. This can be seen from the symbolism of *in order that you may know* as an intent for them to see. *I am Jehovah* means that the Lord is the only God. This is because [in the original language] *Jehovah* means "he is," so it means the source from

which comes the existence and emergence of everything, of which there can be only one. For the idea that Jehovah is the Lord, see §§1343, 1736, 2921, 3023, 3035, 5663, 6303, 6905, 6945, 6956. For the idea that these words mean he is the only God, §§7401, 7444, 7544, 7598.

7637 *And Moses came to Pharaoh, as did Aaron* symbolizes the presence of divine truth. This is clear from the symbolism of *coming to* or approaching as presence (as above at §7631) and from the representation of *Moses* and *Aaron* as divine truth, Moses representing inner truth and Aaron outer truth (discussed in §§7089, 7382).

7638 *And they said to him* symbolizes a perception. This can be seen from the symbolism of *saying* as perceiving, as discussed in §§1791, 1815, 1819, 1822, 1898, 1919, 2080, 2619, 2862, 3395, 3509, 5743, 5877. The reason *they said* means perception here is that Moses and Aaron represent divine truth, "coming" represents its presence, and the presence of divine truth creates perception.

7639 *This is what Jehovah, God of the Hebrews, says,* symbolizes a command from the Lord, who is the God of the church. This can be seen from the symbolism of *saying,* when Jehovah addresses the persecutors, as a command (as above at §7630), and from that of *Hebrews* as people in the church (discussed in §§5136, 6675, 6684, 6738). For the idea that Jehovah God is the Lord, see above at §7636.

7640 *How long will you refuse to be humble before me?* symbolizes disobedience. This is evident from the symbolism of *refusing to be humble* as not obeying. The reason it symbolizes this is that the question is addressed to people committed to evil, and they are incapable of humility before the Divine. Humility has two factors: acknowledging one's own nature, which is pure evil and is nothing in comparison with divinity, and acknowledging the nature of the Divine, which is pure goodness and is infinite. The evil cannot make these two acknowledgments, because they love themselves. If they do humble themselves, it is either because they are afraid or because they seek prestige and wealth. So they adopt a humble attitude only with their body, not in their heart, which sometimes derides the humility; such is the nature of humility inspired by fear or humility aiming at riches and high rank. It is the same with these people's humility before the Divine, although they do not realize it. The inner habit of people driven to evil by self-love is to regard themselves alone, puff themselves up, and turn their back on anyone who does not show them favor.

Since humility is impossible in the evil, in an inner sense being humble symbolizes obedience, so refusing to be humble symbolizes disobedience.

Send my people away and let them serve me means to leave people of the spiritual church alone to worship the Lord. This can be seen from the earlier treatment at §7500, where the same words occur. 7641

Because if you refuse to send them away means if they did not leave them alone. This is established by the symbolism of *sending them away* as leaving them alone, as many times before. *Refusing* to send them away, then, means being unwilling to leave them alone. 7642

Here now, I am bringing the locust into your border means that falsity would occupy their most remote parts. This can be seen from the symbolism of a *locust* as falsity in the most remote parts (discussed below), from that of a *border* as the most remote parts themselves, and from that of *bringing* as occupying (since it applies to falsity). 7643

It says that Jehovah would bring the locusts, but the meaning is that they would be brought, namely, by the evil. This is the same as blaming Jehovah (the Lord) for making Pharaoh's heart leaden, when it is people themselves and the evil in them that harden a heart; see above at §7632.

Evil does not come from the Lord but rather springs from humankind because we take the goodness that flows in from the Lord and divert it to our own purposes. Instead of focusing on the Lord and his qualities at every opportunity, we focus on ourselves. That is why we yearn to control everyone and to possess everything others have. That is why we look down on others and display hatred, vengefulness, and cruelty toward people who decline to fawn on us and to devote their energies to us. That is why we despise anything that has to do with faith or neighborly love—because when it flows in from the Lord, we turn it in our direction, away from the Lord.

[2] From this you can see that we take goodness itself, which flows in from the Lord, and turn it into evil.

That is why the evil in the other life move as far away as they can from heaven. When heaven draws near them—that is, when goodness and truth flow in more powerfully—they hurl themselves forcefully in the opposite direction, into evil and falsity. To the extent that evil and falsity increase in them, they push truth away and subject themselves to devastation. To the same extent they then plunge into the evils involved in punishment, because evil and punishment are bound up together in the other world.

[3] The Lord is constantly putting the heavens in order and is always summoning new inhabitants, to whom he gives homes and property. When he does, heaven approaches, or flows in more powerfully. So hellish spirits

hurl themselves more forcefully into evil and falsity and into the associated punishment. Since they hurl themselves into evil and falsity, they subject themselves to devastation, as just mentioned, and the process does not end until they have stripped themselves completely bare [of goodness and truth] and thrown themselves deep into hell.

Clearly, then, nothing but good emanates from the Lord, and evil comes from the people themselves who are devoted to evil.

This now shows how to understand the statement that Jehovah (the Lord) made Pharaoh's heart leaden and (here) that he would bring the locust, which symbolizes falsity-from-evil on the outermost surface.

[4] Where the Word deals with the devastation of the evil, it mentions locusts and grasshoppers a number of times. In those passages, the locust in an inner sense means falsity that devastates the outermost parts. As I have shown before, a person's earthly plane has inner and outer levels. Falsity in the most remote parts of the earthly plane is meant by the locust, and the evil there is meant by the grasshopper.

Since a locust means falsity in the most remote parts of the earthly plane, the text says that it will be brought *into the border* and cover the *surface* of the land. Verses 14 [and 15] below say, "The locust went up onto the land of Egypt and came to rest *on the whole border* of Egypt and covered the *surface* of the whole land." The border and surface symbolize the outermost, most remote parts, on which the inner levels rest, or where they end.

[5] That is what the locust and grasshopper mean in David:

> He sent against them a swarm that *devoured* them and frogs that destroyed them, *and gave to the grasshopper* their produce, and their labor *to the locust.* (Psalms 78:45, 46)

And in another place:

> He said that the *locust* and *grasshopper* should come, so that there would be no counting them. (Psalms 105:34)

These passages are talking about Egypt, and they mention grasshoppers, even though Moses never refers to them, only to locusts. The reason grasshoppers are also mentioned is that they symbolize evil, while locusts symbolize falsity—both of them as they exist in the most remote parts of the earthly level. When only locusts are mentioned, though [Deuteronomy 28:38; Judges 6:5; 7:12; Job 39:20; Psalms 109:23; Jeremiah 46:23], they symbolize both falsity and evil, because they stand for falsity that grows out of evil. [6] In Nahum:

> There fire will consume you, the sword will cut you off. It will eat you as the *grasshopper* does. Multiply like the *grasshopper,* multiply like the *locust!* You multiplied your merchants beyond the number of stars in the heavens. The *grasshopper* spread out and flew away. Your crowned [monarchs] are like the *locust;* your rulers are like the *locust of locusts.* (Nahum 3:15, 16, 17)

This is about the "blood-soaked city," which symbolizes a theology teaching what is false. It is especially in the most remote parts of the earthly level that falsity and evil multiply, because that is the place for sensory illusions rising out of objects found in the world and on earth, and for physical pleasures rising out of various kinds of appetite. For this reason grasshoppers and locusts also depict the proliferation of evil and falsity, as they do again in Judges 6:5; 7:12; Jeremiah 46:23. For the idea that the sensory level—the outermost level of the earthly plane—is absolutely full of illusions and therefore of falsities, see §§5084, 5089, 5094, 6310, 6311, 6313, 6318, 6598, 6612, 6614, 6622, 6624, 6948, 6949. [7] In Joel:

> What the caterpillar leaves *the locust eats,* and what the *locust* leaves the beetle eats, and what the beetle leaves the *grasshopper* eats. Wake up, drunkards, and cry and howl because of the new wine, all you wine bibbers, since it has been cut off. For a nation will come up over my land—strong and no counting them—and *will reduce my grapevine to a ruin and my fig tree to scum.* (Joel 1:4, 5, 6, 7)

In the same author:

> The threshing floors are full of pure grain, and the presses overflow with new wine and oil. And I will make up to you for the years that the *locust,* the beetle, the *grasshopper,* and the caterpillar *consumed.* (Joel 2:24, 25)

The locust stands for falsity in the most remote parts laying waste to truth and goodness. In Moses:

> You will bring much seed out to the field but gather little, because *the locust will devour it.* You will plant a vineyard but not drink wine or collect [grapes], because the worm will eat it. (Deuteronomy 28:38, 39)

The locust stands for falsity that results from evil. [8] In John:

> From the smoke of the opened abyss went *locusts* out into the earth, to whom was given authority as the scorpions of the earth have authority. They were told not to harm the grain of the earth nor any tree but only whichever people did not have God's seal on their foreheads. It was granted to them not to kill them but to torment them five months. The *figures of the locusts* were like horses prepared for war. And on their heads was something similar to crowns, like gold. Their faces were like people's faces. They had hair like women's hair, and their teeth were like lions' teeth. They had breastplates of something like iron. And the sound of their wings was like the sound of chariots with many horses running to war. Lastly, they had tails like scorpions, and stings were in their tails to harm people five months. They have over them a monarch, the angel of the abyss, whose name in Hebrew is *Abaddon.* But in Greek the angel has the name Apollyon. (Revelation 9:3–11)

What all this symbolizes no one can see except from the inner meaning. When the quotation is viewed in detail according to its inner meaning, it becomes clear that the locusts symbolize twisted reasoning based on illusions and therefore on falsity, and on philosophical proofs too. Because they symbolize this, they also symbolize the falsity found in the most remote parts of a person, which is more earthly and more body-centered than any other kind of falsity. It can easily fool us and lead us astray, because anything that is plain to our senses we grasp, but anything that contradicts them is hard for us to understand. [9] To see that locusts symbolize these things, let me explain the elements of the above quotation one by one.

The *abyss* the locusts came from is hell. The *grain of the earth* they were not to harm is knowledge. The *tree* is concepts of what is good and true. The *people* are desires for what is good. The fact that they were to harm the people but not the grain of the earth or the trees means that we can understand what is true and good even if we do not live by it. People who *have the seal on their foreheads* are people who have been reborn. *Tormenting for five months* the people who did not have God's seal on their foreheads means inflicting devastation on them. *Locusts like horses prepared for war* are twisted reasoning based on falsity that is used to combat religious truth. *Crowns like gold on their heads* and *faces like people's faces* means that the reasoning seems plausible and well intended. *Hair like women's* and *teeth like lions' teeth* are external elements of the earthly level, or sense impressions—that is, earthly-level illusions—that present an appearance of goodness. *Iron breastplates* are external elements that present the appearance of truth. A *sound of wings as of chariots with many horses running to war* is falsity in their religious teachings, from which and for which they fight. *Tails like scorpions, and stings in their tails* are poisonous traits that cause all the above to happen. The *monarch of the abyss* is falsity from hell. *Abaddon* is destruction. *Apollyon* is reasoning based on falsity that appears to be based on truth, especially when people who are considered wise prove the validity of such reasoning through a misuse of philosophy. Blind admiration for their wisdom persuades listeners to believe them.

[10] In a positive sense a locust symbolizes truth on the outermost level—very generalized truth—and the delight it affords. That is why John had *locusts* as his sustenance, and field honey (Matthew 3:4; Mark 1:6). These served as John's sustenance because he represented the Word. His food and his clothing—which was of camel hair with a leather belt—represented the Word in its outer meaning. Outer delight is symbolized by locusts and field honey (§5620), and outer truth by a garment of camel hair and a leather belt (§3301). That is why John is referred to as the Elijah who was to come and announce the Lord's Coming. For the idea that Elijah means the Word, see the preface to Genesis 18 and §§2762, 5247 at the end; and that locusts are among the insects that could be eaten, Leviticus 11:22.

And it will cover the surface of the land means the outermost levels of their earthly mind. This can be seen from the symbolism of a *surface* as the external and therefore outermost levels and from that of the *land* (in this case the land of Egypt) as the earthly mind (dealt with in §§5276, 5278, 5280, 5288, 5301). 7644

And no one will be able to see the land symbolizes the obscuring of the entire earthly mind as a result. This can be seen from the symbolism of *not being able to see* as obscureness, or an inability to perceive truth, and from that of the *land* of Egypt as the earthly mind (as directly above at §7644). 7645

I must explain briefly how it is that devastation of the outermost surface of the earthly plane obscures the entire earthly mind. Our inner levels terminate in our outermost or most remote levels, where the sequential levels in us coexist. When nothing but falsity and evil fills the outermost levels, truth and goodness flowing from the inner depths into the outermost levels flow into evil and falsity there, turning into evil and falsity themselves as a result. So nothing is visible anywhere on the earthly level except falsity and evil. That is what is meant by the obscuring of the entire earthly mind, as symbolized by not being able to see the land.

[2] That is also why hellish spirits who have undergone devastation are on the outermost edges of the earthly plane. In their case, the light that is called intellectual light is not unlike the light of this world, which in the other world turns pitch black at the presence of heaven's light.

So the most remote part of the earthly level (called the sensory plane) is filled with illusions and therefore falsities, and with sensual pleasures and therefore evils (§§6844, 6845). Because of this, and because the hells have the kind of light described, the Lord grants us the ability to rise up out of that sensory plane toward inner levels when we are being reborn; see §§6183, 6313, 7442.

7646 *And it will eat the rescued remainder left to you by the hail* symbolizes the obliteration of everything that has any truth to it. This is clear from the symbolism of *eating* as obliterating and from that of the *rescued remainder left by the hail* as truth unobliterated by the earlier kind of falsity that hail symbolizes. For the symbolism of hail as falsity, see §§7553, 7574. The kind of falsity hail symbolizes is on the outer earthly level, while the kind a locust symbolizes is in the very outermost parts of that level. The latter kind of falsity is what obliterates the most generalized kinds of truth and goodness. What is relatively superficial is also relatively general, and what is very superficial is very general. When anything general is destroyed, the particulars disperse, because general ideas are containers, and particular ideas are the contents.

7647 *And it will eat every tree sprouting from the field for you* symbolizes the consequent obliteration of any concepts they had received from the church. This is clear from the symbolism of *eating* as obliteration (as just above at §7646), from that of a *tree* as perceptions and as concepts of what is true and good (discussed in §§2722 at the end, 2972), and from that of a *field* as the church (discussed in §§2971, 3317, 3766, 4440, 7502, 7571).

7648 *And your houses will be filled, and the houses of all your servants, and the houses of all Egyptians, [with locusts]* means that falsity will prevail in each and every part of the earthly plane, from its inner depths to its outermost surface. This is clear from the symbolism of *being filled* as prevailing (discussed below) and from that of *Pharaoh's house, the houses of all his servants, and the houses of all Egyptians* as each and every part of the earthly plane (discussed in §§7353, 7355). In this case it means from the inner depths to the outermost surface, in keeping with the explanation above at §7645.

Why does *being filled* mean prevailing? When our mind is full of the falsity that grows out of evil, to the point where we enjoy misleading others with falsity and doing evil, this tendency is said to prevail in us, and the desire behind it is described as predominant. That which fills our whole mind, both our thoughts and our will, is said to reign supreme. Whatever we love more than anything else and take as our ultimate goal is this kind of predominant trait, and it dwells in the very smallest components of our will and thought. The exact identity of our prevailing trait can be known from the exhilaration we feel when it meets with success and the disappointment we feel when it does not.

What reigns supreme in us presents a portrait of our spirit, whose countenance is in perfect harmony with our dominant attribute. If that attribute consists of evil and falsity, our spirit is in the form of a devil, but if it consists of goodness and truth, our spirit is in the form of an angel. The spirit is basically a desire that has taken form. Our dominant passion is our truest shape, and the rest of our desires conform to it.

That your parents have not seen, nor your parents' parents, from the day 7649
they were on the ground till this day means that the kind of falsity found among them had not existed in the church from ancient times on, as the following shows: *That they have not seen*—referring to the locust—means that such falsity had not existed. For the symbolism of a locust as falsity in the most remote parts, see above at §7643. *Parents* and *parents' parents* mean from ancient times. And the *ground* symbolizes the church, as discussed in §§566, 1068. *From the day they were on it till this day* symbolizes the state the church was in from that time to this. For the meaning of a day as a state, see §§23, 487, 488, 493, 2788, 3462, 4850. For a discussion of the overall concept, see §7686.

And he looked away and went out from Pharaoh symbolizes being 7650
deprived of perception and cut off, as the following shows: Moses, who is the one being said to have looked away and gone out, represents truth imparted by the Divine, and *Pharaoh* represents the persecutors (mentioned above at §7631). *Looking away* means being deprived of perception, which happens when truth imparted by the Divine looks away, or turns its back—that is, when *we* turn our back on *it*—and *going out* symbolizes being cut off (discussed in §§6100, 7404).

Exodus 10:7–11. *And Pharaoh's servants said to him, "How long will* 7651
this be a snare for us? Send the men away and let them serve Jehovah their God. Do you not yet know that Egypt is perishing?" And Moses was brought back—as was Aaron—to Pharaoh, and he said to them, "Go serve Jehovah your God. Who exactly is going?" And Moses said, "With our young and with

our old we will go, with our sons and with our daughters, with our flock and with our herd we will go, because it is a feast to Jehovah for us." And he said to them, "Right, Jehovah will be with you when I send you and your little children away! See? There is evil in your faces. No! Go, please, you young men, and serve Jehovah, because that is what you seek." And he sent them away from the face of Pharaoh.

And Pharaoh's servants said to him symbolizes a warning delivered by the fearful. *How long will this be a snare for us?* means that under the circumstances they would be caught in their own evil. *Send the men away and let them serve Jehovah their God* means that the best policy is to leave [their victims] alone to worship the Lord their God. *Do you not yet know that Egypt is perishing?* means that recent events show that everyone annoying those simpletons is cast into hell, from which there is no escape. *And Moses was brought back—as was Aaron—to Pharaoh* symbolizes the consequent presence of divine truth. *And he said to them* symbolizes an inclination. *Go serve Jehovah your God* means that they would be left alone to worship the Lord. *Who exactly is going?* means, will anyone stay behind? *And Moses said,* symbolizes the answer. *With our young and with our old we will go* symbolizes the simple and the wise. *With our sons and with our daughters* symbolizes people who desire truth and people who desire goodness. *With our flock and with our herd we will go* symbolizes people with inner goodness and people with outer goodness. *Because it is a feast to Jehovah for us* symbolizes worship of the Lord by every individual. *And he said to them* symbolizes derision. *Right, Jehovah will be with you when I send you and your little children away* means as if the Lord would be with them if they were left alone! *See? There is evil in your faces* means that there is no goodness in their wish. *No!* means turning them down. *Go, please, you young men, and serve Jehovah* means that any who have confirmed the truth for themselves will be left alone to worship the Lord. *Because that is what you seek* means that this gives them what they want. *And he sent them away from the face of Pharaoh* means that the persecutors set their will firmly against divine truth.

7652 *And Pharaoh's servants said to him* symbolizes a warning delivered by the fearful, as the following shows. *Saying* symbolizes a warning, when people facing their demise address fellow community members who are being obstinate. And *Pharaoh's servants* symbolize persecutors who are on a lower rung and are fearful. Their fearfulness is evident from these words of theirs: "How long will this be a snare for us? Send the men away and let them serve Jehovah their God. Do you not yet know that Egypt is perishing?" Clearly these are words of fear. Besides, "Pharaoh's servants" means evil people who inflict harassment, and it is only out of fear that the evil argue in favor of anything good. See §7280.

How long will this be a snare for us? means that under the circumstances they would be caught in their own evil. This is evident from the symbolism of *this being a snare* as being caught in their own evil and paying the consequent penalty. 7653

Send the men away and let them serve Jehovah their God means that the best policy is to leave [their victims] alone to worship the Lord their God. This can be seen from the symbolism of *sending away* as leaving alone and from that of *serving Jehovah* as worshiping the Lord their God (as before in §§7500, 7540, 7641). 7654

Do you not yet know that Egypt is perishing? means that recent events show that everyone annoying those simpletons is cast into hell, from which there is no escape, as the following shows: *Do you not yet know* means that recent events show. *Perishing* means being cast into hell, from which there is no escape. Perishing has this meaning in a spiritual sense just as dying and death do, and to see that dying and death mean damnation and hell, see §§5407, 6119, 7494. And *Egypt* symbolizes persecution, as discussed at §7278, so it also symbolizes the persecutors. The persecutors are the ones speaking, though, so I describe them as annoying rather than persecuting their victims, because evil people excuse and downplay their evil. I also describe their victims as "those simpletons" rather than as people in the spiritual church, because evil people use the term "simpleton" for everyone in the church who lives by what the church holds to be true and good—that is, who lives a life of faith and neighborly love. 7655

And Moses was brought back—as was Aaron—to Pharaoh symbolizes the consequent presence of divine truth. This is clear from the symbolism of *being brought back* as standing present and from the representation of *Moses* and *Aaron* as divine truth, Moses being the inner form of it and Aaron the outer form (discussed in §§7089, 7382). 7656

And he said to them symbolizes an inclination. This can be seen from the next words, showing that, driven by fear, he wanted to send them away. This wish or inclination is contained in the words *he said to them.* 7657

Go serve Jehovah your God means that they would be left alone to worship the Lord. This can be seen from the symbolism of *serving Jehovah* as worshiping the Lord, as in §§7500, 7540, 7641, 7654. *Go,* when Pharaoh says it to Moses in reference to the children of Israel, plainly means that they would be left alone. 7658

7659 *Who exactly is going?* means will anyone stay behind? This is self-evident.

7660 *And Moses said,* obviously symbolizes the answer.

7661 *With our young and with our old we will go* symbolizes the simple and the wise. This can be seen from the symbolism of the *young,* when followed up with the *old,* as the simple, since the old symbolize the wise (§§3183, 6524, 6890).

7662 *With our sons and with our daughters* symbolizes people who desire truth and people who desire goodness, as the following shows: *Sons* symbolize religious truth (dealt with in §§489, 491, 533, 1147, 2623, 3373), so they symbolize a desire, because truth is nothing if we have no desire for it. And *daughters* symbolize goodness (dealt with in §§489, 490, 491), so they symbolize a desire for goodness (§§2362, 3963).

7663 *With our flock and with our herd we will go* symbolizes people with inner goodness and people with outer goodness. This is established by the symbolism of a *flock* as inner goodness and of a *herd* as outer goodness, which are dealt with in §§5913, 6048.

In an inner sense, the words of this verse—that they would go with young and old, with sons and daughters, and with flock and herd—mean everything belonging to the church, on both the outside and the inside. What belongs to the outer part of the church is meant by the young, the sons, and the herd, and what belongs to the inner part is meant by the old, the daughters, and the flock. The old stand for wisdom, the daughters for a desire for goodness, and the flock for goodness itself, which belong to the inner part of the church. But the young stand for simplicity, the sons for a desire for truth, and the herd for outer goodness, which belong to the outer part of the church.

7664 *Because it is a feast to Jehovah for us* symbolizes worship of the Lord by every individual. This can be seen from the symbolism of a *feast* as gladhearted worship, which is discussed at §7093. The reason it symbolizes worship of the Lord is that *Jehovah* in the Word is the Lord (§§1343, 1736, 2921, 3023, 3035, 5663, 6303, 6905, 6945, 6956). The fact that the worship is by every individual is evident from the statement just above that they would go with young and old, with sons and daughters, and with flock and herd.

7665 *And he said to them* symbolizes derision. This is clear from the words Pharaoh says—"Right, Jehovah will be with you when I send you and your little children away!"—which are derisive.

7666 *See? There is evil in your faces* means that there is no goodness in their wish. This can be seen from the symbolism of *faces* as inner levels and the feelings and consequent thoughts there (§§358, 1999, 2434, 3527, 3573, 4066, 4796, 4797, 5102, 5165, 5168, 5695, 6604). Since faces symbolize feelings, they also symbolize wishes. That is why *there is evil in your faces* means that there is no goodness in their feelings or their wish.

No! means turning them down, as is self-evident. 7667

Go, please, you young men, and serve Jehovah means that any who have 7668
confirmed the truth for themselves will be left alone to worship the Lord. This can be seen from the symbolism of *go* as an assurance that they will be left alone (as above at §7658), from that of *young men* as confirmed truth (dealt with below), and from that of *serving Jehovah* as worshiping the Lord (as above in §§7654, 7664).

The reason *young men* means people who have confirmed truth for themselves is that sons, boys, young men, adult men, and old men symbolize consecutive stages of understanding and wisdom. That is what heaven takes them to mean. The inhabitants of heaven engage in spiritual thinking, and what belongs purely to nature and the world cannot enter into such thinking without immediately being stripped away and changed into something compatible with heavenly wisdom and angelic thoughts. Sons, boys, young men, adult men, and old men, then, cannot mean such people in a spiritual sense. They can only symbolize the corresponding spiritual traits, which are stages of understanding and wisdom. The inner meaning of Scripture passages mentioning them makes it quite clear that this is their symbolism.

[2] Young men in the Word stand for people with understanding or, in the abstract thinking of angels, understanding itself. Since they stand for understanding, they also stand for confirmed truth, because confirmation of truth requires understanding.

In addition, the word used for young men here in the original language comes from [a word for] strength and power, which belong to truth but come from goodness and therefore belong to *confirmed* truth.

That is why the term is assigned to the Lord as a name in Zechariah:

> Sword, rise against my shepherd and against my neighbor, a (young) *man.* Strike the shepherd, and let the sheep scatter. (Zechariah 13:7)

For confirmation that this is about the Lord, see Matthew 26:31. In Jeremiah, too:

> How long are you wandering around, rebellious daughter? Jehovah has created something new in the earth: a woman has encircled a (young) *man.* (Jeremiah 31:22)

[3] In Amos, another word for young men in the original language stands for understanding and accordingly for truth understood:

> I sent contagion among you as in Egypt; *with the sword I killed your young men,* along with the captured horses. (Amos 4:10)

"As in Egypt" stands for corrupt knowledge; the young men who were killed stand for truth destroyed by that knowledge; the captured horses stand for the intellect led astray. [4] In the same author:

> They will wander from sea to sea, and from the north all the way to the east; they will dash about to seek Jehovah's word and will not find it. On that day the beautiful young women and the *young men* will faint with thirst. (Amos 8:12, 13)

The beautiful young women stand for a desire for truth; the young men stand for understanding. Fainting with thirst stands for being deprived of truth. That is why it says, "They will dash about to seek Jehovah's word and will not find it." Obviously the passage is not talking about young women or young men or fainting with thirst. In Jeremiah:

> Death climbed through our windows, it came into our palaces, to cut off the toddler in the street, the *young men in the avenues.* (Jeremiah 9:21)

In the same author:

> In what way have they not abandoned the city of glory, the city of my joy! *So its young men will fall in its streets.* (Jeremiah 49:25, 26; 50:30)

In the same author:

> Listen, please, all you peoples; look at my grief: my young women and *my young men* have gone into captivity. (Lamentations 1:18)

In these passages the young men stand for truth understood.

7669 *Because that is what you seek* means that this gives them what they want, as can be seen without explanation.

7670 *And he sent them away from the face of Pharaoh* means that the persecutors set their will firmly against divine truth, as the following shows: Moses and Aaron, the ones driven away, represent divine truth, as noted above at §7637. *Pharaoh* represents the persecutors, as also noted above, at §7631. A *face* symbolizes inner levels and the desires there, as discussed at §7666, so it symbolizes the will, because desire belongs to the will (and thoughts belong to the intellect). The opposition put up by this will is symbolized by *he sent them away from his face,* because anything that goes against a person's will—against the desires composing the will—is sent away.

Exodus 10:12, 13, 14, 15. *And Jehovah said to Moses, "Stretch your hand out over the land of Egypt to bring the locust, and it will go up over the land of Egypt and will eat all the grass of the land, everything that the hail has left." And Moses stretched his staff out over the land of Egypt, and Jehovah brought an east wind into the land that whole day and whole night. Morning came, and the east wind brought the locust. And the locust went up onto all the land of Egypt and came to rest on the whole border of Egypt very heavily. There was no locust like it before that, and there will be none after it. And it covered the surface of the whole land, and the land was overshadowed, and it ate all the grass of the land and all the tree fruit that the hail had left remaining. And there was nothing green remaining on the trees or in the grass of the field in all the land of Egypt.* 7671

And Jehovah said to Moses symbolizes instruction. *Stretch your hand out* symbolizes a wielding of power. *Over the land of Egypt to bring the locust* means so that falsity will take over the entire earthly level of the persecutors. *And it will go up over the land of Egypt* symbolizes total permeation on that level. *And will eat all the grass of the land* symbolizes the obliteration of any truth. *Everything that the hail has left* means which falsity had not already obliterated. *And Moses stretched his staff out over the land of Egypt* symbolizes a wielding of the power of divine truth over the entire earthly plane of the persecutors. *And Jehovah brought an east wind [into the land]* symbolizes the means of destruction. *That whole day and that whole night* means upon all perception, dim or not, on the part of the harassers. *Morning came* symbolizes a state of order in heaven. *And the east wind brought the locust* symbolizes falsity, brought by the means of destruction, swarming thickly among the harassers. *And the locust went up onto all the land of Egypt* symbolizes falsity totally permeating the earthly level. *And came to rest on the whole border of Egypt* means starting with its most remote parts. *Very heavily* means that it reached into each and every corner. *There was no locust like it before that, and there will be none after it* means that such falsity never had existed from the earliest [days] of the church and never would again. *And it covered the surface of the whole land* means that it took over the outermost levels of the earthly mind. *And the land was overshadowed* means that falsity was brought in to replace truth. *And it ate all the grass of the land* means that it obliterated all knowledge about truth. *And all the tree fruit [that the hail had left remaining]* symbolizes every concept of goodness. *And it left nothing green remaining* symbolizes a wiping out of all sensory perception of truth. *On the trees or in the grass of the field* means from the store of concepts and knowledge in the church. *In all the land of Egypt* means anywhere on the earthly plane.

7672 *And Jehovah said to Moses* symbolizes instruction. This can be seen from the symbolism of *saying* as instruction, when *Jehovah* is telling *Moses* (who represents divine truth) what to do—a symbolism discussed in §§6879, 6881, 6883, 6891, 7186, 7267, 7304, 7380.

7673 *Stretch your hand out* symbolizes a wielding of power. This is clear from the symbolism of *stretching out,* a word used for the wielding of power (discussed below), and from the symbolism of a *hand* as power itself (discussed in §§878, 3387, 4931–4937, 5327, 5328, 5544, 6292, 6947, 7011, 7188, 7189, 7518).

Stretching out a hand means wielding power because a hand or arm has power when it is extended. When Jehovah is said to stretch out his hand or arm, then, it symbolizes unlimited or infinite power in action.

That is why Jehovah so often told Moses to stretch out his hand or his staff when miracles were being done. Such instances include Exodus 7:19, "*Stretch your hand out* over the waters of Egypt and they will be blood"; Exodus 8:5, 6, "*Stretch your hand out* over the streams and bring the frogs up"; Exodus 8:16, 17, "*Stretch out your staff* and strike the dust of the land and it will become lice"; Exodus 9:22, 23, "*Stretch your hand out* toward the sky and there will be hail." These things would never have been said if the stretching out of a hand had not in the highest sense symbolized Jehovah's omnipotence.

[2] The meaning was similar when Joshua was told to stretch out his javelin, as recorded in the Book of Joshua this way:

> Jehovah said to Joshua, "*Stretch out the javelin that is in your hand* toward Ai." So when Joshua *stretched out the javelin that was in his hand* toward Ai, the ambushers rose quickly from their place and ran—*as soon as he stretched out his hand*—and came to the city and seized it. Joshua *did not draw back his hand that he had stretched out with the javelin* until all the residents of Ai had been given over to destruction. (Joshua 8:18, 19, 26)

Because this gesture represented divine omnipotence, it too had force, as did all the representational acts that were commanded in those days.

[3] Many passages depict omnipotence as the stretching out of Jehovah's hand and as his outstretched hand and outstretched arm.

It is depicted as the *stretching out of Jehovah's hand.* In Isaiah:

> His anger against his people kindled, and he *stretched his hand out over them* and struck them, and the mountains shook. (Isaiah 5:25)

In Ezekiel:

> I will *stretch my hand out against him* and destroy him. (Ezekiel 14:9, 13)

In the same author:

> I will *stretch my hand out* against you and give you to the nations as prey. (Ezekiel 25:7)

> I will *stretch my hand out* over Edom and cut humans and animals off from it. I will *stretch my hand out* over the Philistines and cut them off. (Ezekiel 25:13, 16)

Likewise in Ezekiel 35:3; Isaiah 31:3; Zephaniah 1:4; 2:13.

Omnipotence is depicted as his *outstretched hand.* In Isaiah:

> *Jehovah's hand is outstretched* over all the nations; who is going to push it away? (Isaiah 14:26, 27)

In Jeremiah:

> I will fight with you *by an outstretched hand* and by a strong arm and in anger and in fury. (Jeremiah 21:5)

In Isaiah:

> *His hand is* still *outstretched.* (Isaiah 9:12, 17; 10:4)

And it is depicted as his *outstretched arm.* In Jeremiah:

> I myself made the earth, the humans, and the animals by my great power and *by my outstretched arm.* (Jeremiah 27:5)

In the same author:

> You have made heaven and earth by your great power and *your outstretched arm;* no word is impossible for you. (Jeremiah 32:17)

The outstretched arm in these passages obviously symbolizes omnipotence. The same is true in many other passages that say "by a strong hand

and an outstretched arm," such as Deuteronomy 4:34; 5:15; 7:19; 9:29; 11:2; 26:8; 1 Kings 8:42; 2 Kings 17:36; Jeremiah 32:21; Ezekiel 20:33, 34.

[4] Jehovah is also said to *stretch out the heavens,* and in that case too stretching out symbolizes omnipotence: it means the almighty power to enlarge heaven's borders and fill its inhabitants with life and wisdom. In Isaiah, for example:

> Jehovah [is] the *one who stretches the heavens out like thin [fabric]* and spreads them out like a tent to be inhabited. (Isaiah 40:22)

In the same author:

> *Jehovah is stretching out the heavens,* spreading out the earth, giving a soul to the people on it, and spirit to everyone walking on it. (Isaiah 42:5)

In Jeremiah:

> [He is] the one who makes the earth by his power, prepares the world by his wisdom; and by his understanding he *stretches out the heavens.* (Jeremiah 51:15)

In Zechariah:

> *Jehovah is stretching out the heavens* and founding the earth and forming a person's spirit within. (Zechariah 12:1)

There are other passages like this too, such as Isaiah 44:24; 45:12; Psalms 104:2.

This discussion now shows why Moses was commanded to stretch out his hand and his staff, and that when he did, miracles were done. Stretching a hand out, then, symbolizes a wielding of power, and in the highest sense, omnipotence.

7674 *Over the land of Egypt to bring the locust* means so that falsity will take over the entire earthly level of the persecutors. This is clear from the symbolism of the *land of Egypt* as the earthly mind (discussed in §§5276, 5278, 5280, 5288, 5301) and Egypt as the earthly plane (discussed in §§6147, 6252), and from that of a *locust* as falsity on the outermost levels of the persecutors (discussed at §7643).

7675 *And it will go up over the land of Egypt* symbolizes total permeation on that level, as the following shows: *Going up* symbolizes permeation. A locust symbolizes falsity on the outermost surface, and "go up" is used for movement from the surface toward inner levels, since inner levels are the same as higher levels. For the idea that falsity occupies inner levels whenever it occupies outer levels, see §7645. And the *land of Egypt* symbolizes the earthly mind, as mentioned directly above at §7674.

And will eat all the grass of the land symbolizes the thorough obliteration of any truth. This can be seen from the symbolism of *eating* as obliterating and from that of the *grass of the land* as truth known to the church (discussed at §7571). 7676

Everything that the hail has left means which falsity had not already obliterated. This can be seen from the symbolism of *has left* as "did not obliterate" and from that of *hail* as falsity-from-evil on the outer earthly level (discussed in §§7553, 7574). 7677

And Moses stretched his staff out over the land of Egypt symbolizes a wielding of the power of divine truth over the entire earthly plane of the persecutors. This is established by the symbolism of *stretching out a staff* as a wielding of power (discussed above at §7673), by the representation of *Moses* as divine truth (discussed in §§6752, 7010, 7014, 7382), and by the symbolism of the *land of Egypt* as the earthly plane in the persecutors (mentioned above at §7674). 7678

The divine power that Moses' hand depicts is the power of divine truth. All power belongs to truth; see §§3091, 5623, 6344, 6423, 6948. In fact, divine truth emanating from divine goodness contains such power that it was the means of creating everything in the universe. This kind of truth is symbolized in John by the Word:

> In the beginning there was the Word, and the Word was with God, and the Word was God; everything was made by him. (John 1:1, 3)

That is why it was through Moses that miracles were done, since Moses represents divine truth.

Many believe that the Word, or divine truth, is merely speech by Jehovah—his command for this or that to happen—and nothing more. But it is *the* essential, the source and means of everything. The essence that comes from Jehovah and the emergence of everything from that essence is what is meant by divine truth.

Angels provide an illustration. They give off an aura of neighborly love and faith that is perceptible to the senses, and this too produces amazing effects. From them we can form some idea of the divine truth that radiates from the Lord's divine goodness.

7679 *And Jehovah brought an east wind [into the land]* symbolizes the means of destruction. This can be seen from the symbolism of an *east wind* as a means of destruction. The east wind has this symbolism because, being dry and turbulent, it withered the produce of that land and was strong enough to shatter trees and ships at sea. So it depicts the means through which divine power has an effect.

Besides, the east symbolizes the doing of good out of love and charity, because in its highest sense the east is the Lord (§§101, 1250, 3708). Since the doing of good out of love and charity is divine in origin, it is very gentle, so it is also gentle as it radiates into heaven. When it filters down to the hells, though, it becomes cruel and rough, because the inhabitants make it so. As a consequence, the inflow and presence of that divine goodness in the hells not only tortures the inhabitants but also puts them through the process of devastation. This too explains why a wind from the east—an east wind—symbolizes a means of destruction.

[2] The symbolism of the east wind as a means of destruction is clear from Scripture passages mentioning it. In Jeremiah, for example:

> Like an *east wind I will scatter them* before their enemy. (Jeremiah 18:17)

In Ezekiel:

> The transplanted grapevine will not prosper. *When the east wind touches it, will it not utterly wither?* (Ezekiel 17:10)

In the same author:

> The grapevine was torn out in anger, was tossed onto the earth; *the east wind dried up its fruit.* (Ezekiel 19:12)

In Hosea:

> He will be fierce among his brothers. An *east wind, Jehovah's gale,* will come rising from the desert, and his fount will *dry up,* and his spring will *evaporate.* (Hosea 13:15)

In David:

> *With an east wind you will shatter the ships of Tarshish.* (Psalms 48:7)

In Ezekiel:

> Into many waters your despisers led you; *the east wind broke you in the heart of the seas.* (Ezekiel 27:26)

These passages show that an east wind symbolizes a means of destruction because it was dry and turbulent. As a result of this symbolism it also symbolizes a means of devastation, as in Hosea:

> Ephraim is grazing on a breeze and *pursues an east wind;* every day he multiplies lies and devastation. (Hosea 12:1)

Ephraim stands for the church's intellect (§§5354, 6222, 6234). To graze on a breeze is to multiply lies, while to pursue an east wind is to multiply devastation. In addition, a state of devastation and trial is called the *day of the east wind* in Isaiah 27:7, 8.

That whole day and that whole night symbolizes [upon] all percep- **7680**
tion, dim or not, on the part of the harassers. That is, all such perception was destroyed. This is evident from the symbolism of a *day* as a state of perception that is not dim and from the symbolism of a *night* as a state of perception that *is* dim. Times of day, such as morning, afternoon, evening, and night, correspond to different kinds of enlightenment, which are forms of understanding and wisdom (§§5672, 6110), so they correspond to different kinds of perception. Day and night correspond to general kinds.

I refer to it here as perception rather than enlightenment because evil beings who inflict harassment do not have enlightenment but still do have perception. However, they remain perceptive only so long as they retain some knowledge of truth and goodness, received from the church in whose sphere they had lived. This is because truth and goodness are the means by which they communicate with the inhabitants of heaven. When such knowledge is taken from them—which happens after they have been through the process of devastation—they no longer have any perception.

Hellish individuals do have the ability to justify their evils and their false ideas, admittedly, but that is not perception. Perception is to see truth as true, and goodness as good, evil as evil, and falsity as false. Perception does not consist in seeing truth as false or goodness as evil, or conversely in seeing evil as good or falsity as true. People who do this replace perception with delusion, which mimics perception by enabling them to justify falsity and evil with empirical evidence that favors their selfish desires.

Morning came symbolizes a state of order in heaven. This can be seen **7681**
from the symbolism of *morning* as the Lord's kingdom and in the highest

sense the Lord himself (discussed in §§22, 2333, 2405, 2540, 2780), and as a state of enlightenment (§§3458, 3723, 5740, 5962). Here, though, it symbolizes heaven in a state of order.

The discussion at §7643 explains the case: as the Lord brings heaven into order, the evil undergo devastation. The inflow of goodness and truth that originate in heaven sparks this devastation, so when the Lord reorganizes the heavens, the hells opposed to them spontaneously fall into order. They move away from heaven in proportion to their degree of evil and are allotted places according to their type of evil. You can see, then, that from the Lord comes nothing but goodness. Evil comes from people who oppose what is good and in the end cannot bear goodness.

This shows that *morning came* symbolizes a state of order in heaven.

7682 *And the east wind brought the locust* symbolizes falsity, brought by the means of destruction, swarming thickly among the harassers. This is evident from the symbolism of an *east wind* as a means of destruction (discussed just above at §7679) and from that of a *locust* as falsity in the outermost parts (discussed at §7643). Here the locust symbolizes falsity swarming thickly, because it is taking over the entire earthly plane (§7645).

7683 *And the locust went up onto all the land of Egypt* symbolizes falsity totally permeating the earthly level. This can be seen from remarks above in §§7674, 7675, where similar words appear.

7684 *And came to rest on the whole border of Egypt* means starting with its most remote parts. This can be seen from the symbolism of a *border* as the most remote parts. *Came to rest on the whole border* therefore means that falsity reached from the outer edges into every corner of the earthly plane and then terminated back at the outer edges, in keeping with the explanation at §7645.

7685 *Very heavily* means that it reached into each and every corner, as can be seen from the exegesis directly above at §7684.

7686 *There was no locust like it before that, and there will be none after it* means that such falsity never had existed from the earliest days of the church and never would again. This can be seen from the symbolism of a *locust* as falsity in the outermost parts, as discussed at §7643. For the idea that such falsity never had existed and never would again, see also §7649 above [in addition to the discussion below].

The facts of this matter need explaining. The specific inner meaning has to do with spirits who were in the underground realm before the Lord's Coming and who could not be taken up to heaven until the Lord had come into the world, adopted a human nature, and made it divine;

see §§6854, 6914. In the meantime they were harassed by evil people who had also been part of the church and had championed religious truth but had lived an evil life.

[2] People who had been part of the church before the Lord's Coming and whose lives had been evil possessed a kind of falsity that had not existed before and will not exist afterward. This was because the people called Nephilim, Anakim, and Rephaim, who were among the last descendants of the earliest church, had not yet been shut up in hell but wandered around spreading their appalling, deadly convictions everywhere they could. One of the places they spread them was therefore to evil people in the church. That is why the latter possessed this kind of falsity. Concerning the Nephilim and their appalling delusions, see §§310, 560, 562, 563, 570, 581, 586a, 607 at the end, 660, 805, 808, 1034, 1120, 1265–1272, 1673.

While the Lord was in the world, he threw the Nephilim into a hell that is on the left and a little way out in front. Had he not, very few people could have been saved, because the falsity the Nephilim disgorged came with a persuasiveness more fearful and deadly than had ever existed before or ever can again. This is the kind of falsity absorbed by spirits who persecuted members of the spiritual church before the Lord's Coming.

That is what is meant in the inner sense of the current words. That is what it concerns specifically. More generally it is about everyone who is part of the church and attacks the upright in the other life. Many of that kind exist today.

And it covered the surface of the [whole] land symbolizes the outermost 7687
levels of the earthly mind. This can be seen from the symbolism of a *surface* as the outermost part, because the surface is the outside or end of the land, and from the symbolism of the *land*—the land of Egypt in this case—as the earthly mind (noted above at §7674).

And the land was overshadowed means that falsity was brought in to 7688
replace truth. This can be seen from the symbolism of shadows, [or darkness,] as falsity, which is discussed in §§1839, 1860, 4418, 4531. Since shadows symbolize falsity, *being overshadowed* means subscribing to falsity. The focus is currently on the devastation undergone by people who [before death] had been part of the church and had known truth but had led an evil life, so the *overshadowed land* symbolizes falsity in place of truth.

Truth is symbolized in an inner sense by light, so falsity is symbolized by shadow. After all, truth and falsity are opposites, as light and shadow are. What is more, people who know truth really do have light, and people with false thinking are in actual shadow. The glimmer of light in the other world that shines on people subject to falsity grows dark at the presence of heaven's light, especially with those who had been in the church, because the falsity they had adopted contradicted Christian truth. As the Lord says in Matthew:

> *If the light that is in you is shadow, how immense the shadow!* (Matthew 6:23)

And in the same author:

> The children of the kingdom will be cast out *into outer shadow.* (Matthew 8:12)

The children of the kingdom are people in the church. Outer shadow is worse falsity. The shadow is described as outer because the falsity on outermost levels is worse.

[2] The fact that falsity is called shadow is clear from many passages in the Word, such as John:

> The light came into the world *but people loved shadow more than light,* since their deeds were evil. (John 3:19)

In the same author:

> Walk, as long as you have light, *to prevent the shadows from overtaking you.* I have come into the world as the light so that *no* one who believes in me should *stay in shadow.* (John 12:35, 46)

In Isaiah:

> Doom to those who call evil good and goodness evil; *who put shadow for light* and *light for shadow.* (Isaiah 5:20)

In Jeremiah:

> Give glory to Jehovah your God before he *brings on the shadows* and before your feet stumble *on the dusky mountains;* then you will wait for light, but he will turn it *into the shadow of death,* he will turn it into blackness. (Jeremiah 13:16)

In Ezekiel:

> *When I extinguish* you I will cover the heavens and *blacken* their stars; the sun *I will cover with a cloud,* and the moon will *not make its glimmer*

> *shine.* All the lamps of light I will *blacken* above you, *and I will bring shadow* over your land. (Ezekiel 32:7, 8)

In Joel:

> The day of Jehovah has come, it is near: a *day of shadow and darkness,* a day of *cloud* and *haze.* (Joel 2:1, 2; Amos 5:18, 20)

In Zephaniah:

> A day of wrath is this day, a day of waste and devastation, a *day of shadow* and *darkness.* (Zephaniah 1:15)

The shadows mentioned in these passages symbolize falsity.

Shadows in the Word also symbolize ignorance of truth—the type of ignorance that characterizes nations who do not have the Word and know nothing about the Lord.

And it ate all the grass of the land means that it obliterated all knowl- **7689**
edge about truth. This can be seen from the symbolism of *eating* as obliterating and from that of the *grass of the land* as knowledge about truth. The grass of a field symbolizes truth known to the church (§7571), since a field means the church; but the grass of the land symbolizes knowledge about truth, since the land here means the earthly mind, and the kind of truth the earthly mind contains is knowledge. Besides, the evil have no religious truth, just knowledge *about* it. Evil people in the church do convince themselves they are in possession of religious truth, but they are not. They are in possession of falsity and stand opposed to faith with its truth. Their allegiance to falsity lies hidden inside as long as they are in the world, but this concealed falsity emerges and reveals itself in the other life when they are stripped of all the religious truth they had known about.

And all the tree fruit [that the hail had left remaining] symbolizes every **7690**
concept of goodness, as the following shows: *Fruit* symbolizes deeds of faith, or of neighborly love, so it symbolizes instances of goodness, which is why being fruitful is mentioned in connection with goodness (§§43, 55, 913, 983, 2846, 2847). And a *tree* symbolizes perceptions and also concepts, as discussed in §§103, 2163, 2722, 2972.

Fruit means deeds of neighborly love and therefore instances of goodness because a tree begins with a fruit containing seed and ends with a fruit containing seed. In between come its branches and leaves. This is like love with its goodness and faith with its truth. When we are being reborn, or planted, we start with love and goodness, and we end with them too. In between come faith and truth, which spring from a loving goodness as their seed and are always looking to a loving goodness as their final goal—just as the middle stages of a tree look forward to the fruit and the seed inside it.

The symbolism of fruit as goodness is plain from many passages in the Word, such as Matthew 3:8, 10; 7:16–20; 12:33; 21:43; Luke 3:8, 9; 6:43–49; 13:6–10; John 15:2–8, 16; Isaiah 37:31; Jeremiah 17:8; 32:19; Revelation 22:2.

7691 *And it left nothing green remaining* symbolizes a wiping out of all sensory perception of truth. This can be seen from the symbolism of *leaving nothing* as wiping everything out and from that of *greenery* as items of knowledge and sense impressions. In this case the green symbolizes sensory perception of truth, since the tree fruit symbolizes a concept of goodness (§7690), and since the clause speaks of everything green on the trees and in the grass of the field.

The reason *greenery* symbolizes sensory perception of truth is that grass, grain, and tree leaves symbolize truth, and the green in them is therefore a sensory perception of truth. ("Sensory perception" means perception on the outermost level.)

Greenery also symbolizes sensory perception of truth in Isaiah:

> The waters of Nimrim will be wastelands, because the grain has dried out, the grass has been consumed, *greenery does not exist.* (Isaiah 15:6)

And in John:

> The fifth angel trumpeted, and locusts went out. They were told not to harm the grain of the earth *nor any greenery.* (Revelation 9:4)

7692 *On the trees or in the grass of the field* means from the store of concepts and knowledge in the church. This is established by the symbolism of a *tree* as concepts of goodness (discussed just above at §7690) and by that of the *grass of the field* as knowledge about truth (also discussed above, at §7689).

7693 *In all the land of Egypt* means anywhere on the earthly plane. This is established by the symbolism of the *land of Egypt* as the earthly mind and therefore the earthly plane, as noted at §7674.

As the locusts referred to in this verse symbolize falsity in the outermost parts, or on a person's sensory level, "sensory" should be defined here, in order to suggest what falsity in the outermost parts is. Sensory people, or people who think and act from their senses, are people who believe nothing but their own empirical evidence. They are led exclusively by physical appetites, sensual pleasures, and cravings, not by reason. Reason in their view is whatever supports these urges. This being what sensory people are like, they reject all possibility of inner depth, so much so that in the end they do not even want to hear anyone speak of it. At heart, then, they deny anything connected with heaven. They flatly disbelieve in life after death, because they locate life in the body alone; they suppose they will die just as animals do.

They think on the surface, so to speak—on the most remote, outermost levels—and have no idea a person can think deeply, in accordance with a perception of truth and goodness. The reason they do not know this, and do not even know there is such a thing as the inner self, is that their inner reaches look down toward the realm of the world, the body, and the earth and are in unison with that realm. Such people's inner plane is therefore far from looking up toward heaven, because it faces in the opposite direction.

Looking up toward heaven is not the same as thinking about heavenly subjects. No, it means having heavenly goals, that is, loving what is heavenly above all else. Wherever love turns, there a person's inner depths turn; and thought follows along.

This shows what a person's sensory level is like, or what the earthly plane is like at its outermost edges. *Sensory* is the word for a person who thinks on the basis of the senses.

Exodus 10:16–20. *And Pharaoh hurried to call Moses and Aaron and said, "I have sinned against Jehovah your God and against you. And now please forgive my sin just this time and plead to Jehovah your God and have him remove from me such great death as this." And [Moses] went out from Pharaoh and pleaded to Jehovah. And Jehovah turned a very strong sea wind and took away the locust and hurled it into the Suph Sea; not one locust was left within the whole border of Egypt. And Jehovah hardened Pharaoh's heart, and he did not send the children of Israel away.* **7694**

And Pharaoh hurried to call Moses and Aaron symbolizes fear felt at that time over truth imparted by the Divine. *And said, "I have sinned against Jehovah your God and against you,"* symbolizes a confession that he had disobeyed the Divine and the truth. *And now please forgive my sin just this time* is a request that they pay no regard to the disobedience. *And plead to Jehovah your God* symbolizes intervention. *And have him remove from me such great death as this* means in order to prevent this type of falsity from causing torment. [*And Moses went out from Pharaoh* symbolizes separation. *And pleaded to Jehovah* symbolizes intervention.] *And Jehovah turned a very strong sea wind* symbolizes a halt to the divine inflow through heaven. *And took away the locust* symbolizes the end of that state. *And hurled it into the Suph Sea* means into hell. *Not one locust was left within the whole border of Egypt* means that this kind of falsity was no longer visible in the outermost parts. *And Jehovah hardened Pharaoh's heart* means that the harassers made themselves obstinate. *And he did not send the children of Israel away* means against leaving the people of the spiritual church alone.

7695 *And Pharaoh hurried to call Moses and Aaron* symbolizes fear felt at that time over truth imparted by the Divine, as the following shows: *Hurrying* means with fear. All hurry arises from the stirring of some emotion, and here, from the emotion of fear, as is plain from Pharaoh's words: "I have sinned against Jehovah your God and against you. Plead that he remove from me such great death as this." *Pharaoh* represents the harassers, as noted many times. And *Moses* and *Aaron* represent truth imparted by the Divine, Moses representing inner truth and Aaron outer truth, as discussed in §§7089, 7382.

7696 *And said, "I have sinned against Jehovah your God and against you,"* symbolizes a confession that he had disobeyed the Divine and the truth. This can be seen from the symbolism of *sinning* as going contrary to divine order (discussed at §5076), turning in aversion from it and therefore from goodness and truth, and developing a rift with them (§§5229, 5474, 5841, 7589). As a result it also symbolizes disobeying the Divine and the truth, because anyone who disobeys them turns away from them. The Divine is what is meant by *Jehovah your God,* and truth is what is meant by Moses and Aaron (§7695).

7697 *And now please forgive my sin just this time* is a request that they pay no regard to the disobedience, as the following shows: *Forgiving* means paying no regard, because to forgive is to regard someone not with a malevolent eye but with a kind eye. And a *sin* symbolizes disobedience, as directly above at §7696.

7698 *And plead to Jehovah your God* symbolizes intervention. This can be seen from the symbolism of *pleading to Jehovah,* when the plea is on someone else's behalf, as intervention (as at §§7396, 7462).

7699 *And have him remove from me such great death as this* means in order to prevent this type of falsity from causing torment. This can be seen from the symbolism of *having him remove this death* as preventing it from causing torment. After all, *death* symbolizes damnation and hell (§§5407, 6119), so it also symbolizes torment.

The reason the harassers begged to have this falsity removed is that they no longer had any ability to reason against religious truth. They had been purged of the ability and were consequently in the dark of hell, which tormented them. (See §7392 on the point that the hellish do not enjoy arguing from utter falsity but do enjoy arguing from truth distorted by illusions and appearances.)

And [Moses] went out from Pharaoh symbolizes separation. This can 7700
be seen from the discussion in §§6100, 7404 of the symbolism of *going out* as separation.

And pleaded to Jehovah symbolizes intervention, as above at §7698. 7701

And Jehovah turned a [very] strong sea wind symbolizes a halt to the 7702
divine inflow through heaven. This is evident from the symbolism of a *sea wind,* or west wind, as a halt to the divine inflow through heaven. The east wind symbolized a means of destruction by reason of the divine inflow through heaven (see §7679), so a sea wind, or west wind, which blows in the opposite direction, symbolizes a halt to that inflow.

And took away the locust symbolizes the end of that state. This can be 7703
seen from the symbolism of a *locust* as falsity in the outermost parts, as discussed at §7643. Lifting a state marked by this falsity—and therefore the end of the state—is symbolized by *taking away* the locust, as in earlier passages about the hail, §§7597, 7610.

And hurled it into the Suph Sea means into hell. This is clear from the 7704
symbolism of the *Suph Sea* as hell, to be treated of later, by the Lord's divine mercy, where I discuss the Israelites' passage through that sea and the Egyptians' death in it [§§8099, 8125, 8137, 8138, 8210].

"Hurled into hell" does not mean that falsity was removed from the persecutors and cast elsewhere. It means that the falsity stayed with them and connected them to the hells that are its home. In the other life, each state of evil and falsity that the evil enter connects them with the hell where the attributes of that state are found. So they form ties with many hells in succession before they complete the process of devastation. For a discussion of this on the basis of experience, see elsewhere.

Not one locust was left within the whole border of Egypt means that this 7705
kind of falsity was no longer visible in the outermost parts. This can be seen from the symbolism of a *locust* as falsity; and because it symbolizes falsity in the outermost parts (§7643), the verse says *within the whole border of Egypt*—a border meaning the outermost part, and Egypt the

earthly plane. That *no locust was left* obviously means that it was not visible. It was the same with the hail; see §7611.

7706 *And Jehovah hardened Pharaoh's heart* means that the harassers made themselves obstinate. This can be seen from the symbolism of *hardening someone's heart* as making themselves obstinate, as mentioned in §§7272, 7300, 7305.

For the idea that when it says "Jehovah hardened Pharaoh's heart" it means in an inner sense that Pharaoh hardened his own heart, see §7632. For the idea that any evil attributed to Jehovah in the Word comes from humankind, see §§2447, 6071, 6991, 6997, 7533.

7707 *And he did not send the children of Israel away* means against leaving the people of the spiritual church alone. This is plain from the symbolism of *sending away* as leaving alone and from the representation of the *children of Israel* as people of the spiritual church, as in §§7474, 7515, 7617.

7708 Exodus 10:21, 22, 23. *And Jehovah said to Moses, "Stretch your hand out to the sky, and there will be darkness on the land of Egypt, and people will feel about in the dark." And Moses stretched his hand out to the sky, and there was thick darkness in all the land of Egypt for three days. A man could not see his brother and none got up out of place for three days. But all the children of Israel had light in their dwellings.*

And Jehovah said to Moses symbolizes instruction. *Stretch your hand out to the sky* symbolizes a wielding of the power of divine truth in heaven. *And there will be darkness on the land of Egypt* symbolizes being wholly deprived of truth and goodness. *And people will feel about in the dark* symbolizes a thick mass of falsity from evil. *And Moses stretched his hand out to the sky* symbolizes the power of divine truth wielded in heaven. *And there was thick darkness in all the land of Egypt* symbolizes being wholly deprived of truth and goodness. *For three days* symbolizes a full state. *A man could not see his brother* means that they could not perceive any truth-from-goodness. *And [none] got up out of place* means that their minds were not lifted up at all. *For three days* symbolizes a full state. *But all the children of Israel had light in their dwellings* means that people of the spiritual church had enlightenment in every corner of their mind.

7709 *And Jehovah said to Moses* symbolizes instruction, as before at §7672.

7710 *Stretch your hand out to the sky* symbolizes a wielding of the power of divine truth in heaven. This can be seen from the symbolism of *stretching a hand out* as a wielding of power (discussed above at §7673), from the representation of Moses, the one stretching out his hand, as divine truth (discussed in §§6723, 6752, 7010, 7014, 7382), and from the symbolism of the *sky* as heaven.

How it is that the power divine truth wielded in heaven produced a new state in the persecutors—a state symbolized by darkness—can be seen from points made in §§7643, 7679, as follows: The Lord is constantly reorganizing heaven and granting heavenly and spiritual goodness to its inhabitants and to newcomers there, and the reorganizing causes evil spirits to undergo the gradual steps of devastation. The reason it does this is that the heavenly and spiritual goodness then flow more directly into the evil spirits opposed to it. (Divine inflow reaches all the way to its opposite, which is how it keeps the hells connected and restrained.) Because the wicked turn everything good into evil, they take the goodness that is flowing in more directly and turn it into greater evil. The more they do, the more strongly they resist truth and goodness, which is to say that they inflict heavier persecution. That is why devastation goes step by step, until the evil are eventually thrown into hell—the final step.

These remarks show that nothing but goodness comes from the Lord, that he does not put the evil through devastation, let alone throw them into hell, and that they do so themselves instead.

And there will be darkness on the land of Egypt symbolizes being wholly 7711
deprived of truth and goodness. This is evident from the symbolism of *darkness* as complete deprivation of truth and goodness.

The Word sometimes mentions shadows and darkness together, and in those places the shadows have to do with falsity and the darkness with evil. However, the term this verse uses for darkness means the deepest darkness, which on an inner level symbolizes the kind of falsity that wells up out of evil. This kind of falsity exists in people who [before death] had been part of the church and had lived an evil life, in violation of the religious rules they knew. The evil from which it wells up opposes the church, heaven, and the Lord, so it categorically opposes goodness and truth. This, then, is the state depicted as darkness.

[2] The following passages show that the Word mentions shadow and darkness together and that where it does, shadow means deprivation of truth and darkness means deprivation of both truth and goodness. In Isaiah:

> Rightful judgment is far away from us, and justice does not reach us. We wait for light, *but here, now, shadows;* and for brilliant days, *but we walk in darkness.* Like the blind we *touch* the wall, and like the eyeless

> we *feel about.* We stumble at midday as if at twilight; among the living as if dead. (Isaiah 59:9, 10)

"Rightful judgment is far away from us, and justice does not reach us" means that there is no truth or goodness. (Judgment has to do with truth, and justice with goodness; see §§2235, 3997.) Waiting for light stands for awaiting truth, and waiting for brilliant days stands for awaiting goodness born of truth, because light takes its brilliance from goodness. Plainly the shadows there contrast with the light and judgment and therefore with truth, while the darkness contrasts with the brilliance and justice and therefore with goodness. The shadows, then, are deprivation of truth, and the darkness is deprivation of both truth and goodness. In Amos:

> *Is the day of Jehovah not shadow* and lack of light? And *is there not darkness* rather than radiance on it? (Amos 5:20)

The meanings are similar. In Joel:

> The day of Jehovah has come, a *day of shadow* and *darkness,* a day of cloud and haze. (Joel 2:2)

[3] In Zephaniah:

> The day of Jehovah is a day of waste and devastation, a *day of shadow and darkness.* (Zephaniah 1:15)

The shadow stands for being deprived of truth, and the darkness for being deprived of both truth and goodness. If darkness did not symbolize something different from shadow, this would be empty repetition, which is foreign to the holy Word. In Scripture it is common to see a single concept expressed by a pair of terms, one relating to truth or falsity, the other to goodness or evil. The same thing occurs in Isaiah:

> To the earth they will look, and here, anguish *and shadow!* They will be rendered gloomy with distress *and* a colliding *darkness.* (Isaiah 8:22)

[4] In Isaiah shadow also symbolizes ignorance of truth (the kind of ignorance existing among people outside the church), and darkness, ignorance of what is good:

> On that day the deaf will hear the words of the book, *and out of the darkness* and *out of the shadows* the eyes of the blind will see. (Isaiah 29:18)

In the same author:

> If you satiate an afflicted soul, *in the shadows* your light will rise, and *your darkness* will be like midday. (Isaiah 58:10)

For the meaning of shadow as falsity, see §7688.

And people will feel about in the dark symbolizes a thick mass of falsity from evil. This can be seen from the symbolism of *feeling about in the dark* as falsity-from-evil so thick there is no knowing what is true or good. If one tries to find out, one is in effect feeling about in the dark, stumbling and colliding with things everywhere. That is why the darkness is called a *colliding darkness* in Isaiah 8:22 and why the same author offers this description: 7712

> *We walk in darkness,* like the blind we *touch* the wall, and like the eyeless *we feel about. We stumble* at midday as if at twilight; among the living as if dead. (Isaiah 59:9, 10)

And Moses stretched his hand out to the sky symbolizes the power of divine truth wielded in heaven. This is evident from the comments just above at §7710, where the same words appear. 7713

And there was thick darkness in all the land of Egypt symbolizes being wholly deprived of truth and goodness. This is evident from the comments above at §7711. 7714

For three days symbolizes a full state. This is evident from the discussion in §§2788, 4495 of the symbolism of *three days* as a full state. A full state means an entire state from beginning to end. Every state has its beginning, its stages of development, and its greatest intensity. That cycle is what is meant by a full state and is symbolized by the three days. 7715

A man could not see his brother means that they could not perceive any truth-from-goodness. This is evident from the symbolism of *seeing* as understanding and perceiving (treated of in §§2150, 2325, 2807, 3764, 3863, 4403–4421, 4567, 4723, 5400), from that of a *man* as truth (treated of at §3134), and from that of a *brother* as goodness (treated of in §§2360, 3303, 3803, 3815, 4121, 5409, 5686, 5692, 6756). A man with his brother symbolizes the goodness that comes of truth (§3459). Clearly, then, *a man could not see his brother* means that they could not perceive any truth-from-goodness. 7716

And [none] got up out of place means that their minds were not lifted up at all. This can be seen from the symbolism of *getting up* as rising to inner levels and therefore as a lifting up of the mind, as discussed in 7717

§§2401, 2785, 2912, 2927, 3171, 3458, 3723, 4103, 4881, 6010. *[None] got up,* then, means that there was no lifting up.

7718 *For three days* symbolizes a full state, as just above at §7715.

7719 *But all the children of Israel had light in their dwellings* means that people of the spiritual church had enlightenment in every corner of their mind, as the following shows: The *children of Israel* represent people of the spiritual church, as discussed in §§6426, 6637, 6862, 6868, 7035, 7062, 7198, 7201, 7215, 7223. *Light* symbolizes enlightenment. After all, light from the Lord enlightens the intellect, because understanding and wisdom rely on that light; see §§1521, 1524, 1619–1632, 2776, 3138, 3167, 3190, 3195, 3222, 3223, 3339, 3636, 3643, 3993, 4302, 4408, 4413, 4415, 5400, 6608. And *dwellings* symbolize the contents of the mind. A house symbolizes the human mind (3538, 4973, 5023, 7353), and bedrooms symbolize its inner depths (7353), but dwellings symbolize everything in the mind. Besides, settling in a dwelling in an inner sense means living (1293, 3384, 3613, 4451, 6051). So dwellings are the location for issues of life, which is to say for issues requiring understanding and wisdom, and everyone knows that understanding and wisdom belong to the mind. What is more, light in the other life shines on the angels' dwellings or living spaces in proportion to the understanding and wisdom of their minds. And the amount of light shining on them is the same as the amount of darkness surrounding the spirits opposed to them—that is, the spirits who inflicted persecution.

7720 Exodus 10:24–29. *And Pharaoh called to Moses and said, "Go serve Jehovah. Only your flock and your herd must stay. Even your little children will go with you." And Moses said, "You yourself will put sacrifices and burnt offerings into our hand, and we will perform them to Jehovah our God. And our livestock must also go with us; not a hoof will be left behind, because we must take from [our livestock] to serve Jehovah our God, and we won't know what we must use to serve Jehovah till we come there." And Jehovah hardened Pharaoh's heart, and he did not want to send them away. And Pharaoh said to him, "Go away from me; be careful not to see my face again, because on the day of your seeing my face you will die." And Moses said, "You have spoken rightly; I will no longer see your face."*

And Pharaoh called to Moses symbolizes the presence of divine law. *And said, "Go serve Jehovah,"* means that [people of the spiritual church] were to be left alone to worship the Lord their God. *Only your flock and your herd must stay* means but not in a spirit of goodness. *Even [your] little children will go with you* means only from truth. *And Moses said,* symbolizes the answer. *You yourself will put sacrifices and burnt offerings into our hand* means that [the persecutors] would have to let go of everything that was to be used for worship. *And we will perform them to Jehovah our God* means which is welcome to the Lord. *And our livestock must also go with us* means in a spirit of goodness based on truth. *Not a hoof will be left behind* means that truth based on goodness must not be missing at all. *Because we must take from [our livestock] to serve Jehovah our God* means that this will be the source for worship of the Lord. *And we won't know what we must use to serve Jehovah our God* means that they will have no idea how to worship. *Till we come there* means until they leave spirits committed to utter falsity-from-evil completely behind. *And Jehovah hardened Pharaoh's heart* means that [the persecutors] set themselves obstinately against the Divine. *And he did not want to send them away* means that they had no intention of leaving [people of the spiritual church] alone. *And Pharaoh said to him* symbolizes blazing up with anger at divine truth then. *Go away from me* means that [they] did not want to know anything about it. *Be careful not to see my face again* means that it would not enter their heart and mind. *Because on the day of your seeing my face you will die* means that if it entered their heart and mind, it would be erased. *And Moses said,* symbolizes the answer. *You have spoken rightly* means that it is really true. *I will no longer see your face* means that divine truth would no longer enter their heart and mind.

And Pharaoh called to Moses symbolizes the presence of divine law. 7721
This can be seen from the symbolism of *calling* someone to oneself as presence (discussed in §§6177, 7390, 7451) and from the representation of *Moses* as divine law (discussed in §§6723, 6752, 7014, 7382).

The presence of divine law among the persecutors means that they perceived where the plagues were coming from. In this case they could tell the source of the incredibly thick falsity-from-evil symbolized by the darkness.

When evil spirits are undergoing devastation in the other life, they are often allowed to sense where the miseries of their punishment come from, so as to learn that they themselves are to blame, not the Divine. Similar experiences often visit the inhabitants of hell, too, but only when they are in a state of rest. This happens for many reasons, a main reason being to remind them of the evil they had committed in the world.

And said, "Go serve Jehovah," means that [people of the spiritual church] 7722
were to be left alone to worship the Lord their God, as above at §7658.

Only your flock and your herd must stay means but not in a spirit of 7723
goodness. That is, they were not to worship the Lord in a spirit of goodness. This is established by the symbolism of a *flock* as inner goodness and by that of a *herd* as outer goodness, which are discussed in §§5913, 6048.

7724 *Even [your] little children will go with you* means only from truth, as the following shows: A *little child* symbolizes truth here, because it refers to boys, youths, young men—in short, to sons, who symbolize characteristics of an understanding mind and therefore symbolize truth; see §7668. And *going with you* means that they are to be left alone to worship the Lord their God.

I need to say what it means to worship the Lord in a spirit of goodness, and what it means to worship him from truth devoid of goodness, as symbolized here by the flock and herd that were to stay and the little children who were to go. Genuine worship grows out of goodness by way of truth, because the Lord is present in goodness. Worship from truth devoid of goodness, on the other hand, is not worship but only a superficial ritual or practice lacking depth. Truth without goodness is nothing more than information. In order to develop into faith, this information has to be united with goodness, at which time it makes the transition to a person's inner self and turns into faith. Faith without neighborly love is not faith, as I have shown many times [§§345, 379, 724, 1162, 2325, 2839, 3121].

This clarifies what worship in a spirit of goodness is and what worship from truth devoid of goodness is.

When I speak of worship in a spirit of goodness, I mean the goodness shown in a person's life, which becomes spiritual by being united with truth. Spiritual goodness takes its quality from truth, and truth takes its essence from goodness, which means that goodness is the soul of truth. This too shows what truth is like without goodness; it is a body without a soul and is therefore a corpse.

7725 *And Moses said,* obviously symbolizes the answer.

7726 *You yourself will put sacrifices and burnt offerings into our hand* means that [the persecutors] would have to let go of everything that was to be used for worship, as the following shows: *Putting into someone's hand* means letting go, because a hand symbolizes power. Putting something into the hand of others means ceding it to their power, which means letting go of it. And *sacrifices and burnt offerings* symbolize worship in general, so they symbolize everything involved in worship, as discussed in §§923, 6905. The reason sacrifices and burnt offerings symbolize everything involved in worship is that the main way of worshiping God used to be sacrifices, as the books of Moses make plain. (For earlier discussions of sacrifices, see §§922, 923, 1128, 1343, 1823, 2165, 2180, 2187, 2776, 2784, 2805, 2807, 2812, 2818, 2830, 3519, 6905.)

7727 *And we will perform them to Jehovah our God* means (worship) which is welcome to the Lord. This is evident from the preceding explanations: that sacrifices and burnt offerings symbolize worship (§7726) and that the flock and herd used for the sacrifices symbolize goodness that inspires worship (§§7723, 7724). "Performing sacrifices and burnt offerings to Jehovah," then, symbolizes worship in a spirit of goodness, which is welcome. (On the point that *Jehovah* in the Word is the Lord, see §§1343, 1736, 2921, 3023, 3035, 5041, 5663, 6280, 6281, 6303, 6905, 6945, 6956.)

And our livestock must also go with us means (worship) in a spirit of goodness based on truth. This can be seen from the symbolism of *livestock* as goodness based on truth, as discussed in §§6016, 6045. *Going with us* expresses a desire to use [the livestock] for worship, in the form of sacrifices and burnt offerings, as is self-evident. **7728**

Not a hoof will be left behind means that truth based on goodness must not be missing at all. This can be seen from the symbolism of a *hoof* as truth stemming from goodness (discussed below) and from that of *not being left behind* as not being absent—not absent from worship of the Lord. **7729**

In the first layer of inner meaning, "not a *hoof* will be left behind" means that absolutely nothing may be missing, because all livestock animals have a hoof. In a deeper sense, though, a hoof symbolizes truth on the outermost level, so it symbolizes truth gained through the senses—the lowliest form of truth. In a negative sense it symbolizes falsity. The reason a hoof symbolizes these things is that the lower leg symbolizes the earthly plane, and the foot with its sole symbolizes the outermost level of that plane (§§2162, 3147, 3761, 3986, 4280, 4938–4952, 5328). A hoof has the same symbolism, because it is the foot of a livestock animal's leg. Since a hoof, like the sole of a foot, symbolizes the outermost level of the earthly plane, it also symbolizes the truth that forms that outermost level. When I speak of the earthly plane, I am referring to truth and goodness, or in a negative sense, falsity and evil. These are what form the earthly plane, which would be devoid of attributes without them.

[2] The following passages show that a hoof, especially a horse's hoof, symbolizes truth on the outermost level, and therefore truth acquired through the senses, or in a negative sense, falsity on the outermost level. In Isaiah:

> . . . whose arrows are sharp, and all their bows bent. The *hooves of their horses* are considered to be like rock; their wheels like a windstorm. (Isaiah 5:28)

This is about a people coming to wreak devastation. Arrows symbolize false theological teachings used as weapons, and bows symbolize the theology itself (§§2686, 2709). Horses symbolize intellectual capacities, and in this case corrupt ones (§§2761, 2762, 3217, 5321, 6125, 6534). Clearly, then, the horses' hooves symbolize falsity on the outermost level. [3] In Jeremiah:

> . . . *over the sound of the thud of the hooves of his mighty ones,* because of the commotion of his chariot, the din of its wheels. (Jeremiah 47:3)

This is about a people laying waste to the Philistines. The thud of the hooves of his mighty ones—meaning horses—stands for open warfare waged against truth by falsity. The chariot stands for a false theology. For the idea that a chariot means a theology teaching either truth or falsity, see §§5321, 5945. [4] In Ezekiel:

> Because of the great number of his horses, their dust will blanket you. Because of the noise of rider and wheel and chariot, your walls will shake. *With the hooves of his horses* he will trample all your streets. (Ezekiel 26:10, 11)

This is about Nebuchadnezzar in the act of laying waste to Tyre. The horses stand for intellectual capacities corrupted, as they do above, and the rider for the use of such capacities (§6534). The chariot wheels stand for the false tenets of a theology—a chariot meaning a theology, as above—and the streets for true ideas (§2336). From this it is plain that the horses' hooves mean falsity. If there were no such symbolism, what would it mean to say, "Because of the great number of his horses, their dust will blanket you. Because of the noise of rider and wheel and chariot, your walls will shake. With the hooves of his horses he will trample all your streets"? Without an inner sense, would this be anything more than hollow verbiage? Whereas in reality, every word in Scripture carries weight, because it comes from the Divine. [5] In the same author:

> They will devastate the haughtiness of Egypt, to have its throng destroyed. And I will obliterate every animal of the place along many waters, so that the foot of a human may not churn [the waters] any longer, *nor the hoof of an animal churn them.* Then I will sink their waters in the deep and make their rivers flow like oil. (Ezekiel 32:12, 13, 14)

This too is unintelligible unless you know what is meant by Egypt, by the foot of a human, by the hoof of an animal, and by the waters along which the animals will be obliterated, and which the foot of a human and the hoof of an animal will churn, and which will be sunk in the deep. The waters and rivers of Egypt are truth in the form of knowledge. The hoof of an animal is falsity on the outermost level of the earthly plane, which churns up that truth in the form of knowledge. [6] In Micah:

> Get up and thresh, daughter of Zion, because your horn I will turn to iron, *and your hooves I will turn to bronze,* so that you may pulverize many peoples. (Micah 4:13)

Again, no one can tell what this is about without an inner meaning. One needs to know therefore what is meant by threshing, by the daughter of Zion, by the horn that will become ironlike, and by the hoof that will become bronzelike, which will be used to pulverize many peoples. The daughter of Zion is a heavenly religion (§2362). A horn is the potential that truth from goodness has (2832). Iron is earthly truth strong enough to destroy falsity (425, 426). A hoof is truth-from-goodness on the outermost level. Bronze is earthly goodness strong enough to withstand evil (425, 1551). [7] In Zechariah:

> I myself will raise up a shepherd in the land [who] will not visit [the sheep] that are becoming stranded, will not go look for those that are tender in age, and will not heal those that are broken. He will, however, eat their richest flesh, *and their hooves he will split.* (Zechariah 11:16)

This is about a stupid shepherd. Eating the richest flesh stands for turning goodness into evil. Splitting hooves stands for turning truth into falsity.

[8] You can see how much more understanding ancient people had than we do today from the fact that in many cases they knew which qualities in heaven the objects of the world corresponded to and therefore what they symbolized. It was people not only in the church but also outside it who had the knowledge. Take, for example, the people of Greece, whose earliest ancestors depicted concepts through the use of symbolism that we today call myth because we know nothing about it. Their ancient sages were obviously knowledgeable in the subject, because they used a winged horse called Pegasus to depict the origin of understanding and wisdom. They said that with *its hoof* the horse struck open a spring at which sat nine maidens, and they set the scene on a hill. They knew that a horse symbolized the intellect; its wings, the spiritual plane; hooves, truth on the outermost level, where understanding takes its rise; maidens, the arts and sciences; a hill, unity, and in a spiritual sense neighborly love; and so on. But these things are among today's lost knowledge.

Because we must take from [our livestock] to serve Jehovah [our God] 7730
means that this will be the source for worship of the Lord, as is evident

from the symbolism of *serving* as worshiping. For the fact that Jehovah is the Lord, see above at §7727.

7731 *And we won't know what we must use to serve Jehovah our God* means that they will have no idea how to worship. This can be seen from the symbolism of *serving Jehovah* as worship of the Lord, as above at §7730.

7732 *Till we come there* means until they leave spirits committed to utter falsity-from-evil completely behind. This can be seen from the fact that *coming there,* into the wilderness, means putting distance between themselves and the Egyptians. So it means putting distance between themselves and people committed to utter falsity-from-evil, who are the ones currently symbolized by the Egyptians. For this symbolism—that going into the wilderness to sacrifice means being at a stage in which falsity has been left completely behind—see §6904.

7733 *And Jehovah hardened Pharaoh's heart* means that [the persecutors] set themselves obstinately against the Divine, as above at §7706.

7734 *And he did not want to send them away* means that they had no intention of leaving [people of the spiritual church] alone. This is clear from the symbolism of *not wanting* as having no intention and from that of *sending away* as leaving alone, as above at §7707, where similar words occur.

7735 *And Pharaoh said to him* symbolizes blazing up with anger at [divine] truth then. This can be seen from the symbolism of *saying,* which includes the next few phrases and therefore means blazing up with anger. After all, what follows is "Pharaoh said to Moses, 'Go away from me; be careful not to see my face again, because on the day of your seeing my face you will die.'" These are words of anger at the divine truth that Moses represents.

7736 *Go away from me* means that they did not want to know anything about it—about divine truth. This can be seen from the symbolism of *go away from me,* when the evil say it about divine truth, as not wanting to know anything about it, because they reject it.

7737 *Be careful not to see my face again* means that it would not enter their heart and mind. This can be seen from the symbolism of *not seeing someone's face again* as no longer entering that person's heart and mind. A *face* symbolizes the inner depths (§§1999, 2434, 3527, 3573, 4066, 4796, 4797, 4798, 5102, 5165, 5168, 5695) and especially the inner desires, so it symbolizes the heart and mind.

7738 *Because on the day of your seeing my face you will die* means that if it entered their heart and mind, it would be erased. This is evident from the symbolism of *seeing someone's face* as entering that person's heart and mind (as directly above at §7737) and from that of *dying* as being erased.

The reason Pharaoh now tells Moses to go away from him and says Moses will die if he sees Pharaoh's face is this: What is now being depicted is the state of the persecutors when they are immersed in utter falsity-from-evil, the kind of falsity symbolized by the darkness. The more deeply the hellish are immersed in falsity as a result of evil, the more they loathe truth, until they reach a point where they do not even want to hear anything true. Truth contradicts falsity, and falsity delights them, because the evil desires that give rise to it are the core pleasure of their life. As a consequence, they reject truth with all their heart and mind, since it opposes the central delight and pleasure of their life. If they do hear anything true, it torments them (§7519). This is the reason they shun the divine truth represented by Moses, because they are in a state of falsity from evil, symbolized by the darkness. That explains why Pharaoh told Moses just above to go away from him and not see his face and said that if he did see it he would die. It also explains why Moses answered, "You have spoken rightly; I will no longer see your face."

And Moses said, obviously symbolizes the answer. 7739

You have spoken rightly means that it is really true. This can be seen 7740 from the symbolism of *speaking rightly* as being true. "Rightly" also means "really" (§§5434, 5437).

"It is really true" means that they are indeed in a state now in which all they want is to know nothing about divine truth. If such truth entered their heart and mind they would expel it, in keeping with the explanation just above at §7738.

I will [no longer] see your face means that [divine truth] would no 7741 longer enter their heart and mind. This is evident from the symbolism of *not seeing someone's face* as not entering that person's heart and mind, in keeping with the comments above at §§7737, 7738.

The Inhabitants and Spirits of Mars (Continued)

AT the end of the previous chapter [§§7620–7622] I told about a 7742 beautiful bird that appeared and eventually turned to stone. I said it represented the state of Mars' inhabitants so far as their heavenly and spiritual love was concerned. Regarding that state and its various changes I was allowed to learn the following.

7743a The inhabitants of Mars display heavenly love, as I have already mentioned. They were represented by a flame that sparkled with beautifully changing colors, and also by a bird with the same iridescence. Many of today's inhabitants are starting to back away from that heavenly love, to prefer knowledge alone, and to equate the life of heaven with knowledge. This was represented by the transformation of that bird into stone. A bird symbolizes spiritual life, and its turning to stone symbolizes a life of knowledge devoid of love. Such a life is no longer spiritual but rather as cold as stone, and nothing heavenly flows into it. These inhabitants still believe they live in the Lord, just like those inhabitants who live a life of heavenly love, and this was symbolized and demonstrated by a spirit who rose up from below and wanted to take the bird away [§7621].

7743b The petrified bird also represented inhabitants of that planet who have a strange way of turning the vital energy of their thoughts and feelings into something almost lifeless. The following is what I saw and heard in this regard.

7744 Once there was a spirit above my head who spoke with me, and from his tone I could tell he was in a sleeplike state. Talking in this state, he kept asking questions, which he did with such good sense that he could not have done better wide awake. I was able to perceive that he was a delegate through whom angels were speaking and that in that state he understood what they were saying and conveyed it to others. He spoke nothing but the truth. If an idea from elsewhere flowed into his mind, he let it in, to be sure, but he did not verbalize it.

I asked him about his state. "It is a peaceful state for me," he said, "and I am completely free of worry about the future. What is more, I fill a role that puts me in touch with heaven."

I was told that in the universal human, spirits like this relate to the longitudinal fissure in the brain that lies between its two hemispheres, where conditions are quiet, no matter how turbulent the brain is on either side.

7745 While I was conversing with this spirit, some others moved toward the front part of my head, where that spirit was. They pressed in on him, so he withdrew to one side and let them have the space.

The new spirits talked among themselves, but the spirits around me could not understand what they were saying, and neither could I. Angels taught me that they were spirits from the planet Mars, who knew how to talk to each other in such a way that spirits standing by could not understand any of it or catch what they were saying.

I was surprised such a manner of speaking could exist. For one thing, all spirits share a single language. For another, all speech flows from thought, and thought consists of individual ideas, which serve as words in the spiritual world. For a third thing, inhabitants of the other world perceive these word-ideas clearly, along with the thought behind them before it is expressed. I was told that these spirits have a way of using their lips and face to form ideas incomprehensible to others. Any time they speak to each other by this method, they cleverly withhold their thoughts from third parties, making especially sure no sign of emotion leaks out. If any hint of emotion were perceived, you see, the thought would come out into the open, since thought flows from emotion.

I learned further that this language was invented by inhabitants of Mars who identify heavenly life with knowledge alone, not with a life of love. Not all inhabitants [use the language]. The inhabitants who do use it keep it when they become spirits.

These are the people specifically symbolized by the bird of stone. After all, to produce speech by manipulating one's face and lips while at the same time draining it of emotion and withholding one's thoughts from others is to rob speech of its soul—to make a lifeless statue out of it and gradually out of oneself as well.

However, although they imagine that others cannot understand what 7746
they are saying to each other, angelic spirits pick up every bit of it. That is because no kind of thinking can be withheld from an angelic spirit, and this was demonstrated to them by direct experience. I found myself contemplating the fact that spirits from our planet feel no shame when they harass others, and this line of thought came to me from angelic spirits. The spirits from Mars then acknowledged that that was what they had been discussing. They were stunned. An angelic spirit also disclosed many other conversations and thoughts the spirits from Mars were having, even though they were working hard to keep their thoughts from that spirit.

Later on some spirits from Mars flowed from above into my face. The 7747
inflow felt like streaks of light rain, which was a sign that they did not like anything true or good—this distaste being what streaks represent.

Then they spoke to me openly, saying, "The inhabitants of our planet talk to each other the same way we do."

"That is bad," I answered, "because that way you block anything deep and move away from it to a superficial message, which you also rob of its vitality. And more importantly, it is dishonest to talk that way. Those who are honest don't want to say or even think anything they wouldn't want others to know—including the public at large, or even the whole of heaven! But if you don't want others to know what you are saying, you are judging them. You are thinking badly of them and well of yourself. And eventually the habit pushes you to the point where you think and speak ill even of the church and heaven and the Lord himself."

7748 I was told that people who love religious knowledge alone, rather than a life in keeping with it, correlate with the brain's inner membrane. People who grow used to talking without emotion, though, and who keep their thoughts to themselves, hidden from others, correlate with a bony version of that membrane, because they go from having some spiritual life to having none.

7749 People who love religious knowledge alone, and not a life in keeping with it, usually glory in that knowledge and see themselves as wiser than anyone else. In other words, they love themselves and look down on others, especially on people devoted to what is good, whom they regard as uneducated and simplistic. In the other life, though, the tables are turned: the ones who seem wise to themselves become stupid, and the simple become wise.

7750 Since the bird of stone represented people who are intent on knowledge alone, not on a life of love, and since this leaves them with almost no spiritual life, let me add a postscript. I will show that the only people with spiritual life are those with heavenly love and *therefore* with knowledge and that this love contains within it all knowledge relevant to itself.

Take land animals and those animals of the sky called birds as an example. They possess all knowledge relevant to what they love. What they love is to feed themselves, keep themselves safe, reproduce, and raise their young, and therefore they have all the information they need. The information is embedded in those different kinds of love and flows into those loves as containers designed just for it. In some animals the knowledge is so astounding that it can only leave a human speechless. It is said to be inborn and is called instinct, but it belongs to the love the animals have.

[2] If our own proper loves—love for God and love for our neighbor, the types of love that distinguish us from animals—were active in us, we would have all necessary knowledge. Not only that, we would also possess all understanding and wisdom, without any need to learn them. They would flow down from heaven (or rather from the Divine through heaven) into our love for God and for our neighbor.

These two kinds of love are not active in us, though. What is active instead is their opposites: love for ourselves and love of worldly advantages.

So we cannot help being born into all ignorance and unawareness. Still, we are led by divine means to some measure of understanding and wisdom, but we do not actually adopt them unless we put self-love and materialism aside, opening the way for love for the Lord and love for our neighbor.

[3] Here is some evidence that love for the Lord and love for one's neighbor hold all understanding and wisdom within them: When people who had those kinds of love in the world enter heaven in the next life, they find themselves in possession of knowledge and wisdom on subjects they knew nothing about before. In fact, like the other angels, they think and say what no ear has ever heard or mind has known—in other words, the ineffable. This is because the ability to receive such things is inherent in those two kinds of love.

The end of the next chapter will be devoted to the spirits and inhabitants of Jupiter [§§7799–7813]. 7751

Exodus 11

Teachings on Neighborly Love

7752 GOODNESS and truth are the qualities to which everything in the universe relates. Anything that does not relate to them lies outside the divine design, and anything that does not relate to both at the same time is unproductive. Goodness is what produces something, and truth is its means.

7753 Here is an example illustrating how matters stand with spiritual goodness and truth, or charity and faith, as they are called: Everything about the church relates to these, and anything that does not relate to them has nothing of the church in it. What does not contain both produces no fruit. That is, it does not produce anything good that comes of neighborly love or of faith.

7754 For anything to develop, there have to be two forces, one called active and the other called passive. Neither one without the other gives birth to anything. In a religious person, these forces or vital energies are neighborly love and faith.

7755 The primary quality of the church is goodness; truth comes second. To put it another way, the primary quality of the church is neighborly love, and faith comes second. This is because the truth embodied in teachings concerning faith exists for the sake of goodness in a person's life. The purpose for which a thing exists is primary.

7756 Regarding the union in us of the goodness embodied in neighborly love and the truth embodied in faith: The former enters us through our soul, the latter through our ears. Goodness comes to us directly from the Lord; truth comes indirectly through the Word. The path by which neighborly love with its goodness enters, then, is called an inner route, while the path by which faith with its truth enters is called an outer route.

What enters by an inner route is imperceptible, because it is not openly accessible to the senses, but what enters by an outer route is perceptible, because it *is* openly accessible. (That is why people attribute all of religion to faith.) Not so for people who have been reborn, though. For them the goodness of neighborly love is clearly perceived.

Charity and its goodness bond with faith and its truth in our inner reaches. Goodness, which flows in from the Lord, actually adopts truth and makes truth its own, deep within us. This causes the goodness in us to be good and the truth in us to be true, the neighborly love to be neighborly love and the faith to be faith. Without this bond, charity is not charity but mere earthly-level goodness. Faith is not faith but mere book learning on religious topics. Sometimes faith means persuading oneself that what one has learned is true, in a quest for undue wealth or prestige. 7757

When truth unites with goodness it is no longer called truth but goodness. So when faith unites with neighborly love, it is no longer called faith but charity. The reason is that we then want to act on truth and do act on it, and what we want and do is called good. 7758

Further regarding the union of charity's goodness with faith's truth: Charitable goodness takes its character from truth, and truth takes its essence from goodness. It therefore follows that the quality of the goodness depends on the kind of truth it unites with. Goodness consequently becomes genuine if the truth with which it unites is genuine. Genuine religious truth can exist within the church but not outside it, because the church is where the Word is. 7759

Moreover, it is also the amount of such truth and the connection of one truth with another that gives such goodness its nature. That is how spiritual goodness forms in us. 7760

It is important to distinguish properly between spiritual and earthly-level goodness. As just mentioned, spiritual goodness takes its character from religious truths and from the amount of and connection between them. Earthly-level goodness, on the other hand, is something we are born with and also comes about through happenstance such as misfortune, illness, and so on. 7761

Earthly goodness saves no one; spiritual goodness saves everyone. This is because goodness molded by religious truth is a platform on which heaven (or rather the Lord through heaven) can operate, guiding us, keeping us from harm, and then taking us up to heaven. Earthly goodness does not provide such a platform. As a result, people with earthly-level goodness can be as easily swept away by falsity as by truth, as long as the falsity appears in the guise of truth. They can be as easily led by evil as by goodness, as long as the evil is presented as good. They are like feathers in the wind.

The confidence or trust that is said to be integral to faith and is called faith is confidence or trust on an earthly rather than a spiritual level. Spiritual confidence or trust takes its essence and life from a loving 7762 goodness, not from abstract religious truth. The trust belonging to faith alone is dead. Real trust is therefore impossible in people who have lived an evil life.

The confidence that the Lord's merit confers salvation no matter how one had lived [on earth] is not even based on truth.

Exodus 11

1. And Jehovah said to Moses, "One more plague I will bring on Pharaoh and on Egypt. After that he will send you away from here. When he sends everything away, he will actually drive you out of here.

2. Come, say in the ears of the people that they should ask—a man of his companion, and a woman of her companion—for vessels of silver and vessels of gold."

3. And Jehovah gave favor to the people in the eyes of the Egyptians. In addition, the man Moses was very great in the land of Egypt in the eyes of Pharaoh's servants and in the eyes of the people.

4. And Moses said, "This is what Jehovah has said: 'Around the middle of the night I myself will go out into the middle of Egypt.

5. And every firstborn in the land of Egypt will die, from the firstborn of Pharaoh who was to sit on his throne to the firstborn of the slave woman who is behind the millstones, and every firstborn of the animals.

6. And there will be a great outcry in the whole land of Egypt such as there has never been and such as will not be again.

7. And toward all the children of Israel, from man to animal, not a dog will move its tongue, so that you may know that Jehovah distinguishes between the Egyptians and Israel.

8. And all these servants of yours will come down to me and bow to me, saying, "Go out, you and all the people that are at your feet," and after that I will go out.'" And he went out from Pharaoh in a wrath of anger.

9. And Jehovah said to Moses, "Pharaoh will not listen to you [two], so that my portents may multiply in the land of Egypt."

10. And Moses and Aaron performed all these portents before Pharaoh. And Jehovah hardened Pharaoh's heart, and he did not send the children of Israel away from his land.

Summary

THE inner meaning of this chapter is about the damning of faith detached from neighborly love, as symbolized by the many firstborn of Egypt put to death in the middle of the night. It is also about knowledge of truth and goodness that was to be transferred to the people of the spiritual church. That knowledge is symbolized by the vessels of silver and gold that the children of Israel were to borrow from the Egyptians. 7763

Inner Meaning

EXODUS 11:1, 2, 3. *And Jehovah said to Moses, "One more plague I will bring on Pharaoh and on Egypt. After that he will send you away from here. When he sends everything away, he will actually drive you out of here. Come, say in the ears of the people that they should ask—a man of his companion, and a woman of her companion—for vessels of silver and vessels of gold." And Jehovah gave favor to the people in the eyes of the Egyptians. In addition, the man Moses was very great in the land of Egypt in the eyes of Pharaoh's servants and in the eyes of the people.* 7764

And Jehovah said to Moses symbolizes instruction. *One more plague I will bring on Pharaoh and on Egypt* symbolizes the damnation in which the devastation ends. *After that he will send you away from here* means that [people of the spiritual church] will then be left alone. *When he sends everything away, he will actually drive you out of here* means that [the harassers] will leave them completely alone and will loathe and flee their presence. *Come, say in the ears of the people* symbolizes instructions, and obedience to them. *That they should ask—a man of his companion, and a woman of her companion—for vessels of silver and vessels of gold* means that the knowledge of truth and goodness taken away from evil people in the church is to be awarded to good people in the church. *And Jehovah gave favor to the people in the eyes of the Egyptians* symbolizes the fear felt by those immersed in evil toward people of the spiritual church, on account of the plagues. *In addition, the man Moses was very great in the land of Egypt* symbolizes due respect now for divine truth. *In the eyes of [Pharaoh's] servants and in the eyes of the people* means among the subordinates.

7765 *And Jehovah said to Moses* symbolizes instruction, as in §§7186, 7267, 7304, 7380.

7766 *One more plague I will bring on Pharaoh and on Egypt* symbolizes the damnation in which the devastation ends. This can be seen from the symbolism of *one more plague* as the final stage of devastation.

The explanation of earlier chapters has made it plain that the plagues imposed on Egypt symbolized the series of stages in the process of devastation. What follows will show that it ends in damnation—the damnation of faith detached from neighborly love. All the firstborn put to death in Egypt symbolize the damning of that faith (the damnation being symbolized by death, and that faith by the firstborn).

Faith is said to be damnable when its tenets are used to support falsity and evil. When faith supports these, it takes their side and shifts over to reinforcing them. That is what happens in people who detach faith from neighborly love in both their theology and their life. Faith is not faith in such people, however; it is mere knowledge of faith's tenets, though they call it faith. That is what is meant by a damnable faith.

[2] What is more, the believers themselves in whom the tenets of faith had been connected to falsity and evil arrive at damnation after undergoing devastation. Damnation manifests itself as a foul, rotten stench that wafts more strongly from them than from people who never had been in possession of faith's teachings.

This particular situation reflects the general rule: In general an evil spirit gives off an unmistakable odor upon approaching a heavenly community that possesses neighborly love. The same is true in the particular case of a believer in whom elements both of heaven (or faith) and of hell coexist.

This now demonstrates that the one further plague about to be brought on Pharaoh and on Egypt symbolizes the damnation in which the devastation ends. Pharaoh represents the harassers, who at this point in the text are facing damnation, and Egypt symbolizes the earthly mind (§§5276, 5278, 5280, 5288, 5301, 6147, 6252).

After that he will send you away from here means that [people of the spiritual church] will then be left alone. This is established by the symbolism of *sending away* as leaving alone, mentioned many times before. 7767

When he sends everything away, he will actually drive you out of here means that [the harassers] will leave them completely alone and will loathe and flee their presence. This can be seen from the symbolism of *sending everything away* as leaving them completely alone and from that of *actually driving you out* as loathing and fleeing people in the spiritual church, whom they had harassed. If you loathe someone's presence, you also flee it and drive the person away. 7768

The reason the persecutors now loathe and flee people of spiritual religion is that the inflow of goodness and truth now tortures them. The situation is like painful sores that cannot stand even the touch of warm water or a breath of air, or like an injured eye that cannot bear even gentle sunshine. So it is for the persecutors; their earthly mind is now equally raw, because after they have been devastated—after they reject what they used to believe in—the least breath of goodness and truth hurts. That is the reason for their avoidance.

Come, say in the ears of the people symbolizes instructions and obedience to them. This is evident from the symbolism of *saying* in this case as instructions, because Jehovah here says what the children of Israel are to do when they leave Egypt. Obedience is symbolized by saying *in the ears,* because ears correspond to and therefore symbolize obedience (§§2542, 3869, 4551, 4652–4660). 7769

That they should ask—a man of his companion, and a woman of her companion—for vessels of silver and vessels of gold means that the knowledge of truth and goodness taken away from evil people in the church is to be awarded to good people in the church. This can be seen from the symbolism of *vessels of silver and vessels of gold* as knowledge of truth and goodness. Silver is truth, and gold is goodness (see §§1551, 1552, 2954, 5658, 6112), and vessels are items of knowledge (§§3068, 3079). 7770

Items of knowledge are called vessels for truth and goodness because they hold truth and goodness within them. People believe that knowledge of truth and goodness is the truth and goodness itself that constitutes faith. However, a desire for truth and goodness, not knowledge of them, is what constitutes faith. Desires pour into items of knowledge as their containers.

Asking the Egyptians for silver and gold clearly means taking it away and appropriating it. That is why an earlier chapter says that the children of Israel were to plunder the Egyptians (Exodus 3:22), and the next chapter, that they robbed them (Exodus 12:[36]).

The reason the text says that a man should ask his companion and a woman her companion is that a man correlates with and symbolizes truth and a woman correlates with and symbolizes goodness.

[2] To understand what this is about, see the explanation at Exodus 3:21, 22, §§6914, 6917. The treatment there shows that there is knowledge of truth and goodness that once belonged to people in the church who knew the secrets of faith and yet lived an evil life, and that this knowledge is actually transferred from them to people in the spiritual church. See §6914 to learn how the transfer takes place. This is what is symbolized by the Lord's words in Matthew:

> The master said to the one who went off and hid a talent in the earth, "*Take the talent from him* and *give it to the one who has ten talents.* Because all who *have something will be granted to overflow with it. But from those who do not have anything, even what they have will be taken. But cast the useless slave into outer darkness.*" (Matthew 25:25, 28, 29, 30; Luke 19:24, 25, 26)

Likewise in the same author:

> *Those who have something will be granted to overflow with it; but from those who do not have anything, even what they have will be taken.* (Matthew 13:12; Mark 4:24, 25)

[3] The reason for the transfer is that evil people use concepts of goodness and truth for evil purposes, while good people use them for good purposes. The concepts are the same, but the purposes to which they are applied determine their quality in every individual. It is like worldly wealth: one person puts it to good use, another to evil use. Our wealth is therefore as good as the use to which we put it.

This comparison also shows that the same concepts that once belonged to wicked people (like the same wealth that once belonged to them) can belong to good people and serve good purposes.

From this evidence you can now see what is represented by the command for the children of Israel to borrow vessels of silver and vessels of gold from the Egyptians and in the process, to rob and plunder them. Jehovah would never have ordered such theft and pillage had it not had this representation in the spiritual world.

[4] The following passage in Isaiah is similar:

> In the end, Tyre's merchandise and its *harlot's wages* will be *holy to Jehovah.* They will not be hoarded or kept back; instead, *the people living in view of Jehovah will have its merchandise for eating,* for *filling up on,* as will *the ancient ones covering themselves up.* (Isaiah 23:18)

This is about Tyre, which symbolizes knowledge of goodness and truth (§1201). The merchandise and harlot's wages stand for knowledge used for evil purposes. The knowledge was to be given to good people, who would use it for good purposes, and this is symbolized by the words "The people living in view of Jehovah will have its merchandise for eating, for filling up on, as will the ancient ones covering themselves up." [5] In Micah, too:

> Get up and thresh, daughter of Zion, because your horn I will turn to iron, and your hooves I will turn to bronze, so that you may pulverize many peoples. And I have *devoted their profit to Jehovah and their riches to the Lord of the whole earth.* (Micah 4:13)

Pulverizing many peoples stands for putting them through devastation. The profit devoted to Jehovah and to the Lord of the whole earth is knowledge of truth and goodness. There is similar significance to this:

> *David consecrated to Jehovah the silver and gold he had taken from the nations* that he had subdued: from the Syrians, from Moab, from the children of Ammon, from the Philistines, from Amalek, and from the plunder of Hadadezer. (2 Samuel 8:11, 12)

And to this:

> Solomon *put the consecrated items* of his *father among the treasures of Jehovah's House.* (1 Kings 7:51)

And Jehovah gave favor to the people in the eyes of the Egyptians symbolizes the fear felt by those immersed in evil toward people of the spiritual church, on account of the plagues. This can be seen from the earlier explanation at §6914, where similar words appear. **7771**

In addition, the man Moses was very great in the land of Egypt symbolizes due respect now for divine truth, as the following shows: *Moses* represents divine truth, as noted many times. *Very great* symbolizes due respect. Here it symbolizes respect born of fear, because the only respect **7772** that the evil who are in hell have for something divine is fearful. "Very great" plainly means respect, because the text says "in the eyes of the servants and in the eyes of the people." And the *land of Egypt* symbolizes the earthly mind, as discussed in §§5276, 5278, 5280, 5288, 5301, 6147, 6252.

This shows that *the man Moses was very great in the land of Egypt* symbolizes due respect for divine truth in the mind of the persecutors.

7773 *In the eyes of [Pharaoh's] servants and in the eyes of the people* means among the subordinates. This can be seen from the symbolism of the *servants* and *people* as subordinates. Pharaoh represents the main persecutors, to whom the rest were subordinate.

The reason subordinates are meant is that there is a form of government just as much among the evil as among the good, or in hell as in heaven. That is to say, there are higher-ups and people under them, without which society would not be cohesive. However, hierarchy works in an entirely different way in heaven than in hell.

In heaven all are equal; they love each other as sisters and brothers do. Nonetheless, some promote others over themselves, if those others excel in understanding and wisdom. In and of itself, love for what is good and true makes everyone yield almost automatically to people who have more wisdom about goodness and more understanding of truth.

In hell, on the other hand, hierarchy has to do with power and therefore with brutality. Those in charge bully anyone who does not cater to their every whim. They view all others as their enemies, though outwardly they treat them as their friends, for the sake of banding together against violence from outsiders. Such an alliance is like the bond among thieves. Underlings constantly aspire to gain power and often do burst out into rebellion. When they do, conditions there are grievous, because savagery and cruelty abound. This cycle repeats itself.

From this you can see how subordination works in the next life.

7774 Exodus 11:4, 5, 6, 7, 8. *And Moses said, "This is what Jehovah has said: 'Around the middle of the night I myself will go out into the middle of Egypt. And every firstborn in the land of Egypt will die, from the firstborn of Pharaoh who was to sit on his throne to the firstborn of the slave woman who is behind the millstones, and every firstborn of the animals. And there will be a great outcry in the whole land of Egypt such as there has never been and such as will not be again. And toward all the children of Israel, from man to animal, not a dog will move its tongue, so that you may know that Jehovah distinguishes between the Egyptians and Israel. And all these servants of yours will come down to me and bow to me, saying, "Go out, you and all the people that are at your feet," and after that I will go out.'" And he went out from Pharaoh in a wrath of anger.*

And Moses said, "This is what Jehovah has said" symbolizes instruction. *Around the middle of the night* means when the devastation would be total. *I myself will go out into the middle of Egypt* means that the Divine would then be present everywhere. *And every firstborn in the land of Egypt will die* means that faith detached from neighborly love would then be damned. *From the firstborn of Pharaoh who was to sit on his throne* symbolizes falsified religious truth of the first rank. *To the firstborn of the slave woman who is behind the millstones* symbolizes falsified religious truth of the last rank. *And every firstborn of the animals* symbolizes adulterated religious goodness. *And there will be a great outcry in the whole land of Egypt* symbolizes inner mourning. *Such as there has never been and such as will not be again* symbolizes conditions so bad that they could not be equaled. *And toward all the children of Israel not a dog will move its tongue* means that among people of the spiritual church there would be no damnation or mourning in the least. *From man to animal* means neither in respect to anything true nor in respect to anything good. *So that you may know that Jehovah distinguishes between the Egyptians and Israel* means so as to reveal what kind of distinction is drawn between people who dwell in evil and people who dwell in goodness. *And all these servants of yours will come down to me* symbolizes the subordinates. *And bow to me* symbolizes due respect for divine truth, born of fear. *Saying, "Go out, you and all the people that are at your feet,"* symbolizes a plea for the departure of those who possess truth from the Divine, from highest to lowest. *And after that I will go out* means that divine truth will leave. *And he went out from Pharaoh in a wrath of anger* means that the presence of divine truth was wrested from spirits about to be damned.

And Moses said, "This is what Jehovah has said" symbolizes instruction, 7775
as above at §7765.

Around the middle of the night means when the devastation would be 7776
total. This can be seen from the symbolism of the *middle of the night* as the time of the deepest darkness—in other words, of utter falsity. Night symbolizes a state of falsity (§§2353, 6000), and the middle of it is the peak of that state. So midnight means total devastation.

I myself will go out into the middle of Egypt means that the Divine 7777
would then be present everywhere. This can be seen from the symbolism of *going out* through the *middle,* when Jehovah is said to do it, as the presence of the Divine. "Everywhere" is symbolized by the *middle,* when

it means the middle of the land, because going out through the middle of Egypt means going into all of Egypt.

7778 *And every firstborn in the land of Egypt will die* means that faith detached from neighborly love would [then] be damned. This is established by the symbolism of *dying* as being damned (discussed in §§5407, 6119) and from that of a *firstborn* as faith within the church leading to neighborly love (discussed in §§352, 2435, 6344, 7035). A firstborn *in the land of Egypt,* though, symbolizes faith without neighborly love (about which, see above at §7766).

[2] I need to say a little more about faith without neighborly love. Faith devoid of neighborly love is not faith but mere knowledge of faith's tenets. Faith and its truth look to neighborly love as their ultimate goal, and once that goal is reached, they flow from neighborly love as their primary goal. Plainly, then, faith and all that it implies is impossible among people who lack charity, although as everyone knows a knowledge of faith's truth is still possible. This knowledge is what such people call faith. When they use what they know about faith's truth and goodness to support falsity and evil, they lose that truth and goodness, because the truth and goodness start to resemble the falsity and evil they serve. The falsity and evil they support appear within the truth and goodness.

[3] Genuine faith in all its ramifications looks upward to heaven and the Lord, but everything involved in a faith detached from charity looks downward. If it supports evil and falsity, it looks all the way down to hell. This too makes it plain that faith separated from neighborly love is not faith.

From these considerations you can see what is meant by the damnation of faith detached from neighborly love: it means the damnation of falsified truth and adulterated goodness as the components of faith. When truth has been falsified it is no longer true but false, and when goodness has been adulterated it is no longer good but evil. Faith itself is no longer a belief in what is true and good but in what is false and evil, regardless of what it looks or sounds like on the outside.

I will tell you a secret: one's faith actually matches one's life. If we live a damnable life, then, our faith is also damnable; our faith consists of falsity when our life consists of evil. The falsity of a person's beliefs is not visible in the world, but it reveals itself in the other life when the evil there are deprived of what they know about truth and goodness. Falsity that had previously lain hidden in them then comes out into the open.

[4] Some of the wicked talk themselves into believing that religious truth is true. This persuasion too is thought to be faith, although it is not

faith. They stamp it on their minds to use as a means of garnering affluence, rank, and reputation. So long as the truth they have accepted serves as a means, they love it for the goal they have, which is evil, but when it no longer serves, they abandon it. In fact, they regard it as false. This persuasion is what is called dogmatism. It is what is meant by the Lord's words in Matthew:

> Many will say to me on that day, "Lord! Lord! Haven't we prophesied in your name and cast out demons in your name and exercised many powers in your name?" But then I will proclaim to them, "I do not know you. Leave me, you evildoers!" (Matthew 7:22, 23)

The same kind of faith is also meant by the oilless lamps that the five stupid young women had. They too said, "'Lord! Lord! Open up to us!' But answering, he said, 'Truly, I say to you: I do not know you'" (Matthew 25:11, 12). The lamps symbolize truth that leads to faith, and the oil, good that is done out of charity, so oilless lamps symbolize faith's truth without charity's goodness.

From the firstborn of Pharaoh who was to sit on his throne symbolizes falsified religious truth of the first rank, as the following shows: A *firstborn* symbolizes faith, as discussed in §§352, 2435, 6344, 7035. *Pharaoh* represents knowledge in general that corrupts truth known to the church, as discussed in §§6015, 6651, 6679, 6683, 6692. So the *firstborn of Pharaoh* symbolizes a faith consisting of such knowledge and therefore a faith consisting of falsified truth. And a *throne* symbolizes the reign of truth and in a negative sense the reign of falsity, as discussed in §5313. **7779**

The meaning of Pharaoh's firstborn who was to sit on his throne as falsified religious truth of the first rank can be seen from the fact that the text adds, "to the firstborn of the slave woman who is behind the millstones," symbolizing falsified religious truth of the last rank. Besides, the child of a monarch symbolizes something that occupies first place, because a monarch is the head [of a country].

[2] Falsified truths of the first rank are those considered essential. Here are some examples: Faith saves us, no matter how we lived, and saves us in the final hour of our life. Once saved, we are purified of sin, which is instantly wiped away, as dirt is washed from our hands by water. These notions presuppose that faith can exist in the absence of neighborly love, that the way we live makes no difference to our salvation, and that a person who is a devil can instantly become an angel of God. Such propositions and others like them are falsified truths of the first rank. Propositions derived directly from them come second, while more distant inferences

come last. Every truth is full of long series of inferences, some of which apply directly and some indirectly. Inferences that only touch on the original proposition come last.

[3] It is quite obvious that these ideas and others like them are falsified religious truths. After all, what person who thinks properly cannot see that living a life of faith is what makes us spiritual? Faith does not make us spiritual, except to the extent that we plant its seed in our life. Our life consists in what we love, and what we love we hold as our desire and intent, and what we hold as our desire and intent we put into action. This is our core being. What we know and contemplate without desiring it is not.

We cannot possibly change this core of ours into another kind of core by thinking about intercession and salvation, only by being born anew, which takes most of our life. After all, we have to be conceived again and born again and grow up again. This is accomplished not by thinking and talking but by intending and acting.

[4] I mention all this because the firstborn of Pharaoh and of the Egyptians symbolize faith detached from neighborly love. As was shown in the previous section, this faith is not faith but is rather a knowledge of faith's tenets.

The reason the Egyptians' firstborn represented that faith is that Egyptians knew more about religious ritual than any others constituting the representative church that came after the era of the Flood (§§4749, 4964, 4966, 6004). At that time all ritual represented the spiritual attributes of heaven. The Egyptians knew more on this subject than anyone else. As time passed, though, they started to love knowledge alone. Eventually they came to consider knowledge of religious matters to be the whole of religion (as people do today) rather than equating religion with a life of neighborly love. So they turned the entire structure of religion on its head, and once they had done that they could not help falsifying the truth that people identify with faith. When we use truth to violate the divine design—which we do when we use it for evil purposes, and which the Egyptians did when they used it for their magic—it is no longer true for us. The evil purposes to which we apply it make it false.

[5] For example, take the worship of calves among the Egyptians, who knew that a calf represented neighborly kindness. As long as they knew and thought about this, then when they saw calves or prepared them for the love feasts typical of the ancients—and later when they used calves for sacrifice—their thinking was sound. It also joined with the thinking of angels in heaven, to whom a calf is neighborly kindness. But when they

started to make golden calves and to put them in their temples and worship them, their thinking was unsound, and it joined with that of hell's inhabitants. So they were upending representative truth, turning it into representative falsity.

To the firstborn of the slave woman who is behind the millstones symbolizes falsified religious truth of the last rank, as the following shows: A *firstborn* symbolizes faith, as discussed directly above at §7779, and since it symbolizes faith, it symbolizes the whole range of truth. Truth is a matter of faith, because we ought to believe it. A *slave woman* symbolizes an outer desire for truth, or a desire for information, as discussed in §§1895, 2567, 3835, 3849. A slave woman *behind the millstones* symbolizes the outermost possible desire for information, because "behind the millstones" symbolizes what occupies last place. 7780

The text says "behind the millstones" because a mill is used to portray aspects of faith. Millstones are used to grind grain into flour and so to prepare it for bread. Flour symbolizes truth that yields goodness, and bread symbolizes the actual goodness yielded.

Sitting at the millstones, then, means being taught about and trained in the kinds of ideas that are capable of serving faith, and through faith, neighborly love. That is why the ancients used the phrase "sitting at the millstones" to depict the first rudiments of a theology concerning faith, and the phrase "sitting behind the millstones" to depict theological ideas that were even more rudimentary.

As this was the symbolism, in passages in which the Lord is teaching about the final days of the church he says:

> *Two grinding in the mill; one will be taken and the other left.* (Matthew 24:41)

This he would never have said had a mill not symbolized aspects of faith. For what a mill and grinding mean in an inner sense, see §4335.

Regarding religious truth of the first rank and the last, keep this in mind: Religious truths that develop directly out of charitable goodness are in first place, because they *are* goodness—goodness given shape. The lowest-ranking truths, by contrast, are basic. As one truth is derived from another in turn, they move further away from goodness, step by step, until finally they become stripped down. This is the kind of truth symbolized by slave women behind the millstones.

And every firstborn of the animals symbolizes adulterated religious goodness. This is established by the symbolism of a *firstborn* as faith, and 7781 by the symbolism of *animals* as desires for what is good, and in a negative sense as desires for what is evil, as discussed in §§45, 46, 142, 143, 246, 714, 715, 719, 776, 2179, 2180, 3519, 5198, 7424. This symbolism of animals comes from representations in the other life (§3218). That is why sacrificial animals had the same symbolism (§§2180, 2805, 2807, 2830, 3519). Because this was the symbolism of animals, their firstborn symbolize goodness that grows out of truth. In this case they symbolize goodness-from-truth adulterated, because the animals belonged to the Egyptians, who corrupted all truth and goodness by using it for evil purposes.

7782 *And there will be a great outcry in the whole land of Egypt* symbolizes inner mourning. This can be seen from the symbolism of an *outcry* over the death of the firstborn (in an inner sense, over damnation) as mourning. A *great* outcry is inner mourning, because the greater the mourning is, the deeper it goes.

7783 *Such as there has never been and such as will not be again* symbolizes conditions so bad that they could not be equaled. This can be seen from explanations at §§7649, 7686.

7784 *And toward all the children of Israel not a dog will move its tongue* means that among people of the spiritual church there will be no damnation or mourning in the least, as the following shows: The *children of Israel* represent people of the spiritual church, as discussed in §§6426, 6637, 6862, 6868, 7035, 7062, 7198, 7201, 7215, 7223. And *not a dog will move its tongue* means that there will be no damnation or mourning at all, because this is the opposite of the great outcry that was to take place in the land of Egypt. The outcry means inner mourning (§7782) over the damnation symbolized by the death of the firstborn.

[2] The fact that damnation is not at all the lot of people in the spiritual church (that is, people who display the goodness characteristic of that church) should not be taken to mean they are completely free of evil. It only means that the Lord holds them back from evil and keeps them on a good path. Their selfhood is pure evil and is completely damned, but the Lord's selfhood, which they receive from him, is good and therefore carries no damnation. The meaning, then, is that people who live in the Lord incur no damnation.

[3] It is expressed as "not a dog will move its tongue" because of the symbolism of a *dog*. A dog symbolizes the lowliest, most menial people of all in the church. It also symbolizes people outside the church, and people who bark on and on about church matters but understand little. In a

negative sense a dog symbolizes people entirely outside the church's faith who vilify religious thinking.

The symbolism of dogs as people outside the church can be seen in Matthew:

> Jesus said to the Greek woman—the Syrophoenician—"It is not good to take the children's bread and *throw it to the dogs."* But she said, "Yes, Lord, but even *the pups eat some of the crumbs that fall from their masters' table."* Then, answering, Jesus said to her, "Woman, your faith is abundant. You may have what you want." And [the daughter of] the woman was healed. (Matthew 15:26, 27, 28; Mark 7:27, 28)

By the children here are meant people in the church, and by the dogs, people outside it. The *dogs* that licked Lazarus' sores (Luke 16:21) have the same meaning. In the latter story, the rich man in an inner sense means someone who is in the church and who is therefore well supplied with spiritual riches, which are concepts of truth and goodness.

[4] [In the following passages] dogs stand for people in the church who are at its lowest level, for people who bark on and on about church matters but understand little, and, in a negative sense, for people who vilify religious thinking. In Isaiah:

> His sentries are all blind; they do not know; *they are all mute dogs; they cannot bark,* watching, lying down, loving to sleep. (Isaiah 56:10)

In David:

> *They create a commotion, as a dog does.* They roam around the city, because *they bay with their mouth; swords are on their lips.* (Psalms 59:6, 7, 14)

In the same author:

> . . . so that your foot can press the *tongue of your dogs* into blood. (Psalms 68:23)

In Matthew:

> *Don't give what is holy to the dogs;* don't strew your pearls before the pigs; or they may trample them with their feet and, *turning, tear you apart.* (Matthew 7:6)

So whatever is the very lowliest, anything that deserves to be discarded, is symbolized by a dead dog (1 Samuel 24:14; 2 Samuel 9:8; 16:9).

7785 *From man to animal* means neither in respect to anything true nor in respect to anything good. This is evident from the symbolism of a *man* as truth (discussed at §3134) and from that of an *animal* as a desire for goodness and therefore as goodness itself (discussed just above at §7781).

7786 *So that you may know that Jehovah distinguishes between the Egyptians and Israel* means so as to reveal what kind of distinction is drawn between people who dwell in evil and people who dwell in goodness, as the following shows: *Knowing* symbolizes being revealed. The *Egyptians* represent people who dwell in evil. Earlier they symbolized people under the sway of falsity, but now that they have been stripped of the religious truth they knew, they symbolize people under the sway of evil. After all, the death of the firstborn symbolizes damnation, which is a state of evil. And the children of *Israel* represent people of the spiritual church, as mentioned above at §7784, so they represent people dwelling in goodness. This is because people of the spiritual church are led by faith to neighborly love and therefore by truth to goodness.

7787 *And all [these] servants of yours will come down to me* symbolizes the subordinates. This is clear from the symbolism of *Pharaoh's servants* as subordinates, which is discussed above at §7773.

7788 *And bow to me* symbolizes due respect for divine truth, born of fear. This can be seen from the representation of Moses as divine truth (noted many times before) and from the symbolism of *bowing* as humility—although in this case it symbolizes respect born of fear, since it is ascribed to people devoted to evil.

I speak of respect born of fear because evil people have no other respect for divine truth or even for the Divine itself than the kind inspired in them by fear. Hell's inhabitants love only themselves, and people who love only themselves have no respect for anyone else. All regard for others and even for the Divine itself they redirect to themselves. Where there is love, there is respect. Where there is no love, there is no respect except the kind born of fear.

That is why wicked people in the other life undergo repeated punishment until they finally do not dare to rise up against good people and persecute them. There is no other way to deter them from evildoing than through fear of punishment.

7789 *Saying, "Go out, you and all the people that are at your feet,"* symbolizes a plea for the departure of those who possess truth from the Divine, from highest to lowest, as the following shows: *Going out* means leaving. Moses—*you*—represents divine truth. The *people* symbolize those with truth from the Divine. This is because the children of Israel—the people meant here—represent participants in the spiritual church. So they represent individuals with truth that grows out of goodness and with goodness that grows out of truth. In this case they represent individuals who possess truth from the Divine, because they are called "the people that are at your [Moses'] feet," Moses representing divine truth. And *at your feet* symbolizes the lowlier ones and consequently the subordinates. Feet symbolize the lower planes, because they symbolize what is earthly, since the earthly realm lies below the spiritual realm. For the symbolism of feet as the earthly dimension, see §§2162, 3761, 3986, 4280, 4938–4952. That is why the text speaks of the *people that are at your feet.*

The symbolism also includes the idea of highest to lowest. Divine truth and therefore the highest is symbolized by Moses, while the entire mass of those who subscribe to truth from the Divine is symbolized by "the people at your feet."

And after that I will go out means that divine truth will leave. This is 7790
evident from the symbolism of *going out* as leaving and from the representation of Moses as divine truth.

This means that when spirits who have been persecuting the upright are finally damned, all divine truth departs from them, because their evil is then active in them, and evil rejects and snuffs out all divine truth.

Earlier, before they were damned, they did know religious truth, but they did not have the truth inside them. It lay in their mouth, not in their heart. Once they have been stripped of that truth, then, evil remains, and the falsity-from-evil that had lain hidden in them emerges. Even though they had proclaimed the truth, you see, they had not subscribed to it but rather to falsity. What is more, even their avowal of the truth had come not from the origin of truth, which is goodness, but from evil. It was for the sake of riches, honors, and reputation and consequently for the sake of themselves and their worldly advantage that they had championed the truth.

Truth that descends from such an origin stays on the surface and drops off like scales when it is being laid waste. When it drops off, it leaves behind areas that stink and reek with the falsity that wafts from the evils there.

Such is the lot of people who knew religious truth but lived a life contrary to it. As the Lord says in Luke:

> Those servants who know their master's will but neither prepare themselves nor do his will, will be beaten with many [blows]. But as for

those who do not know, even if they do deeds worthy of blows they will be beaten with few. (Luke 12:47, 48)

7791 *And he went out from Pharaoh in a wrath of anger* means that the presence of divine truth was wrested from spirits about to be damned, as the following shows: *Going out* means leaving, and in this case, being wrested away, because the text says "in a wrath of anger." (Besides, at the end, when damnation sets in, the two parties are wrenched apart, because when spirits start to loathe divine truth, to fear it, and ultimately to be terrified by its presence, they tear themselves away from it.) Moses represents divine truth, as noted many times. *Pharaoh* represents spirits who harassed people of the spiritual church, as also noted many times, but here he represents spirits about to be damned (damnation being symbolized by the fact that the firstborn were to be put to death, §7778). And a *wrath of anger* symbolizes revulsion and aversion, as discussed in §§3614, 5034, 5798. When aversion is attributed to the Divine, as it is here to the divine truth represented by Moses, the meaning is not that the Divine feels any loathing but that people committed to evil do (5798). (Wrath has to do with falsity; anger, with evil, 3614.)

7792 Exodus 11:9, 10. *And Jehovah said to Moses, "Pharaoh will not listen to you [two], so that my portents may multiply in the land of Egypt." And Moses and Aaron performed all these portents before Pharaoh. And Jehovah hardened Pharaoh's heart, and he did not send the children of Israel away from his land.*

And Jehovah said to Moses symbolizes instruction. *Pharaoh will not listen to you [two]* symbolizes disobedience. *So that my portents may multiply in the land of Egypt* means in order to prove that, far from caring about faith, they were intent on evil. *And Moses and Aaron performed all these portents before Pharaoh* means that all this devastation and all the consequent proof that they are dedicated to evil was generated through truth coming from the Divine. *And Jehovah hardened Pharaoh's heart* means that they were obstinate. *And he did not send the children of Israel away from his land* means that they did not leave people of the spiritual church alone.

7793 *And Jehovah said to Moses* symbolizes instruction. This is plain from the symbolism of *saying,* when Jehovah predicts what is going to happen, as instruction.

7794 *Pharaoh will not listen to you [two]* symbolizes disobedience. This can be seen from the symbolism of *listening* as obedience (discussed in §§2542, 3869, 4652–4660, 5017, 7216) and from the representation of *Pharaoh* as spirits who harassed the upright in the other life—the same spirits who are now about to be damned.

So that my portents may multiply in the land of Egypt means in order to prove that, far from caring about faith, they were intent on evil. This can be seen from the symbolism of the *portents* and signs performed in Egypt as instances of devastation and therefore as proof that they are intent on evil, a symbolism noted at §7633. Each of these portents symbolized a new level in the devastation of people who were part of the church [when they were in the world] and knew faith's tenets but lived evil lives. Because these are the ones who persecute the upright in the other life, it is their current state that is being symbolized. (See §7465.) The *multiplying* of the portents symbolizes the way these states build on one another. 7795

There are two reasons for the large number of steps. One is to prove to the evil that they are devoted to evil. The other is to enlighten the good about the state of people who were in the church but lived evil lives (§7633). Were it not for these two aims, the evil could be damned and sent to hell immediately, without such a long series of changes in state.

[2] The world has no idea that the wicked go through so many stages before being damned and sent to hell. People think we are either damned or saved immediately, without undergoing any process. But the reality is quite different: justice carries the day there. We are not damned until we know with deep conviction that we are committed to evil and that it is impossible for us to be in heaven. In addition, our evilness is displayed openly to us, in keeping with the Lord's words in Luke:

> Nothing is concealed that will not be revealed, or hidden that will not be known. So whatever you said in the dark will be heard in the light. And what you spoke in the ear in your private rooms will be proclaimed on the roofs. (Luke 12:2, 3; Matthew 10:26; Mark 4:22)

What is more, we are also warned to desist from evil, but when evil rules us so thoroughly that we cannot stop, the power to do harm by falsifying truth and pretending to be good is taken from us. It is removed gradually, one step at a time, until we end by being damned and sent to hell. That is what happens when we are left to the wickedness of our life.

[3] The wickedness of our life is the evil we have in our will and consequently in our thoughts. It is therefore the kind of person we are inside, and the kind of person we would be on the outside if we were not hampered by the law and by the fear of forfeiting our wealth, position, reputation, and life. This inner life is what follows us beyond the grave.

Our outer life does not, unless it springs from our inner life. On the outside we pretend to be just the opposite. So when we are stripped of our facade after death, it becomes obvious what we were like in regard to both our will and our thoughts. This is the state to which an evil person is reduced by the various steps of devastation. All devastation in the other life progresses from outer to inner levels.

This discussion clarifies what kind of justice exists in the other world and what kind of process precedes the damnation of an evil person.

That my portents may multiply in the land of Egypt, then, plainly means to prove that, far from caring about faith, they were intent on evil. For the idea that people devoted to evil are without faith, see above at §7778.

7796 *And Moses and Aaron performed all these portents before Pharaoh* means that all this devastation and all the consequent proof that they are dedicated to evil was generated through truth from the Divine, as the following shows: *Moses* and *Aaron* represent divine truth, Moses representing truth that comes directly from the Divine, and Aaron, truth that comes indirectly, as dealt with in §§7010, 7089, 7382. And the *portents performed* in Egypt—*before Pharaoh*—symbolize so many steps in the devastation of people who were part of the church but lived evil lives. This symbolism of the portents of Egypt can be seen from the symbolism of each portent. For the fact that the portents also symbolize proof of their dedication to evil rather than to faith, see directly above at §7795.

[2] The verse says that Moses and Aaron performed the portents, even though it was not they but the Divine that performed them. It is phrased this way because Moses and Aaron represent divine truth, and the portents were performed by the Divine through truth radiating from itself. Everything that the Divine itself does is done through truth emanating from it. The Divine itself is the core essence of everything, but truth radiating from it is the consequent manifestation of everything. Goodness itself, which is the divine essence, brings everything into existence through the truth belonging to it.

I am saying the devastation was generated through truth from the Divine, but it needs to be understood that divine truth is not the cause, because the Divine does not inflict devastation on anyone. No, it is the evil who devastate themselves, by setting themselves obstinately against divine truth—snuffing it out or rejecting or corrupting it—and by taking divine goodness, which flows in continuously, and turning it into evil. This is what creates the devastation. You can see, then, why it is that the inflow of goodness and truth from the Divine is not the cause of devastation, because without their inflow there is no life. The fault lies rather in the conversion of goodness and truth into evil and falsity, which is done by a person dedicated to evil.

And Jehovah hardened Pharaoh's heart means that they were obstinate. This can be seen from the symbolism of *hardening one's heart* as being obstinate, which is mentioned in §§7272, 7300, 7305. For the idea that Jehovah does not harden anyone's heart or do any kind of evil, even though evil is attributed to him in the Word's literal meaning, see §§7533, 7632, 7643. 7797

And he did not send the children of Israel away from his land means that they did not leave people of the spiritual church alone. This can be seen from the symbolism of *sending away* as leaving alone and from the representation of the *children of Israel* as people of the spiritual church (discussed in §§6426, 6637, 6862, 6868, 7035, 7062, 7198, 7201, 7215, 7223). 7798

The Spirits and Inhabitants of Jupiter

I have been allowed to interact with the spirits and angels of Jupiter over a longer period than with spirits from the other planets, so I have more to say about their state and the state of their planet's inhabitants. 7799

The planet Jupiter itself is not visible to anyone in the next life, but spirits from Jupiter are. They appear out in front, to the left, some distance away, and always in that position. Spirits and angels picture the planet too as being there. 7800

The spirits of all the planets individually are separated from each other and are located near their own globe. The reason they are separated is that they differ in character and occupy different areas of the universal human. Those who differ in character appear as distant from others as they are different. When it comes to the location of spirits and angels in the other world and to distances among them, all separation and distinction reflect differences in their nature and character. After all, place corresponds to state (§§2625, 2837, 3356, 3387, 4321, 4882, 5605, 7381).

There are many kinds of spirits from Jupiter, but there are three kinds with whom I have spent time and spoken often. One kind—the 7801 lowliest—looks dark, almost pitch black. These spirits are despised by others and are called disciplinarians, because they discipline those inhabitants of their planet who live wicked lives. They are always wanting to go to heaven.

The second kind has a face that glows as if it were reflecting candlelight. These spirits appear seated and resemble idols, because they let themselves be worshiped by others, especially by the servants they had in the world, where they convinced the servants they were mediators between the servants and the Lord. The servants call them saints and masters.

The third kind—the best—has more understanding and wisdom than the others. These spirits are seen wearing sky-blue clothes interwoven with flecks of gold.

However, the actual angels from that planet live in the same place as the angels of the other planets, because all true angels constitute a single, inclusive heaven.

7802 It is common on that planet for spirits to speak with the inhabitants, teach them, and also chastise them if they have done wrong. Their angels have told me a lot about it, so I would like to lay out some of it here.

The reason the spirits talk with people there is that they think a lot about heaven and life after death, without worrying much about life in the world. They know they will live on after they pass away, in a happy state that matches the state of their inner self, as formed in the world.

On our planet too, in ancient times, it was common to talk with spirits and angels, for the same reason: that people thought about heaven but not very often about the world. This living communication with heaven closed off after a while, though, as people changed from being deep to being shallow—that is, as they started to think about the world and stopped thinking much about heaven. It closed off even more tightly when people stopped believing that heaven and hell existed or that they themselves were essentially spirit-people who would live on after death.

Today people believe that the body has life on its own, not from its spirit. So if they could not believe they will rise again with their body, they would not believe in a resurrection at all.

7803 In regard to the way spirits talk with inhabitants of Jupiter, there are spirits who chastise, spirits who teach, and spirits who supervise.

The spirits who chastise the inhabitants come up close to their left side, leaning around toward the back. In that position they dredge up out of people's memory everything they have done or thought. This is easy for spirits, because when they come to people they instantly penetrate every corner of their memory (§§6192, 6193, 6198, 6199, 6214). If they find that the people have done or thought something bad, they denounce them for it and punish them with pain in the joints of their feet or hands or in their epigastric region. This too they can do with skill, when allowed to.

When spirits of this kind come to people, they strike horror and fear into them. That is how people know of their arrival. Instilling fear is something that evil spirits—especially those who were robbers when they were alive in the world—know how to do when they approach someone.

[2] To show me how those spirits behave when they visit an inhabitant of their planet, such a spirit was permitted to approach me. When he got near, a palpable horror and fear seized me, but the dread I felt was not deep but rather superficial, because I knew he was that type of spirit. I also took a look at him. He resembled a dark cloud with tiny free-floating stars inside it. Floating stars symbolize falsity, whereas fixed stars symbolize truth.

The spirit attached to my left side toward my back. He also began to denounce me for deeds and thoughts he had dredged up from my memory that he was interpreting negatively. He was stopped, though, by some angels who were also present.

When he realized he was with someone who was not an inhabitant of his own planet, he started talking to me, saying that when he comes to people, he knows every single thing they have done or thought. He also said he criticizes them harshly and punishes them with different kinds of pain.

The teaching spirits likewise stand near an inhabitant's left side, but 7804
farther forward. They chastise too, but gently, and they quickly switch to teaching how a person should live. They also look dark, but unlike the previous spirits they do not resemble clouds. Instead they seem to be wearing sackcloth. They are called teachers, while the previous set are called disciplinarians.

When those spirits are present, angelic spirits from their same planet 7805
are also present. They sit by a person's head, which they have a special way of filling up, so to speak. Their presence there comes across as a gentle breath of air, because they are afraid of causing a person the slightest pain or anxiety when they approach and flow in.

They supervise both the punishing spirits and the teaching spirits, to keep the former from treating a person any worse than the Lord allows, and to make sure the latter tell the truth.

I had the privilege of speaking with these angelic spirits too.

There are two signs that appear to those spirits when they are with 7806
a person. They see a white-faced man of times long past, which is a sign that they should not speak anything but the truth. They also see a face

in a window, which is a sign for them to leave. I saw both the man of the past and the face in the window. When the face appeared, the spirit immediately left me.

7807 While the disciplinary spirit was with me, the angelic spirits kept a constant smile of good cheer on my face. They made the area around my lips jut out and held my mouth open. This is very easy for angels to do by flowing in. They said they produce the same expression on the faces of their planet's inhabitants when present with them.

7808 Sometimes after being corrected and instructed, the inhabitants do wrong again, or think of doing wrong, and the truth they have been commanded does not make them restrain themselves. If the chastising spirit then returns, they are punished more severely. Angelic spirits temper the punishment, though, depending on the intent behind the person's deeds and the desire behind the person's thoughts.

7809 The spirits there talk with the people, but the people do not talk with the spirits in return. All they say (in response to a lesson) is, "I won't do that anymore."

They are also forbidden to tell anyone connected with them that a spirit has spoken with them. If they tell, they are severely punished.

When the spirits of Jupiter were with me, they initially thought they were with a person of their own planet. But when I answered them and when I contemplated a desire I had to make these experiences public, they were not allowed either to rebuke or to teach me. They then realized they were with another kind of person.

7810 A disciplinary spirit came to me another time as well, attached himself to my left side below my waist as before, and once again wanted to punish me. Their angels, though, who were also present at the time, prevented him.

The spirit then showed me different kinds of punishment they are allowed to inflict on inhabitants of their planet who do wrong or form an intent to do wrong. In addition to joint pain [§7803], there was a painful squeeze at the waist that feels like the pinch of a tight belt. Then there was an off-and-on stoppage of the breath, to the point of distress, and a prohibition against eating anything but bread. As a last resort there was the threat that if the malefactors did not cease doing as they had been, they would die, which would deprive them of the joys of spouse, children, and friends. Grief on that account is instilled at the same time.

7811 From all this you can see that the angels of theirs who sit by a person's head have a certain power of judgment over people, because the angels flow in and permit some things, regulate others, and forbid still others. However, I was given the opportunity to tell them not to believe they sit in judgment. "Only the Lord is Judge," I said. "All the orders and commands you give the punishing and teaching spirits come to you from him. They just *seem* to come from you."

Besides all the spirits just mentioned, there are dissuading spirits. They are people who were banished from the society of others when they lived in the world, because they were evil. When they approach, a sort of hovering flame appears and drops down near one's face. They position themselves down behind a person and project their voices up from there. **7812**

They contradict whatever a teaching spirit has relayed from the angels; they tell people not to live the way they have been taught but rather to do whatever they want and so on. They usually arrive right after the previous spirits have left. The inhabitants there know who those spirits are, though, and what they are like, so they pay no attention. Still, the experience teaches them what evil is and therefore what goodness is. From evil one learns what is good, since the nature of goodness is recognized from its opposite. All our perception of some issue comes from reflecting on things that contrast with it in various ways and to different degrees.

More will be said about the spirits and inhabitants of Jupiter at the end of the following chapter [§§8021–8032]. **7813**

Exodus 12

Teachings on Neighborly Love

7814 WE were created in such a way that we can look up above ourselves and also down below ourselves. Looking above ourselves means focusing on our neighbor, our country, our religion, heaven, and most of all the Lord. Looking below ourselves means focusing on the earth, the world, and most of all ourselves.

7815 The reason looking above ourselves means focusing on our neighbor, country, and religion is that this means focusing on the Lord. The Lord dwells in neighborly love, and it is an act of neighborly love to have regard for one's neighbor, country, and religion—in other words, to wish them well. People who turn their back on these and wish only themselves well are the ones who look below themselves.

7816 To look above ourselves is to be lifted up by the Lord. We cannot look above ourselves without being raised up by the one who dwells above. Looking below ourselves is something we do ourselves, because we are then refusing to be lifted up.

7817 People with a goodness born of charity and faith look above themselves, because they are lifted up by the Lord. People without a goodness born of charity and faith look below themselves, because they are not lifted up by the Lord.

It is when we take the stream of truth and goodness flowing from the Lord and bend it in our own direction that we look below ourselves. When we bend it in our own direction, we see ourselves and the world before our eyes. We fail to see the Lord with his goodness and truth at all, because we put them behind us, where they are so hard to see that we lose interest in them and eventually deny they exist.

7818 Looking to something above or below means adopting it as a goal, or loving it more than anything else. Looking up therefore means adopting qualities of the Lord and of heaven as a goal, or loving them more than anything else. Looking down means adopting self-centered and worldly qualities as a goal and loving them more than anything else. What is more, our inner reaches actually turn in the same direction our love turns.

People with a goodness born of charity and faith also love themselves and worldly advantages, but only the way one loves the means of achieving a goal. Their self-love aims at love for the Lord, because they love themselves as a means of achieving the goal of being able to serve the Lord. Their love for worldly advantages aims at love for their neighbor, because they love those advantages as a means of achieving the goal of being able to serve their neighbor. When we love a means for the sake of achieving a goal, it is not the means but the goal that we love. 7819

From these remarks you can see that people blessed with worldly glory—with more prominence and wealth than others have—can look up to the Lord just as much as people who lack prominence and wealth can. They look up when they view prestige and riches as a means rather than a goal. 7820

Looking up is proper to humankind, but looking down is proper to animals. It follows, then, that the more one looks down below oneself, the more one is an animal and an image of hell. The more one looks up above oneself, the more one is a human and an image of the Lord. 7821

Exodus 12

1. And Jehovah said to Moses and to Aaron in the land of Egypt, saying,

2. "This month is the head of the months for you; it is the first in the months of the year for you.

3. Speak to the whole congregation of Israel, saying, 'On the tenth of this month they shall each take themselves a member of the flock for the household of their fathers, a member of the flock for a household.

4. And if the household is too small for a flock animal, [the householder] and his fellow townsman closest to his house [shall] take [one] according to the number of souls; each according to what his or her mouth will eat shall be counted for the flock animal.

5. A sound animal, a male, the son of a year it shall be for you; from among the lambs or from among the goats you shall take it.

6. And it will be in safekeeping for you till the fourteenth day of this month. And the whole assembly of the congregation of Israel shall slaughter it between the evenings.

7. And they shall take some of the blood and put it on the two doorposts and on the lintel on their houses in which they are going to eat it.

8. And they shall eat the flesh on that night, roasted with fire; and [with] unleavened loaves on bitter herbs they shall eat it.

9. You are not to eat any of it raw or by any means cooked in water but rather roasted with fire, its head atop its legs and atop its middle.

10. And you shall not leave any of it till morning. And what remains of it till morning you shall burn with fire.

11. And this is how you shall eat it: your hips girded, your shoes on your feet, and your staff in your hand; and you shall eat it in a hurry. It is a Passover [offering] to Jehovah.

12. And I will pass through the land of Egypt on this night and strike every firstborn in the land of Egypt from human to animal. And on all the gods of Egypt I will pass judgment; I am Jehovah!

13. And the blood will serve you as a sign on the houses, [to show] where you are, and should I see the blood, I will pass by you, and the plague will not come as a destroyer on you, in my striking the land of Egypt.

14. And that day shall serve you as a reminder, and you shall celebrate it as a feast to Jehovah throughout your generations; by an eternal statute you shall celebrate it.

15. Seven days you shall eat unleavened loaves. Yes, on the first day you shall make yeast cease from your houses, because anyone eating yeast bread, that soul shall be cut off from Israel. [This shall last] from the first day up to the seventh day.

16. And on the first day you shall have a holy convocation, and on the seventh day a holy convocation. No work shall be done on those days, only [the provision of] something to eat for every soul; this alone shall be done by you.

17. And you shall observe [the practice of] the unleavened loaves, because on that same day I led your armies out of the land of Egypt; and you shall keep this day throughout your generations by an eternal statute.

18. In the first [month], on the fourteenth day of the month in the evening, you shall eat unleavened loaves, up to the twenty-first day of the month in the evening.

19. For seven days yeast shall not be found in your houses, because anyone eating yeast bread, that soul shall be cut off from the congregation of Israel, both an immigrant and a native of the land.

20. No yeast bread shall you eat; in all your dwellings you shall eat unleavened loaves.'"

21. And Moses called all the elders of Israel and said to them, "Haul forth and take for yourselves an animal of the flock according to your clans and slaughter the Passover.

22. And you shall take a bundle of hyssop, and you are to dip it in the blood that is in the basin and touch it to the lintel and to the two doorposts with the blood that is in the basin. And you yourselves shall not go out—not one—from the doorway of your house till morning.

23. And Jehovah will pass through to inflict a plague on Egypt, and should he see the blood on the lintel and on the two doorposts, Jehovah will pass by the doorway and not let the destroyer come to your houses to inflict the plague.

24. And you shall keep this word as a statute for yourself and for your children forever.

25. And it will happen that you will come to the land that Jehovah is going to give you, as he spoke, and you shall keep this service.

26. And it will happen that your sons will say to you, 'What is this service you have?'

27. And you shall say, 'It is the Passover sacrifice to Jehovah—that he passed by the houses of the children of Israel in Egypt in his inflicting a plague on Egypt and delivered our houses.'" And the people bent and bowed.

28. And the children of Israel went and did as Jehovah had commanded Moses and Aaron; that is what they did.

29. And it came about in the middle of the night that Jehovah struck every firstborn in the land of Egypt, from the firstborn of Pharaoh who was to sit on his throne to the firstborn of the prisoner who was in the house of the pit, and every firstborn of the animals.

30. And Pharaoh rose that night, as did all his servants and all the Egyptians, and there was a great outcry in Egypt, because there was no house where no one was dead.

31. And he called Moses and Aaron by night and said, "Rise, go out from the middle of my people, both you and the children of Israel, and go serve Jehovah according to what you have spoken.

32. Take both your flocks and your herds, as you have spoken, and go; and may you bless me, too."

33. And Egypt prevailed on the people, hurrying to send them away from the land, because [the Egyptians] said, "We are all dying."

34. And the people carried off their dough before it had been leavened, their kneading troughs tied up in their clothes on their shoulder.

35. And the children of Israel did according to the word of Moses and asked the Egyptians for vessels of silver and vessels of gold and for clothes.

36. And Jehovah gave favor to the people in the eyes of the Egyptians. And [the Egyptians] lent to them, and they robbed the Egyptians.

37. And the children of Israel traveled from Rameses to Succoth, something like six hundred thousand men on the march, besides children.

38. And a multitudinous rabble also went up with them, and flocks and herds—a very weighty acquisition.

39. And the dough that they had brought out of Egypt they cooked into unleavened cakes, because it had not been leavened, because they were driven out of Egypt and could not wait. And they had not even prepared provisions for themselves.

40. And the residence of the children of Israel during which they resided in Egypt [was] four hundred thirty years.

41. And it happened at the end of four hundred thirty years—and it happened on that same day—that all Jehovah's armies went out from the land of Egypt.

42. It is a night of watchkeeping for Jehovah, to lead them out of the land of Egypt. This is the very night for Jehovah of watchkeeping for all the children of Israel throughout their generations.

43. And Jehovah said to Moses and Aaron, "This is the statute for Passover: any offspring of a foreigner shall not eat it.

44. And any man's slave, anyone purchased with silver—you shall circumcise him; then he shall eat it.

45. A temporary resident or a hired servant shall not eat it.

46. In a single house it shall be eaten; you shall not take any of the flesh outside the house. And not a bone shall you break in it.

47. The whole congregation of Israel shall perform it.

48. And when an immigrant resides with you and would perform the Passover to Jehovah, every male of his shall be circumcised, and then he shall approach to perform it, and he will be as a native of the land. And anyone foreskinned shall not eat it.

49. One law there shall be for the native and for the immigrant residing in your midst."

50. And all the children of Israel did as Jehovah had commanded Moses and Aaron; that is what they did.

51. And it happened on that same day that Jehovah led the children of Israel out of the land of Egypt according to their armies.

Summary

THE inner meaning of this chapter is about the deliverance of people in the spiritual church and the damnation of people whose faith is detached from neighborly love. The damnation of the one group and the deliverance of the other is represented by the Passover. The state of neighborly love and faith characterizing the ones who were delivered is represented by the practices to be observed on the days of Passover. 7822

In the highest sense, the Passover represents the damnation of the faithless and the deliverance of the faithful by the Lord when he was glorified. In that highest sense, the statutes for Passover depict the state of these people as it was at the time and as it was to be afterward, both in general and in every particular. 7823

Inner Meaning

EXODUS 12:1, 2. *And Jehovah said to Moses and to Aaron in the land of Egypt, saying, "This month is the head of the months for you; it is the first in the months of the year for you."* 7824

And Jehovah said to Moses and to Aaron symbolizes instructions given by divine truth. *In the land of Egypt* means while the people belonging to the spiritual church were still in the vicinity of the persecutors. *Saying, "This month is the head of the months for you,"* means that this state was the most important of all. *It is the first in the months of the year for you* symbolizes the starting point, the source of all subsequent states forever.

And Jehovah said to Moses and to Aaron symbolizes instructions given by divine truth, as the following shows: *Saying* symbolizes instructions, when Jehovah is talking about measures to be taken up by the church (since *saying* includes the words that follow it). And *Moses* and *Aaron* 7825 represent divine truth, Moses representing truth that emanates directly from the Divine, and Aaron, truth that emanates indirectly, as discussed in §§7009, 7010, 7089, 7382.

7826 *In the land of Egypt* means while the people belonging to the spiritual church were still in the vicinity of the persecutors. This can be seen from the symbolism of the *land of Egypt* as the place where the persecutors were. After all, Pharaoh and the Egyptians represent and symbolize people in the church who believed in faith detached from neighborly love [when they lived in the world] and who in the other life harass the upright (§§6692, 7097, 7107, 7110, 7126, 7142, 7317). The land of Egypt symbolizes the persecution itself (7278). The children of Israel represent people of the spiritual church who were being harassed (6426, 6637, 6862, 6868, 7035, 7062, 7198, 7201, 7215, 7223). For the fact that they were in the vicinity of the persecutors in the other life, see §7240. Their nearness is symbolized by the fact that the children of Israel were in the middle of the land of Egypt (in the land of Goshen), and the persecution is symbolized by burdens laid on them.

This now shows that "Jehovah said to Moses and to Aaron in the land of Egypt" symbolizes instructions given by divine truth while the people belonging to the spiritual church were still in the vicinity of the persecutors.

7827 *Saying, "This month is the head of the months for you,"* means that this state was the most important of all, as the following shows: A *month* symbolizes the end of a previous state and the start of the next, so it symbolizes a new state, as discussed at §3814. And when a *head* is mentioned in connection with months of the year and (in an inner sense) with states of life, it means the most important. Clearly, then, *this month is the head of the months for you* means that this state was the most important of all.

The reason it was the most important state of all is contained in the next section.

7828 *It is the first in the months of the year for you* symbolizes the starting point, the source of all subsequent states forever, as the following shows: *Being first* symbolizes a starting point, when it applies to the months of the year and, in an inner sense, to states of life. *Months* symbolize states, as noted directly above at §7827. And a *year* symbolizes a period of life from beginning to end, as discussed at §2906. Here the word is used of people in the spiritual church who were in the other world, and their period of life has a beginning but no end, so in this case a year symbolizes a period of life from its starting point to eternity. For this additional meaning of a year, see the end of §2906.

Why was this month made the head of the months and the first of all the months? Because it symbolizes the start of deliverance for people of the spiritual church who so far had been in a captive state, held as they were in the underground realm, where the evil spirits represented by Pharaoh and the Egyptians persecuted them.

[2] Here is why their state when they were first delivered was the most important of all and the starting point, the source of all their subsequent states forever: The inhabitants of the underground realm were delivered by the Lord's coming into the world, and without his coming into the world, they could not possibly have been saved. It was when he rose again that they were delivered. So that state, when they were delivered, was plainly the most important of all for them.

Likewise for everyone in the spiritual church ever since, who never could have been saved if the Lord had not come into the world and glorified his human nature, or made it divine.

(For the idea that people of the spiritual church were held in the underground realm till the Lord's Coming and that the Lord delivered and saved them, see §§6854, 6914. For the general idea that the people of the spiritual church were saved by the Lord's Coming, see §§2661, 2716, 6372, 7035, 7091 at the end.)

In the highest sense, then, these words mean that the glorification and resurrection of the Lord's human side is the source of all salvation.

Exodus 12:3, 4, 5, 6. *"Speak to the whole congregation of Israel, saying,* **7829**
'On the tenth of this month they shall each take themselves a member of the flock for the household of their fathers, a member of the flock for a household. And if the household is too small for a flock animal, [the householder] and his fellow townsman closest to his house [shall] take [one] according to the number of souls; each according to what his or her mouth will eat shall be counted for the flock animal. A sound animal, a male, the son of a year it shall be for you; from among the lambs or from among the goats you shall take it. And it will be in safekeeping for you till the fourteenth day of this month. And the whole congregation of Israel shall slaughter it between the evenings.'"

Speak to the whole congregation of Israel, saying, symbolizes an inflow instructing everyone in the spiritual church. *On the tenth of this month* symbolizes a state in which the inner levels are initiated. *They shall each take themselves a member of the flock* means into innocence. *For the household of their fathers, a member of the flock for a household* means in keeping with the goodness unique to each. *And if the household is too small for a flock animal* means if that individual variety of goodness is not enough for innocence. *[The householder] and his fellow townsman closest to his house shall take [one]* means combining with the neighboring variety of goodness from truth. *According to the number of souls; [each] according to what his or her mouth will eat shall be counted for the flock animal* means in this way making goodness sufficient for innocence by filling it with the amount of truth-from-goodness necessary for [innocence] to be adopted. *A sound animal* symbolizes spotless innocence. *A male* means which comes of a faith grounded in neighborly love. *The son of a year it shall be for you* symbolizes a full state. *From among the lambs or from among the goats you shall take it* symbolizes inner and outer innocent goodness. *And it will be in safekeeping for you* symbolizes a time and state of initiation. *Till the fourteenth [day] of [this] month* means reaching a holy state. *And the whole assembly of the congregation of Israel shall slaughter it* symbolizes preparation for enjoyment by everyone in the spiritual church collectively. *Between the evenings* symbolizes the last state and the first.

7830 *Speak to the whole congregation of Israel, saying,* symbolizes an inflow instructing everyone in the spiritual church, as the following shows: *Speaking* symbolizes an inflow, as mentioned in §§2951, 5481, 5743. It also symbolizes instructions—instructions on observances they are to keep once they are delivered—as is evident from the verses that follow. And the *congregation of Israel* symbolizes all truth and goodness in their entirety. After all, "the congregation of Israel" means all the tribes, which stand for everything true and good, or all facets of faith and neighborly love, as may be seen in §§3858, 3926, 4060, 6335. Since the congregation of Israel symbolizes these things, it symbolizes people of the spiritual church (§6337), because the church consists of truth and goodness. For the idea that the children of Israel represent the spiritual church, see §§6426, 6637, 6862, 6868, 7035, 7062, 7198, 7201, 7215, 7223.

7831 *On the tenth of this month* symbolizes a state in which the inner levels are initiated. This can be seen from the symbolism of the *tenth* (day) as the state of one's inner levels, since a day symbolizes a state (§§23, 487, 488, 493, 893, 2788, 3462, 3785, 4850, 5672) and ten symbolizes a remnant (576, 1738, 1906, 2284), that is, truth and goodness that the Lord stores up in our inner levels (1050, 1906, 2284, 5135, 5897, 7560, 7564). Since the remnant lies on our inner levels and is the means by which we are prepared for and initiated into the reception of goodness and truth from the Lord, the tenth day here symbolizes a state in which the inner levels are initiated. For the idea that a remnant is the means by which we are regenerated and consequently initiated into the reception of goodness and truth flowing in from the Lord, see §§5342, 5898, 6156. Our remnant is also the means by which we communicate with heaven (7560). This is because the stored-up goodness and truth come from the Lord, not from us (7564). A *month* means a whole state from its beginning to its end (3814) and therefore the entire state of deliverance symbolized by the overall Passover celebration. This shows that *on the tenth of this month* symbolizes a state in which the inner levels are initiated.

This state, in which the inner levels are initiated, lasted from the tenth day of the month to its fourteenth day, during which time the Passover animal was held in safekeeping. The Passover animal symbolizes the inmost core of innocent goodness, so [the meaning is] that this core, together with the inner levels surrounding it, was shut away in the meantime and kept free of contaminants. This state is a state in which the inner levels are initiated, or are prepared for receiving an inflow of goodness and truth from the Lord.

The content of these words is sacred, because if there had not been something holy hidden inside them, the people would not have been required to take a Passover animal on the tenth of the month and keep it till the fourteenth day. They would not then have had to slaughter it between the evenings, eat it roasted with fire rather than cooked in water, leave none of it till morning, burn with fire what remained, break not a bone of it, and so on. Anyone who ponders the matter can see that these details involve holy qualities no one yet knows about, that these holy qualities are spiritual ones belonging to the church and heaven, and that they relate to the Divine, from whom everything in the Word descends.

They shall each take themselves a member of the flock means into innocence. This is clear from the symbolism of a lamb or goat (the *member of the flock* here), as innocence, a lamb symbolizing innocence in the inner self and a goat innocence in the outer self (§3519). 7832

For the household of their fathers, a member of the flock for a household means in keeping with the goodness unique to each. This can be seen from the symbolism of the *household of one's fathers,* which stands for the good quality of one clan as distinguished from that of another. This is because the household of one's father symbolizes a person's inner goodness (§3128). 7833

Here is the situation: All the tribes of Israel [taken together] symbolize the entire range of truth and goodness belonging to faith and neighborly love, and each tribe symbolizes one category of goodness or truth;

see §§3858, 3926, 3939, 4060, 6335, 6337, 6640. Each clan within its tribe therefore symbolized a unique kind of goodness, so the goodness in one particular clan was distinct from the goodness in another. And the household of one's fathers within a clan symbolized an individual variety of goodness within that kind.

The tribes, clans, and households into which the children of Israel were divided had this symbolism so as to represent heaven, where different kinds of goodness are distinguished into general categories, particular types, and individual varieties. The bonds angels form with each other mirror this system of classification.

Be advised that one person's good quality is never exactly the same as another's. No, such qualities are all different, so different that they are divided into higher-level, universal categories and then into lower-level subcategories, all the way down to individual varieties and subvarieties. On the point that there is this much variety among the different sorts of goodness arising from love and faith, see §§684, 690, 3241, 3267, 3744, 3745, 3746, 3986, 4005, 4149, 5598, 7236.

This now clarifies why the people were required to "each take themselves a member of the flock for the household of their fathers, a member of the flock for a household."

7834 *And if the household is too small for a flock animal* means if that individual variety of goodness is not enough for innocence. This can be seen from the symbolism of a *household* as an individual variety of goodness (discussed directly above at §7833), from that of *being too small* as not being enough, and from that of a *flock animal* as innocence (also mentioned just above, at §7832).

7835 *[The householder] and his fellow townsman closest to his house shall take [one]* means combining with the neighboring variety of goodness from truth. This can be seen from the symbolism of *taking* (taking one flock animal together with the closest fellow townsman) as combining, and from that of the *townsman closest to his house* as the neighboring variety of goodness from truth. One's closest fellow townsman is obviously one's direct neighbor; and a *house,* [or household,] symbolizes goodness (see above at §7833).

I describe it as goodness from truth because the subject here is people in the spiritual church, who possess truth-based goodness. Truth-based goodness is truth in our will and our actions. When we accept the truth composing faith along with a feeling of neighborly love, that seed of truth is planted in the inner depths of our mind. When it reproduces, the feeling to which it was connected also reproduces and appears in the form of goodness. That is why the goodness in a spiritual religion is goodness from truth, which is also called spiritual goodness.

According to the number of souls; [each] according to what his or her mouth will eat shall be counted for the flock animal means in this way making goodness sufficient for innocence by filling it with the amount of truth-from-goodness necessary for [innocence] to be adopted, as the following shows: The *number of souls* symbolizes the amount of truth-from-goodness necessary. (In the Word, a *number* has to do with truth, and a *soul* with spiritual goodness.) *[Each] according to what his or her mouth will eat* means for it to be adopted. (For the symbolism of eating as adopting, see §§3168, 3513, 3596, 3832.) And a *flock animal* symbolizes innocence, as mentioned above at §7832. Making goodness sufficient for innocence by filling it up is symbolized by taking in [souls] from the house of the closest fellow townsman in numbers large enough for a flock animal. For the meaning of a house as goodness, see above at §7833. **7836**

I use the term "truth-from-goodness," by which I mean truth that arises out of goodness. When people of the spiritual church are being reborn, faith and its truth introduce them into charity and its goodness. Once they have been introduced, though, the truth that is then born of their charitable goodness is called truth from goodness.

[2] Regarding the contents of this verse, no one can see how the matter stands without knowing how matters stand with the communities of heaven. These communities are what the grouping of the children of Israel by tribe, clan, and household represented.

Here is the situation with communities in heaven: Heaven as a whole is one community, which is governed as one individual by the Lord. There are as many general communities within that one community as there are limbs, viscera, and organs in an individual. There are as many specialized communities as there are substructures within the structure of each limb or organ. And there are as many particular communities as there are smaller parts making up the larger parts within those substructures. The fact that this is so is evident from the correspondence of the human body and its limbs, organs, and viscera with the universal human, or heaven, as has been described from personal experience at the end of many chapters.

This discussion shows just how heaven is divided up into communities.

[3] Here is the case with each community in particular: A community consists of many angels with compatible kinds of goodness. There are all different kinds of goodness, because the angels each have their

own unique type. But the Lord arranges the different types of compatible goodness in such a pattern that together they present the appearance of a single goodness.

These are the communities represented by the fathers' households among the children of Israel.

That is why the children of Israel were divided not only into tribes but also into clans and households. It is also why the names of an Israelite's ancestors going back to the original tribe are given when that person is named. For instance, in 1 Samuel 1:1 Samuel's father is said to have been from Mount Ephraim and to have had the name Elkanah son of Jeroham son of Elihu son of Tohu son of Zuph. In 1 Samuel 9:1 Saul's father is said to have been from Benjamin and to have had the name Kish son of Abiel son of Zeror son of Becorath son of Aphiah son of a Jeminite man. Many others are introduced in a similar way. A person's lineage was mentioned this way so that heaven could see what kind of goodness—derived in progressive stages from an initial kind—was represented by the person.

[4] Furthermore, the way things work in heaven is that if a community is not as complete as it needs to be, members are brought in from a neighboring community in numbers large enough to fill out the form of goodness there. This is done in keeping with the needs of each state and each change in that state (since the form of goodness varies as the state changes).

[5] Another thing to know is that innocence reigns supreme in the third or inmost heaven, which is directly above the heaven inhabited by the spiritual, who constitute the middle or second heaven. The Lord, who is innocence itself, flows directly into the third heaven. In the second heaven, where the spiritual live, he flows in with his innocence indirectly, through the third heaven. It is by means of this inflow that he arranges or organizes the communities of the second heaven according to their different kinds of goodness. So the inflow of innocence governs the way states of goodness change there and consequently the way the bonds among the communities vary.

This discussion shows how to understand the message of this verse's inner meaning: that if one's individual variety of goodness is not enough for innocence, one must combine it with the neighboring variety of goodness from truth, to make it sufficient for innocence by filling it with the amount of truth-from-goodness necessary for [innocence] to be adopted.

7837 *A sound animal* symbolizes spotless innocence. This can be seen from the symbolism of an *animal* of the flock as innocence (mentioned above at §7832) and from that of *sound* as meaning without blemish and therefore spotless. The reason it was spotless and without blemish is that in the spiritual world, every blemish symbolizes something false or evil.

A male means which comes of a faith grounded in neighborly love. 7838
This is clear from the symbolism of a *male* as the truth taught by faith (discussed at §§2046, 4005) and therefore as a faith grounded in neighborly love. The truth belonging to faith is not true and does not belong to faith unless it is accompanied by the goodness belonging to neighborly love, or better, unless it grows out of that goodness.

The reason the Passover animal was male was that it symbolized the innocence of people in the spiritual church. People in the spiritual church have no other kind of goodness than goodness that is essentially the truth taught by faith. This truth is called goodness when it is acted on in a spirit of neighborly love (§7835). That is why the animal was male.

In other sacrifices, female members of the flock were also used, if what was being represented was worship inspired by goodness.

The son of a year it shall be for you symbolizes a full state. This is 7839
established by the symbolism of a *son* as truth (discussed in §§489, 491, 533, 1147, 2623, 2803, 2813, 3373, 3704) and by the symbolism of a *year* as a whole period from beginning to end (discussed at §2906) and therefore as a full state.

I should say what a full state is. A state can be called full when goodness lacks nothing it needs for accepting the inflow of innocence. Religious truth united to charitable goodness is what fills goodness up in this way, because spiritual goodness takes its character from religious truth. This is what I mean by the full state that a son of a year symbolizes.

A state lacks fullness when truth has not yet given goodness a character that enables it to welcome a corresponding state of innocence. The state first becomes full when truth is regarded from the viewpoint of goodness, and it is not yet full when goodness is regarded from the viewpoint of truth. People who are regenerating are in this latter state; people who have already regenerated are in the former. Those who are regenerating possess truth that leads to goodness; those who have regenerated possess truth that grows out of goodness. In other words, those who are regenerating simply obey the truth; those who have regenerated actually want to put truth into practice. So the regenerating belong to the outer church, but the regenerated to the inner church.

It is because the son of a year symbolized a full state that a lamb or kid, the *son of a [single] year,* was so often required for sacrifices, as in

Exodus 29:38; Leviticus 9:3; 12:6; 14:10; 23:12, 18, 19; Numbers 6:12; 7:15 and following verses up through 87, 88; 15:27; 28:9, 11. And in Ezekiel's description of the new temple:

> *The ruler shall prepare a lamb, a sound son of its [first] year, as a burnt offering* daily to Jehovah; each morning he shall prepare it. (Ezekiel 46:13)

The new temple means the Lord's spiritual kingdom. The ruler stands for people dedicated to genuine truth and therefore to goodness. The burnt offering of a lamb means worshiping the Lord with innocent goodness. And the son of a year means a full state.

7840 *From among the lambs or from among the goats you shall take it* symbolizes inner and outer innocent goodness. This can be seen from the symbolism of a *lamb* as innocent goodness (dealt with at §3994) and from that of a *goat* or kid as truth-based goodness containing innocence (dealt with in §§3995, 4005, 4006, 4871). For the fact that a lamb symbolizes inner innocent goodness and a kid or goat outer innocent goodness, see §3519.

Let me briefly say what is meant by inner and outer innocent goodness. All goodness must contain innocence to be good. Without innocence, goodness has no soul. This is because innocence is the means by which the Lord flows in and by which he brings goodness alive in people who are being reborn.

Goodness animated by innocence can be inner or outer. Inner goodness exists with people who are said to belong to the inner part of the church, outer goodness with those who belong to the outer part. People who have used inner truth (the kind of truth found in the Word's inner meaning) to give their goodness its character belong to the inner part of the church. People who have used outer truth (the kind found in the Word's literal meaning) to give their goodness its character belong to the outer part of the church. People belonging to the inner part of the church are those who do good to their neighbor because they are moved by love for their neighbor, but people belonging to the outer part are those who do so out of obedience.

When being reborn, everyone starts by becoming part of the outer church but later becomes part of the inner church. People in the inner part of the church have more understanding and wisdom than people in the outer part, so they also live farther within heaven.

These remarks illustrate what inner and outer innocent goodness are.

And it will be in safekeeping for you symbolizes a time and state of initiation. This can be seen from the symbolism of the tenth day—the start of the period lasting till the fourteenth day during which the animal was to *be in safekeeping*—as a state in which the inner levels are initiated (discussed at §7831). 7841

Till the fourteenth [day] of [this] month means reaching a holy state. This can be seen from the symbolism of the *fourteenth day* as a holy state. For the symbolism of a day as a state, see above at §7831. As for the number fourteen, it has the same symbolism as seven (for the symbolism of seven as something holy, see §§395, 433, 716, 881, 5265, 5268), because the multiples of numbers have the same symbolism as their factors (§§5291, 5335, 5708). That is why Passover was to start on the fourteenth day of the month, last seven days, and end on the twenty-first day—a day that also symbolized something holy, because twenty-one is the product of three times seven. This was why there was to be a *holy convocation* on the first day of Passover and a *holy convocation* on the twenty-first day [of the month] (verse 16). 7842

And the whole assembly of the congregation of Israel shall slaughter it symbolizes preparation for enjoyment by everyone in the spiritual church collectively, as the following shows: *Slaughtering* (when it applies to the lamb or goat used in performance of the Passover) symbolizes preparation for enjoyment (enjoyment of the innocent goodness symbolized by the lamb or goat). And the *whole assembly of the congregation of Israel* means by everyone in the spiritual church collectively, as dealt with above at §7830. The assembly of the congregation symbolizes truth-from-goodness possessed by the people of that church, since an *assembly* has to do with truth (§6355) and a *congregation* with goodness. 7843

Between the evenings symbolizes the last state and the first. This is clear from the symbolism of *evening* as a state of falsity and also a state in which truth is unknown, because the shadows of evening stand for falsity and also for ignorance of the truth. On a spiritual level, all times of day, like all times of the year, symbolize cyclical changes of state in respect to truth and goodness (§§5672, 5962, 6110). The end and the beginning of those changes is evening, so when the text says "between the evenings," it is including all states. Here the phrase symbolizes a state of deliverance for people committed to the truth that comes of goodness, and a state of damnation for people committed to the falsity that comes of evil. These are the states symbolized by the departure of the children of Israel from 7844

Egypt when the firstborn of that land were being killed. The following words in Moses show that this moment is called evening:

> You shall sacrifice the Passover *in the evening, when the sun sets, at the set time of your departure from Egypt.* (Deuteronomy 16:4, 6)

[2] This discussion makes clear what *between the evenings* means. For the people represented by the children of Israel it means the end of a state of persecution and the beginning of a state of deliverance. From this beginning their state moves toward morning, that is, toward being lifted into heaven. For the people represented by the Egyptians it means the end of a state of persecuting and the beginning of a state of damnation. Their state moves toward night, that is, toward being sent down to hell. The lowering of the latter into hell is represented by the drowning [of the Egyptians] in the Suph Sea. The raising of the former into heaven is represented by the entry [of the children of Israel] into the land of Canaan.

[3] In various passages where the Word speaks of evening it symbolizes the last days and the first days of the church. It symbolizes the last days for people among whom the church ceases to exist, and the first days for people among whom it is just commencing. So above all, evening symbolizes the Lord's Coming, because that is when the previous religion ended and a new one began. The first state of a new religion too is called evening because the people in it start off in dim light and advance from there to bright light, which is their morning.

[4] The symbolism of evening and morning as the Lord's coming into the world can be seen in Daniel:

> I heard a holy one speaking: "How long will the vision, the perpetual offering, and the transgression, the trampling of the Holy Place and the army, continue?" And he said to me, "*Up till evening [and] morning,* two thousand three hundred times, for then the Holy Place will be set right." (Daniel 8:13, 14)

Plainly the evening here means the last days, when the church was utterly laid waste and the Lord came into the world, while the morning means light and the dawn of a new religion from him. [5] Likewise in Zechariah:

> There will be a single day, which will be known to Jehovah, not day or night, *because around the time of evening there will be light.* (Zechariah 14:7)

In Zephaniah:

> In the end let the region be for the survivors of the house of Judah; on those places they will graze. In the houses of Ashkelon, *in the evening they will have rest, when* Jehovah their God *visits them* and brings them back from captivity. (Zephaniah 2:7)

The evening stands for the first state of the dawning church.

Because evening symbolized the last state of the old religion and the first state of a new one, Aaron and his sons were commanded to make [the fire of] the lamp go up before Jehovah from *evening till morning* (Exodus 27:20, 21).

[6] The meaning of evening as the last state of a religion, when falsity crowds thickly because there is no faith, and evil crowds thickly because there is no neighborly love, is clear in Jeremiah:

> Doom to you! For day departs, *for the shadows of evening have fallen.* (Jeremiah 6:4)

In Ezekiel:

> I spoke to the people in the morning, and *my wife died at evening.* (Ezekiel 24:18)

His wife stands for the church. In David:

> Toward dawn [the grass] will blossom and pass away; *toward evening you will cut it back, it will wither.* (Psalms 90:6)

Exodus 12:7, 8, 9, 10, 11. *"And they shall take some of the blood and put it on the two doorposts and on the lintel on their houses in which they are going to eat it. And they shall eat the flesh on that night, roasted with fire; and [with] unleavened loaves on bitter herbs they shall eat it. You are not to eat any of it raw or by any means cooked in water but rather roasted with fire, its head atop its legs and atop its middle. And you shall not leave any of it till morning. And what remains of it till morning you shall burn with fire. And this is how you shall eat it: your hips girded, your shoes on your feet, and your staff in your hand; and you shall eat it in a hurry. It is a Passover [offering] to Jehovah."* **7845**

And they shall take some of the blood symbolizes sacred truth arising from innocent goodness. *And put it on the two doorposts and on the lintel* symbolizes truth and goodness on the earthly plane. *On their houses* means which characterize a will to do good. *In which they are going to eat it* symbolizes enjoyment. *And they shall eat the flesh* symbolizes enjoyment of what is good. *On that night* means when the evil are damned. *Roasted with fire* symbolizes a loving goodness. *And [with] unleavened loaves* means purified of all falsity. *On bitter herbs* means by times of trial, in all their unpleasantness. *They shall eat it* symbolizes enjoyment. *You are not to eat any of it raw* means not without love. *Or by any means cooked in water* means that it must not evolve out of truth. *But rather roasted with fire* means from love. *Its head atop its legs and atop its middle* means from the inmost core out. *And you shall not leave any of it till morning* symbolizes the length of time this state lasts till a state of enlightenment in heaven arrives. *And what remains of it till morning you shall burn with fire* symbolizes a state midway to a goal through times of trial. *And this is how you shall eat it* symbolizes enjoying it while separated from the evil spirits who inflicted persecution, and being saved at that time. *Your hips girded* means in regard to inner levels. *Your shoes on your feet* means in regard to outer levels. *And your staff in your hand* means in regard to everything in between. *And you shall eat it in a hurry* symbolizes eagerness to separate. *It is a Passover [offering] to Jehovah* symbolizes the Lord's presence, and deliverance by him.

7846 *And they shall take some of the blood* symbolizes sacred truth arising from innocent goodness. This is established by the symbolism of *blood* as sacred truth radiating from the Lord (discussed in §§4735, 6978, 7317, 7326). This blood was from a lamb, and a lamb symbolizes innocent goodness (§3994), so the blood stands for sacred truth arising from innocent goodness.

7847 *And put it on the two doorposts and on the lintel* symbolizes truth and goodness on the earthly plane. This can be seen from the symbolism of *doorposts* as truth on the earthly plane and of a *lintel* as goodness on that plane.

Doorposts and a lintel have this symbolism because a house symbolizes the human being as a whole, or the human mind. The parts of a door symbolize qualities that serve as an entryway, and these qualities are obviously earthly-level truth and goodness. After all, our earthly self has to be taught before our rational self can be, and what we learn at that preliminary stage is earthly lessons that gradually have deeper, spiritual lessons instilled into them. From this you can see how truth and goodness on the earthly plane serve as an entryway.

What is more, a lintel and doorposts have the same symbolism as a brow piece, [or phylactery,] and hands on a human being. Angels' thoughts routinely draw a connection between earthly phenomena and parts of the human body. The reason is that the spiritual world, or heaven, is in the form of a human being. So everything in that world—everything spiritual, which means truth and goodness—relates to the human form (as shown at the end of many chapters, where correspondence was discussed). Since earthly concepts turn into spiritual ones in an angel's thoughts, so does the concept of a house, which to them is the human mind. The rooms and chambers are the inner reaches of the mind, and the windows, doors, doorposts, and lintels are outer parts of the mind, which allow entry. Because this is the nature of angelic thoughts, they are alive. So when the dead objects of the physical world cross into the spiritual world, they come to life. Everything that is spiritual is alive, because it comes from the Lord.

[2] These words in Moses show that doorposts and a lintel have the same symbolism—when it comes to the human form—as a brow piece and hands:

> You shall love Jehovah your God with all your heart and with all your soul and with all your powers. You are to bind these [words] *onto your hand* as a sign; and let them be *as brow pieces* between your eyes. And you are to write *them on the doorposts of your house* and on *your gates.* (Deuteronomy 6:5, 8, 9; 11:13, 18, 20)

Because they hold the same meaning, both [pairs] are mentioned.

[3] The fact that a lintel and doorposts in a spiritual sense are earthly-level goodness and truth that provide an entry to spiritual attributes is clear in Ezekiel's description of the new temple, which symbolizes a spiritual religion. The description makes frequent mention of doorposts and lintels and of their measurements. Such details would never have been noted if they did not symbolize some aspect of the church and of heaven—in other words, something spiritual. Take for instance the following words in that prophet:

> The priest shall take some of the blood of the sin offering *and put it on the doorpost of the House* and on the four corners of the ledge of the altar *and on the doorpost of the gate of the inner court* on the first day of the month. (Ezekiel 45:19)

In the same prophet:

> The ruler shall enter by way of the porch outside and stand at the *doorpost of the gate,* and the priests shall sacrifice his burnt offering; then he shall worship *on the threshold of the gate.* (Ezekiel 46:2)

Anyone can see that the temple, [or "House,"] here does not mean a temple but the Lord's church. After all, many chapters in that book describe events that never happened and never will. [4] In the highest sense, the temple means the Lord in his divine humanity, as he himself teaches in John 2:19, 21, 22; so in a representative sense it means his church. An angel measured the *lintels* of the new temple (see Ezekiel 40:9, 10, 14, 16, 21, 24), and this measuring would not be worth mentioning if lintels and numbers did not symbolize some aspect of religion.

Since doorposts and a lintel symbolized truth and goodness on the earthly plane that serve as an entryway, they were made square in cross-section in this new temple (Ezekiel 41:21). For the same reason the *doorposts* in Solomon's temple were made of olive wood (1 Kings 6:31, 33). Olive wood was used to symbolize goodness stemming from truth, or the goodness that marks a spiritual religion.

7848 *On their houses* means which characterize a will to do good. This can be seen from the symbolism of a *house* as a person (dealt with at §3128) and as the human mind (§§3538, 4973, 5023, 7353) and therefore as characteristics of the will. Here it symbolizes the characteristics of a will to do good.

The reason a house also symbolizes the will is that it symbolizes a human being, and the main thing that makes us human is our will.

Besides, it is all the same whether you speak of a human being or the human mind. It is not our physical makeup but our mind that makes us human. Our quality as a person is the same as the quality of our mind—in other words, of our intellect and will, especially our will.

7849 *In which they are going to eat it* symbolizes enjoyment. This is evident from the symbolism of *eating* as adopting something (discussed in §§3168, 3513 at the end, 4745) but in this case as coming into the enjoyment of it, since the subject under discussion is a state of initiation.

Let me explain: When the spirits who were held in safekeeping in the underground realm until the Lord's Coming (§§6854, 6914, 7091 at the end, 7828) were being delivered, they had to undergo preparation for receiving an inflow of goodness and truth from the Lord. They were passing through the middle of hell, and during that crossing they would be threatened by an inflow of evil and falsity from hellish beings on all sides. That is why they had to undergo preparation, so that the state of truth and goodness in them would then be full. With the Lord's divine mercy, I will say more later about this crossing [§§8039, 8099, 8185, 8321, 8322].

The preparation for or initiation into a state in which they could accept what was good and true is depicted by the steps they were to take between the tenth and fourteenth days of the month and by the practices they were to observe in eating the Passover lamb.

And they shall eat the flesh symbolizes enjoyment of what is good, as the following shows: *Eating* symbolizes enjoyment, as noted directly above at §7849. And *flesh* symbolizes human autonomy brought to life by the Lord's divine humanity, so it symbolizes all heavenly and spiritual goodness in us, as discussed in §§3813, 6968. **7850**

This symbolism of flesh was very well known to the ancients, but today it is so little known that the reader must inevitably wonder at my claiming such a symbolism for flesh. If you describe it as a spiritual concept that corresponds, no one understands. If you describe it as symbolism, people do understand, but not in the sense of correspondential symbolism. They take the symbol and its meaning as utterly separate, when in reality a corresponding spiritual concept or corresponding symbolic meaning is bound up with the object to which it corresponds. It is like the bond between our eyesight and our eye, or between our hearing and our ear. It is like the bond connecting our thoughts (which are spiritual) with the form of our interiors and through this with the organs of speech. Or it is like the bond connecting our will (which is also spiritual) with the muscle fibers we use when we act. That is the relationship that every corresponding spiritual attribute or symbolic meaning has with the earthly counterpart to which it corresponds.

[2] Surely no one can fail to see that by flesh the Lord does not mean flesh, and by blood he does not mean blood, in John:

> Truly, truly, I say to you: unless you *eat the flesh of the Son of Humankind* and *drink his blood* you will not have life in you. Whoever *eats my flesh* and *drinks my blood* has eternal life, and I will revive that person on the last day, because *my flesh* is truly food, and *my blood* is truly drink. (John 6:53, 54, 55, 56)

Flesh means the divine goodness of the Lord's divine love, which comes from his divine humanity, and blood means the divine truth radiating from his divine goodness. A response on our part to his goodness and truth is also meant. Few today know any of this, and the ones who are capable of knowing it do not want to. The reason they do not want to know it is that they do not desire truth for its own sake but for other, worldly purposes.

Another reason is that people oriented toward the earthly realm want to see everything in earthly terms.

[3] These remarks are intended to show what is symbolized by the eating of flesh in the Passover meal and consequently in the holy supper established at that time. On the bread and wine of the [Christian] Holy Supper, which have the same symbolism as flesh and blood, see §§2165, 2177, 2187, 3464, 3478, 3735, 3813, 4211, 4217, 4735, 4976, 5915.

Leaving aside other passages, the following in John makes it quite plain that flesh is not flesh in the Word's spiritual meaning:

> Come and gather to the supper of the great God, so that you can *eat the flesh* of commanders, and the *flesh* of the mighty, and the *flesh* of horses and of the people sitting on them, and the *flesh* of all, free people and slaves, both small and great. (Revelation 19:17, 18)

The flesh symbolizes goodness of different kinds.

7851 *On that night* means when the evil are damned. This can be seen from the symbolism of *night* as a state in which truth and goodness are stripped away (discussed in §§221, 709, 2353, 7776) and therefore as damnation. When there is no longer any truth or goodness, only falsity and evil, damnation has arrived. The damned here are spirits who persecuted members of the spiritual church.

7852 *Roasted with fire* symbolizes a loving goodness. This can be seen from the symbolism of *roasted with fire* as a loving goodness because *fire* symbolizes love (§§934, 4906, 5215, 6314, 6832, 6834, 6849, 7324) and *roasted* symbolizes that which is permeated with love, so it symbolizes goodness.

The Word distinguishes roasted food from boiled food—roasted food symbolizing goodness because roasting uses fire, and boiled food meaning truth because boiling uses water. It distinguishes them here, since it says, "You are not to eat any of it raw or *by any means cooked in water* but rather *roasted with fire*" (verse 9). The reason for this requirement is that the Passover lamb symbolizes innocent goodness, which is goodness that embodies love for the Lord.

[2] These comments show what is meant in a spiritual sense by the *roasted fish* in Luke 24:42, 43, and by the fish sitting on the fire when the Lord appeared to the disciples, as described in John:

> After the disciples got out onto the land, they see a *fire laid* and a *small fish lying on it,* and bread. Jesus comes and takes the bread and gives it to them, and the *small fish* likewise. (John 21:9, 13)

A fish symbolizes earthly-level truth (§991), and a fire symbolizes goodness, so the small fish lying on it symbolizes truth associated with spiritual goodness, as it exists on the earthly plane. People who disbelieve in an inner meaning to the Word of course deny there is any secret hidden in the fact that there was fish on a fire when the Lord appeared to his disciples and that he gave it to them to eat.

[3] Since "roasted with fire" symbolizes the goodness that goes with heavenly and spiritual love, in a negative sense it symbolizes the evil that goes with self-love and love of worldly advantages. In Isaiah:

> Part of [the tree] they *burned with fire,* on part of it they ate meat, they *roasted a roast* to fill up on, they also *warmed themselves.* And they said, "Friend, I have *warmed myself, I have seen fire.* Part of it I *burned with fire,* I also cooked bread *on* its *embers,* I *roasted meat* and am eating it." (Isaiah 44:16, 19)

This is about worshipers of an idol. The idol symbolizes falsity from evil, which is what the passage is depicting. Roasting a roast and roasting meat means doing evil deeds at the prompting of an unclean love. For the negative meaning of fire as the evil that goes with self-love and love of worldly advantages, or with the cravings stirred by those two kinds of love, see §§1297, 1861, 2446, 5071, 5215, 6314, 6832, 7324, 7575.

And [with] unleavened loaves means purified of all falsity. This can be **7853**
seen from the symbolism of *unleavened* or flat bread as something purified of falsity, which is discussed in §2342. The reason unleavened loaves have this symbolism is that yeast symbolizes falsity, as discussed below [§7906].

On bitter herbs means by times of trial, in all their unpleasantness. This **7854**
is evident from the symbolism of *bitter things* or bitterness as something unpleasant, and here, as the unpleasantness of trials. No one can adopt the innocent goodness the Passover lamb represents except by undergoing trials. Unleavened bread symbolizes this kind of goodness, and since it is through being tested that we make it our own, the people were required to eat it on bitter herbs. In addition, this bread was "the bread of affliction" for them, just as the manna was (Deuteronomy 8:15, 16; 16:3), because it had no yeast, that is, no falsity-from-evil. Pure truth and pure goodness are unbearable to us.

[2] The symbolism of bitterness as something unpleasant is plain in Isaiah:

> Doom to those who call evil good and goodness evil; *who put bitter for sweet and sweet for bitter.* (Isaiah 5:20)

And in the same author:

> They will not drink wine with a song; *the strong drink will be bitter for those drinking it.* (Isaiah 24:9)

The symbolism of bitterness as times of trial, in all their unpleasantness, is plain from the following. In Exodus:

> Finally they came *to Marah* but could not drink the water *for bitterness,* because *it was bitter.* So the people murmured against Moses, and when he cried out to Jehovah, Jehovah showed him a piece of wood that he threw into the water, and *the water became sweet.* There he set them a statute and judgment, *because there he tested them.* (Exodus 15:23, 24, 25)

And in John:

> There fell out of the sky a large star burning like a lamp; the name of the star is called *Wormwood,* and many people died of the water, because *it was embittered.* (Revelation 8:10, 11)

The bitter water stands for the unpleasantness involved in times of trial. The people who died of the water stand for those who succumbed in their trials.

7855 *They shall eat it* symbolizes enjoyment, as is evident from the remarks above at §7849.

7856 *You are not to eat any of it raw* means not without love. This can be seen from the symbolism of *eating* as enjoyment (as above at §7849) and from that of *raw* as devoid of a loving goodness. This symbolism of "raw" is clear from the symbolism of "roasted with fire," which means a loving goodness, as discussed above at §7852. "Raw" means that something has not been roasted with fire, so it means something devoid of love.

7857 *Or by any means cooked in water* means that it must not evolve out of religious truth. This is clear from the symbolism of *water* as religious truth, which is discussed in §§2702, 3058, 3424, 4976, 5668. What has been *cooked in water* consequently means what results—that is, goodness that grows out of religious truth. This kind of goodness is distinguished from the kind that grows out of love, as symbolized by "roasted with fire" (§7852).

Spiritual goodness always comes either from faith (which is to say *through* faith) or from love. While we are being reborn, the goodness in us comes from religious truth; during that time we live by the truth not out of any desire for truth but out of obedience, because so it has been commanded. Later, though, once we have been reborn, we do good because we want to and therefore out of love.

The Word draws a strict distinction between these two states in a person because we cannot be in both at once. If we are in the first state, we cannot enter the second until we have been reborn. If we are in the second state, we must not resort to the first. People who do that lose any inclination to do good out of love and relapse into the state of faith that served to start them on the path to goodness. In fact, they relapse beyond that point.

That is the inner-level meaning of the Lord's words in Matthew about the Last Judgment:

> Then those on top of the house should not go down to take anything from their house. And those in the field should not turn back behind to take their clothes. (Matthew 24:17, 18)

It is also meant by the story in which Lot's wife looked back behind her (Luke 17:31, 32).

From this you can see what it means to enjoy goodness that comes from love but not goodness that comes from faith's truth, as symbolized by the instruction that people eat the flesh roasted with fire, not cooked in water.

[2] Sacrifices and burnt offerings symbolized worshiping the Lord in faith and love—sacrifices, in faith, and burnt offerings, in love. And eating the consecrated foods together symbolized giving glory to the Lord and rejoicing at the chance to enjoy good things from him. It was therefore acceptable to boil flesh on those occasions. After all, a desire for religious truth is what inspires people to give the Lord glory and to rejoice in the opportunity to enjoy what is good. In fact, all acclamation of the Lord rises out of such a desire. (To see that the flesh of a sacrifice was boiled, read Exodus 29:31, 32; 1 Samuel 2:13, 15; 1 Kings 19:21.)

The same thing is symbolized by the boiling mentioned in Zechariah:

> On that day, *every pot* in Jerusalem [and] in Judah will be holiness to Jehovah Sabaoth, and *everyone sacrificing* will come and *take of [the pots] and boil [meat] in them.* (Zechariah 14:21)

But rather roasted with fire means from love. This is established by the symbolism of *roasted with fire* as goodness marked by love, which is discussed above at §7852. **7858**

7859 *Its head atop its legs and atop its middle* means from the inmost core out, as the following shows: When the *head* is said to be atop the legs and the middle, it symbolizes the inmost core, because the head is highest, and the highest part means the inmost part, in a spiritual sense (§§2148, 3084, 4599, 5146; for the symbolism of the head as inner levels and of the body as outer levels, see §6436). The *legs* symbolize outer levels, because the legs are lower in relation to the head, and just as higher parts symbolize inner levels, lower parts symbolize outer levels. And the *middle* symbolizes levels that are still lower, such as the plane of the stomach and intestines.

[2] The command to roast the head atop the legs and atop the middle represented the idea that the inner and outer planes must unite, or act as one. The inner planes belong to the inner self, the outer planes to the outer self; that is, the inner planes belong to the spiritual self but the outer planes to the earthly self. They must unite, or act as one, if a person is to be a kingdom of the Lord. They separate when the earthly, outer self acts differently than the spiritual, inner self wants it to.

[3] This discussion shows what was symbolized by the requirement that the Passover lamb be roasted with fire, the head atop the legs and middle. (The middle means the earthly plane in an even more external aspect, which is that of the senses.)

These commands hold a divine secret, as anyone can see, since the Passover lamb was one of the holiest objects in that religion. The only way to see this holy secret is to understand the concepts and words in a spiritual way, which is the way described here.

7860 *And you shall not leave any of it till morning* symbolizes the length of time this state lasts till a state of enlightenment in heaven arrives. This can be seen from the symbolism of *morning* as heaven and a state of enlightenment there, as discussed in §§2405, 3458, 3723, 5740, 5962. *Leaving none of it till then* stands for the length of time the state lasts, of course, because that is when the earlier state will end.

As shown already [§§7822–7823, 7828, 7844], the inner meaning is about the deliverance from persecution of people in the spiritual church. The state during which they were delivered is represented by Passover, but the state in which they were lifted to heaven is represented by entry into the land of Canaan. The latter state is what the morning means. The two states are entirely different, just as a state midway to a goal is entirely different from the state of having reached the goal. The events that happen during a state midway to a goal will be over and done with when the goal state arrives.

This makes plain the reason for commanding that the people leave none of it till morning.

And what remains of it till morning you shall burn with fire symbolizes a state midway to a goal through times of trial, as the following shows: *What remains till morning* symbolizes a state midway to the goal state of being lifted into heaven. After all, *morning* symbolizes elevation into heaven and enlightenment there (see directly above at §7860), so the period just before morning symbolizes a state midway to it. Enjoying the remainder by eating it was allowable in that state, but not afterward. And *burning something with fire* means undergoing times of trial. The reason it has this symbolism is that fire is what purifies things. A further reason is that people who are being tried are subjected to their cravings, and cravings burn. **7861**

And this is how you shall eat it symbolizes enjoying it while separated from the evil spirits who inflicted persecution, and being saved at that time. This can be seen from the symbolism of *eating* as enjoyment, which is mentioned above at §7849. Since the theme here is the departure from Egypt, which symbolizes separation from the spirits who inflicted persecution, that is the stage meant by *this is how you shall eat it.* That it means being saved as well is clear. **7862**

Your hips girded means in regard to inner levels. This can be seen from the symbolism of the *hip* area as aspects of marriage love (§§3021, 4277, 4280, 5050–5062) and therefore as that which relates to love for goodness and truth. Marriage love, you see, develops out of a love for what is good and true (§§686, 2618, 2727–2759, 4434, 5053). For this reason, and because the hips are above the feet, which stand for outer levels (as discussed just below), the hips symbolize inner levels. **7863**

The requirement that people's hips be *girded* symbolizes a readiness to accept an inflow of goodness and truth from the Lord and to act according to that inflow. Any instance of putting on clothes and fastening them symbolizes a state in which one prepares to receive and act, because everything is then held in good order. Not so when the clothes are not fastened.

Your shoes on your feet means in regard to outer levels. This is clear from the symbolism of *shoes* as the outer or last levels of the earthly plane, which provide a general covering for its inner levels, and from the symbolism of the *feet* as the earthly plane (discussed in §§2162, 3147, 3761, 3986, 4280, 4938–4952). **7864**

7865 *And your staff in your hand* means in regard to everything in between. This is clear from the symbolism of a *staff in hand.* When the subject is travels or journeys, and the text mentions hips, and shoes on the feet, meaning inner and outer levels, a staff in hand symbolizes everything in between.

7866 *And you shall eat it in a hurry* symbolizes eagerness to separate. This can be seen from the symbolism of a *hurry* as eagerness, because haste results from an emotion, as noted at §7695. Here the emotion is eagerness to separate, because the separation was from the persecutors symbolized by the Egyptians.

7867 *It is a Passover [offering] to Jehovah* symbolizes the Lord's presence, and deliverance by him. This is evident from the discussion so far, especially remarks about the way people in the spiritual church were delivered by the Lord's Coming (§§6854, 6914, 7035, 7091 at the end, 7828; for Jehovah in the Word being the Lord, see §§1343, 1736, 2921, 3023, 3035, 5041, 5663, 6281, 6303, 6905).

7868 Exodus 12:12, 13, 14, 15, 16. *"And I will pass through the land of Egypt on this night and strike every firstborn in the land of Egypt from human to animal. And on all the gods of Egypt I will pass judgment; I am Jehovah! And the blood will serve you as a sign on the houses, [to show] where you are, and should I see the blood, I will pass by you, and the plague will not come as a destroyer on you, in my striking the land of Egypt. And that day shall serve you as a reminder, and you shall celebrate it as a feast to Jehovah throughout your generations; by an eternal statute you shall celebrate it. Seven days you shall eat unleavened loaves. Yes, on the first day you shall make yeast cease from your houses, because anyone eating yeast bread, that soul shall be cut off from Israel. [This shall last] from the first day up to the seventh day. And on the first day you shall have a holy convocation, and on the seventh day a holy convocation. No work shall be done on those days, only [the provision of] something to eat for every soul; this alone shall be done by you."*

And I will pass through the land of Egypt symbolizes his presence among the persecutors. *On this night* symbolizes a state of evil for them. *And strike every firstborn in the land of Egypt* symbolizes the damnation of people who subscribe to a faith detached from neighborly love. *From human to animal* symbolizes their inner and outer evil cravings. *And on all the gods of Egypt I will pass judgment* symbolizes their damnable falsities. *I am Jehovah* means that the Lord alone is God. *And the blood* symbolizes truth that comes from innocent goodness. *Will serve you as a sign on the houses, [to show where you are]* means that it testifies to a will to do good. *And should I see the blood* symbolizes awareness of that truth on the part of those who bring damnation. *I will pass by you* means that it will flee away. *And the plague will not come as a destroyer on you* means that damnation from the hells will not affect them. *In my striking the land of Egypt* means when people who subscribe to a faith detached from neighborly love are damned. *And that day shall serve you as a reminder* symbolizes the quality of that state during worship. *You shall celebrate it as a feast to Jehovah* symbolizes worship of the Lord because of being delivered from damnation. *Throughout your generations* means with all that faith and neighborly love imply. *By an eternal statute you shall celebrate it* symbolizes worship of the Lord that reflects the way heaven is arranged, worship intended for people in the spiritual church. *Seven days* symbolizes what is holy. *You shall eat unleavened loaves* symbolizes purification from falsity. *Yes, on the first day you shall make yeast cease from your houses* means that their goodness must be completely free of falsity. *Because anyone eating yeast bread* symbolizes people who adopt falsity. *That soul shall be cut off from Israel* means that they will be separated from members of the spiritual church and will be damned. *[This shall last] from the first day up to the seventh day* symbolizes a complete and holy state. *And on the first day you shall have a holy convocation* means that at the beginning they will all be together. *On the seventh day a holy convocation* means at the end of the state too. *No work shall be done on those days* means being held back from earthly and worldly concerns during that state. *Only [the provision of] something to eat for every soul* means when spiritual and heavenly goodness are being adopted. *This alone shall be done [by you]* means that this is all they will then concentrate on.

And I will pass through the land of Egypt symbolizes his presence among 7869
the persecutors. This can be seen from the symbolism of *passing*—when Jehovah is the one who passes, and when he passes *through the land*—as presence, and from that of the Egyptians as spirits who harassed the people of the spiritual church (discussed in §§6692, 7097). In this case it is the *land of Egypt* that stands for the persecutors.

On this night symbolizes a state of evil for them. This can be seen 7870
from the symbolism of *night* as a state in which there is nothing but evil and falsity. After all, night is the opposite of day, and darkness, of light; and day and light symbolize a state in which there is truth and goodness. As a consequence night also symbolizes the church's last days, because at that stage there is no faith or neighborly love, so falsity and evil take over; see §§2353, 6000. Night symbolizes total devastation as well (§7776) and damnation too (§7851).

These remarks show that the state of people in hell is called night. Not that they live in nocturnal darkness, because after all they are able to see each other. Rather, since the state of truth and goodness found in the heavens is called day, a state of falsity and evil is called night. Besides, it really is dark there when any light shines in from heaven. At those times, the meager light by which the hells see disappears and darkness falls.

[2] Surprisingly, the glimmer they see by derives from light that comes from the Lord through heaven. There is no other source for any of the light in the next world. However, the inhabitants of hell receive this light within their faculty for understanding truth. They retain an ability to understand truth (as we all do) no matter how deeply they immerse themselves in evil or falsity. But this heavenly light passes from that faculty into their will (that is, into an unwillingness to understand) and from there into the evil and falsity they possess. When that happens, it turns into the kind of dull glow given off by a coal fire, and as I said, when the light of heaven flows in, it turns that glow into thick darkness. (For the idea that the hells have a dim light like that given off by a coal fire, see §§1528, 3340, 4418, 4531. For the idea that it turns into darkness at the presence of heaven's light, see §§1783, 3412, 4533, 5057, 5058, 6000.)

This discussion shows that everyone in the other world enjoys a light that matches her or his faculty of understanding, as supplied either with truth-from-goodness or with falsity-from-evil.

7871 *And strike every firstborn in the land of Egypt* symbolizes the damnation of people who subscribe to a faith detached from neighborly love, as the following shows: *Striking* symbolizes damnation, because it means killing, or putting to death, and death in a spiritual sense means damnation; see §6119. The *firstborn,* when ascribed to the Egyptians (who represent people committed to falsity that rises out of evil), symbolize faith detached from neighborly love (§§3325, 7039, 7766, 7778, 7779). In a positive sense, when the term is used of the spiritual church, a firstborn means faith that comes of neighborly love; see §§352, 2435, 3325, 3494, 6344, 7035. In a negative sense, then, it means faith devoid of neighborly love.

7872 *From human to animal* symbolizes their inner and outer evil cravings. This can be seen from the symbolism of *from human to animal* as a desire for inner and outer goodness, as discussed in §§7424, 7523. A *human* symbolizes a desire for inner goodness, and an *animal,* a desire for outer goodness, so in a negative sense (as in this verse, which speaks of the firstborn of the Egyptians) it symbolizes evil desires, or inner and outer cravings. For the meaning of animals as positive desires, and in the opposite sense as negative desires, or cravings, see §§45, 46, 142, 143, 246, 714, 715, 719, 776, 1823, 2179, 2180, 2781, 3218, 3519, 5198.

And on all the gods of Egypt I will pass judgment symbolizes their dam- 7873
nable falsities. This can be seen from the symbolism of *gods* as falsities (discussed below) and from that of *passing judgment* as being damned. Judging (passing judgment) results in a verdict of either life or death. A verdict of life is salvation, a verdict of death, damnation.

Gods are mentioned many times in the Word. When angels are called gods, truth is being symbolized; see §§4295, 4402, 7268. In a negative sense, then, the gods of the non-Jewish nations symbolize falsity (§§4402, 4544).

The reason truths are called gods is that truth issues from divinity itself and is inherently divine. People who accept it are therefore called gods. Not that they are gods but that the truth in them is divine. That is why God is called *Elohim* in the plural in the original language.

Divinity itself is divine goodness, but what issues from it is divine truth, which fills the whole of heaven.

Since God means truth, then, in a negative sense it means falsity.

I am Jehovah means that the Lord alone is God, as can be seen from 7874
explanations above in §§7401, 7444, 7544, 7598, 7636.

And the blood symbolizes truth that comes from innocent goodness. 7875
This is established by the discussion in §7846 of the symbolism of the *blood* of a lamb as truth that comes from innocent goodness.

Will serve you as a sign on the houses, [to show] where you are means 7876
that it testifies to a will to do good. This can be seen from the symbolism of *serving as a sign,* which means testifying, and from that of *houses* as characteristics of a will to do good (mentioned above at §7848).

And should I see the blood symbolizes awareness of that truth on the 7877
part of those who bring damnation, as the following shows: *Seeing* means understanding and perceiving, as discussed in §§2150, 2325, 2807, 3764, 4403–4421, 4567, 4723, 5400. The idea that the awareness is on the part of those who bring damnation is discussed below. And *blood* symbolizes truth that comes of innocent goodness, as above at §7846.

[2] I need to define the truth that comes of innocent goodness. Innocent goodness is goodness that embodies love for the Lord, because people who love the Lord are innocent. That is why inhabitants of the third or inmost heaven are more innocent than the others, because they love the Lord. Their innocence makes them look like little children to others.

Yet they are the wisest of all in heaven (see §2306), because innocence dwells in wisdom (§§2305, 3494, 4797).

The truth-from-innocent-goodness they have is not truth as taught by faith but is a goodness inspired by neighborly love. The inhabitants of the third heaven do not know what faith is, so they also do not know what the truth associated with it is. They have a perception of religious truth that tells them instantly that something is so. They never reason over its validity, much less argue about it. Nothing that is perceived in this fashion is susceptible to being known intellectually. The case is very different with the spiritual inhabitants of the second heaven. They are led by faith with its truth to neighborly love and its goodness, so they use reason to figure out whether an idea is true or not, since they lack a perception of it. Truths are consequently a matter of knowledge for them and are called religious teachings.

[3] For the idea that inhabitants of the third or inmost heaven live in a state in which they perceive religious truth and therefore do not classify it as knowledge, see §§202, 337, 2715, 2718, 3246, 4448.

Let me now address the idea that when Jehovah, referring to himself, says, *should I see,* it symbolizes awareness on the part of those who bring damnation, or hellish beings. The situation is plain from earlier explanations to the effect that people attribute evil to Jehovah, or the Lord, whereas in reality nothing bad comes from him, only from hell; see §§2447, 6071, 6991, 6997, 7533, 7632, 7643. When the one who is capable of doing away with evil tolerates it, the appearance is that it comes from him. That is the case here, where the firstborn of the Egyptians were put to death. Jehovah is described as responsible, since the text says, "'I will pass through the land of Egypt on this night and strike every firstborn in the land of Egypt.' And it came about in the middle of the night that Jehovah struck every firstborn in the land of Egypt, from the firstborn of Pharaoh who was to sit on his throne to the firstborn of the prisoner who was in the house of the pit" (verses 12, 29). Yet the one who does it is called a destroyer in the current verse: "The blood will serve you as a sign on the houses, [to show] where you are, and should I see the blood, I will pass by you, and the *plague will not come as a destroyer on you."* [4] It is the same when the evil undergo devastation in the other world, and when they are damned and thrown into hell—which is what is meant in an inner sense by the plagues, the death of the firstborn, and the drowning in the Suph Sea. Jehovah (the Lord) puts no one through devastation, let alone damns anyone or throws anyone into hell. It is the evil spirits themselves who do it to themselves; it is the evil in them. So it is that *should I see the blood* symbolizes awareness on the part of those who bring damnation.

[5] This "toleration" cannot be explained briefly, because it involves many, many secrets. When the ungodly are damned and tormented, the Lord's toleration of it is the toleration not of one who wishes it but of one who does not wish it. It is the toleration of one who cannot bring relief, because the purpose, which is the salvation of the whole human race, urges otherwise. To help would be to do evil, which goes against everything divine.

More about this elsewhere [§§7926, 7930], with the Lord's divine mercy.

I will pass by you means that (damnation from the hells) will flee away. **7878**
This can be seen from the symbolism of *passing by,* when the word applies to damnation, as fleeing away. In addition, the damning atmosphere that pours out of the hells flees right past anyone surrounded by the Lord with truth and goodness. Damnation affects people immersed in evil and falsity, because they are in a receptive state, but not people surrounded by truth and goodness. These traits are opposed to each other, so the one flees the other.

All the rules laid down so far for the Passover lamb, the cooking and eating of it, and the blood on the doorposts and lintel relate to this promise that the destroyer will pass by their houses, or in an inner sense, that they will be untouched by damnation. It was for this goal—the flight of damnation away from them—that they were prepared. The process of preparation is what the rules laid down for the Passover lamb depict in an inner sense.

And the plague will not come as a destroyer on you means that dam- **7879**
nation from hell will not affect them, as the following shows: A *plague* symbolizes damnation here, because this plague was the death of all the firstborn in Egypt. For the symbolism of their death as damnation, see §7778. And the *destroyer* symbolizes hell, which brings damnation.

Here is how matters stand with hell as the bringer of damnation: The process of devastation that the evil undergo in the other life, their damnation, and their consignment to hell come not directly from the spirit dedicated to evil but from the hells. Everything bad that happens there results from an inflow from the hells, and none of it without that inflow. Evil happens according to the state of evil in the spirits being devastated and damned, and this state matches the extent to which they are stripped of goodness and truth. The state of the spirits' evil determines the degree to which they communicate with the hells, and the hells are more than ready to inflict evil. Doing so is the highest pleasure of their life.

[2] Because the hells are like this, the Lord keeps them closed. If they lay open, the entire human race would be destroyed, because the hells are always seeking the ruin of everyone. When seventy thousand men perished in a contagion because David had counted the people (2 Samuel 24) and when one hundred eighty-five thousand were killed in the camp of the Assyrians in one night (2 Kings 19:35), it was the work of the hells, which then lay open. It would be the same today if they were open now, so the Lord keeps them shut tight.

For the idea that damnation from the hells cannot affect people whom the Lord holds in goodness and truth—the symbolic meaning of *the plague will not come as a destroyer on you*—see §7878 directly above.

7880 *In my striking the land of Egypt* means when people who subscribe to a faith detached from neighborly love are damned. This is evident from the discussion above at §7871.

7881 *And that day shall serve you as a reminder* symbolizes the quality of that state during worship. This can be seen from the symbolism of a *day* as a state (discussed in §§23, 487, 488, 493, 2788, 3462, 3785, 4850, 5672, 5962, 6110) and from that of a *reminder,* [or memorial,] as the quality of something in worship (noted at §6888).

7882 *You shall celebrate it as a feast to Jehovah* symbolizes worship of the Lord because of being delivered from damnation. This can be seen from the symbolism of *celebrating a feast to Jehovah* as worship of the Lord, specifically on account of being delivered from damnation, since that was the reason this day was a feast. For the idea that Passover was established on account of the Lord's deliverance of people in the spiritual church, see §7867.

7883 *Throughout your generations* means with all that faith and neighborly love imply. This can be seen from the symbolism of *generations* as successive generations of faith and neighborly love, as discussed in §§613, 2020, 2584, 6239.

7884 *By an eternal statute you shall celebrate it* symbolizes worship of the Lord that reflects the way heaven is arranged, worship intended for people in the spiritual church. This can be seen from the symbolism of an *eternal statute* as the arrangement ordained for heaven (discussed below) and from that of *celebrating* as worship of the Lord (as just above at §7882). Since it is the children of Israel who are being told to celebrate it, people of the spiritual church are meant.

An *eternal statute* means the arrangement ordained for heaven because all the statutes commanded for the children of Israel were of a kind that resulted from arrangements in heaven, so they also represented something heavenly.

Worship that reflects the way heaven is arranged means every instance in which we do the good the Lord has commanded. When people today talk about worship of God, they mainly mean worshiping with one's lips in a church and [in private prayers] morning and evening. However, it is not these that are the essential components in worship of God, but rather a life of useful activity. Worshiping by living a useful life accords with the arrangement ordained for heaven. Worship of the lips too is worship, but it does no good whatever unless we worship with our lives, because that is heartfelt worship. If worship of the lips is really to be worship, it must grow out of living worship.

Seven days symbolizes what is holy. This is established by the symbolism of *seven* as implying something holy and of seven *days* as meaning that which is holy. On the point that seven implies something holy, see §§395, 433, 716, 881, 5265, 5268. **7885**

You shall eat unleavened loaves symbolizes purification from falsity. This is clear from the discussion in §2342 of the symbolism of *unleavened loaves* as purification from falsity. **7886**

Yes, on the first day you shall make yeast cease from your houses means that their goodness must be completely free of falsity. This is clear from the symbolism of the *first day* as the beginning of that state (for the meaning of a day as a state, see just above at §7881), from that of *yeast* as falsity (discussed below [§7906]), and from that of a *house* as goodness (discussed in §§2233, 2559, 3652, 3720, 7833, 7834, 7835, 7848). This shows that *on the first day you shall make yeast cease from your houses* means that from the very beginning of the state, their goodness must be free of falsity. **7887**

Let me explain about goodness: Goodness comes in an infinite variety of types, and these types take their nature from truth. The quality of goodness is therefore determined by the quality of the truth it assimilates. The truth it assimilates is rarely genuine. Instead it is an appearance of truth, or is even false, but without being opposed to truth. This truth flows into goodness when we live according to it. If we do so out of ignorance, and the ignorance harbors innocence, and if our aim is to do good, then the Lord and heaven nonetheless regard it not as false but as truthlike and accept it as truth, depending on the nature of the innocence. This is where goodness takes its character from.

This shows what is meant by the requirement that their goodness be free of falsity.

7888 *Because anyone eating yeast bread* symbolizes people who adopt falsity. This is plain from the symbolism of *eating* as adopting (discussed in §§2187, 2343, 3168, 3513 at the end, 3596, 4745) and from that of *yeast* as falsity (as above at §7887).

7889 *That soul shall be cut off from Israel* means that they will be separated from members of the spiritual church and will be damned. This can be seen from the symbolism of *being cut off* as being separated and being damned and from the representation of the children of *Israel* as people of the spiritual church (mentioned many times).

Why is it that people who have falsity in their goodness will be separated and damned? When the falsity symbolized by yeast is present within goodness, it turns goodness into something that inevitably embraces the evil coming from those hells that bring damnation. When the time comes for [people of the spiritual church] to be delivered from the spirits who harassed them, damnation will flow in from all sides. People with genuine goodness, though, or with goodness free of falsity, will pass through the middle of this damnation unharmed; see above at §7878.

7890 *[This shall last from] the first day up to the seventh day* symbolizes a complete and holy state. This can be seen from the symbolism of *seven days* as a holy state (mentioned above at §7885) and as a complete state (§6508), which is also symbolized by a week. For the meaning of a week as a whole span of time, large or small, from beginning to end, see §§2044, 3845.

7891 *And on the first day you shall have a holy convocation* means that at the beginning they will all be together, as the following shows: The *first day* symbolizes the beginning—the beginning of deliverance from the spirits who persecuted them and consequently from damnation. And a *holy convocation* means that they will all be together.

Convocations were called so that the whole congregation of Israel could come together and represent heaven this way, since everyone was then divided into tribes and the tribes into clans and the clans into households. (See §7836 for the idea that the tribes, clans, and households of the children of Israel represented heaven with all its communities.) That is why the convocations were called holy and took place at every feast (Leviticus 23:27, 36; Numbers 28:26; 29:1, 7, 12). Accordingly, the feasts were actually called holy convocations, since all males were required to attend them. The fact that the feasts were called holy convocations can be seen in Moses:

> These are the set feasts to Jehovah, *which you shall call holy convocations,* to offer a fire offering to Jehovah. (Leviticus 23:37)

The fact that all males were then present can be seen in the same author:

> *Three times a year every male of yours shall appear before Jehovah your God* in the place that he chooses: in the feast of unleavened bread and in the feast of weeks and in the feast of booths. (Deuteronomy 16:16)

On the seventh day a holy convocation means at the end of the state too. This can be seen from the symbolism of the *seventh day,* the final day of the feast, as its end. For the meaning of a *holy convocation,* see directly above at §7891. 7892

No work shall be done on those days means being held back from earthly and worldly concerns during that state. This can be seen from the symbolism of *work* as labors and pursuits that have worldly and earthly advantages as their goal. *No work shall be done on those days,* then, means being held back from those concerns. 7893

The purpose behind ordering the people so harshly not to do any work on feasts and Sabbaths was to put them in a fully representational state on those occasions, that is, to involve them in activities that represented something heavenly and spiritual. If they had done work aimed at worldly and earthly goals, it would have disturbed the state. Religious representation was established among Jacob's descendants as a means of communication between heaven and humankind. That is the purpose for which the church exists. Such communication would not have succeeded if Jacob's descendants had not been forbidden on pain of death to do any work on feast days and Sabbath days. Their attention was monopolized by worldly and earthly interests in which they immersed themselves wholeheartedly. That is what they were like. So if they had been free to pursue those interests on those days, the communication that their representative practices facilitated would have broken off entirely and died.

The same feasts were kept in practice after that era ended, though, because of the heavenly life people then enjoy and because of the opportunity to teach them what faith and charity are.

Only [the provision of] something to eat for every soul means when spiritual and heavenly goodness are being adopted. This can be seen from 7894 the symbolism of *eating* as adopting, which is discussed in §§2187, 2343, 3168, 3513 at the end, 3596, 4745. The adoption of something spiritual and heavenly is meant by the practices established for the Passover lamb.

7895 *This alone shall be done [by you]* means that this is all they will [then] concentrate on, as needs no explanation.

7896 Exodus 12:17, 18, 19, 20. *"And you shall observe [the practice of] the unleavened loaves, because [on] that same day I led your armies out of the land of Egypt; and you shall keep this day throughout your generations by an eternal statute. In the first [month], on the fourteenth day of the month in the evening, you shall eat unleavened loaves, up to the twenty-first day of the month in the evening. For seven days yeast shall not be found in your houses, because anyone eating yeast bread, that soul shall be cut off from the congregation of Israel, both an immigrant and a native of the land. No yeast bread shall you eat; in all your dwellings you shall eat unleavened loaves.'"*

And you shall observe [the practice of] the unleavened loaves means that there must be no falsity. *Because on that same day I led your armies out of the land of Egypt* means because there will then be a state of neighborly love and faith that creates a divide with people devoted to evil and falsity. *And you shall keep this day throughout your generations by an eternal statute* symbolizes worship inspired by faith and neighborly love that reflects the design of heaven. *In the first [month], on the fourteenth day of the month* means at the start of the holy state. *In the evening* symbolizes the end of the previous state and the beginning of a new one. *You shall eat unleavened loaves* symbolizes the adoption by goodness of truth purified of falsity. *Up to the twenty-first day of the month* symbolizes the end of that holy state. *In the evening* symbolizes the end of the previous state and the start of a new one. *For seven days* symbolizes the whole span of this state. *Yeast shall not be found in your houses* means that no falsity may go anywhere near goodness. *Because anyone eating yeast bread, that soul shall be cut off from the congregation of Israel* means that people who join falsity with their goodness will be damned. *Both an immigrant and a native of the land* means who are part of the church, whether or not they were born into it. *No yeast bread shall you eat* means that utmost care must be taken not to adopt falsity. *In all your dwellings you shall eat unleavened loaves* means that truth must be adopted in the inner levels where goodness resides.

7897 *And you shall observe [the practice of] the unleavened loaves* means that there must be no falsity. This is clear from the symbolism of *unleavened loaves* as something purified of all falsity, which is discussed at §2342.

Because on that same day I led your armies out of the land of Egypt means because there will then be a state of neighborly love and faith that creates a divide with people devoted to evil and falsity, as the following shows: A *day* symbolizes a state, as noted above at §7881. *Armies* symbolize the qualities that go to make up neighborly love and faith, as discussed in §§3448, 7236. *Leading out* means being separated. And the *Egyptians* symbolize people devoted to evil and falsity, as frequently mentioned. 7898

And you shall keep this day throughout your generations by an eternal statute symbolizes worship inspired by faith and neighborly love that reflects the divine design, as the following shows: *Keeping* symbolizes worship, because that day was "kept" when Passover was observed on it. *Generations* symbolize aspects of faith and neighborly love, as dealt with above at §7883. And an *eternal statute* means that it reflects the divine design, as also dealt with above, at §7884. 7899

In the first [month], on the fourteenth day of the month means at the start of the holy state. This is clear from the symbolism of *in the first [month]* as the beginning (as above at §§7887, 7891) and from that of the *fourteenth day* as a holy state. The number fourteen means something holy (see above at §7842), and a day means a state (§7881). 7900

The number fourteen means something holy because it is a product of seven. When the Word mentions *seven,* it symbolizes something holy. (Factors and multiples have the same meaning as each other, §§5291, 5335, 5708.)

Since Passover was the holiest of the feast days, the command was that it be celebrated on the fourteenth day of the month, last for seven days, and end on the twenty-first day, which also symbolizes something holy.

Therefore it was also decreed that people unable to celebrate Passover in the first month celebrate it the next month, again on the fourteenth day. The statute appears this way in Moses:

> When any man is unclean on account of a soul or is on a distant road, among you or your [future] generations, he shall still perform the Passover [offering] to Jehovah; *in the second month, on the fourteenth day,* between the evenings they shall perform it. (Numbers 9:10, 11)

In the evening symbolizes the end of the previous state and the beginning of a new one. This can be seen from the discussion in §7844 of the symbolism of *evening* as the end of a previous state and the start of the next. 7901

You shall eat unleavened loaves symbolizes the adoption by goodness of truth purified of falsity, as the following shows: *Eating* symbolizes 7902 adoption, as treated of in §§2187, 2343, 3168, 3513 at the end, 3596, 4745. The reason it means the adoption of truth by goodness is that truth is adopted by that which is good, and (as shown many times before [§§3804, 4149, 4301, 6916, 7759, 7760, 7839, 7887]) goodness takes its quality from truth. So for truth to be adopted, goodness is the necessary agent, and for goodness to be adopted, truth is the necessary means. And an *unleavened loaf* symbolizes truth purified of all falsity, as treated of at §2342.

[2] In respect to truth purified of all falsity, you need to know that in a human being no such thing as pure truth is possible. For one thing, falsity is constantly gushing from the evil we inhabit and are inhabited by. For another, truths are interconnected, so if one link in the chain is false (and especially if many are), the other, genuine truths end up sullied and partake somewhat of the falsity.

Truth is said to be purified of falsity when we are capable of being held by the Lord in innocent goodness. Innocence means acknowledging that there is nothing but evil in us and that everything good comes from the Lord. It also means believing that we do not know or perceive anything—including religious truth—on our own, only under the Lord's power. When we are in this state, falsity can be removed from us, and truth from the Lord can be instilled.

This is the state symbolized by the unleavened loaves and also by the eating of the Passover lamb.

7903 *Up to the twenty-first day of the month* symbolizes the end of that holy state. This can be seen from the symbolism of the *twenty-first day* as a holy state and as the end of that state. It means a holy state because [twenty-one] is the product of seven times three, and seven symbolizes something holy, as does three. The meaning of this twenty-first day as the end of the state is obvious, since it was the final day.

7904 *In the evening* symbolizes the end of the previous state and the start of a new one, as above at §7901.

7905 *For seven days* symbolizes the whole span of this state. This can be seen from the symbolism of *seven days* as a holy state (as above at §7885) and as a whole span of time from beginning to end, or a complete state (§§728, 6508), which is what a week symbolizes too (§§2044, 3845). Because of all this symbolism, the feast was set up to last seven days.

7906 *Yeast shall not be found in your houses* means that no falsity may go anywhere near goodness. This can be seen from the symbolism of *yeast* as falsity (discussed below) and from that of a *house* as goodness (discussed in §§3652, 3720, 4982, 7833, 7834, 7835).

The meaning of *yeast* as falsity can be seen from passages mentioning yeast and yeast bread, and also unleavened bread and yeast-free goods. In Matthew, for instance:

> Jesus said, "Watch and *beware of the yeast of the Pharisees and Sadducees.*" Afterward the disciples understood that he had not said *to beware of the yeast in bread* but *of the teaching of the Pharisees and Sadducees.* (Matthew 16:6, 12)

In this case the yeast obviously stands for false teachings.

Since yeast symbolized falsity, *offering the blood of a sacrifice on yeast bread* was forbidden (Exodus 23:18; 34:25), because the blood of a sacrifice symbolized sacred truth and therefore truth purified of all falsity (§§4735, 6978, 7317, 7326, 7846, 7850). It was also decreed that the *minha* offered on the altar *should not be cooked with yeast* (Leviticus 6:16, 17) and that *cakes and wafers were also to be free of yeast* (Leviticus 7:11, 12, 13).

[2] In further regard to leavened and unleavened bread, be aware that the truth in us can never be purified of falsity without so-called fermentation—that is, without a fight put up by falsity against truth and by truth against falsity. After the fight is finished and truth has conquered, falsity drops away like the waste products of fermentation, and truth stands purified, like wine, which clarifies upon fermentation, the dregs settling to the bottom.

The main occasion for this "fermentation" or fight is when our state changes, when our actions start to be motivated not by faith and truth (as they previously were) but by neighborly love and goodness. When we act on religious truth, our state has not yet been purified. It is when we act out of neighborly kindness that our state has been purified, because we then act on our will, where before we acted only on our understanding.

[3] Spiritual battles, or trials, are fermentations in a spiritual sense, because during them, falsity seeks to unite with truth. But truth spurns falsity and eventually sends it down to the bottom, which means that the dregs are removed.

This is the sense in which to understand the Lord's teaching in Matthew about yeast:

> *The kingdom of the heavens is like yeast* that a woman, taking it, hid in three pecks of flour *until the whole was leavened.* (Matthew 13:33)

The flour is truth from which goodness develops. And in Hosea:

> They are all committing adultery like an oven fired up by the baker; *the stirrer ceases from kneading the dough until it is leavened.* (Hosea 7:4)

As just mentioned, the kinds of personal struggles symbolized by fermentation crop up in the state just preceding a new stage of life. For this reason there was also a statute requiring that when a *new minha* was brought to the *Feast of Firstfruits [in the form of] waved bread, it was to be cooked with yeast,* and that this constituted the firstfruits to Jehovah (Leviticus 23:16, 17).

7907 *Because anyone eating yeast bread, that soul shall be cut off from the congregation of Israel* means that people who join falsity with their goodness will be damned, as the following shows: *Eating* symbolizes adopting (discussed in §§2343, 3168, 3513 at the end, 3596, 4745) and therefore uniting (§2187), because anyone who adopts something unites with it. *Yeast bread* symbolizes falsity, as discussed directly above at §7906. *Being cut off* symbolizes being separated and damned, as discussed at §7889. A *soul* symbolizes a person. And the *congregation of Israel* symbolizes people of the spiritual church, as mentioned in §§7830, 7843. This shows that *anyone eating yeast bread, that soul shall be cut off from the congregation of Israel* means that people who join falsity with their goodness will be separated from the spiritual church and will be damned.

7908 *Both an immigrant and a native of the land* means who are part of the church, whether or not they were born into it, as the following shows: An *immigrant* symbolizes a person who is taught about the true ideas and good desires of the church and accepts them (discussed in §§1463, 4444), so it symbolizes people who were not born within the church but found their way to it nonetheless. And a *native of the land* symbolizes people who were born within the church.

7909 *No yeast bread shall you eat* means that utmost care must be taken not to adopt falsity. This can be seen from the symbolism of *yeast bread* as falsity (discussed above at §7906) and from that of *eating* as adopting (also mentioned above, at §7907).

The text's frequent warning that yeast bread was not to be eaten (in verses 15, 17, 18, 19, for example) carries the message that we should guard against falsity with utmost care. The point in being so wary of it is to protect the goodness we possess. Falsity is not compatible with goodness but rather destroys it, because falsity belongs to evil, and truth to goodness. If we adopt falsity, or believe firmly in it, we are completely unreceptive to innocent goodness, with the consequence that we cannot be delivered from damnation.

Adopting falsity and entertaining it are two very different things, however. If people who entertain falsity possess goodness, then when the truth becomes visible to them, they reject the false thinking. People who adopt falsity as their own, though, hold on to it, and if real truth appears to them, they oppose it.

Now you can see why the text so often warns against eating yeast bread.

In all your dwellings you shall eat unleavened loaves means that truth 7910
must be adopted in the inner levels where goodness resides, as can be seen from the following: *Dwellings* symbolize the contents of the mind and therefore matters of understanding and wisdom (as discussed at §7719), so they symbolize inner levels, since that is where understanding and wisdom reside, as does goodness. And *eating unleavened loaves* means adopting truth, as stated several times before [§§7886, 7887, 7897, 7902].

About inner levels as the place where truth is adopted and where goodness resides: It is important to realize that when people live in the Lord (meaning when they live a life of faith and neighborly love), goodness dwells in their inner depths. The deeper it lies, the purer and more heavenly it is. Truth, on the other hand, lodges on the outer surface, and the shallower its lodging in those people, the more bereft it is of goodness. This is because our inner reaches are in heaven, and our inmost core is near the Lord, but our outer surface is in the world. That is why truth, which has to do with faith, enters along an outer route, while goodness enters along an inner route (§§7756, 7757). It is also why the inner levels, in which goodness resides, are where truth is adopted.

Exodus 12:21, 22, 23, 24. *And Moses called all the elders of Israel and said* 7911
to them, "Haul forth and take for yourselves an animal of the flock according to your clans and slaughter the Passover. And you shall take a bundle of hyssop, and you are to dip it in the blood that is in the basin and touch it to the lintel and to the two doorposts with the blood that is in the basin. And you yourselves shall not go out—not one—from the doorway of your house till morning. And Jehovah will pass through to inflict a plague on Egypt, and should he see the blood on the lintel and on the two doorposts, Jehovah will pass by the doorway and not let the destroyer come to your houses to inflict the plague. And you shall keep this word as a statute for yourself and for your children forever."

And Moses called all the elders of Israel means that the intellect of people in the spiritual church was enlightened through the inflow and presence of divine truth. *And said to them* symbolizes a perception. *Haul forth* means that they should force themselves. *And take for yourselves an animal of the flock* means into accepting innocent goodness. *According to your clans* means in keeping with the truth-based goodness of each individual. *And slaughter the Passover* symbolizes preparation for the Lord's presence and consequent deliverance. *And you shall take a bundle of hyssop* symbolizes an outer means of purification. *And dip it in the blood* symbolizes sacred truth coming from innocent goodness. *That is in the basin* means which is present in earthly-level goodness. *And touch it to the lintel and to the two doorposts* symbolizes goodness and truth on the earthly plane. *With the blood that is in the basin* symbolizes the sacred truth belonging to innocent goodness, present on the earthly plane. *And you yourselves shall not go out—not one—from the doorway of your house* means that they have to stay grounded in goodness, which must not be regarded from the viewpoint of truth. *Till morning* means till a state of enlightenment. *And Jehovah will pass through* symbolizes the presence of the Divine. *To inflict a plague on Egypt* means which resulted in damnation for people in the church who adhered to a faith detached from neighborly love. *And should he see the blood on the lintel and on the two doorposts* symbolizes an awareness of the sacred truth that comes from innocent goodness and is present on the earthly plane. *Jehovah will pass by the doorway* means that damnation will flee away. *And not let the destroyer come to your houses* means that falsity and evil from the hells must not come anywhere near the will. *To inflict the plague* symbolizes damnation that they actually bring on themselves. *And you shall keep this word as a statute for yourself and for your children forever* means that from then on, this will all be according to the divine arrangement for people of the spiritual church.

7912 *And Moses called all the elders of Israel* means that the intellect of people in the spiritual church was enlightened through the inflow and presence of divine truth, as the following shows: *Calling,* when divine truth is said to do it, symbolizes inflow and presence, as discussed in §§6177, 6840, 7390, 7451, 7721. *Moses* represents the divine law and therefore the Word and divine truth, as discussed in the preface to Genesis 18 and §§4859 at the end, 5922, 6723, 6752, 6771, 6827, 7010, 7014, 7089, 7382. *Elders* symbolize the leading elements of wisdom and understanding, which harmonize with truth and goodness, as discussed in §§6524, 6525, 6890. Calling them, or causing them to be present, means enlightening the intellect. And *Israel* represents the spiritual church, as discussed in §§4286, 6426, 6637. This shows that *Moses called all the elders of Israel* means that the intellect of people in the spiritual church was enlightened through the inflow and presence of divine truth.

And said to them symbolizes a perception. This is clear from the symbolism of *saying* in the Word's narratives as a perception, which is discussed in §§1791, 1815, 1819, 1822, 1898, 1919, 2080, 2619, 2862, 3395, 3509, 5687, 5743, 5877, 6251. 7913

Haul forth means that they should force themselves. This can be seen from the symbolism of *hauling forth* as forcing oneself, when it refers to the innocent goodness that people of the spiritual church are to receive from the Lord. People whose religion is spiritual do not accept innocent goodness—goodness embodying love for the Lord—unless they compel themselves to. They have difficulty believing that the Lord is the only God and that his humanity is divine. Lacking belief in him, then, they also lack love for him, so they cannot experience innocent goodness unless they force themselves. For the idea that we ought to force ourselves, and that when we do, we are acting freely, though we are not acting freely when forced from the outside, see §§1937, 1947. This is what hauling forth (the Passover animal) symbolizes. 7914

Hauling it forth plainly holds some secret invisible in the literal meaning.

And take for yourselves an animal of the flock means into accepting innocent goodness. This can be seen from the symbolism of the Passover lamb—the *animal of the flock* here—as innocent goodness, which is discussed in §§3519, 3994, 7840. 7915

According to your clans means in keeping with the truth-based goodness of each individual. This can be seen from the symbolism of *clans* as truth-based goodness when the word applies to the children of Israel, who represent the spiritual church, because "truth-based goodness" is the name for the goodness characterizing that church. The reason clans have this symbolism is that nothing but spiritual attributes are meant in the inner sense. That is, nothing is meant but attributes of heaven and the church and therefore attributes of faith and neighborly love. Clans in an inner sense therefore are what develops out of goodness by means of truth and are truth-based goodness. 7916

And slaughter the Passover symbolizes preparation for the Lord's presence and consequent deliverance. This can be seen from the symbolism of *slaughtering* as preparation (as above at §7843) and from that of the *Passover* as the Lord's presence and the deliverance of people in the spiritual church. 7917

7918 *And you shall take a bundle of hyssop* symbolizes an outer means of purification. This can be seen from the symbolism of *hyssop,* which stands for outer truth as a means of purification, as discussed below. The text says to *take a bundle of* hyssop because a bundle has to do with truth and the arrangement of it (§§5530, 5881, 7408).

The reason hyssop stands for outer truth as a means of purification is that all spiritual purification is brought about by truth. We do not recognize the earthly and worldly types of love from which we need to be purified except through truth. When the Lord instills this truth in us, he instills along with it a horror for those types of love as something unclean and damnable. When anything of the kind flows into our thoughts, the horror returns, which causes us to turn away in loathing. That is how we are purified by truth as an outer means.

This being so, flint knives or daggers were decreed as the instrument for circumcision. Flint daggers or knives stand for religious truth through which purification is accomplished (see §§2799, 7044), and circumcision stands for purification from filthy kinds of love (§§2039, 2632, 3412, 3413, 4462, 7045).

[2] Because hyssop had this symbolism, it was used in cleansings, which in an inner sense symbolized purification from falsity and evil. An example is the cleansing of a person from leprosy, in Moses:

> The priest shall take *for the leper who is to be cleansed* two live, clean birds and *cedar wood* and scarlet cloth and *hyssop.* And he shall dip them into the blood of the slaughtered bird and spatter it on the person to be cleansed. (Leviticus 14:4, 5, 6, 7)

Likewise *for the cleansing of a house* if there was leprosy in it (Leviticus 14:49, 50, 51). Preparation of the *water for removing [sin],* by which people were cleansed, also involved the use of *cedar wood* and *hyssop* (Numbers 19:6, 18). Cedar wood symbolized inner spiritual truth, and hyssop, outer spiritual truth, so cedar symbolized an inner means of purification, and hyssop, an outer means.

It is quite plain in David that hyssop is a means of purification:

> *You will purge me with hyssop,* and I will become clean; you will wash me, and I will be whiter than snow. (Psalms 51:7)

Purging with hyssop and becoming clean stands for outward purification. Washing and being whiter than snow stands for inward purification.

Snow and whiteness are mentioned in connection with truth (§§3301, 3993, 4007, 5319).

The following words in 1 Kings show that hyssop means the lowliest form of truth, and cedar, a higher form:

> Solomon spoke about types of wood, *from the cedar that is in Lebanon to the hyssop that is growing out of the wall.* (1 Kings 4:33)

The cedar stands for truth as a component of intelligence on an inner level, and the hyssop for truth as a component of intelligence on an outer level.

And dip it in the blood symbolizes sacred truth coming from innocent goodness. This can be seen from the symbolism of *blood,* in this case the blood of a lamb, as sacred truth coming from innocent goodness, as discussed above at §§7846, 7877. For a definition of the truth that comes from innocent goodness, see §7877. 7919

That is in the basin means which is present in earthly-level goodness. This can be seen from the symbolism of a *basin* as earthly-level goodness. Vessels in general symbolize items of knowledge on the earthly plane (§3068) because items of knowledge are containers for inflowing goodness and truth. Since they symbolize knowledge, they also symbolize the earthly plane itself, because knowledge goes to make up that plane, and the earthly plane is a comprehensive container. More particularly, though, vessels of wood and bronze symbolize goodness on the earthly level, because wood means goodness, as does bronze. That is why a basin means earthly-level goodness. 7920

It needs to be understood that by worldly goodness I mean one thing and by earthly-level goodness another. Worldly goodness is something we receive by heredity, but earthly-level goodness is something we receive from the Lord by being reborn. (Concerning worldly goodness, see §7197.)

And touch it to the lintel and to the two doorposts symbolizes goodness and truth on the earthly plane. This can be seen from the symbolism of a *lintel* as earthly-level goodness and from that of *doorposts* as earthly-level truth, as discussed at §7847. 7921

With the blood that is in the basin symbolizes the sacred truth belonging to innocent goodness, present on the earthly plane. This is evident from the symbolism of *blood* (lamb's blood) as sacred truth coming from innocent goodness (dealt with at §7919) and from that of a *basin* as the earthly plane (dealt with just above at §7920). 7922

7923 *And you yourselves shall not go out—not one—from the doorway of your house* means that they have to stay grounded in goodness, which must not be regarded from the viewpoint of truth, as the following shows: *Not going out* means staying. A *house* symbolizes goodness, as discussed in §§2233, 2559, 3652, 3720, 7833, 7834, 7835, 7848. This makes it clear that *you yourselves shall not go out—not one—from the doorway of your house* means that they have to stay grounded in goodness.

Here is why it means that goodness must not be regarded from the viewpoint of truth: Staying in the house means staying grounded in goodness, but going out from the doorway of the house means leaving goodness for truth, because goodness lies inside, while truth lies on the outside (§7910). (For what it means to regard truth from the viewpoint of goodness, see §§5895 at the end, 5897 [near the end], 7857.) To regard goodness from the viewpoint of truth is to regard what is within from an outer viewpoint, whereas to regard truth from the viewpoint of goodness is to regard what is outward from an inner viewpoint. As just mentioned, goodness is inward, but truth is outward. It is orderly to look from goodness to truth, because all divine inflow acts on the outer surface through the inner depths, but it is not orderly to look from truth to goodness. So when we are being reborn, the order switches and goodness, or neighborly love, is seen as being in first place, and truth, or faith, in second.

7924 *Till morning* means till a state of enlightenment. This is established by the symbolism of *morning* as a state of enlightenment, as mentioned in §§3458, 3723, 5740, 7860.

7925 *And Jehovah will pass through* symbolizes the presence of the Divine. This can be seen from the symbolism of *passing through* the land of Egypt, when *Jehovah* is being said to do it, as the presence of the Divine, which is noted above at §7869.

7926 *To inflict a plague on Egypt* means which resulted in damnation for people in the church who adhered to a faith detached from neighborly love. This can be seen from the symbolism of this *plague* (the death of the firstborn) as the damnation of people in a religion that was detached from neighborly love, as discussed in §§7766, 7778. After all, *Egypt,* or Egyptians, symbolizes people immersed in the knowledge of religious subjects who nonetheless separated theology from life—in other words, faith from neighborly love. That is just what the Egyptians were like, too, because they were versed in the knowledge belonging to the church of that era, which was a representational religion. They knew which spiritual qualities were represented by the earthly practices that constituted the church's rituals in those days, so they knew what corresponded to what. This is manifest from their hieroglyphics, which were images of earthly objects that represented spiritual qualities.

That is why Egyptians also symbolize people who know matters of faith but live an evil life.

In the other world, people like this are purged of everything that constitutes faith, that is, everything having to do with religion, and in the end are damned. This damnation is what the death of the firstborn in Egypt means in an inner sense.

[2] Since the text says that Jehovah will pass through to inflict a plague on Egypt, and it symbolizes the presence of the Divine, which resulted in the damnation of people in the church who adhered to a faith detached from neighborly love, I need to explain this. Jehovah (the Lord) does not present himself among the inhabitants of hell to inflict damnation, but it is still his presence that brings their damnation about. You see, the hells relentlessly try to harass the good and relentlessly seek to climb into heaven and agitate its inhabitants, although they cannot make it past the inhabitants of heaven's outermost bounds. They harbor an enmity from which hostility and violence are constantly exuding. The Lord, though, always provides for the inhabitants of heaven's outer limits to enjoy safety and quiet. This he accomplishes through his presence with them. When hellish spirits of their own accord go to where the Lord is present—that is, into his presence—they are exposing themselves to the evils involved in spiritual devastation and finally to damnation. The Lord's presence, which they are running up against, carries those consequences with it, as I have shown a number of times before [§§2447, 4299, 6849, 7679, 7710, 7877]. This makes it plain that the Lord does not present himself to them to inflict the miseries of punishment on them but that, on the contrary, they cast themselves into those miseries.

These remarks demonstrate that from the Lord comes nothing but goodness and that all evil comes from the very people who are intent on it. The evil therefore bring devastating experiences, damnation, and hell on themselves.

You can see, then, how to understand the statement that Jehovah will pass through to inflict a plague on Egypt.

And should he see the blood on the lintel and on the two doorposts symbolizes an awareness of the sacred truth that comes from innocent goodness and is present on the earthly plane. This can be seen from the symbolism 7927 of *seeing* as understanding and perceiving (discussed in §§2150, 2325, 2807, 3764, 4403–4421, 4567, 4723, 5400), from that of *blood* as sacred truth coming from innocent goodness (as above at §7919), and from that of the *lintel* and the *two doorposts* as goodness and truth on the earthly level (also discussed above, at §7847).

7928 *Jehovah will pass by the doorway* means that damnation will flee away. This can be seen from the discussion above at §7878, where similar words occur.

7929 *And not let the destroyer come to your houses* means that falsity and evil from the hells must not come anywhere near the will, as the following shows: *Not let [it come]* means that it must not come near. The *destroyer* symbolizes hell, as discussed at §7879, so it symbolizes falsity and evil generated by the hells, which actually consist of falsity and evil. And *houses* symbolize something belonging to the will, as discussed in §§710, 7848. A house symbolizes a human being, so it also symbolizes the human mind, because what makes us human is our understanding of truth and our will to do good, which are mental functions. It is particularly the part of the mind called the will that makes us human, so a house also symbolizes the will. Which of these is being symbolized can be seen from the series of concepts in the inner meaning.

7930 *To inflict the plague* symbolizes damnation that they actually bring on themselves. This can be seen from the symbolism of this *plague* as the damnation of people in the church who adhered to a faith detached from neighborly love, as discussed in §§7879, 7926. For the idea that the evil bring on their own damnation, see just above at §7926.

7931 *And you shall keep this word as a statute for yourself and for your children forever* means that from then on, this will all be according to the divine arrangement for people of the spiritual church, as the following shows: *Keeping this word forever* means that this was all to be observed from then on. *As a statute* means according to the arrangement, as discussed at §7884. And the children of Israel represent people in the spiritual church, as discussed in §§4286, 6426, 6637, 6862, 6868, 7035, 7062, 7198, 7201, 7215, 7223.

By an arrangement I mean the way matters stood in heaven starting at the time right after the resurrection when the Lord in his divine humanity began to reorganize everything in heaven and on earth (Matthew 28:18). According to this arrangement, people in the spiritual church could now be taken up to heaven to enjoy eternal bliss, which they could not under the previous order. Before this, the Lord had managed everything through heaven, but afterward he did so through his human side, which he had glorified and made divine while he was in the world. The change brought him such a great increase in strength that people were now taken up to heaven who could not be taken up before, while the wicked fell back on all sides and were locked up in their hells. This is the arrangement meant.

Exodus 12:25, 26, 27, 28. *"And it will happen that you will come to the land that Jehovah is going to give you, as he spoke, and you shall keep this service. And it will happen that your sons will say to you, 'What is this service you have?' And you shall say, 'It is the Passover sacrifice to Jehovah—that he passed by the houses of the children of Israel in Egypt in his inflicting a plague on Egypt and delivered our houses.'" And the people bent and bowed. And the children of Israel went and did as Jehovah had commanded Moses and Aaron; that is what they did.* **7932**

And it will happen that you will come to the land that Jehovah is going to give you means to heaven, given them by the Lord. *As he spoke* means according to his promise in the Word. *And you shall keep this service* symbolizes worship on account of being delivered. *And it will happen that your sons will say to you* symbolizes an inner perception of truth on the part of conscience. *What is this service you have?* means in the midst of worship. *And you shall say,* symbolizes a thought. *It is the Passover sacrifice to Jehovah* symbolizes worship of the Lord on account of being delivered. *That he passed by the houses of Israel* means that damnation fled from the goodness in which the Lord anchored them. *In Egypt* means when they were near evil spirits. *In his inflicting a plague on Egypt* means when people in the church who had subscribed to a faith detached from neighborly love were damned. *And delivered our houses* means yet nothing damnable would touch [people of the spiritual church], because the Lord filled them with goodness. *And the people bent and bowed* symbolizes humility on the lips and in the heart. *And the children of Israel went and did as Jehovah had commanded Moses and Aaron* means that people in the spiritual church obeyed divine truth. *That is what they did* symbolizes an act of the will.

[2] *And it will happen that you will come to the land that Jehovah is going to give you* means to heaven, given them by the Lord. This can be seen from the symbolism of the *land*—the land of Canaan, for which they were headed—as the Lord's kingdom and therefore as heaven, which is discussed in §§1607, 1866, 3038, 3481, 3705, 4116, 4240, 4447, 5757. The children of Israel represented people of the spiritual church who had lived in the world before the Lord's Coming, who could not be saved without him, and who were therefore held in safety in an underground realm, the

hells around them tormenting them all the while. Eventually the Lord did come into the world and made his human nature divine, and when he rose again, he freed the people who had been kept under protection in that realm. After they had undergone certain trials, he brought them up to heaven. That is the story contained in the inner meaning of Moses' second book, Exodus. The Egyptians symbolize the spirits who inflicted the persecution. The escape from Egypt symbolizes deliverance. The forty years the people lived in the wilderness symbolize times of trial. And their entry into the land of Canaan symbolizes their elevation to heaven. See earlier remarks on this subject in §§6854, 6914, 7091 at the end, 7828.

This discussion shows that *when you will come into the land* means to heaven, given them by the Lord.

7933 *As he spoke* means according to his promise in the Word. This can be seen from the symbolism of *speaking.* When the Lord is said to have spoken, and to have spoken about heaven, which people in the spiritual church are going to reach, the term symbolizes a promise given in the Word. The Word's inner meaning—in the books of Moses as well as the Prophets—deals with the deliverance of people who were kept in the underground realm until the Lord's Coming, where they were persecuted by evil spirits, and about their elevation into heaven. They are the people meant there by the children of Israel. The promise that this would happen is what is symbolized here by *as Jehovah spoke.*

[2] In various passages the Lord says that everything in Scripture either will be or has been fulfilled in him. What he is talking about there is the contents of the Word's inner meaning, which deal only with his kingdom and in the highest sense with the Lord himself. Take for instance this passage in Luke:

> Jesus said to the disciples, "*These are the words that I spoke to you while I was still with you: that everything that has been written in the Law of Moses and the Prophets and the Psalms concerning me had to be fulfilled." Then he opened their mind to understand the Scriptures.* (Luke 24:44, 45)

In the same author:

> *Here, we are going up into Jerusalem, where everything that has been written by the prophets about the Son of Humankind will be completed.* (Luke 18:31)

And in Matthew:

> *Don't think that I came to undo the Law and the Prophets. I did not come to undo but to fulfill them. Truly, I say to you: until heaven and earth pass*

> *away, not one jot or one serif will pass away in the law till everything comes to pass.* (Matthew 5:17, 18)

[3] Again, these statements and what the Lord says elsewhere about the fulfilling of the law or Scripture contain predictions about him in their inner meaning. Everything, down to each jot or the smallest tip of any letter, has to do with the Lord in its inner meaning, which is the reason for the statement that not one jot or one serif will pass away in the law till everything comes to pass. And in Luke:

> *It is easier for heaven and earth to pass away than for one tip of a letter in the law to fail.* (Luke 16:17)

Anyone who does not know that everything down to the smallest detail of all has to do in its inner meaning with the Lord and his kingdom, and that this makes the Word supremely sacred, cannot possibly understand what it means to say that not one tip of a letter will fail, that not one jot or serif will pass away, and that it is easier for heaven and earth to pass away. What is visible in the outer meaning does not appear to be worth much. But the inner text is so seamless that not even one small word could be left out of it without breaking up the line of thought.

And you shall keep this service symbolizes worship on account of being delivered. This can be seen from the symbolism of *keeping* as a practice to be observed, as above at §7931, and from the symbolism of serving, or a *service,* as worship of the Lord. **7934**

And it will happen that your sons will say to you symbolizes an inner perception of truth on the part of conscience. This is established by the symbolism of *saying* as a perception (mentioned above at §7913) and from that of *sons* as truth (discussed in §§489, 491, 533, 1147, 2623, 3373, 4257). The reason it means an inner perception on the part of conscience is that the theme here is the subsequent or future state of people in the spiritual church who were delivered by the Lord. That state was one in which the idea that they owed their salvation to the Lord alone was to become fixed in their minds. The perception of this truth is a function of conscience. People whose religion is spiritual do not have the kind of perception that people whose religion is heavenly do; instead, they have conscience. **7935**

[2] The conscience they have is created and formed out of the truth taught by the religion into which they were born—truth that they absorbed in youth and beyond, solidified by the way they lived, and therefore incorporated into their faith. To abide by this kind of truth is to abide by

conscience, and to violate it is to violate conscience. It lodges in their inner memory as if engraved there. Eventually such truth comes to resemble the kinds of traits stamped on us in early childhood, which later appear to be second nature or even inborn. Such traits include various speech patterns, thoughts, memories, and reflections, and (more superficially) gait, gestures, facial expressions, and so on, which we are not born with but rather develop as habits.

When religious truth is stamped on us this same way, in our inner self, it too becomes second nature. In the end it makes us think, intend, and act in accordance with itself, as if it were innate. This form of vital energy is called conscience, and it is the life force of a spiritual person. The worth of conscience is determined by the extent to which genuine religious truth inspires our thinking and genuinely charitable goodness motivates our actions, as well as by the extent to which this truth and goodness guide us.

The subsequent story line too shows that these words symbolize an inner perception on the part of conscience.

7936 *What is this service you have?* means (a perception on the part of conscience) in the midst of worship. This can be seen from the symbolism of a *service* as worship, as above at §7934.

7937 *And you shall say,* symbolizes a thought. This is evident from the symbolism of *saying* as thought, which is mentioned in §§3395, 7094. The reason saying means a thought here is that just above at §7935 it symbolized a perception on the part of conscience, and this is the answer, which comes to conscience's awareness as a thought.

7938 *It is the Passover sacrifice to Jehovah* symbolizes worship of the Lord on account of being delivered. This can be seen from the symbolism of a *sacrifice* as worship (discussed in §§922, 6905) and from that of *Passover* as the Lord's presence and the deliverance of people in the spiritual church (discussed in §§7093 at the end, 7867).

7939 *That he passed by the houses of Israel* means that damnation fled from the goodness in which the Lord anchored them. This can be seen from the symbolism of *Jehovah will pass by,* which means that damnation will flee away (as above in §§7878, 7928), from the symbolism of *houses* as goodness (discussed in §§3652, 3720, 4982, 7833, 7834, 7835), and from the representation of *Israel* as people of the spiritual church (mentioned often).

I say that they were anchored in goodness by the Lord because when upon being delivered they were passing through scenes of damnation (through the hells, in other words), the Lord kept them anchored in goodness. That was the reason for preparing them. The process of preparation is depicted in the rules about the blood and about the Passover lamb and the eating of it, as laid down in verses 3–11, 15–20, 22, 43–48 of this chapter.

The fact that they passed through scenes of damnation (or hell) upon being delivered will be seen below [§§8039, 8099, 8125, 8131, 8155, 8181, 8205].

In Egypt means when they were near evil spirits. This can be seen from the symbolism of the Egyptians as the evil spirits who persecuted people of the spiritual church, which is mentioned many times. *Egypt* therefore symbolizes the state or place those spirits were in. Obviously they were nearby, because this took place in the land of Goshen. 7940

To learn what is involved in this, see the discussion above at §7932.

In his inflicting a plague on Egypt means when people in the church who had subscribed to a faith detached from neighborly love were damned. This is evident from the symbolism of *inflicting a plague on Egypt* as the damnation of people committed to a faith detached from neighborly love, as discussed in §§7766, 7778, 7926. 7941

And delivered our houses means yet nothing damnable would touch [people of the spiritual church], because the Lord filled them with goodness. This can be seen from the explanation above at §7939. 7942

And the people bent and bowed symbolizes humility on the lips and in the heart. This can be seen from the symbolism of *bending* as outer humility and therefore humility on the lips and from that of *bowing* as inner humility and therefore humility in the heart, as discussed in §§5682, 7068. 7943

And the children of Israel went and did as Jehovah had commanded Moses and Aaron means that people in the spiritual church obeyed divine truth. This can be seen from the symbolism of *going and doing* as obeying, from the representation of the *children of Israel* as people in the spiritual church (mentioned often), and from the representation of *Moses and Aaron* as divine truth, Moses representing inner truth and Aaron outer truth (discussed in §§7089, 7382). 7944

That is what they did symbolizes an act of the will. This can be seen from the fact that *they did* is a repetition. The previous instance symbolizes an act of the intellect, but this instance symbolizes an act of the will. In the Word it is common to find something that looks like the doubling of a single item, but one mention relates to truth in the intellect and the other to goodness in the will. The purpose is for every detail in the Word to display the heavenly marriage, which is a marriage of goodness and truth (§§683, 793, 801, 2173, 2516, 2712, 4137, 5138, 5502, 6343), and in the 7945 highest sense, the divine marriage, which is the marriage of the divine goodness in the Lord with the divine truth radiating from him (§§3004, 5502, 6179). This makes it plain that the Word is very holy.

7946 Exodus 12:29, 30, 31, 32, 33, 34. *And it came about in the middle of the night that Jehovah struck every firstborn in the land of Egypt, from the firstborn of Pharaoh who was to sit on his throne to the firstborn of the prisoner who was in the house of the pit, and every firstborn of the animals. And Pharaoh rose that night, as did all his servants and all the Egyptians, and there was a great outcry in Egypt, because there was no house where no one was dead. And he called Moses and Aaron by night and said, "Rise, go out from the middle of my people, both you and the children of Israel, and go serve Jehovah according to what you have spoken. Take both your flocks and your herds, as you have spoken, and go; and may you bless me, too." And Egypt prevailed on the people, hurrying to send them away from the land, because [the Egyptians] said, "We are all dying." And the people carried off their dough before it had been leavened, their kneading troughs tied up in their clothes on their shoulder.*

And it came about in the middle of the night symbolizes a state of utter falsity-from-evil. *That Jehovah struck every firstborn in the land of Egypt* symbolizes the damnation of a faith detached from neighborly love. *From the firstborn of Pharaoh who was to sit on his throne* symbolizes falsified religious truth of the first rank. *To the firstborn of the prisoner who was in the house of the pit* symbolizes falsified religious truth of the last rank. *And every firstborn of the animals* symbolizes adulterated goodness belonging to faith. *And Pharaoh rose that night, as did all his servants and all the Egyptians* means that when the people who were damned were brought into a state of utter falsity-from-evil, each and every one of them felt a loathing and fear of people in the spiritual church. *And there was a great outcry in Egypt* symbolizes inner mourning. *Because there was no house where no one was dead* means because no one [there] was not damned. *And he called Moses and Aaron by night* symbolizes contact with truth from the Divine in that state. *And said, "Rise, go out from the middle of my people,"* means that they should leave them. *Both you and the children of Israel* means taking with them the truth they had from the Divine, and also truth leading to goodness, and truth coming from goodness. *Go serve Jehovah* means that they were to worship the Lord. *According to what you have spoken* means as they wished. *Take both your flocks and your herds* symbolizes inner and outer neighborly kindness. *As you have spoken* means as they wished. *And go* means that they were unquestionably to leave. *And may you bless me, too* symbolizes a request for them to intervene. *And Egypt prevailed on the people, hurrying to send them away from the land* means that in their loathing and fear they urged them to leave. *Because [the Egyptians] said, "We are all dying,"* symbolizes hell for them as a result. *And the people carried off their dough before it had been leavened* symbolizes a first state of truth-from-goodness containing no falsity. *Their kneading troughs tied up in their clothes* symbolizes pleasures rising out of positive desires, adhering to truth. *On their shoulder* means with all their might.

And it came about in the middle of the night symbolizes a state of utter **7947**
falsity-from-evil. This is evident from the symbolism of the *middle of the night* as total devastation (treated of at §7776), that is, a stripping away of everything good and true, which results in a state of utter falsity-from-evil. For the meaning of night as a state of nothing [but] evil [and falsity], see §§2353, 6000, 7870.

That Jehovah struck every firstborn in the land of Egypt symbolizes the **7948**
damnation of a faith detached from neighborly love. This can be seen from the symbolism of *striking* as damnation (as at §7871) and from that of the *firstborn in the land of Egypt* as faith separated from neighborly love (discussed in §§7039, 7766, 7778).

From the firstborn of Pharaoh who was to sit on his throne symbolizes **7949**
falsified religious truth of the first rank. This is established by the explanation at §7779, where the same words occur.

To the firstborn of the prisoner who was in the house of the pit symbolizes **7950**
falsified religious truth of the last rank, as the following shows: The *firstborn* in the land of Egypt symbolize faith detached from neighborly love (as just above at §7948) and therefore faith's truth when falsified, too (discussed below). And the *prisoner who is in the house of the pit* symbolizes one who ranks last, because it is set against the firstborn of Pharaoh who was to sit on his throne, symbolizing falsified religious truth of the first rank (§§7779, 7949). In the first layer of spiritual meaning, a prisoner in the house of the pit means people engrossed in the physical senses. They are totally in the dark concerning truth and goodness, because they do not have even the power of perception possessed by people who are on the inner sensory level. That is why they symbolize people who rank last.

[2] The reason the firstborn in the land of Egypt stand for falsified religious truth is that the firstborn of Egypt stand for faith detached from neighborly love (§7948). People with this kind of faith are in utter shadow and darkness about religious truth. No light is available to them, so they

cannot in the least perceive what is true or whether it is true. All spiritual light comes from the Lord by way of goodness and consequently by way of charity, because charitable goodness is like a flame that sheds light. After all, goodness is a matter of love, and love is spiritual fire, the source of enlightenment. It is a serious mistake to think that people who lead evil lives can at the same time have any light on faith and its truths. They can take a confirmatory stance—can prove the teachings of their religion, sometimes with skill and cleverness—but they cannot see whether the propositions they are confirming are true or not. Even falsity can be proved convincingly enough to look like truth, and the role of a wise person consists not in constructing proofs but in seeing whether a thing is so; see §§4741, 5033, 6865, 7012, 7680.

[3] People given to evil in their lives, then, are given to the falsity that goes along with their evil. The truth, even if they know it, they do not believe. They sometimes think they believe it, but they are wrong. They will learn of their disbelief in the other life, when their perceptions are forced to match their will. They will then deny, reject, and spurn the truth and acknowledge its opposite, falsity, as true. That is why people who subscribe to a faith detached from neighborly love cannot help falsifying religious truth.

7951 *And every firstborn of the animals* symbolizes adulterated goodness belonging to faith, as before at §7781.

7952 *And Pharaoh rose that night, as did all his servants and all the Egyptians* means that when the people who were damned were brought into a state of utter falsity-from-evil, each and every one of them felt a loathing and fear of people in the spiritual church, as the following shows: *Night* symbolizes a state of utter falsity-from-evil, as above at §7947, so it symbolizes damnation. It makes no difference whether you say a state of utter falsity-from-evil or damnation, because people in that state are damned. *Pharaoh, his servants, and all the Egyptians* means each and every one. The rest of the meaning—that they felt a loathing and fear of people in the spiritual church—can be seen from what comes next, because Pharaoh called Moses and Aaron and told them to go from the midst of his people; and the Egyptians drove them out (verse 39).

7953 *And there was a great outcry in Egypt* symbolizes inner mourning, as at §7782, where similar words occur.

7954 *Because there was no house where no one was dead* means because no one [there] was not damned. This can be seen from the symbolism of *there was no house [where] no one was* as no one there was not and from the meaning of *dead* as damned (discussed in §§5407, 6119, 7494, 7871).

And he called Moses and Aaron by night symbolizes contact with truth 7955
from the Divine in that state, as the following shows: *He called* symbolizes presence and an inflow, as discussed in §§6177, 6840, 7390, 7451, 7721. Here it symbolizes contact, because the action is being attributed to people in a state of damnation, or of utter falsity-from-evil. They are not open to any inflow of truth or goodness on the inside, only on the outside, which is mere contact. *Moses* and *Aaron* represent truth from the Divine, as mentioned in §§6771, 6827. I describe it as truth from the Divine rather than divine truth because the text is talking about people in a state of damnation. And *by night* symbolizes a state of damnation, as discussed above in §§7851, 7870.

And said, "Rise, go out from the middle of my people," means that they 7956
should leave, as is self-evident.

Both you and the children of Israel means taking with them the truth 7957
[they had] from the Divine, and also truth leading to goodness, and truth coming from goodness, as the following shows: Moses represents truth from the Divine, as noted just above at §7955. And the *children of Israel* represent people of the spiritual church (noted many times), so they represent people focused on truth that leads to goodness and on truth that comes from goodness. What distinguishes a spiritual religion from a heavenly religion is the fact that the truth taught by faith leads people of a spiritual religion to the doing of good out of neighborly love. So they take truth to be the critical element. Truth is what gets them started, because it teaches them what to do. When they do it, that truth is called goodness. This goodness in turn, once they have been introduced into it, shows them what is true, and they again act on it. Clearly, then, it is all the same whether you speak of people in the spiritual church or of people who focus on truth that leads to goodness and on truth that comes from goodness.

Go serve Jehovah means that they were to worship the Lord. This can 7958
be seen from the symbolism of *serving* as worshiping. For the idea that where the Word mentions *Jehovah* it means the Lord, see §§1343, 1736, 2921, 3023, 3035, 5041, 5663, 6281, 6303, 6905.

According to what you have spoken means as they wished. This can be 7959
seen from the symbolism of *speaking* as the will, which is dealt with at §2626.

7960 *Take both your flocks and your herds* symbolizes inner and outer neighborly kindness. This can be seen from the symbolism of *flocks* as inner neighborly kindness and of *herds* as outer neighborly kindness, as discussed in §§2566, 5913, 6048.

7961 *As you have spoken* means as they wished, as just above at §7959.

7962 *And go* means that they were unquestionably to leave. This can be seen from the symbolism of *going* away as leaving. Since it is a repetition of the command to go, it means that they were unquestionably to leave.

7963 *And may you bless me, too* symbolizes a request for them to intervene. This is evident from the symbolism of *blessing* as intervening, because in this case it means a request to plead for him. On the point that pleading for Pharaoh means intervening, see §§7396, 7462.

7964 *And Egypt prevailed on the people, hurrying to send them away from the land* means that in their loathing and fear they urged them to leave. This is clear from the symbolism of *prevailing on the people, hurrying to send them away* as urging them to leave. Plainly loathing and fear are involved, because people devoted to utter falsity-from-evil loathe people devoted to truth from goodness so much that they cannot even bear the latter's presence. That is why people immersed in evil throw themselves down into hell to a depth that matches the nature and amount of their evil, so as to stay far away from goodness. It is not only loathing that motivates them but fear as well, since the presence of goodness tortures them.

7965 *Because [the Egyptians] said, "We are all dying,"* symbolizes hell for them as a result. This can be seen from the symbolism of *dying* as hell. For the spiritual meaning of death as hell, see §§5407, 6119.

7966 *And the people carried off their dough before it had been leavened* symbolizes a first state of truth-from-goodness containing no falsity, as the following shows: *Dough* symbolizes truth from goodness. Meal and flour, you see, symbolize truth; the dough made from them symbolizes truth from goodness; and the bread made from the dough symbolizes a loving goodness. Since bread symbolizes a loving goodness, the rest (the dough and the meal) symbolize forms of goodness and truth in their order. For the meaning of bread as a loving goodness, see §§276, 680, 2165, 2177, 3464, 3478, 3735, 3813, 4211, 4217, 4735, 4976, 5915. And *before it had been leavened* symbolizes something free of falsity. For the meaning of yeast as falsity, see above at §7906.

[2] You can see that it is a first state—the first after deliverance—because it says that the people carried off the dough, meaning they carried it off when they left. The second state is depicted in verse 39 below,

in the words "the dough that they had brought out of Egypt they cooked into unleavened cakes, because it had not been leavened." The symbolism there is that truth from goodness produced another round of goodness free of falsity.

These are the two states the Lord maintains in people of the spiritual church when they are devoted to goodness. In the first, they observe and think about truth from the viewpoint of the goodness in their will. In the second, from that marriage of goodness and truth they bring forth new truth, which they again turn into goodness by embracing it with their will and acting on it. The cycle repeats indefinitely. That is what comes forth and develops out of truth in people whose religion is spiritual. In the spiritual world the process is presented visually in the image of a tree with leaves and fruit. The leaves on the tree are truth; the fruit is goodness from truth; the seeds are goodness itself, from which everything else springs.

Their kneading troughs tied up in their clothes symbolizes pleasures ris- **7967**
ing out of positive desires, adhering to truth. This can be seen from the symbolism of *kneading troughs* as pleasures rising out of positive desires (mentioned at §7356), from that of being *tied up* as adhering, and from that of *clothes* as truth (discussed in §§1073, 2576, 4545, 4763, 5248, 5319, 5954, 6914, 6917).

I need to say what I mean by pleasures rising out of positive desires that adhere to truth. Any truth that penetrates a person's mind is bound up with some pleasure. Without pleasure, truth has no vitality. The pleasure bound up with the truth indicates the status of that truth in the person's mind. If the pleasure rises out of negative desires, the truth is ailing, but if the pleasure rises out of positive desires, the truth is in good shape. The angels with us constantly flow in with positive emotions, and when they do, they stir up the true ideas joined to those emotions; and the reverse. If truth is not bound up with the positive emotions, the angels labor in vain to stir up the thoughts and feelings in which faith and neighborly love consist.

This shows what is meant by pleasures rising out of positive desires and adhering to truth, symbolized by the *kneading troughs tied up in their clothes.*

On their shoulder means [adhering] with all their might. This can be **7968**
seen from the symbolism of a *shoulder* as all their might, which is discussed in §§1085, 4931–4937.

Exodus 12:35, 36. *And the children of Israel did according to the word of* **7969**
Moses and asked the Egyptians for vessels of silver and vessels of gold and for

clothes. And Jehovah gave favor to the people in the eyes of the Egyptians. And [the Egyptians] lent to them, and they robbed the Egyptians.

And the children of Israel did according to the word of Moses means that they obeyed divine truth. *And asked the Egyptians for vessels of silver and vessels of gold and for clothes* means that knowledge of truth and goodness was taken away from evil people in the church, to be awarded to good people in the church. *And Jehovah gave favor to the people in the eyes of the Egyptians* symbolizes the fear felt by the damned toward people in the spiritual church. *And [the Egyptians] lent to them* means that the knowledge was handed over. *And they robbed the Egyptians* means that people under damnation were stripped bare of that knowledge.

7970 There is no need to explain all this in detail, because it has already been explained twice, at verses 21, 22 of Exodus 3 (§§6914–6920) and at verses 2, 3 of the previous chapter (§§7769–7773).

7971 Exodus 12:37, 38, 39. *And the children of Israel traveled from Rameses to Succoth, something like six hundred thousand men on the march, besides children. And a multitudinous rabble also went up with them, and flocks and herds—a very weighty acquisition. And the dough that they had brought out of Egypt they cooked into unleavened cakes, because it had not been leavened, because they were driven out of Egypt and could not wait. And they had not even prepared provisions for themselves.*

And the children of Israel traveled from Rameses to Succoth symbolizes the first state after departure, and the nature of that state. *Something like six hundred thousand men on the march* symbolizes all religious truth and goodness taken together. *Besides children* symbolizes innocent goodness. *And a multitudinous rabble also* symbolizes nongenuine truth [and goodness]. *Went up with them* means alongside. *And flocks and herds—a very weighty acquisition,* symbolizes inner and outer goodness acquired in great abundance through truth. *And the dough that they had brought out of Egypt they cooked into unleavened cakes* means that truth from goodness produced another round of goodness that was free of falsity. *Because it had not been leavened* means because the truth from goodness had no falsity in it. *Because they were driven out of Egypt and could not wait* means because they were removed from people ruled by falsity from evil. *And they had not even prepared provisions for themselves* means that they had no other truth or goodness with them to nourish them.

7972 *And the children of Israel traveled from Rameses to Succoth* symbolizes the first state after departure, and the nature of that state. This can be seen from the symbolism of *traveling* as the pattern and customs of a life, as discussed in §§1293, 3335, 4882, 5493, 5605. The travels of the children of Israel reported in Exodus, then, are states of life and the changes that occur between the first and last of them. This journey from Rameses to Succoth symbolizes the first state and its nature, because all place-names, like all names of people, symbolize things of all kinds and their quality; see §§768, 1224, 1264, 1876, 1888, 3422, 4298, 4310, 4442, 5095, 6516.

Something like six hundred thousand men on the march symbolizes all religious truth and goodness taken together. This can be seen from the symbolism of the number *six hundred thousand* as everything that goes to make up faith, taken together. Six hundred thousand is a multiple of six and of twelve, and twelve symbolizes all aspects of faith and neighborly love (§§577, 2089, 2129 at the end, 2130 at the end, 3272, 3858, 3913). That is why Jacob's sons were twelve, why their descendants divided into twelve tribes, and why the Lord took twelve disciples: to represent all facets of faith and neighborly love. (About the tribes, see §§3858, 3862, 3926, 3939, 4060, 6335, 6337, 6640, 7836, 7891. About the disciples, 3354, 3488, 3858 at the end, 6397.) [2] Six hundred thousand has the same symbolism here because a larger or smaller number—a multiple or fraction—holds the same meaning as the simple numbers from which it comes (5291, 5335, 5708). This is obvious from the number twelve. Whether it is divided to produce six or multiplied to produce seventy-two or one hundred forty-four (twelve times twelve) or twelve thousand or one hundred forty-four thousand, it has the same symbolism. Take for instance the one hundred forty-four thousand in John: **7973**

> I heard the number of those sealed: *one hundred forty-four thousand* sealed from every tribe of Israel. *From each tribe twelve thousand.* (Revelation 7:4, 5, and following verses)

In these verses the children of Israel do not mean the children of Israel, the tribes do not mean tribes, a number does not mean a number. Instead they mean the kinds of things contained in the inner meaning, or all aspects of faith and neighborly love. Each tribe in particular therefore means one type or category, as explained at Genesis 29 and 30. [3] Likewise in the same author:

> Look! A Lamb standing on Mount Zion, *and with him, one hundred forty-four thousand having his Father's name* written on their foreheads. They were singing a new song before the throne, and no one could learn the song *except the one hundred forty-four thousand purchased from the earth.* They are the ones who follow the Lamb where he goes. *They were*

> *purchased from among humankind, firstfruits to God and to the Lamb.* (Revelation 14:1, 3, 4)

This description shows plainly that the one hundred forty-four thousand means people who are loving. It also shows that the number is actually a symbol for a state and its quality. It marks out the same territory as twelve, because it is the product of twelve thousand times twelve. [4] It is like the smaller number one hundred forty-four (twelve times twelve) in the same author:

> He measured the wall of the holy Jerusalem, as it came down from God out of heaven, at *one hundred forty-four cubits,* which is the measure of a human, that is, of an angel. (Revelation 21:2, 17)

The wall of the holy Jerusalem in a spiritual sense is not a wall but rather religious truth defending the church and all it stands for; see §6419. So it is described as having been one hundred forty-four cubits. This meaning is quite plain, because it says that the measure is the measure of a human, that is, of an angel. A human and an angel symbolize all the truth and all the goodness taught by faith. [5] The meaning is also plain from the *twelve* precious stones making up the wall's foundation and from the *twelve* gates, each of which was a pearl (Revelation 21:19, 20, 21). Precious stones symbolize faith's truth that comes from the goodness of neighborly love (§§643, 3720, 6426). The same thing is symbolized by a gate and by a pearl.

This demonstrates that a smaller or larger number has the same meaning as the simple number from which it arises. For the idea that all numbers in the Word have a symbolic meaning, see §§482, 487, 575, 647, 648, 755, 813, 1963, 1988, 2075, 2252, 3252, 4264, 4495, 4670, 5265, 6175.

[6] From this you can now see that the number of men leaving Egypt—six hundred thousand—has the same kind of symbolism.

Hardly anyone can believe this number has this symbolism, because it is a narrative detail. All narrative keeps the mind fixed steadily on the superficial meaning and distracts it from the deeper meaning. Still, the number does also have a symbolic meaning; in Scripture there is not even one small word, in fact, there is not one jot or tip of a letter that is not intrinsically holy because of enfolding within itself some sacred meaning. There is nothing sacred in mere history, as everyone can see.

7974 *Besides children* symbolizes innocent goodness. This is evident from the discussion in §§430, 1616, 2126, 2305, 3183, 3494, 4797, 5608 of the symbolism of a *child* as innocent goodness.

And a multitudinous rabble also symbolizes nongenuine [truth and] goodness. This can be seen from the symbolism of a *multitudinous rabble* as nongenuine [truth and] goodness. Since the children of Israel represent genuine goodness and truth in the spiritual church (§7957), the rabble accompanying them symbolizes truth and goodness that are not genuine. 7975

With people whose religion is spiritual, the way matters stand is that they possess genuine goodness and truth, and they possess nongenuine goodness and truth. This is because people whose religion is spiritual have no perception of goodness and truth. Instead what they acknowledge and believe to be good and true is what the teachings of their religion teach. That is why they know a lot of truth that is not genuine, with the consequence that they also have goodness that is not genuine—since goodness takes its character from truth. (On the point that the spiritual accept much truth that is not genuine, see §§2708, 2715, 2718, 2831, 2849, 2935, 2937, 3240, 3241, 3246, 3833, 4402, 4788, 5113, 6289, 6500, 6639, 6865, 6945, 7233; and that they therefore have goodness that is not pure, see §6427.) Nonetheless, the Lord maintains the most genuine possible goodness in them, using an inflow that comes by way of inner levels (§6499). Truth and goodness that are not genuine are then divided off and cast to the sides, and they are what is symbolized by the very multitudinous rabble.

[2] The rabble likewise symbolizes people who align with the church but are not part of it, such as non-Christians who live lives of obedience and of love shared with each other. They too lack genuine truth, because they do not have the Word. These people, and nongenuine truth itself, are also symbolized by the numerous crowd in John:

> I heard the number of those sealed: one hundred forty-four thousand sealed from every tribe of Israel. After these things, I looked, when there! a *numerous crowd that no one could count,* of every nation and of [all] tribes and peoples and tongues, standing before the throne and before the Lamb, dressed in white robes, with palms in their hands. (Revelation 7:4, 9)

Went up with them means alongside. This can be seen from the symbolism of *going up with them,* when it is talking about goodness and truth, as being alongside. Nongenuine truth and goodness is indeed divided off from genuine goodness and truth in a spiritual person, but it is not removed. It remains attached off to the side, where it was cast (§7975). 7976

The same applies to the Lord's church among non-Christians, who have nongenuine truth. In heaven, non-Christians similarly live alongside people who possess genuine truth and goodness.

7977 *And flocks and herds—a very weighty acquisition,* symbolizes inner and outer goodness acquired in great abundance through truth. This is established by the symbolism of a *flock* as inner goodness and from that of a herd as outer goodness, as discussed in §§2566, 5913, 6048, 7960. The fact that this goodness is acquired is symbolized by an *acquisition.* All goodness in people of a spiritual religion is gained through truth; without the truth taught by faith they do not know what spiritual truth or spiritual goodness is.

They do often know about truth on the plane of public life and of private morality and about the virtues associated with that truth, because these are consistent with a worldly perspective. So they even have a feel for this level of truth and goodness. Spiritual truth and the goodness associated with it, though, are not consistent with a worldly perspective and in fact depart radically from it in many respects, so people of a spiritual religion need to be taught about them.

The purpose of this digression is to show that all goodness in people of the spiritual church must be acquired through truth. The fact that *very weighty* means in great abundance is plain.

7978 *And the dough that they had brought out of Egypt they cooked into unleavened cakes* means that truth from goodness produced another round of goodness that was free of falsity. This can be seen from the symbolism of *cooking* as producing, when it applies to the truth-from-goodness symbolized by the dough; from that of *dough* as truth from goodness (discussed above at §7966); and from that of *unleavened cakes* as goodness free of falsity. For the symbolism of unleavened goods as something free of falsity, see §§2342, 7906.

This is the second state of truth-from-goodness experienced by the people upon their deliverance; see above at §§7966, 7972.

The reason *cakes* mean goodness is that these are cakes of bread, and in an inner sense bread is a loving goodness, as discussed in §§276, 680, 2165, 2177, 3464, 3478, 3735, 3813, 4211, 4217, 4735, 4976, 5915. Bread in the form of cakes is distinguished from bread in general by the fact that cakes of bread symbolize goodness born of love for one's neighbor and therefore spiritual goodness, whereas bread in general symbolizes goodness born of love for the Lord and therefore heavenly goodness. Spiritual goodness was symbolized by the minha offered and burned with a sacrifice on the altar, because the minha was cooked into cakes and wafers, as shown in Exodus 29:2, 3, 23, 24, 32; Leviticus 2:2 and following verses; 6:20, 21; Numbers 6:15, 19; 15:18, 19, 20, 21.

[2] The same thing was symbolized by the twelve loaves of showbread, which were also cooked as cakes. Moses has this to say about them:

> You shall take flour and *cook* it into *twelve cakes; one cake* shall be of two tenths [of an ephah]. And you shall place them in two rows, six in each row, on the clean table, before Jehovah. And you shall put pure frankincense on the row. And it shall serve as loaves for a memorial, a fire offering to Jehovah. (Leviticus 24:5, 6, 7, 8, 9)

This shows that the loaves symbolized something holy; otherwise such a procedure would never have been commanded. Since they symbolized something holy, they are also called "most holy" (Leviticus 24:9). These loaves symbolized goodness born of heavenly love, and the fact that they were cooked into cakes symbolized goodness born of spiritual love.

From this discussion and from comments in the sections cited above, it can be seen that the bread in the Holy Supper has the same meaning.

Because it had not been leavened means because the truth from goodness had no falsity in it. This can be seen from the symbolism of dough— **7979**
the thing being said not to have been leavened—as truth from goodness (discussed above at §7966) and from that of *not having been leavened* as being free of falsity (discussed in §§2342, 7906).

Because they were driven out of Egypt and could not wait means since **7980**
they were removed from people ruled by falsity from evil, as the following shows: *Being driven out* means being removed, because anyone who is driven out is removed; see above at §7964. *Egypt* symbolizes people devoted to falsity from evil, as mentioned before. And *not being able to wait* symbolizes the need to remove them.

And they had not even prepared provisions for themselves means that they **7981**
had no other truth or goodness with them to nourish them, that is, no other truth and goodness than that symbolized by the unleavened dough, which stands for truth-from-goodness containing no falsity (see §7966). This can be seen from the symbolism of *provisions* as nourishment by truth and goodness, mentioned in §§5490, 5953.

Exodus 12:40, 41, 42. *And the residence of the children of Israel during* **7982**
which they resided in Egypt [was] four hundred thirty years. And it happened

at the end of four hundred thirty years—[and] it happened on that same day—that all Jehovah's armies went out from the land of Egypt. It is a night of watchkeeping for Jehovah, to lead them out of the land of Egypt. This is the very night for Jehovah of watchkeeping for all the children of Israel throughout their generations.

And the residence of the children of Israel during which they resided in Egypt symbolizes the length of time the persecution lasted. *[Was] four hundred thirty years* symbolizes the nature and state of the persecution. *And it happened at the end of four hundred thirty years* symbolizes the time when the Lord came into the world and delivered them. *And it happened on that same day* means then. *That all Jehovah's armies went out from the land of Egypt* means that the people who were detained there despite their dedication to truth and goodness were released. *It is a night of watchkeeping for Jehovah* symbolizes the Lord's presence among people intent on truth and goodness and among people intent on evil and accordingly on utter falsity. *To lead them out of the land of Egypt* symbolizes deliverance from spiritual captivity. *This is the very night for Jehovah of watchkeeping* means that they were then withheld from everything false and evil. *For all the children of Israel throughout their generations* symbolizes people of the spiritual church, who have goodness-from-truth and truth-from-goodness in them.

7983 *And the residence of the children of Israel during which they resided in Egypt* symbolizes the length of time the persecution lasted. This can be seen from the symbolism of *residence* as a state of life, as discussed in §§1293, 3384, 3613, 4451, 6051. In this case it symbolizes a state of persecution, because that is the state of life currently under discussion and is the state of life symbolized by the four hundred thirty years to which these words refer.

7984 *[Was] four hundred thirty years* symbolizes the nature and state of the persecution, as the following shows: *Thirty* symbolizes a state that is complete in regard to remaining traces [of goodness and truth], because it is the product of three times ten. Three symbolizes a complete state (§§2788, 4495, 7715), and ten symbolizes a remnant (576, 1906, 2284). (A complete state will be defined below.) And *four hundred* is a symbol for the length of time spiritual devastation lasts (discussed in §§2959, 2966), so it symbolizes the union of goodness and truth (4341). (For the idea that all numbers symbolize inner qualities and states and that a multiple has the same symbolism as the factors going into it, see above at §7973.)

[2] Regarding the devastation symbolized by four hundred years, there are two kinds: a loss of evil and falsity, and a loss of goodness and truth. People who are being damned have their goodness and truth devastated, but people who are being saved have their evil and falsity devastated. This devastation is a stripping away.

The explanation so far has shown that in evil people who had been part of the church, everything good and true is laid waste, because the plagues in Egypt symbolized progressive levels of devastation. In good people, however, everything evil and false is laid waste. In them, evil and falsity are gradually detached—are cast to the sides—and goodness and truth are gathered and put at the center. This gathered store of goodness and truth is meant by a "remnant." When their state is complete in regard to this remnant, they are taken up to heaven. That is the state symbolized by the number thirty, and the devastation is symbolized by the number four hundred.

Persecution and trials are the means by which evil and falsity are laid waste and goodness and truth are instilled in good people. Through times of persecution and trial, falsity and evil are shoved to the side and goodness and truth are imparted, until the state is complete.

[3] Let me briefly define a complete state as well. Whether we are being damned or saved, we all have a certain capacity we can reach. Evil people, or people who are being damned, have a certain capacity for evil and falsity, while good people, or people being saved, have a certain capacity for goodness and truth. In the other life we each achieve our capacity, but some have a larger capacity, some have a smaller. We acquire our capacity in the world through our desires that come from love. The more we loved evil and therefore falsity [in the world], the larger a capacity for them we acquired. The more we loved goodness and therefore truth, the greater a capacity we have for them. In the next life, others can see plainly what the limits of our capacity are and how far we expanded them. We cannot exceed our capacity there, but we can and do fill it. People who have desired goodness and truth achieve their capacity for goodness and truth, and people who have desired evil and falsity achieve their capacity for evil and falsity. From this it is plain that our capacity is the ability we developed in the world to accept either evil and falsity or goodness and truth.

[4] This is the condition meant by a complete state, symbolized by the number thirty. The Lord depicts that state in the parable of the talents

(Matthew 25:14–30) and the parable of the minas (Luke 19:13–25), specifically in these closing words [from the parable] in Matthew:

> All who have something will be granted to overflow with it, but from those who do not have anything, even what they have will be taken from them. (Matthew 25:29)

And [from the parable] in Luke:

> To those standing by he said, "Take the mina from him and give it to the one who has ten minas." They said to him, "Lord, he has ten minas." I say to you that to everyone who has, something will be given, but from those who do not have anything, even what they have will be taken from them. (Luke 19:24, 25, 26)

The Lord also teaches elsewhere in the same author that everyone's measure gets filled:

> Give, and something will be given to you; good measure pressed down, shaken, and overflowing they will put into your lap. (Luke 6:38)

These remarks now show what is meant by a complete state.

7985 The text says that the residence of the children of Israel during which they resided in Egypt was four hundred thirty years and that at the end of four hundred thirty years, on that same day, all Jehovah's armies went out from the land of Egypt. In reality, though, the children of Israel lived there no more than half that time, or two hundred fifteen years, from the point at which Jacob went down into Egypt to the exodus of his descendants that is currently under discussion. This is quite clear from the chronological details given in Sacred Scripture. Moses was born to Amram, and Amram to Kohath, and Kohath to Levi; and Kohath went to Egypt at the same time as his father, Levi (Genesis 46:[6,] 11). Kohath lived one hundred thirty-three years (Exodus 6:18); Amram, who fathered Aaron and Moses, lived one hundred thirty-seven years (Exodus 6:20); and Moses was a man of eighty years when he stood before Pharaoh (Exodus 7:7). The text does not say how old Kohath was when Amram was born or how old Amram was when Moses was born, but clearly the total was not four hundred thirty years, since not even their full ages amount to four hundred thirty years, only to three hundred fifty. This can be seen if Kohath's lifetime of one hundred thirty-three is added to Amram's of one hundred thirty-seven, and this sum to Moses' eighty years when he stood before Pharaoh. It comes to even less if you add only the years between their births. It was two hundred fifteen years, as the chronology shows.

However, it was indeed four hundred thirty years from the point at which Abraham went down into Egypt to the point at which the children of Israel left it; on this too, see the chronological details. Clearly, then, this four hundred thirty years means the entire span of time starting with Abraham, not Jacob. The reason for specifying these years as the years when the children of Israel resided in Egypt has to do with the inner meaning. In the inner meaning, those years are a symbol for a complete state and for the duration of the spiritual devastation experienced by people who were part of the spiritual church and who were kept in the underground realm till the Lord's Coming, when they were rescued. On this subject, see §§6854, 6914, 7035, 7091, 7828, 7932.

And it happened at the end of four hundred thirty years symbolizes the 7986
time when the Lord came into the world and saved them, as the following shows: *Four hundred thirty years* is a symbol for a complete state and for the length of time devastation or persecution lasted for people of the spiritual church who were kept in the underground realm till the Lord's Coming, when they were delivered. (This symbolism is discussed directly above at §7985 and in §§6854, 6914, 7035, 7091, 7828, 7932.) *At the end* of those years consequently symbolizes the time when the Lord came into the world and saved them.

And it happened on that same day means then. This is clear from the 7987
symbolism of a *day* as a state, which is discussed in §§23, 487, 488, 493, 2788, 3462, 3785, 4850, 5672, 5962, 7680. *On that same* day, then, means in that state. So it means then, when the Lord came (symbolized by "at the end of four hundred thirty years") and people of the spiritual church were delivered (symbolized by "all Jehovah's armies went out from the land of Egypt").

That all Jehovah's armies went out from the land of Egypt means that 7988
the people who were detained there despite their dedication to truth and goodness were released, as the following shows: *Going out from the land of Egypt* means being released and delivered from persecution. (The idea that going out means being released is self-evident. See §7278 for the symbolism of the land of Egypt as persecution.) And *Jehovah's armies* symbolize truth and goodness as it exists in a spiritual religion, so they symbolize people dedicated to truth and goodness, as discussed in §§3448, 7236.

The meaning of *Jehovah's armies* as truth and goodness can be seen in Daniel:

> One horn went out from a small [horn] of the buck [of the goats] and grew immensely toward the south and toward the sunrise and toward the ornament [of Israel], and it grew *right to the armies of the heavens* and threw down to the ground *some of the army* and some of the stars and trampled them. In fact [the horn] exalted itself right *to the leader of the army.* And the *army was handed over, along with the perpetual offering, for transgression,* because it cast *truth* to the ground. Then I heard a holy one speaking: "How long are both the Holy Place and the *army* being given over for trampling?" He said to me, "Up till evening and morning two thousand three hundred times; then the Holy Place will be set right." (Daniel 8:9–14)

It is obvious here that the army means truth and goodness. After all, the passage says that some of the army and some of the stars were thrown down to the ground and then that *truth* was cast to the ground. It also says that the army was [given over] for trampling up till evening and morning, which means till the Lord's Coming.

[2] Since truth and goodness are the army of Jehovah, angels are called his army in 1 Kings:

> Micaiah the prophet said, "I saw Jehovah sitting on his throne, *and the entire army of the heavens standing next to him."* (1 Kings 22:19)

And in David:

> Bless Jehovah, *you angels of his,* powerful in strength. Bless Jehovah, *all you his armies,* his attendants. (Psalms 103:20, 21)

The angels are being called an army because of the truth and goodness in which they dwell. It is not only angels that were called Jehovah's army but also the lights in the sky, such as the sun, moon, and stars, because the sun symbolized a goodness based on love; the moon, a goodness based on faith; and the stars, a knowledge of what is good and true. The fact that these lights are called an army is plain in Genesis:

> The heavens and the earth were completed, and *all their armies.* (Genesis 2:1)

The armies here mean all the lights in the sky, but in an inner sense (where the subject is the process by which a person is created anew) they mean truth and goodness. [3] Likewise in David:

> Praise Jehovah, all you angels of his! *Praise him, all you armies of his!* Praise him, sun and moon! Praise him, all you shining stars! (Psalms 148:2, 3)

For the meaning of the sun as a goodness born of love, and of the moon as a goodness born of faith, see §§1529, 1530, 2441, 2495, 4060, 4696, 5377, 7083. For the meaning of the stars as a knowledge of what is good and true, §§1808, 2120, 2495, 2849, 4697.

[4] The reason the sun, moon, and stars symbolize goodness and truth is that in heaven the Lord is a sun to the heavenly inhabitants and a moon to the spiritual (§§1521, 1529, 1530, 1531, 3636, 3643, 4300, 4321 at the end, 5097, 7078, 7083, 7171, 7173). It is also because the angels' homes shine like stars, in accordance with these words in Daniel:

> Then those who understand will shine like the radiance of the expanse, and those who *cause many to be righteous* [will shine] *like stars* to eternity and forever. (Daniel 12:3)

[5] Since the name "Jehovah's army" is applied to angels on account of the truth and goodness they have, and to the sun, moon, and stars, and since everything true and good radiates from the Lord, the Word calls him *Jehovah Sabaoth,* or *Jehovah of Armies* (§3448). Another reason for the name is that he fights the hells on our behalf.

All this now shows what Jehovah's army means in an inner sense. The offspring of Jacob who left Egypt were not Jehovah's army but rather *represented* it. This is plain from their life in Egypt: They did not know Jehovah or even his name until it was told to Moses out of the bramble (Exodus 3:13, 14, 15, 16), and they were calf-worshipers just as much as the Egyptians were (as Exodus 32 suggests). The same thing is plain from their life in the wilderness, in that their very nature prevented them from being brought into the land of Canaan. So they were anything but the army of Jehovah.

It is a night of watchkeeping for Jehovah symbolizes the Lord's presence among people intent on truth and goodness and among people intent on evil and accordingly on utter falsity. This can be seen from the symbolism of *night* as a state of damnation (noted at §7851) and from that of *watchkeeping for Jehovah* as the Lord's presence and the protection it 7989 affords. The Lord's presence enlightens people governed by goodness and therefore by truth, and it blinds people governed by evil and therefore by falsity. The Lord's presence leads people who are going to be lifted to heaven out of damnation, because he withholds them from evil and keeps them on a good path, by a mighty force. And it leads people who are going to be cast down to hell *into* damnation, because evil besets them in proportion to the Lord's presence (§§7643, 7926). That is why this state and time is called a night of watchkeeping for Jehovah.

Later in Exodus the Lord's presence is depicted as a pillar of cloud by day and a pillar of fire by night to serve as a guide (Exodus 13:21). His presence both with people intent on goodness and truth and with people intent on evil and falsity is depicted in the positioning of the pillar between the camp of Israel and the camp of the Egyptians, and in the drowning of the Egyptians in the Suph Sea when Jehovah looked out from the pillar at the camp of the Egyptians (Exodus 14:19, 20, 24, 25, 26, 27).

7990 *To lead them out of the land of Egypt* symbolizes deliverance from spiritual captivity. This is clear from the symbolism of *leading out* as delivering and from that of the *land of Egypt* as a place where evil spirits persecuted them and consequently where they were in spiritual captivity (in keeping with information brought forward at §§6854, 6914, 7035, 7091, 7828, 7932, 7985).

People are said to be in spiritual captivity when goodness and truth are kept inwardly active in them by the Lord but evil and falsity are kept outwardly active in them by hell. Such a situation brings the outer self into conflict with the inner self. This is the state that takes hold of people undergoing persecution. The Lord, flowing in through their inner depths, is then fighting for them against an onslaught of evil and falsity from the hells. Under these circumstances they are essentially held captive, because as a result of the Lord's inflow they want to stay with what is good and true, but the onslaught from the hells makes this seem impossible.

The purpose of the struggle is to force the outer self to obey the inner and therefore to place the earthly plane under the control of the spiritual.

7991 *This is the very night for Jehovah of watchkeeping* means that they were then withheld from everything false and evil, as shown by the remarks just above at §7989 about the night of watchkeeping for Jehovah.

7992 *For all the children of Israel throughout their generations* symbolizes people of the spiritual church, who have goodness-from-truth and truth-from-goodness in them. This can be seen from the representation of the *children of Israel* as people of the spiritual church (mentioned often) and from the symbolism of *generations* as aspects of faith and neighborly love (discussed in §§2020, 2584, 6239) and so as people who have goodness-from-truth and truth-from-goodness in them. People of a spiritual religion are led by faith and its truth into neighborly love and its goodness, and once they have reached that point, they are led from goodness to truth. (People led from goodness to truth are the ones who constitute the inner part of the church, while those led by truth into goodness are the ones who constitute the outer part.)

Exodus 12:43–49. *And Jehovah said to Moses and Aaron, "This is the statute for Passover: any offspring of a foreigner shall not eat it. And any man's slave, anyone purchased with silver—you shall circumcise him; then he shall eat it. A temporary resident or a hired servant shall not eat it. In a single house it shall be eaten; you shall not take any of the flesh outside the house. And not a bone shall you break in it. The whole congregation of Israel shall perform it. And when an immigrant resides with you and would perform the Passover to Jehovah, every male of his shall be circumcised, and then he shall approach to perform it, and he will be as a native of the land. And anyone foreskinned shall not eat it. One law there shall be for the native and for the immigrant residing in your midst."* **7993**

And Jehovah said to Moses and Aaron symbolizes instructions delivered through divine truth. *This is the statute for Passover* symbolizes laws laying out the ordained plan for people delivered from damnation and persecution. *Any offspring of a foreigner shall not eat it* means that anyone without truth and goodness will be separate. *And any man's slave* symbolizes a person still [more] focused on the earthly plane. *Anyone purchased with silver* means who has any spiritual truth. *You shall circumcise him* symbolizes purification from unclean kinds of love. *Then he shall eat it* means joining in. *A temporary resident or a hired servant shall not eat it* means that people who do good from innate disposition alone or who do good for the sake of profit will not join in. *In a single house it shall be eaten* symbolizes ties formed among compatible kinds of goodness to create a single good quality together. *You shall not take any of the flesh outside the house* means that this good quality must not be mixed with someone else's. *And not a bone shall you break in it* means that truth in the form of knowledge must also be sound. *The whole congregation of Israel shall perform it* means that this law reflecting the ordained plan is for everyone with goodness from truth and truth from goodness. *And when an immigrant resides with you* symbolizes people who have learned about and accepted the truth and goodness characterizing the church. *And would perform the Passover to*

Jehovah means if they wish to join in. *Every male of his shall be circumcised* means that the truth they know must be rid of impure kinds of love. *And then he shall approach to perform it* means that then they will join in. *And he will be as a native of the land* means that they will be accepted just the same as people born into the truth and goodness of the church who have been purified of unclean types of love. *And anyone foreskinned shall not eat it* means that people with self-love and materialism cannot join in. *One law there shall be for the native and for the immigrant residing in your midst* means that people who have been taught about and then accepted the truth and goodness in the church and who live by it will be like those inside the church who had already been taught and who live a life compatible with all that faith and charity command.

7994 *And Jehovah said to Moses and Aaron* symbolizes instructions delivered through divine truth. This is clear from the symbolism of *Jehovah said,* in relation to religious statutes, as instructions, or being taught (discussed in §§7186, 7267, 7304, 7380, 7517, 7769, 7793, 7825), and from the representation of *Moses and Aaron* as divine truth, Moses representing inner truth and Aaron outer truth (discussed in §§7009, 7010, 7089, 7382).

7995 *This is the statute for Passover* symbolizes laws laying out the ordained plan for people delivered from damnation and persecution. This can be seen from the symbolism of a *statute* as something resulting from the ordained plan (treated of below) and from that of *Passover* as the Lord's presence and delivery from damnation (discussed in §§7093 at the end, 7867).

Regarding the results of the ordained plan, as symbolized by a statute: It needs to be realized that all the statutes commanded of the children of Israel were laws describing the ordained plan in its outward form but that they represented and symbolized laws describing the ordained plan in its inward form. The laws of that plan are truths originating in goodness. The totality of all the laws laying out the ordained plan is the same thing as divine truth radiating from the Lord's divine goodness. Clearly, then, the Lord's divinity itself as it exists in heaven is that plan. Divine goodness is its essence, and divine truth is its form.

7996 *Any offspring of a foreigner shall not eat it* means that anyone without truth and goodness will be separate, as the following shows: A *foreigner* symbolizes people outside the church who do not acknowledge any of the true ideas or good values of the faith (this being what the nations in the land of Canaan were like), as discussed in §§2049, 2115. So it symbolizes people lacking in truth and goodness. And *not eating it* means not communicating or bonding and therefore being separate.

The next few verses talk about the people who will and will not eat the Passover offering together. Passover was a supper that represented the formation of ties among the good in heaven. The statutes that follow tell who was capable of forming ties and who was not.

[2] In ancient times the purpose for which the church held banquets in general, whether at midday or in the evening, was for people to join and unite in love and to instruct each other on the subject of love and faith and accordingly on the subject of heaven (see §§3596, 3832, 5161). Those were the pleasures associated with communal meals in those days, and they were the reason for holding luncheons and dinners. So both the mind and the body were nourished at once and in correspondence with each other. This resulted in good health and long life for the people of that time, it resulted in understanding and wisdom, and it resulted in contact with heaven—sometimes open contact with angels.

But all depth vanishes over time and disappears into superficiality, and this happened to the intent behind banquets and shared meals as well. The point these days is not spiritual connection but worldly connections; the point is to increase one's wealth, improve one's standing, and have a good time. The body is nourished but the mind is not.

The Passover supper represented the way angels in the heavens are **7997**
grouped into communities according to goodness and truth; see above in §§7836, 7996. Because the meal represented this method of grouping, it was decreed not only that each household gather individually to eat on that occasion but also that no people join in other than those who represented the loving kind of bond that unites heavenly communities. So everyone else was kept apart. That included foreigners on one hand and temporary residents and hired servants on the other. Foreigners were kept out because they symbolized people lacking in the goodness and truth that characterize the church. Temporary residents and hired servants were kept out because they represented people who do what is good and true from innate disposition alone or for the sake of profit and boast about it. Neither the latter set of people nor the former can associate with angels in the heavens. During the first stage after their arrival in the other world, before they undergo a purging of anything good or true in them, they are allowed to wander around. When they come to a community of angels, they sense a reverent aura rising out of the truth that comes of innocent goodness, symbolized by the blood of the Passover lamb (§§7846, 7877). Then they cannot approach but rush away instead with fear and loathing.

7998 *And any man's slave* symbolizes a person still [more] focused on the earthly plane. This can be seen from the symbolism of a *slave* as the earthly plane (discussed in §§3019, 3020, 3191, 3192, 3204, 3206, 3209, 5305) and therefore as a person focused on the earthly plane. The earthly self is called a slave because it was created to minister to the spiritual self and obey it as a slave obeys a master.

7999 *Anyone purchased with silver* means who has any spiritual truth. This can be seen from the symbolism of a *purchase* as acquisition and adoption (discussed in §§4397, 4487, 5374, 5406, 5410, 5426) and from that of *silver* as truth (discussed in §§1551, 2954, 5658). In this case the silver symbolizes spiritual truth, because in an inner sense the slave who has been purchased is the earthly self, so that the master who buys the slave is the spiritual self.

The situation here cannot be seen by one who does not know how the spiritual plane "purchases"—acquires and adopts—the earthly plane. When we are being reborn, there is discord at first between our inner and outer planes, or between our spiritual and earthly planes. The spiritual level wants what heaven has to offer; the earthly level, what the world has to offer. However, the spiritual level constantly flows into the earthly level and induces it to agree. The means it uses is truth, and anything on the earthly plane that the spiritual plane appropriates is called something purchased with silver, meaning something acquired and adopted by means of truth.

8000 *You shall circumcise him* symbolizes purification from unclean kinds of love. This can be seen from the symbolism of being *circumcised* as purification from love for oneself and one's worldly advantages and therefore from unclean kinds of love, as dealt with in §§2039, 2056, 2632, 3412, 3413, 4462, 7045.

8001 *Then he shall eat it* means joining in. This can be seen from the symbolism of *eating*—eating the Passover lamb with everyone else—as communicating and uniting, which is treated of in §§2187, 5643. As noted above in §§7836, 7891, 7996, 7997, the Passover supper represented the way angels are grouped according to the goodness and truth they have. In their inner meaning the statutes about the foreigners, slaves, temporary residents, hired servants, and immigrants spoken of here tell who could join in and who could not. That is why eating symbolizes joining in, or grouping together, and why not eating means not joining in, or separating.

8002 *A temporary resident or a hired servant shall not eat it* means that people who do good from innate disposition alone or who do good for the sake of profit will not join in, as the following shows: A *temporary resident* symbolizes people who do good from innate disposition alone, as discussed below. A *hired servant* symbolizes people who do good for the sake of profit, as also discussed below. And *not eating it* means not joining in, as discussed directly above, at §8001.

The reason a *temporary resident* means people who do good from innate disposition alone is that temporary residents were either strangers or settlers from other lands who lived in the same house with a citizen of Israel or Judah. Living together means engaging in what is good together. As mentioned, though, they came from peoples outside the church, so the goodness being symbolized is not the kind found in the church; it is a kind found in what is not the church. This type of goodness is identified with the earthly level, because it comes by birth [and therefore] by heredity. Some people also display such goodness because of being sick or frail. This goodness is the kind I mean when I refer to the good done by the people symbolized by temporary residents.

[2] This goodness is totally different from the kind that characterizes the church, because conscience is formed in us through the latter—conscience being a plane into which angels flow and through which we can keep company with them. Earthly-level goodness, in contrast, does not lead to the formation of any plane for angels to act on. People with goodness of an earthly type do good in the dark, from blind instinct, not in the light of truth shed by heaven's inflow. In the other world they are therefore carried off like straw in the wind by anyone, bad or good, especially by a bad person who knows how to add some emotional coercion to a rational argument. Angels are then unable to rescue them, because angels operate by means of religious truth and goodness, flowing into a plane formed out of this truth and goodness deep inside a person.

From this you can see that people who do good solely from native disposition cannot associate with angels. To read about them and their lot in the other life, see §§3469, 3470, 3518, 4988, 4992, 5032, 6208, 7197.

[3] The fact that temporary residents are people staying not in their own land or house but someone else's can be seen in Moses:

> The land shall not be sold permanently, because the land is mine, but instead you shall be *immigrants* and *temporary residents* with me. (Leviticus 25:23)

In David:

> Hear my prayers, Jehovah; at my tears do not be silent; because *I am an immigrant with you, a temporary resident* like all my ancestors. (Psalms 39:12)

And in Genesis:

> Abraham said to the sons of Heth, "An *immigrant* and *temporary resident* I am with you; give me the possession of a grave." (Genesis 23:4)

An immigrant too means a stranger or settler from another land, just as much as a temporary resident does, but an immigrant symbolizes people who were learning and accepting the truth taught by the church. Temporary residents symbolize people who refused to learn because they refused to accept.

[4] As for *hired servants,* they were people who worked for a wage. They were servants, not slaves. (For evidence that these were the people called hired servants, see Leviticus 19:13; 25:4, 5, 6; Deuteronomy 24:14, 15.) As hired servants were wage earners, in an inner sense they mean people who do good for gain in this world. In an even deeper sense they mean people who do good for the sake of a reward in the other life and consequently who want to earn credit by doing good deeds.

[5] People who do good just to gain something from it in the world cannot possibly associate with angels, because their goal is the world, or wealth and prestige, rather than heaven, or the prosperity and happiness of their souls. The purpose is what determines one's actions and gives those actions their quality.

Concerning people who do good for the sake of profit alone the Lord says this in John:

> I am the good shepherd; the good shepherd lays down his soul for the sheep. But the *hired servant* and one who is not a shepherd, whose own the sheep are not, sees the wolf coming and abandons the sheep and flees, and the wolf seizes the sheep and scatters them, but the *hired servant* flees because of being a *hired servant.* (John 10:11, 12, 13)

And in Jeremiah:

> A very beautiful heifer is Egypt; destruction comes from the north. *Its hired servants are like calves of the fattening stall,* for indeed they have turned, they have fled together, they have not made a stand, because the day of their disaster has come upon them. (Jeremiah 46:20, 21)

[6] Temporary residents and hired servants were not to join in on sacred ceremonies with people who were part of the church, says Moses:

> *No foreigner* shall eat what is holy; neither a *temporary resident* living with a priest nor a *hired servant* shall eat what is holy. (Leviticus 22:10)

He also says that slaves whose service was to be perpetual were to be bought from among the offspring of temporary residents:

> A male slave and a female slave you shall buy from the nations that are around you. And also *from the offspring of temporary residents* staying as immigrants with you—from among them you shall buy, and from their clans that are with you (even if they have given birth in your land), so that they become your possession and you bequeath them to your children after you to inherit as a possession; to eternity you shall be their masters. (Leviticus 25:44, 45, 46)

The offspring of temporary residents symbolize knowledge resulting from earthly light alone. Spiritual truth must be their master, which is symbolized by the fact that slaves from among the offspring of temporary residents were bought as a lasting possession.

[7] As for people who do good to earn a reward in the other life (the other group symbolized by hired servants), they differ from the people I have just been describing. Unlike the latter, they have a life of happiness in heaven as their goal, but this goal directs their divine worship away from the Lord, turning it toward themselves. They wish well to themselves alone, then, not to others except to the extent that those others wish well to them. So self-love rather than love for their neighbor permeates everything about them, which means that they lack genuine charity.

What is more, they cannot form ties with angels, because angels loathe any mention or notion of reward or repayment.

The Lord teaches in Luke that we are to do good without looking for a reward:

> *Love your enemies,* and *do good* and lend, *not hoping for anything out of it;* then your reward will be ample, and you will be children of the Highest One. (Luke 6:32–35)

He also teaches this in Luke 14:12, 13, 14.

To learn what self-righteous goodness is like, see §§1110, 1111, 1774, 1835, 1877, 2027, 2273, 2371, 2380, 3816, 4007 at the end, 4174, 4943, 6388, 6389, 6390, 6392, 6393, 6478.

[8] The reason the Lord so often says that people who do good are going to reap a reward in heaven (as he does in Matthew 5:11, 12; 6:1, 2, 16; 10:41, 42; 20:1–16; Mark 9:41; Luke 6:23, 35; 14:14; John 4:36) is that until we have been reborn, we cannot help thinking about a reward. When we have been reborn, things change. Then we chafe if anyone thinks we are

helping our neighbor for the sake of a reward, because what makes us feel pleased and blessed is helping someone, not being repaid. For the idea that a reward in an inner sense is the pleasure afforded by feelings of neighborly love, see §§3816, 3956, 6388, 6478.

8003 *In a single house it shall be eaten* symbolizes ties formed among compatible kinds of goodness to create a single good quality [together]. This can be seen from the fact that the Passover supper represented the ties that bind angels into communities in heaven and that each *house* of the children of Israel represented some individual community; see §§7836, 7891, 7996, 7997. Angelic communities are all distinguished from each other by their good qualities—in general, in particular, and individually (§§3241, 4625). The angels who are brought together are those with a similar kind of goodness.

They create a single good quality because no united whole derives its existence from a single component, only from a large number of them. From the many—of various kinds but compatible—arises a form. Forms are unified by their harmony, and in heaven, by their spiritual harmony, which is the harmony exhibited by good qualities of a loving kind; see §§3241, 3267, 3744, 3745, 3746, 3986, 4005, 4149, 5598, 7236, 7833, 7836.

From this you can see that *in a single house it shall be eaten* symbolizes ties formed among compatible kinds of goodness to create a single good quality together. For the meaning of *eating* (eating the Passover) as coming together in a group, or joining in, see above at §8001.

8004 *You shall not take any of the flesh outside the house* means that this good quality must not be mixed with someone else's, as the following shows: *Taking it outside the house* means giving it to someone else to eat and therefore symbolizes mixing it with some other type of goodness than the kind in one's own community. And *flesh* symbolizes goodness, as discussed in §§6968, 7850.

Heaven's communities are divided up according to the functions of all the limbs, viscera, and organs of the body, as was shown at the end of many chapters. The function of each limb and organ relates correspondentially to a specific type of goodness, distinct from another type. It is clear, then, that there are many kinds of goodness and that they must never be mixed together if they are to give rise to distinct forms that will come together to make up the utterly perfect form of heaven. If they were mixed together, the differences would disappear. That is what *you shall not take any of the flesh outside the house* symbolizes.

And not a bone shall you break in it means that truth in the form of knowledge must also be sound. This can be seen from the symbolism of a *bone* as the outermost plane, on which inner planes come to rest as their foundation and which serves as a support to keep inner levels from fragmenting. Knowledge serves as this kind of outermost plane in the spiritual realm, because in accordance with the divine design all spiritual truth and goodness flow down to lower levels, finally coming to rest in knowledge, where they make themselves visible to us. Obviously, *you shall not break* it means that it must be sound. **8005**

Knowledge can be called sound when it allows in only such truth as harmonizes with the goodness related to it (knowledge being a general container for truth).

Besides, knowledge resembles bones in the human body. If the bones are not sound or are not in good order (when they are dislocated, for instance, or are crooked), it changes the shape of the body, which affects the way the body moves.

Truths in the form of knowledge are doctrinal teachings.

The whole congregation of Israel shall perform it means that this law reflecting the ordained plan is for everyone with goodness from truth and truth from goodness. This can be seen from the symbolism of the *congregation of Israel* as all truth and goodness in their entirety (§7830). Because the congregation of Israel symbolizes this, it symbolizes people with truth that leads to goodness and with goodness that leads to truth (§7957) and therefore people of the spiritual church. **8006**

The reason they were all to perform the Passover offering was to represent the deliverance of people in the spiritual church who were kept in the underground realm until the Lord's Coming (§§6854, 6914, 7091 at the end, 7828, 7932). By eating it in a single house they were to represent the grouping of angels into communities in heaven (§§7836, 7996, 7997), so since the whole congregation of Israel was to perform it, they were to represent the whole of heaven.

In those days the church did not exist anywhere. There was only a representation of a church, for which Abraham's descendants through Jacob were chosen. The representational practices of the church enabled communication with heaven and through heaven with the Lord. This was why that nation was charged to keep all the statutes and laws with strict fidelity. Especially important were the statutes for Passover, to the point where anyone who was clean but did not perform the Passover was to be cut off (Numbers 9:13).

8007 *And when an immigrant resides with you* symbolizes people who have learned about and accepted the truth and goodness characterizing the church. This can be seen from the symbolism of an *immigrant* as people who were being taught and who were accepting the church's statutes and laws, as discussed in §§2025, 4444, 7908. The text says *when one resides with you* because residing as an immigrant symbolizes learning and living (§§1463, 3672). So the immigrants residing with them symbolize people who were not only learning about and accepting the truth and goodness characterizing the church but were also living out what they had learned.

8008 *And would perform the Passover to Jehovah* means if they wish to join in. This can be seen from the symbolism of *performing the Passover to Jehovah,* or eating it, as joining in, which is discussed at §8001.

8009 *Every male of his shall be circumcised* means that the truth they know must be rid of impure kinds of love. This can be seen from the symbolism of *being circumcised* as being purified or rid of impure kinds of love (dealt with in §§2039, 2056, 2632, 3412, 3413, 4462, 7045) and from that of a *male* as religious truth (dealt with in §§749, 2046, 4005, 7838).

8010 *And [then] he shall approach to perform it* means that then they will join in, as above at §8008.

8011 *And he will be as a native of the land* means that they will be welcome just the same as people born into the truth and goodness of the church who have been purified of unclean types of love. This can be seen from the symbolism of a *native of the land* as someone born within the church who is devoted to the truth and goodness it champions and so as someone purified of unclean types of love. The term is "native of the *land*" because the land symbolizes the church. For the idea that "the land" in the Word means the church, see §§566, 662, 1066, 1068, 1262, 1413, 1607, 1733, 1850, 2117, 2118, 2571, 2928, 3355, 4447, 4535, 5577. The land means the church because in the Word "the land" refers to the land of Canaan, and the land of Canaan symbolizes the Lord's kingdom and the church (§§1413, 1437, 1585, 1607, 1866, 3038, 3481, 3686, 3705, 4116, 4240, 4447, 4454, 4516, 4517, 5136, 5757, 6516).

Whenever a land is mentioned in the Word, angels take it to mean not that land but the nation there, and taking it to mean the nation, they take it to mean the spiritual character of that nation. That is, they take it to mean the kind of religious attributes that nation displays. It is well known that the mention of a land brings up the idea of that nation's character, because this is what happens among people on earth too. But it happens even more among angels, who have a spiritual way of thinking about everything earthly.

And anyone foreskinned shall not eat it means that people with self-love and materialism cannot join in. This is evident from the symbolism of the *foreskinned,* or uncircumcised, as people with self-love and materialism (discussed in §§2056, 3412, 3413, 7045) and from that of *eating* (the Passover) as joining in, as above at §8001. **8012**

One law there shall be for the native and for the immigrant residing in your midst means that people who have been taught about and then accepted the truth and goodness of the church and who live by it will be like those inside the church who had already been taught and who live a life compatible with all that faith and charity command. This can be seen from the following: *One law there shall be* symbolizes impartial justice and therefore means that one person will be like another. The *native* symbolizes people born into the church who commit to the truth and goodness it champions, in both their theology and their life, as mentioned just above at §8011. And an *immigrant residing in your midst* symbolizes someone who learns about and accepts the truth and goodness characterizing the church and lives by it, as also mentioned above, at §8007. **8013**

[2] I speak of the commandments of *faith* and *charity* because of the difference between the two. Before rebirth we live by the commandments of faith, but afterward we live by the commandments of charity. Before rebirth none of us knows about charity from experiencing it, only from learning about it. The precepts we have been taught, which are called the commandments of faith, are what we then live by. After rebirth, though, we know what charity is from experiencing it, because we then love our neighbor and wish our neighbor well with all our heart. We also live then by a law internalized by us, because we act on a feeling of neighborly love. This state is radically different from the previous one. People in the first state are in the dark regarding religious truth and goodness, but people in the later state have relative clarity. The latter see the truth and confirm it in an enlightened way, whereas the former do it not from enlightenment but from the conviction that what their religion teaches is true. Since they do not see it in an enlightened way, they can just as easily confirm falsity as truth, and once they have confirmed something, they view it as absolutely true.

These remarks show what living by the commandments of faith means and what living by the commandments of charity means.

[3] Concerning immigrants: A number of times in the Word it was commanded that no distinction be drawn between natives of the land and the immigrants residing with them. The reason for this is that people outside the church—from among whom the immigrants come—are as likely to go to heaven as people inside the church, once they have learned and accepted the truth taught by the faith. (On non-Christians in the other world, see §§932, 1032, 1059, 2049, 2284, 2589–2604, 2861, 2863, 3263, 4190, 4197.) That is why it was commanded that the same rules apply to the native and the immigrant, as in Moses:

> *For if there resides with you an immigrant* who makes a fire offering for a restful smell to Jehovah—as you do it, so he shall do it; in regard to the congregation, *one statute there shall be for you and for the resident immigrant,* an eternal statute throughout your generations. *As you are, so shall the immigrant be before Jehovah. One law and one judgment shall there be for you and for the immigrant residing with you.* (Numbers 15:14, 15, 16)

In the same author:

> *The immigrant residing with you shall be to you as the native-born of you.* (Leviticus 19:34)

In the same author:

> One judgment there shall be for you; *as for the immigrant, so for the native shall it be.* (Leviticus 24:22)

In the same author:

> *When an immigrant resides with you,* he shall perform the Passover to Jehovah according to the statute of Passover; and according to its statutes, so he shall perform it. *One statute there shall be for you, both for the immigrant and for the native.* (Numbers 9:14)

8014 Exodus 12:50, 51. *And all the children of Israel did as Jehovah had commanded Moses and Aaron; that is what they did. And it happened on that same day that Jehovah led the children of Israel out of the land of Egypt according to their armies.*

And all the children of Israel did as Jehovah had commanded Moses and Aaron symbolizes an act of obedience to divine truth. *That is what they did* symbolizes an act of the will. *And it happened on that same day* symbolizes a state in which the Lord is present. *That Jehovah led the children of Israel out of the land of Egypt* means that the Lord delivered from damnation people intent on goodness from truth and truth from goodness. *According to their armies* means as distinguished from each other according to the quality that truth lent to their goodness.

And all the children of Israel did as Jehovah had commanded Moses and 8015
Aaron symbolizes an act of obedience to divine truth. This can be seen from the comments above at §7944, where similar words appear.

That is what they did symbolizes an act of the will. This can be seen 8016
from the symbolism of *doing,* when the word is repeated, as an act of the will, as above at §7945.

And it happened on that same day symbolizes a state in which the Lord 8017
is present. This can be seen from the symbolism of a *day* as a time and a state, as discussed in §§23, 487, 488, 493, 893, 2788, 3462, 3785, 4850, 7680. The reason it is a state in which the Lord is present is that the day was Passover, which symbolizes the Lord's presence and the deliverance of people in the spiritual church from spiritual captivity and damnation (§7867). The fact that deliverance happened at the same time is symbolized by the rest of the verse: "That day Jehovah led the children of Israel out of the land of Egypt according to their armies." It was the day after Passover, as can be seen in Moses:

> They set out from Egypt on the fifteenth day of the first month, the day after Passover, in the eyes of all the Egyptians—the Egyptians being then engaged in burying the firstborn who had been killed. (Numbers 33:3, 4)

On the point that the Lord's presence delivers from damnation people who focus on goodness, and leads *into* damnation people who focus on evil, see §§7926, 7989.

That Jehovah led the children of Israel out of the land of Egypt means 8018
that the Lord delivered from damnation people intent on goodness from truth and truth from goodness. This is established by the symbolism of *leading out* as delivering, by the representation of the *children of Israel* as people of the spiritual church, or what is the same, people intent on goodness from truth and truth from goodness (noted above at §§7957, 8006), and by the symbolism of the *land of Egypt* as damnation. The land of Egypt symbolizes damnation here because the state of the Egyptians at this point has that symbolism (§§7766, 7778). For the idea that the Lord delivered from damnation people of the spiritual church, or people with goodness from truth and truth from goodness, see §§6854, 6914, 7091 at the end, 7828, 7932.

[2] The fact that the Lord delivered them when he rose again is symbolized by his descent to the lower regions. It was revealed in the raising of the dead from their tombs, as described in Matthew:

> And the tombs opened and many bodies of sleeping saints rose, and leaving their tombs after his resurrection, they entered the holy city and appeared to many. (Matthew 27:52, 53)

The departure of the dead from their tombs, entry into the holy city, and public appearance took place to serve as testimony that the Lord had delivered the people held till then in spiritual captivity and had taken them to heaven. (On an inner level, the holy city symbolizes heaven. That is why Jerusalem is called holy. In reality it was not holy but profane, since its people inflicted such cruel treatment on the Lord himself, who was represented in all the rituals of their religion and described in their Word and was therefore the God of their religion.)

[3] This passage in Daniel has a similar symbolism:

> In that time your people will be rescued—everyone then found written in the book. In the end many of those sleeping in the dust of the earth will wake up: some to eternal life but the rest to reproaches, to eternal disgrace. (Daniel 12:1, 2)

So does this passage in Ezekiel:

> Prophesy and say, "This is what the Lord Jehovih has said: 'Watch! I am going to open your graves and will make you come up out of your graves, my people, and bring you up onto the land of Israel, so that you may know that I am Jehovah, when I open your graves and make you come up out of your graves, my people, and I will put my spirit in you so that you may live and will place you on your land, so that you may know that I, Jehovah, have spoken and done it,' says Jehovah." (Ezekiel 37:12, 13, 14)

The land of Israel, or of Canaan, means heaven (§8011). This prophetic passage depicts a person's re-creation, or rebirth, and the way the Lord brings people of the spiritual church to life.

8019 *According to their armies* means as distinguished from each other according to the quality that truth lent to their goodness. This can be seen from the symbolism of *armies* as goodness and truth, discussed above at §7988. *According to* their armies means that the people the children of Israel represented were distinguished by the quality that truth lent to their goodness. (For the idea that different kinds of goodness are the standard for dividing up all the inhabitants of the other world and creating bonds among them, see §§7833, 7836, 8003.)

I speak of the quality lent to goodness by truth as the standard because all goodness takes its character from truth and is differentiated by it (§§3804, 4149, 6916).

The statutes and laws about the eating of the Passover lamb laid down in this chapter make it quite plain that secrets of heaven dwell hidden in every detail. Without knowledge gleaned from the inner meaning, one can learn only about the bare ritual in its superficial form, not about anything heavenly, let alone divine. For instance, one cannot see why the Passover animal was to be either a lamb or a kid, why it was to be a male and the son of a year, why it was to be slaughtered on the fourteenth day of the month, why its blood was to be spattered on the doorposts and lintel, why it was to be eaten roasted with fire, with unleavened loaves on bitter herbs, and none of it raw or cooked in water, why it was to be roasted with its head atop its legs and atop its middle, why none of it was to be left till morning and the leftover was to be burned with fire, why the people were to eat unleavened loaves seven days and those eating yeast bread were to be cut off, why a foreigner and temporary resident and hired servant were not to eat it but a man's slave (anyone purchased with silver) and an immigrant were, if they had been circumcised, why it was to be eaten in a single house and none of the flesh was to be taken outside the house, and why not a bone in it was to be broken. If one is not to be entirely ignorant of the meaning enfolded in these and many other requirements, and of the reason they were commanded, one needs to know the laws describing the ordained plan for the spiritual world to which these requirements correspond. One also needs to know from the inner meaning what every detail symbolizes in that world, or heaven. Most of all one needs to believe it all holds spiritual content. If something spiritual did not lie within each and every word, then when we read the Word, the angels with us would understand little or nothing in it, because everything the Word describes in an earthly manner angels understand in a spiritual way. 8020

The Spirits and Inhabitants of Jupiter (Continued)

ONE of the spirits of Jupiter whom I described earlier [§7803] as striking terror in people simply by approaching came up to my left side 8021 below my elbow. He talked from there, but his speech had a buzz to it. The words were not terribly distinct or separate, either, so it took quite a while for me to gather the sense. While speaking he was also causing a feeling of terror.

"This is how we do it on our planet," he said. "Before our angels visit anyone, we are sent ahead to prepare the person this way. Welcome our angels kindly yourself, when they come," he warned.

"It is not up to me," I was allowed to answer. "I take everyone just as they are."

8022 Then angels from that planet came, and I could tell from the way they talked to me that they were entirely different from the angels of our planet. Their speech was not verbal speech but thought-speech, which diffused itself throughout my inner reaches. From there it also flowed into my face, so that my face mirrored it perfectly, starting with my lips and continuing out to the edges in every direction. The thoughts that they used as words came in individual units, but the divisions between them were very slight. "That is how we talk to fellow inhabitants of our planet," they said. "There too we have a facial speech that starts at the lips."

8023 Next they spoke to me in thoughts that were even less clearly divided up, so that hardly any gap was perceptible. To me it resembled the meaning words hold for people who pay attention to the sense alone, in isolation from the words. This method of speech was more intelligible to me than the first kind, and also richer.

As before, it had an effect on my face, but the effect, like the speech, was more continuous. It did not start with my lips, as it had earlier, but with my eyes.

"This too is how we speak with fellow inhabitants of our planet," they said, "but only with those who understand and perceive things more deeply than the others do."

8024 Afterward they started talking in a still smoother, fuller way, and then my face was not able to keep up matching its movement to their words. However, I felt their speech act on my brain and sensed it moving my brain in a similar fashion.

8025 Last of all they talked in such a way that their speech reached only the deeper part of my intellect. It poured from them like a stream of highly rarefied air. The inflow itself I perceived but not the individual details. They said that there are also people on their planet to whom they speak this way and that these are the ones taken right to heaven after they die.

These types of speech acted like fluids of different kinds. The first was like liquid water, the second like a thinner fluid, the third like the air [at sea level], and the fourth like the thinner air [at high altitude]. 8026

The spirit at my left side that I mentioned above [§8021] would occasionally interject a remark, usually to warn me to control my behavior with the angels from their planet. This was because there were spirits from our planet who would bring up things that displeased them. He added that he did not understand what the angels were saying until later, after he moved up to my left ear. At that point his speech did not buzz the way it had before but was instead like the speech of other spirits. 8027

This experience showed how things are supposed to work in heaven and therefore in the earthly realm. According to the ordained plan, a spirit is sent ahead to prepare the way when angels are about to visit. The spirit strikes fear in people, warning them to welcome the angels kindly, and interrupts their speech. The spirit does not understand at first what the angels are saying but does understand later when brought into a better state. In short, the spirit is always present, preparing people's minds and trying to head off any unbecoming behavior. 8028

The thought of John the Baptist occurred to me in this connection. It was in accordance with heaven's ordained plan that he was sent ahead to announce the Lord's Coming and prepare the way for the Lord to be received properly, in keeping with what is said in Matthew 3:3; Luke 1:17; 3:4; John 1:23.

From previous remarks in several places about our state after death, it can be seen that few of us go right to heaven when we arrive in the next life. Instead we spend some time below heaven being wiped clean of the taints left by earthly and bodily types of love, brought with us from the world. This prepares and enables us to associate with angels. The same thing happens with the people of all planets; after their departure they first find themselves among spirits below heaven. Later, when they have been prepared, they become angels. On one occasion, I was allowed to watch as spirits from Jupiter became angels. I saw horses that appeared to be alight with fire, which carried them off, as Elijah was carried off. Horses alight with fire symbolize an enlightened intellect. For the symbolism of horses in the Word as the intellect, see §§2760, 2761, 2762, 3217, 5321, 6125, 6534, and for the symbolism of the fiery horses and fiery chariots that carried Elijah off as an understanding of the inner depths of the Word, see §2762. 8029

8030 This heaven of angels to which the inhabitants are carried off is the first heaven, the lowest of three. It appears to the right of their planet, completely separate from the first or lowest heaven of the angels from our own planet.

The inhabitants of their first heaven are seen wearing sky blue studded with tiny golden stars. They consider this blue to be the perfect color for heaven. Back on their planet, when they are looking at the starry sky, they call it the dwelling place of angels, so they love the blue.

8031 The spirits of that planet are totally opposed to keeping company with the spirits of our planet, because they differ in disposition and manners. They say the spirits of our planet are wily, are quick to plot evil and clever at doing so, know and think little about goodness, and unlike them do not acknowledge the one Lord.

In addition, spirits from the planet Jupiter are much wiser than spirits from our planet. They say we talk a lot and think little and therefore cannot perceive much at a deep level, not even what is good. From this the spirits of Jupiter conclude that people on our planet are shallow creatures.

8032 There will be more on the spirits and inhabitants of Jupiter at the end of the next chapter [§§8111–8119].

Exodus 13

Teachings on Neighborly Love

NOW I need to say what neighborly love and faith are in a person. 8033
Neighborly love is an inner desire that consists in this: that we sincerely want to do good to our neighbor, that this is our highest pleasure, and that we want to do it without being repaid.

Faith is an inner desire that consists in this: that we sincerely want to 8034
know what is true and good, not for the sake of theology as our ultimate goal but rather for the sake of our life.

The desire that is faith comes together with the desire that is neighborly love in this: that we want to behave according to the truth and therefore to actually *do* the truth [John 3:21].

People genuinely moved by neighborly love and faith believe that 8035
they have no goodwill on their own and understand nothing true on their own, but that a will for what is good and an understanding of what is true come from the Lord.

This is what neighborly love is, then, and this is what faith is. People 8036
who possess them have the Lord's kingdom and heaven inside them. The church also exists in them. They are people whom the Lord has regenerated and who have received a new will and a new intellect from him.

People who love themselves or their own worldly advantages and 8037
have this as their goal cannot possibly experience charity and faith. People devoted to these two kinds of love do not even know what charity and faith are. They simply cannot grasp that wanting to do good to our neighbor without repayment is heaven in us, or that this desire contains happiness as great as the angels' happiness, which is indescribable. They believe that if they were deprived of the joy they gain from the glory of high position and wealth, they would no longer have any joy at all, when in reality that is the starting point for heavenly joy, which is infinitely superior.

Exodus 13

1. And Jehovah spoke to Moses, saying,

2. "Consecrate to me [every] firstborn, that which opens every womb among the children of Israel, among humans and among animals. It is mine."

3. And Moses said to the people, "Remember this day, on which you went out of Egypt, out of the house of slaves, because with strength of hand Jehovah brought you out from here. And yeast bread shall not be eaten.

4. Today you are going out, in the month of Abib.

5. And it will happen when Jehovah brings you into the land of the Canaanite and the Hittite and the Amorite and the Hivite and the Jebusite—which he swore to your fathers to give you, a land flowing with milk and honey—that you shall observe this service in this month.

6. Seven days you shall eat unleavened loaves, and on the seventh day, a feast to Jehovah.

7. Unleavened loaves shall be eaten the seven days, and yeast bread shall not be seen with you, and yeast shall not be seen with you within your whole border.

8. And you shall tell your son on that day, saying, 'Because of this, [which] Jehovah did for me in my going out of Egypt.'

9. And it will serve you as a sign on your hand and as a reminder between your eyes, so that the law of Jehovah may be in your mouth; because with a strong hand Jehovah brought you out of Egypt.

10. And you shall keep this statute at the set time from year to year.

11. And it shall happen when Jehovah brings you into the land of the Canaanite (as he swore to you and to your fathers) and gives it to you,

12. that you shall hand everything that opens the womb over to Jehovah, and every offspring of an animal that opens [the womb]—the males that you will have—to Jehovah.

13. And everything that opens [the womb] of a donkey you shall redeem with a member of the flock, and if you do not redeem it, you shall break its neck. And every firstborn of a human among your sons you shall redeem.

14. And it will happen that your son will ask you tomorrow, saying, 'What is this?' And you are to say to him, 'With strength of hand Jehovah brought us out of Egypt, out of the house of slaves,

15. and it happened that Pharaoh hardened himself against sending us away, and Jehovah killed every firstborn in the land of Egypt, from the firstborn of a human to the firstborn of an animal; therefore I sacrifice to Jehovah everything that opens the womb (the males), and every firstborn of my sons I redeem.'

16. And it will serve as a sign on your hand and for brow pieces between your eyes, because with strength of hand Jehovah brought us out of Egypt."

17. And it happened in Pharaoh's sending the people away that God did not lead them by way of the land of the Philistines, although it was nearby; because God said, "Maybe the people will have regrets when they see war and will return to Egypt."

18. And God led the people around by way of the wilderness to the Suph Sea. And the children of Israel went up armed from the land of Egypt.

19. And Moses took Joseph's bones with him, because [Joseph] had put the children of Israel under a solemn oath, saying, "God will unfailingly visit you, and you must bring my bones up from this place with you."

20. And they traveled from Succoth and camped in Etham, on the edge of the wilderness.

21. And Jehovah went before them by day in a pillar of cloud to lead them on the way and by night in a pillar of fire to give them light, for going by day and by night.

22. The pillar of cloud did not go away by day or the pillar of fire by night [from] before the people.

Summary

THE inner meaning of this chapter is about faith in the Lord and constant remembrance of being delivered from damnation by him. Faith in the Lord is symbolized by the consecration of the firstborn, and constant remembrance of deliverance by him, by the celebration of the Passover. 8038

What follows in this and later chapters deals with people in the spiritual church who were held in the underground realm until the Lord's Coming. They had to be further prepared before they could be taken to heaven, and for the sake of that goal, first they were led safely through the 8039 midst of damnation, and then they suffered various trials, the Lord being present the whole time. Their passage through the midst of damnation is symbolized by the crossing of the Suph Sea. Their trials are symbolized by their life in the wilderness to which they were led. The Lord's presence is symbolized by the pillar of cloud by day and of fire by night.

Inner Meaning

8040 EXODUS 13:1, 2. *And Jehovah spoke to Moses, saying, "Consecrate to me every firstborn, that which opens every womb among the children of Israel, among humans and among animals. It is mine."*

And Jehovah spoke to Moses, saying, symbolizes instructions from the Divine. *Consecrate to me every firstborn* means that faith comes from the Lord. *That which opens every womb* symbolizes faith that results from neighborly love. *Among the children of Israel* means in the spiritual church. *Among humans and among animals* symbolizes inner and outer forms of goodness prompted by faith. *It is mine* means that it belongs to the Lord.

8041 *And Jehovah spoke to Moses, saying,* symbolizes instructions from the Divine, as the following shows: *Speaking* or saying symbolizes instructions, when Jehovah is talking about religious observances, as dealt with in §§7769, 7793, 7825; and since *Jehovah* was the one speaking, it means instructions from the Divine. And *Moses* represents divine truth, as dealt with in §§6771, 7014, 7382, so *Jehovah spoke to Moses, saying,* symbolizes instructions from the Divine delivered through divine truth.

8042 *Consecrate to me every firstborn* means that faith comes from the Lord. This is indicated by the symbolism of *consecrating something to Jehovah* (the Lord) as attributing it to him—confessing and acknowledging that it comes from him—and by the symbolism of the *firstborn* as faith (discussed in §§352, 2435, 6344, 7035).

When I say faith, I mean all truth known to the spiritual church, and since I mean all truth in the church I also mean the spiritual church itself, because the crucial element in that church is truth. Goodness is admittedly the real essential of the church and is the actual firstborn (§§2435, 3325, 4925, 4926, 4928, 4930), but the goodness that people in a spiritual religion possess is basically truth. When these people act on the truth taught by their theology, such truth is called goodness. It has passed from their intellect into their will and from their will into action, and what the will performs is described as something good.

The reason this goodness in and of itself is still truth is this: To people in a spiritual religion, truth means the teachings of their church. The teachings of the various churches are at odds, so their truths also disagree, but even though these truths differ so much, they are turned into goodness by being willed and acted on, as just mentioned.

[2] While we are being reborn, faith as it exists in our intellect (theology) leads us to faith existing in our will (life). That is, truth taught by our faith leads us to doing good out of neighborly love. When we commit to doing good out of neighborly love, rebirth has been accomplished. From that goodness we then give birth to new truth, which is called truth from goodness. This truth is the genuine religious truth meant by the firstborn. The generations or births of truth from goodness resemble the generations or births of sons and daughters from a parent and then of grandsons and granddaughters and great-grandsons and great-granddaughters and so on. The first, directly occurring generation or birth—the generation of the sons and daughters—is what is symbolized by the firstborn, no matter how many there might be in that generation. The second and third generations or births are not the firstborn, except in relation to their own "parents."

The reason this generation was consecrated to Jehovah (the Lord) is that all truth and goodness derived or descending from something more fundamental draws its essence from those fundamental elements.

This spiritual rule is the basis for the right of the firstborn that is detailed in the Word.

That which opens every womb symbolizes faith that results from neigh- **8043**
borly love. This can be seen from the symbolism of *that which opens the womb* as that which is born directly to a regenerate person and therefore as that which is born directly of neighborly love, in keeping with the remarks right above at §8042. Anyone who is conceived anew re-enters the womb, so to speak, while one who is *born* anew comes out of the womb again. What is conceived in and born from the womb is not the person as a person but faith that comes of neighborly love. This kind of faith is what creates spirituality in a person and therefore creates the actual person anew, because the spiritual dimension is then the source of the person's life. This discussion shows what *that which opens the womb*

means in a spiritual sense. That is exactly how angels (who think solely in spiritual terms) understand it.

For the meaning of a womb and of being in the womb and leaving it, see §§3293 at the end, 3294, 3967, 4904, 4918, 4931, 5052, 5054, 6433.

[2] Because a womb has this symbolism, the Word refers to the Lord as the one who forms us from the womb—that is, regenerates us—as in Isaiah:

> This is what Jehovah has said, your maker and the *one who formed you from the womb* (he helps you): "Don't be afraid, my servant, Jacob, and Jeshurun, whom I have chosen, because I will pour *water* out on thirsty land, and brooklets on dry ground. I will pour *my spirit* out on your seed and a blessing on your offspring." (Isaiah 44:2, 3)

The Lord is called our maker and the one who forms us from the womb because he regenerates us and turns us from earthly beings into spiritual ones. Since truth and goodness are the means of regeneration, the passage says he will pour *water* out on thirsty land and his *spirit* on their seed. Water symbolizes faith with its truth (§§2702, 3058, 3424, 4976, 5668, 7307), and spirit symbolizes neighborly love with its goodness. Water and spirit have the same symbolism in John:

> Jesus said to Nicodemus, "Truly, truly, I say to you: unless one is *born anew,* one cannot see the kingdom of God." Nicodemus said to him, "How can we be born when we are old? *Can we come into our mother's womb a second time?"* Jesus answered, "Truly, truly, I say to you: *unless one has been born of water and spirit* one cannot enter the kingdom of God. What has been born of the flesh is flesh, but what *has been born of the spirit is spirit.* Are you yourself not a *teacher* in Israel, and you do not know this?" (John 3:3, 4, 5, 6, 10)

[3] The Lord is called the one who forms us from the womb in another place in Isaiah as well:

> This is what Jehovah has said, your Redeemer and the *one who formed you from the womb:* "I am Jehovah, making all things, spreading the heavens out on my own and stretching the earth out by myself." (Isaiah 44:24)

The heavens and the earth in a broad sense mean the inner and outer aspects of the church (§§82, 1411, 1733, 1850, 3355, 4535), and in a narrow sense, the inner and outer aspects of the church in a person who has been reborn.

Spreading and stretching them out means using divine power to make or create them (§7673). So the Lord as the Regenerator is called the Maker and the Creator, and regeneration is called a new creation [2 Corinthians 5:17; Galatians 6:15]. [4] Again in the same author:

> Listen to me, house of Jacob, and all you survivors of the house of Israel, carried from the belly, *borne from the womb.* (Isaiah 46:3)

And in David:

> *From the womb,* Lord Jehovih, *I have been laid* on you; *you are the one who brought me forth* from my mother's belly. You are my praise at all times. (Psalms 71:6)

From this evidence it is now clear what is symbolized on an inner level by *that which opens the womb* and therefore by a firstborn.

Among the children of Israel means in the spiritual church. This can be seen from the representation of the *children of Israel* as the spiritual church, as noted in §§4286, 6426, 6637, 6862, 6868, 7035, 7062, 7198, 7201, 7215, 7223. **8044**

Among humans and among animals symbolizes inner and outer forms of goodness prompted by faith, as in §§7424, 7523. **8045**

It is mine means that it belongs to the Lord. This can be seen from the fact that in the Word, Jehovah means the Lord (§§1343, 1736, 2921, 3023, 3035, 5041, 5663, 6281, 6303, 6905, 6945, 6956). So *it is mine* means that it belongs to the Lord. For the idea that the Lord is the source of everything good and true and therefore of neighborly love and faith, and that absolutely none of it comes from us, see §§904 at the end, 2411, 3142, 3147, 4151, 5482, 5649, 6193, 6325, 6466–6495, 6613–6626, 6982, 6985, 6996, 7004, 7055, 7056, 7058, 7270, 7343. **8046**

Exodus 13:3–10. *And Moses said to the people, "Remember this day, on which you went out of Egypt, out of the house of slaves, because with strength of hand Jehovah brought you out from here. And yeast bread shall not be eaten. Today you are going out, in the month of Abib. And it will happen when Jehovah brings you into the land of the Canaanite and the Hittite and the Amorite and the Hivite and the Jebusite—which he swore to your fathers to give you, a land flowing with milk and honey—that you shall observe this service in this month. Seven days you shall eat unleavened loaves, and on the seventh day, a feast to Jehovah. Unleavened loaves shall be eaten the seven days, and yeast bread shall not be seen with you, and yeast shall not be seen with you within your whole border. And you shall tell your son on that day,* **8047** *saying, 'Because of this, [which] Jehovah did for me in my going out of Egypt.' And it will serve you as a sign on your hand and as a reminder between your eyes, so that the law of Jehovah may be in your mouth; because with a strong hand Jehovah brought you out of Egypt. And you shall keep this statute at the set time from year to year."*

And Moses said to the people symbolizes being taught by divine truth. *Remember this day, on which you went out of Egypt, out of the house of slaves* means that it would be especially important for them to recall the state they were in when delivered from spiritual captivity by the Lord. *Because with strength of hand Jehovah brought you out from here* means that they were delivered by the Lord's divine power. *And yeast bread shall not be eaten* means that anything that has been rendered false must not be adopted. *Today you are going out* symbolizes being delivered for all eternity. *In the month of Abib* symbolizes the start of a new state. *And it will happen when Jehovah brings you into the land of the Canaanite and the Hittite and the Amorite and the Hivite and the Jebusite* means into a heavenly region occupied by spirits who are devoted to evil and falsity. *Which he swore to your fathers to give you* means which the Divine promised to people with a devotion to goodness and truth. *A land flowing with milk and honey* means where there is gladness and joy. *That you shall observe this service in this month* symbolizes perpetual worship of the Lord on account of their deliverance. *Seven days you shall eat unleavened loaves* symbolizes being purified of falsity. *And on the seventh day, a feast to Jehovah* symbolizes holy worship of the Lord. *Unleavened loaves shall be eaten the seven days* means that they absolutely must be purified of falsity. *And yeast bread shall not be seen with you* means that they must absolutely not allow any falsification. *And yeast shall not be seen with you* means nor any falsity. *Within your whole border* means wherever truth that is based in goodness extends its reach. *And you shall tell your son on that day, saying,* symbolizes an inner perception of truth on the part of conscience. *Because of this, [which] Jehovah did for me in my going out of Egypt,* means that the Lord delivered them from spiritual captivity and damnation. *And it will serve you as a sign on your hand* means that it will always be present in their will. *And as a reminder between your eyes* means that it will always be present in their intellect. *So that the law of Jehovah may be in your mouth* means in order for divine truth to be present in everything that issues from these faculties. *Because with a strong hand Jehovah brought you out of Egypt* means that they were delivered by divine power. *And you shall keep this statute at the set time from year to year* means that this is the law ordained for that state whenever it arises.

And Moses said to the people symbolizes being taught by divine truth, 8048
as the following shows: *Saying*, when it is done by divine truth and concerns practices the church is to observe, symbolizes instruction, as discussed in §§7186, 7267, 7304, 7380, 7517. And *Moses* represents divine truth, as noted above at §8041.

Remember this day, on which you went out of Egypt, out of the house of 8049
slaves means that it would be especially important for them to recall the state they were in when delivered from spiritual captivity by the Lord, as the following shows: *Remember* means that it is important to recall. A *day* symbolizes a state, as discussed in §§23, 487, 488, 493, 893, 2788, 3462, 3785, 4850, 5672, 5962, 7680. *Going out* means being delivered, because the departure of the children of Israel symbolizes the Lord's deliverance of people in the spiritual church. Concerning this deliverance, see §§6854, 6914, 7091 at the end, 7828, 7932, 8018. *Egypt* and the *house of slaves* symbolize spiritual captivity. After all, Pharaoh and the Egyptians symbolize inhabitants of the other world who used falsity to harass the spiritual (§§7097, 7107, 7110, 7126, 7142, 7220, 7228, 7317), so the land of Egypt symbolized persecution (7278). To be persecuted by falsity is actually spiritual captivity, because when people are being attacked in this way, they are essentially held captive by falsity, from which they constantly labor to be freed. That is why the Word describes them as being imprisoned in a pit (6854). Such spiritual captivity is what is also symbolized by a house of slaves. For the meaning of slavery, [or servitude,] as an assault by falsity, or harassment, see §§7120, 7129.

Because with strength of hand Jehovah brought you out from here means 8050
that they were delivered by the Lord's divine power, as the following shows: *Strength of hand* symbolizes power, and when ascribed to Jehovah, it symbolizes omnipotence. The meaning of strength as power is obvious. For the meaning of a hand too as power, see §§878, 3387, 4931–4937, 5327, 5328, 5544, 6947, 7188, 7189, 7518, 7673. And *bringing out* means delivering. For Jehovah being the Lord, see above at §8046.

And yeast bread shall not be eaten means that anything that has been 8051
rendered false must not be adopted. This can be seen from the symbolism of *eating* as adopting (discussed in §§3168, 3513 at the end, 3596, 4745) and from that of yeast as falsity (discussed in §§2342, 7906), so that *yeast bread* means something rendered false.

A word about the adoption of falsity and of that which is falsified: Keep in mind that nothing false or falsified is adopted as falsity or a falsification by anyone intent on goodness who therefore wants to know the truth, only by a person intent on evil who is therefore unwilling to know the truth. The reason people intent on goodness who want to know the truth do not adopt falsity in the form of falsity is that they think well of God, the kingdom of God, and the life of the spirit. So they apply falsity in such a way as to somehow harmonize rather than clash with these thoughts. They soften it, blocking out its harshness and rigidity.

If this were not so, hardly anyone could be saved, because falsity is more prevalent than truth.

Be aware that people who possess goodness also love truth. When they are taught by angels in the next life, they reject falsity and welcome the truth, so far as they loved the truth when they were in the world.

8052 *Today you are going out* symbolizes being delivered for all eternity. This is established by the meaning of *today* as eternity (discussed in §§2838, 3998, 4304, 6165, 6984) and from that of *going out* as being delivered (as above at §8049).

8053 *In the month of Abib* symbolizes the start of a new state. This can be seen from the symbolism of a *month* as the end of the previous state and the start of the next and therefore as a new state, too, as discussed in §3814. The meaning of the month *Abib* as the starting point for all the states to follow is plain from the previous chapter's description of the month: "This month is the head of the months for you; it is the first in the months of the year for you" (Exodus 12:2); see §§7827, 7828.

8054 *And it will happen when Jehovah brings you into the land of the Canaanite and the Hittite and the Amorite and the Hivite and the Jebusite* means [into] a heavenly region occupied by spirits who are devoted to evil and falsity. This can be seen from the symbolism of the *land of the Canaanite and the Hittite and the Amorite and the Hivite and the Jebusite* as heaven, and in this case as a region of heaven occupied by spirits devoted to evil and falsity. For the meaning of the land of Canaan as the Lord's kingdom in heaven and his kingdom on earth (or the church), see §§1413, 1437, 1585, 1607, 1866, 3038, 3481, 3686, 3705, 4116, 4240, 4447, 4454, 4516, 4517, 5136, 5757, 6516. The nations named here symbolize evil and falsity: A Canaanite symbolizes evil resulting from a false teaching with evil origins (4818). A Hittite symbolizes falsity that gives rise to evil (2913). An Amorite symbolizes evil and the falsity it produces (1857, 6306). A Hivite symbolizes idolatry containing a bit of goodness (6860). And a

Jebusite symbolizes idolatry containing a bit of truth (6860). For the idea that the heavenly region that would later be inhabited by people of the spiritual church was occupied by evil and falsity until the Lord's Coming, see §6858.

[2] To discuss the matter further: It needs to be known that before the Lord's Coming, heaven was not divided into three—a third or inmost heaven, a second or middle heaven, and a first or outermost heaven—as it was after his Coming. Instead it was one, and the spiritual heaven did not yet exist. The area set aside for the spiritual heaven was occupied by spirits immersed in falsity and evil who could nonetheless be held to a certain standard of truth and goodness. Superficial means, and especially the prospect of eminence and prestige, held them to that standard, as happens in the world too. Here in this world, people devoted to evil and falsity are still compelled by the superficial considerations of rank and wealth into more or less thinking and saying what is true and intending and doing what is good.

The reason this part of heaven was occupied by such spirits at that time was that good spirits were lacking and members of the spiritual church had not yet been prepared. Yet every area needed to be filled with spirits, to create a continuous expanse reaching from the Lord to humankind. Had there been a gap, humankind would have perished.

Even today some parts of heaven are occupied by spirits of this kind who are forcefully withheld from doing wrong there. Directly overhead are spirits who use innocence to deceive others and lead them astray, but above them are heavenly angels from the earliest church who restrain them so powerfully that they cannot possibly harm anyone. Behind the head there is another region that once was part of heaven but is currently occupied by evil spirits; and out in front to the left, yet another.

[3] Evil spirits are constantly trying to invade places where good spirits live, and their efforts succeed the moment good spirits cease to fill those places. I have often been given an awareness of such efforts.

Those regions come to be occupied when the number of evil people in the world grows and the number of good people shrinks, because at such times evil spirits come close to us and good spirits back away. The more they back away, the more the areas closest to us are taken over by evil spirits. When this happens on a large scale, the population of those areas changes dramatically.

Such occupations take place when a church nears its end, because evil and falsity then reign supreme. Around the time it fully ends, though, the evil are cast down and the occupied areas are given to the good, who have spent the meantime being prepared for heaven.

That is what is meant by the following passage in John:

> There was war *in heaven:* Michael and his angels fought against the dragon, and the dragon fought, as did his angels, but they did not prevail, *and no place was found for them any longer in heaven.* (Revelation 12:7, 8)

This state of affairs in heaven was represented by the occupation of the land of Canaan by various nations and by their being evicted by the children of Israel. The land of Canaan symbolizes the Lord's kingdom and therefore heaven and the church, as the sections referred to above demonstrate.

8055 *Which he swore to your fathers to give you* means which the Divine promised to people with a devotion to goodness and truth, as the following shows: *Swearing,* when Jehovah is the one who does it, symbolizes irreversible confirmation by the Divine, as treated of in §§2842, 3375, so swearing to *give* something is a promise. And *fathers* symbolize people devoted to goodness and truth. Where the subject is the church, fathers symbolize the ancient people, or the ancient churches, which possessed goodness and truth (§§6050, 6075, 6589, 6876, 6884, 7649).

8056 *A land flowing with milk and honey* means where there is gladness and joy. This can be seen from the symbolism of a *land flowing with milk and honey* as delight and pleasure (discussed in §§5620, 6857) and therefore as gladness and joy. I use the words "gladness" and "joy" because in the Word, gladness is spoken of in connection with truth and joy with goodness. The same is true of delight and pleasure. And *milk* has to do with truth from goodness, while *honey* has to do with goodness from truth.

8057 *That you shall observe this service in this month* symbolizes perpetual worship of the Lord on account of their deliverance, as the following shows: A *service* symbolizes worship, as in §7934. And a *month* symbolizes the end of a previous state and the start of a new one. The month of Abib symbolizes a starting point for all the states to come, as mentioned at §8053, so this month also symbolizes what is perpetual.

8058 *Seven days you shall eat unleavened loaves* symbolizes being purified of falsity, as the following indicates: The symbolism of *seven days* involves something holy (as discussed in §§395, 433, 716, 881, 5265, 5268), and seven days also symbolize a complete state (§6508). And *eating unleavened* *loaves* symbolizes the adoption of truth and purification from falsity, because unleavened bread means goodness purified of falsity and eating means adopting (§§3168, 3513, 3596, 3832, 4745). Unleavened bread means goodness purified of falsity because bread means goodness and yeast means falsity.

And on the seventh day, a feast to Jehovah symbolizes holy worship of the Lord, as the following shows: The *seventh day* symbolizes a holy state, a day being a state (see §§23, 487, 488, 493, 893, 2788, 3462, 3785, 4850, 5672, 5962) and seven being something holy (§§395, 433, 716, 881, 5265, 5268). And a *feast to Jehovah* symbolizes worship of the Lord, a feast being worship with a glad heart (see §7093) and *Jehovah* being the Lord (§8046). 8059

Unleavened loaves shall be eaten the seven days means that they absolutely must be purified of falsity, as the following makes plain: *Eating unleavened loaves* means adopting goodness purified of falsity, as just above at §8058. Because the phrase is repeated, it means that this absolutely must happen. And *seven days* symbolize something holy and a complete state, as noted above at §8058. 8060

And yeast bread shall not be seen with you means that they must absolutely not allow any falsification (to be adopted), in keeping with the explanation above at §8051. The fact that this absolutely must not happen is symbolized by its being repeated. 8061

And yeast shall not be seen with you means nor any falsity. This is evident from the symbolism of *yeast* as falsity (discussed in §7906). The difference between the falsification symbolized by yeast bread and the falsity symbolized by yeast is that a falsification is the use of truth to justify evil, whereas falsity is anything that opposes truth. 8062

Within your whole border means wherever truth that is based in goodness extends its reach. This is evident from the symbolism of a *border* as the reach of truth-from-goodness. All truth has a certain reach, which sometimes presents itself as an aura, and since it has a certain reach, it has its limits. The outreach of truth's aura depends on the nature and amount of goodness. Goodness is like a flame, and truth is like light. 8063

In the spiritual world, an aura reaches out to the communities all around. However far an aura extends in that world, that is how far [the truth and goodness] are communicated. On this subject, see §§6598–6613.

Everyone receives understanding and wisdom—and happiness too—in accordance with the reach of this aura in heaven, specifically in accordance with both the extent and the nature of it.

These considerations show what *within your whole border* symbolizes on a spiritual plane—in this case, that goodness must have no falsity in it. Falsity lies outside the aura; it starts where truth stops. If falsity breaches the aura, it is adopted. The idea that it must not breach the aura is symbolized by "yeast bread and yeast shall not be seen with you within your whole border."

8064 *And you shall tell your son on that day, saying,* symbolizes an inner perception [of truth] on the part of conscience. This can be seen from the explanation at §7935, where similar words occur.

8065 *Because of this, [which] Jehovah did for me in my going out of Egypt,* means that the Lord delivered them from spiritual captivity and damnation. This can be seen from the symbolism of *going out* as being delivered and from that of *Egypt* as spiritual captivity and damnation, all of which is dealt with above at §8049.

8066 *And it will serve you as a sign on your hand* means that it will always be present in their will, as the following shows: A *sign* symbolizes lasting remembrance, because anything that serves as a sign and reminder is intended for lasting remembrance. The reason the sign was on their hand was so that they would remember their deliverance whenever they moved their hand or used it. The reason it served as a reminder between their eyes was so that they would remember their deliverance whenever they looked at anything. And a *hand* symbolizes power, as discussed in §§878, 3387, 4931–4937, 5327, 5328, 5544, 6292, 6947, 7011, 7188, 7189, 7518, 7673. Here it symbolizes the will, because all action and power to act, which takes place through our hand, issues from our will.

8067 *And as a reminder between [your] eyes* means that it will always be present in their intellect, as the following shows: A *reminder* also symbolizes lasting remembrance. It is called a reminder because the Word speaks of a reminder when referring to the intellect and of a sign when referring to the will. And *eyes* symbolize the intellect, as dealt with in §§2701, 3820, 4403–4421, 4523–4534. So a reminder between the eyes means that it will always be present in their intellect, which is to say, in their thoughts.

I need to say briefly how to view the idea that it will always be present in the intellect and always present in the will. What is imprinted on us through faith and charity, or what we thoroughly believe in and love, is unceasingly present in our thought and will. We think about it and desire it even if we are engaged in thinking about and dealing with other matters and suppose that it is not then present in our mind. It actually is there, in among everything else that contributes to the nature of our mind. [2] That this is so is quite plain from the spiritual aura around a spirit or angel. When angels or spirits approach, their aura immediately tells an onlooker what they believe, how they love their neighbor, and what else they care about, even if they are not thinking about those things at all at the time.

These are the kinds of focal points that constitute the vital energy of every individual's mind and take up permanent residence there. The phenomenon could be illustrated by many, many comparisons with our own experience, such as various thought patterns, emotions, and behaviors ingrained in us since childhood, and similar habits that are always present and controlling us, even if we are not thinking about them explicitly.

It is the same with love for our neighbor, love for God, love for what is good and true, and faith. When we are motivated by these, we constantly desire and think about them, because we have internalized them, and when we have internalized them, they are said to reign supreme throughout us; see §§6159, 6571, 7648.

So that the law of Jehovah may be in your mouth means in order for **8068**
divine truth to be present in everything that issues from these faculties. This can be seen from the symbolism of the *law of Jehovah* as divine truth (discussed at §7463) and from that of *being in one's mouth* as being in everything that issues from these faculties—from the intellect and the will. To be in a person's mouth is to be in a person's speech, and to be in a person's speech is to be in both parts of that person's mind, the intellectual and volitional sides alike. The intellectual side is present in the meaning of the words and in the ideas; the volitional side, in the emotions that give life to the speech.

Because with a strong hand Jehovah brought you out of Egypt means **8069**
that they were delivered by divine power. This can be seen from the symbolism of the *strong hand* of *Jehovah* as the divine power of the Lord and from that of *bringing out* as delivering, both of which are mentioned above at §8050.

And you shall keep this statute at the set time from year to year means **8070**
that this is the law ordained for that state whenever it arises, as the following shows: A *statute* symbolizes an ordained law, as discussed in §§7884, 7995. A *time* symbolizes a state, as discussed in §§2625, 2788, 2837, 3254, 3356, 3404, 3827, 3938, 4814, 4882, 4901, 4916, 6110, 7381, so *at the set time* means in that state. And a *year* symbolizes a whole period from beginning to end, as discussed at §2906, so *from year to year* means always.

Exodus 13:11–16. *"And it shall happen when Jehovah brings you into the* **8071**
land of the Canaanite (as he swore to you and to your fathers) and gives it to

you, that you shall hand everything that opens the womb over to Jehovah, and every offspring of an animal that opens [the womb]—the males that you will have—to Jehovah. And everything that opens [the womb] of a donkey you shall redeem with a member of the flock, and if you do not redeem it, you shall break its neck. And every firstborn of a human among your sons you shall redeem. And it will happen that your son will ask you tomorrow, saying, 'What is this?' And you are to say to him, 'With strength of hand Jehovah brought us out of Egypt, out of the house of slaves, and it happened that Pharaoh hardened himself against sending us away, and Jehovah killed every firstborn in the land of Egypt, from the firstborn of a human to the firstborn of an animal; therefore I sacrifice to Jehovah everything that opens the womb (the males), and every firstborn of my sons I redeem.' And it will serve as a sign on your hand and for brow pieces between your eyes, because with strength of hand Jehovah brought us out of Egypt."

And it shall happen when Jehovah brings you into the land of the Canaanite symbolizes a heavenly region occupied by spirits devoted to evil and falsity. *(As he swore to you and to your fathers) and gives it to you* means which the Divine has promised to people governed by goodness and truth. *That you shall hand everything that opens the womb over to Jehovah* means that faith marked by neighborly love—which is a product of rebirth—is the Lord's. *And every offspring of an animal that opens [the womb]* symbolizes all the neighborly love that comes with the new birth. *The males that you will have* means which springs from religious truth. *To Jehovah* means that it is the Lord's. *And everything that opens [the womb] of a donkey you shall redeem with a member of the flock* means that faith existing solely on the earthly level must not be ascribed to the Lord, only the innocent truth it holds inside it. *And if you do not redeem it, you shall break its neck* means that if it holds no innocent truth, it is to be removed and discarded. *And every firstborn of a human among your sons you shall redeem* means that the truth associated with faith is not to be ascribed to the Lord, only the goodness associated with it. *And it will happen that your son will ask you* symbolizes a perception imparted by truth existing in the conscience. *Tomorrow* means whenever such a perception occurs. *What is this?* symbolizes an inquiry into the reason. *And you are to say to him* symbolizes the answer. *With strength of hand Jehovah brought us out of Egypt, out of the house of slaves* means that they were delivered from spiritual captivity by the Lord's divine power. *And it happened that Pharaoh hardened himself against sending us away* means that spirits who were using falsity to inflict persecution obstinately refused to let their victims be delivered.

And Jehovah killed every firstborn in the land of Egypt means that everyone who detached faith from neighborly love was damned. *From the firstborn of a human to the firstborn of an animal* symbolizes the inner and outer falsity that comes of a detached faith. *Therefore I sacrifice to Jehovah everything that opens the womb (the males)* means that faith growing out of neighborly love, which is a product of the new birth, must therefore be attributed to the Lord. *And every firstborn of my sons I redeem* means that the truth associated with faith must not be attributed to the Lord, only the goodness associated with it. *And it will serve as a sign on [your] hand* means that it will always be present in the will. *And for brow pieces between [your] eyes* means that it will always be present in the intellect. *Because with strength of hand Jehovah brought us out from Egypt* means that they were delivered by the Lord's divine power.

And it shall happen when Jehovah brings you into the land of the Canaanite symbolizes a heavenly region occupied by spirits devoted to evil and falsity, as can be seen from the remarks above at §8054. 8072

(As he swore to you and to your fathers) and gives it to you means which the Divine has promised to people governed by goodness and truth, as can be seen from the remarks above at §8055, where similar words occur. 8073

That you shall hand everything that opens the womb over to Jehovah means that faith marked by neighborly love—which is a product of rebirth—is the Lord's, as the following shows: *Handing over,* like "consecrating" above (§8042) and "sacrificing" below (§8088), means attributing. And *that opens the womb* symbolizes faith growing out of neighborly love in a person reborn, as discussed above at §§8042, 8043. For *Jehovah* being the Lord, see §8046. 8074

And every offspring of an animal that opens [the womb] symbolizes all the neighborly love that comes with the new birth, as the following shows: *That opens the womb* symbolizes faith growing out of neighborly love that comes with the new birth, as discussed at §8043. And the *offspring of an animal* symbolizes a desire for what is good, as discussed in §§45, 46, 142, 143, 246, 714, 715, 719, 776, 1823, 2179, 2180, 3218, 3519, 5198, so it symbolizes the goodness urged by neighborly love. 8075

The males that you will have means which springs from religious truth. This is clear from the discussion in §§2046, 4005, 7838 of the symbolism of a *male* as religious truth. 8076

To Jehovah means that it is the Lord's, because in the Word, *Jehovah* refers to none other than the Lord; see §§1343, 1736, 2921, 3023, 3035, 5041, 5663, 6281, 6303, 6905, 6945, 6956. 8077

I will not unfold the contents of these two verses any further, because I have already done so at verse 2 of this chapter, §§8042, 8043, 8044, 8045.

8078 *And everything that opens [the womb] of a donkey you shall redeem with a member of the flock* means that faith existing solely on the earthly level must not be ascribed to the Lord, only the innocent truth it holds inside it, as the following shows: *That opens [the womb]* symbolizes the first thing born to a regenerate person, or such a person's "firstborn," so it symbolizes faith. (The meaning of a firstborn as faith has been shown before [§§352, 2435, 6344, 7035, 8042].) A *donkey* symbolizes the earthly level. After all, a donkey symbolizes knowledge (5492, 5741) and that which is subservient (5958, 6389), so it also symbolizes the earthly level, because knowledge resides on that level, which is subservient to the spiritual level. That which opens [the womb] of a donkey, then, symbolizes faith existing solely on the earthly level, which is discussed below. *Redeeming* something means exchanging something else for it. This symbolism of redemption is plain from the sense of the current clause when it is given in full: "[Everything] that opens [the womb] of a donkey you shall (not hand over to Jehovah but) redeem for a member of the flock." [2] "Handing over to Jehovah" means ascribing to the Lord (as do "consecrating" and "sacrificing"; see just above at §8074), so not handing something over but redeeming it means not ascribing a thing but instead exchanging something else for it. And a *member of the flock* symbolizes innocent truth. A member of the flock symbolizes innocent truth because the term refers to a lamb or a kid, which symbolizes innocence (3519, 3994, 7840). Here it symbolizes innocent truth because the term is not *lamb* or *kid* but *member of the flock.*

These considerations show that *everything that opens [the womb] of a donkey you shall redeem with a member of the flock* means that faith existing solely on the earthly level is not to be ascribed to the Lord, only the innocent truth it holds inside it.

[3] Faith existing solely on the earthly level is faith instilled by an outer rather than an inner route. An example is sensory faith, which is to believe a thing is so because our eye can see it and our hand can touch it. This is the kind of faith about which the Lord said to Thomas:

> Because you have seen, Thomas, you have believed; fortunate are those who do not see, and believe. (John 20:29)

Another example is faith in miracles, which is to believe a thing is so only on the basis of miracles. Concerning this faith, see §7290. There is also faith in authority, which is to believe a thing is so because someone we trust has said it.

[4] Spiritual faith, though, is faith instilled by inner and outer routes at the same time. What is instilled along an inner route enables us to believe, and what is instilled along an outer route then enables us to confirm what we believe. The spiritual aspect of faith is a desire to love our neighbor and therefore a desire for truth we can use to do good and to live a good life. These desires render faith spiritual.

The inner route for instilling faith is to read the Word and then receive enlightenment from the Lord, which he gives us according to the quality of our desire, or according to our goal of seeing the truth.

[5] From this you can now see what merely earthly faith is. You can see that because it is not spiritual, it cannot be attributed to the Lord—the Lord cannot be acknowledged as or believed to be its source, since it is through a desire for truth and goodness that the Lord flows in. For the idea that faith is an inner desire, see §8034.

The innocent truth that can lie within this kind of faith and be accepted by the Lord is whatever we believe in all innocence to be true.

This discussion now shows how to understand the idea that faith existing on the earthly level alone must not be attributed to the Lord, only the innocent truth it holds inside it.

And if you do not redeem it, you shall break its neck means that if it **8079**
holds no innocent truth, it is to be removed and discarded. This can be seen from the symbolism of *not redeeming something* as not ascribing it to the Lord but instead exchanging something else for it (see directly above at §8078) and from that of *breaking its neck* as removing it and casting it aside. The reason breaking a neck has this meaning is that a neck symbolizes the connection between the inner depths and the outer surface (§§3542, 3603, 3695, 3725, 5320, 5328, 5926, 6033). The breaking of a neck therefore symbolizes removal and riddance—the removal and riddance of merely earthly faith if it holds no innocent truth.

And every firstborn [of a human] among your sons you shall redeem **8080**
means that the truth associated with faith is not to be ascribed to the Lord, only the goodness associated with it. This is clear from the symbolism of a *firstborn* as faith (discussed in §§352, 2435, 6344, 7035, 8042), from that of *sons* as truth (discussed in §§489, 491, 533, 1147, 2623, 3373), and from that of *redeeming* as exchanging something else for a thing (as above at §§8078, 8079). The fact that it means a ban on ascribing such truth to the Lord follows from the sense of these words when it is given

in full: "And every firstborn of a human among your sons you shall (not hand over, that is, not sacrifice, but) redeem." Not handing over means not ascribing, as above in §§8074, 8078.

This shows that *every firstborn of a human among your sons you shall redeem* means that the truth associated with faith is not to be ascribed to the Lord but that something else should be ascribed to him in its stead. What is to be substituted is the goodness associated with faith. This can be seen from the fact that a firstborn symbolizes faith with its goodness most of the time (as above at §§8042, 8043) but faith with its truth when the phrase is "the firstborn of a human among your sons." Faith consists of both truth and goodness.

[2] Here is more evidence that the goodness prompted by faith (which is neighborly love) is the substitute that should be ascribed to the Lord in place of the truth taught by faith: it was not the firstborn of the children of Israel who were taken [for the Lord] but the Levites instead. The reason the Levites were taken is that Levi represented faith in the form of goodness—in other words, charity (§§3875, 4497, 4502, 4503). On the point that the tribe of Levi was taken in place of all the firstborn, see Numbers 3:12, 13, 40–end; 8:16, 17, 18.

Still more evidence: Faith is not faith without charity (§§654, 724, 1162, 1176, 2231, 2343, 2349, 2417, 2839, 2982, 3146, 3325, 3849, 3865, 4368, 5351, 7039, 7082, 7083, 7084, 7342 at the end, 7950). The goodness taught by faith is actually in first place, the truth only apparently so (§§3539, 3548, 3556, 3563, 3570, 3576, 3603, 3701, 4925, 4926, 4928, 4930, 4977, 5351, 6256, 6269, 6272, 6273). So charity, [or neighborly love,] is the firstborn (§§3325, 3494, 4925, 4926, 4928, 4930).

[3] The reason faith's truth regarded in itself, without faith's goodness, must not be attributed to the Lord (assigned to him, acknowledged as coming from him) is that none of the truth of faith has any life to it until it becomes goodness inspired by faith. The way faith's truth turns into faith's goodness is that we will it and act on it (§7835). Once it becomes faith's goodness, the Lord acknowledges it as his; it is indirectly, through a goodness embodying faith, that the Lord grants faith to us.

Moreover, when a person whose religion is spiritual is being reborn, all the truth belonging to faith in that person turns into the goodness belonging to faith. That is when it first becomes the Lord's.

[4] The law about redeeming the firstborn of a human was laid down to keep [the children of Israel] from sacrificing their sons. Child sacrifice had become a practice in the surrounding nations, which held on to the

statutes of the ancient church (a religion that was steeped in symbolism) but completely adulterated them over time. A requirement that firstborns be *consecrated* to God came from the ancient statutes, but the nations began to interpret consecration as sacrifice. Jacob's descendants were inclined to do the same, so the law about consecration was made explicit for them, and as just mentioned, the Levites were taken in place of the firstborn, in order to prevent such a thing from happening. In the spiritual world this law is explained according to its correspondential meaning, which is that the truth associated with faith is not holy and therefore ought not to be consecrated or attributed to the Lord, only the goodness.

In later times as well people understood consecration to involve giving their firstborn son to Jehovah—that is, presenting the child—and offering a sacrifice on his behalf, as Luke says:

> When the days of their purification were fulfilled according to the Law of Moses, they brought Jesus into Jerusalem *in order to present him to the Lord,* as it has been written in the Law of the Lord, that every male opening the womb was to be called *sacred to the Lord,* and in order to offer a sacrifice. (Luke 2:22, 23, 24)

And it will happen that your son will ask you symbolizes a perception imparted by truth existing in the conscience. This can be seen from the symbolism of *asking* as knowing something by perception (discussed in §§5597, 5800, 6250) and from that of a *son* as truth (discussed in §§489, 491, 533, 1147, 2623, 3373). The fact that the perception is imparted by truth existing in the conscience is plain from the explanation at §7935, where essentially the same words occur. **8081**

I speak of truth in the conscience because the conscience of people in a spiritual religion consists of truth. They acquire it from religious teachings they consider true, whether those teachings really are true or not. The teachings become part of their conscience when they also become part of their life.

Tomorrow means whenever such a perception occurs. This is evident from the symbolism of *tomorrow* or a future day as eternity (discussed in §3998) and therefore also as something lasting, or as "always." Here it means whenever the thing occurs. **8082**

What is this? symbolizes an inquiry into the reason. *And you are to say to him* symbolizes the answer. This is self-evident. **8083**

With strength of hand Jehovah brought us out of Egypt, out of the house of slaves means that they were delivered from spiritual captivity **8084** by the Lord's divine power, as can be seen from the discussion above at §§8049, 8050.

8085 *And it happened that Pharaoh hardened himself against sending us away* means that spirits who were using falsity to inflict persecution obstinately refused to let their victims be delivered. This can be seen from the symbolism of *hardening oneself* as obstinacy (mentioned in §§7272, 7300, 7305), from the representation of *Pharaoh* as spirits who used falsity to inflict persecution (mentioned in §§7107, 7110, 7126, 7142, 7220, 7228, 7317), and from the symbolism of *sending away* as delivering.

8086 *And Jehovah killed every firstborn in the land of Egypt* means that everyone who detached faith from neighborly love was damned. This can be seen from the symbolism of the *firstborn of Egypt* as faith detached from neighborly love, which is discussed in §§7039, 7779. Their *death* symbolizes the damnation of people with a detached faith who live an evil life; see §§7766, 7778.

8087 *From the firstborn of a human to the firstborn of an animal* is the inner and outer falsity that comes of a detached faith, as the following shows: The *firstborn* of Egypt symbolize faith detached from neighborly love, as directly above at §8086, so they symbolize falsity in one's faith. People who separate faith from neighborly love in their theology and their life cannot help subscribing to falsity, because the evil in their life is always at work persuading them to accept such falsity as conforms with it. When presented with the truth, that evil forces it into agreement by misinterpreting it and in this way renders it false. And *human* and *animal* mean inner and outer, as discussed in §§7424, 7523.

8088 *Therefore I sacrifice to Jehovah everything that opens the womb (the males)* means that faith growing out of neighborly love, which is a product of the new birth, must therefore be attributed to the Lord, as the following shows: *Sacrificing to Jehovah* means attributing to the Lord. "Sacrificing" here has the same symbolism as "consecrating" in verse 2 of the current chapter and "handing over" in verse 12. For the idea that consecrating something to Jehovah stands for attributing something to the Lord, see §8042; and that handing something over does too, §8074. Attributing something to the Lord means not claiming it for oneself but admitting and acknowledging that it comes from him. *That opens the womb* symbolizes what faith growing out of neighborly love produces, as discussed at §8043. For the fact that it comes with the new birth, see above at §8042. And a *male* symbolizes faith with its truth, as discussed in §§2046, 4005, 7838.

And every firstborn of my sons I redeem means that the truth associated with faith must not be attributed to the Lord, only the goodness associated with it. This is clear from the explanation above at §8080, where similar words occur. 8089

And it will serve as a sign on your hand means that it will always be present in the will. *And for brow pieces between [your] eyes* means that it will always be present in the intellect. *Because with strength of hand Jehovah brought us out from Egypt* means that they were delivered by the Lord's divine power. All this can be seen from the explanation above at verse 9 of this chapter (§§8066, 8067, 8069), where similar words occur. 8090

Exodus 13:17, 18. *And it happened in Pharaoh's sending the people away that God did not lead them by way of the land of the Philistines, although it was nearby; because God said, "Maybe the people will have regrets when they see war and will return to Egypt." And God led the people around by way of the wilderness to the Suph Sea. And the children of Israel went up armed from the land of Egypt.* 8091

And it happened in Pharaoh's sending the people away means when the spirits persecuting members of the spiritual church left them alone. *That God did not lead them by way of the land of the Philistines* means that the Divine made sure they would not switch over to religious truth lacking in goodness. *Although it was nearby* means that this is what comes to mind first. *Because God said,* symbolizes divine foresight. *Maybe the people will have regrets when they see war* means that they will turn away from the truth when they come under attack. *And return to Egypt* means descending into falsity that is totally opposed to the truth and goodness taught by faith. *And God led the people around by way of the wilderness* means that under divine protection they were led by their trials to reaffirm the truth and goodness in their faith. *To the Suph Sea* symbolizes the damnation they first passed through. *And the children of Israel went up armed from the land of Egypt* means that they were released from the state of persecution and in the process underwent preparation to endure times of trial.

And it happened in Pharaoh's sending the people away means when the spirits persecuting members of the spiritual church left them alone. This can be seen from the symbolism of *sending away* as leaving alone, from the representation of *Pharaoh* as spirits who used falsity to inflict persecution (noted in §§7107, 7110, 7126, 7142, 7220, 7228, 7317), and from the symbolism of the children of Israel—the *people* here—as members of the spiritual church (noted above at §8044). 8092

8093 *That God did not lead them by way of the land of the Philistines* means that the Divine made sure they would not switch over to religious truth lacking in goodness, as the following shows: *God did not lead them by way of* means that the Divine made sure they would not switch over. After all, any leading done by God symbolizes providence, and a way symbolizes truth (§§627, 2333), or in this case switching over to truth. And *Philistines* (as discussed in §§1197, 1198, 3412, 3413) represent people with a knowledge of religious concepts who do not live a life of neighborly love. So they represent people who possess religious truth lacking in goodness. This symbolism of the Philistines and their land can be seen from passages in the Word mentioning them, especially the depiction of them in Jeremiah 47:1–end, and Joel 3:[4,] 5, 6. It can also be seen from scriptural narratives reporting on wars between the children of Israel and the Philistines and on the Philistines' conquest of the children of Israel at one time and their conquest of the Philistines at another. In these passages the Philistines represent people with a detached faith, people for whom a knowledge of religious concepts rather than a life in keeping with that knowledge is of primary importance—in short, people who teach and believe that faith alone saves.

[2] This opinion about faith alone, or detached faith, is not new. It is not just a modern notion but existed in the ancient churches and grew strong when evil grew strong in people's lives. It is written about here and there in the Word, but under various proper names. The first is *Cain* when he killed his brother Abel (§§337, 340, 1179). In the inner, representative sense of that story, Cain is faith alone, and Abel is neighborly love. Such a faith is also depicted by *Ham* when his father cursed him (1062, 1063), then by *Reuben* when he climbed onto his father's bed (3870, 4601), and by *Simeon* and *Levi* when they killed Hamor and the men of Shechem and were therefore cursed by their father (3870, 6352). The same kind of faith is depicted by the *Egyptians,* whose firstborn were killed (7766, 7778) and who drowned in the Suph Sea. It is depicted by the *Philistines* (3412, 3413) and by *Tyre* and *Sidon* in various passages in the Prophets, where the Philistines symbolize a knowledge of religious concepts, and Tyre and Sidon symbolize the inner and outer concepts themselves. Lastly it is depicted by *Peter* when he three times denied knowing the Lord (6000, 6073 at the end). But see what has been shown before about this faith, in §§36, 379, 389, 916, 1017, 1076, 1077, 1162, 1176, 1798, 1799, 1834, 1844, 2049, 2116, 2228, 2231, 2261, 2343, 2349, 2363, 2383, 2385, 2401, 2435, 2982, 3146, 3242, 3325, 3412, 3413, 3416, 3427, 3773, 4663, 4672, 4673, 4683, 4721, 4730,

4766, 4783, 4925, 5351, 5820, 5826, 6269, 6272, 6273, 6348, 6353, 7039, 7097, 7127, 7317, 7502, 7545, 7623–7627, 7724, 7779, 7790, 7950.

Although it was nearby means that this is what comes to mind first. This 8094
can be seen from the symbolism of *nearby,* when it applies to a detached faith, as that which comes to mind first.

I need to say briefly how to understand the idea that the theory of faith alone (faith detached [from neighborly love]) comes to mind first. An evil life brings related falsity with it. This falsity lies hidden in people whose lives are evil, and sometimes they are unaware it is there, but as soon as they think about the truths of their religion, especially about salvation, the falsity comes out in the open. If they cannot deny genuine truth in its broad outlines, they interpret it in such a way as to justify their evil, and in this way they render the truth false. So when they think about faith and neighborly love (the essential ingredients of religion and salvation), faith springs to mind right away but neighborly love does not, because it opposes the evil in their lives. For this reason they push charity aside and choose faith alone. From these remarks you can see that the truth faith teaches is nearby but the goodness it teaches is not; in other words, religious truth rather than religious goodness occurs to them first.

[2] From this false and mistaken premise many other distortions and errors then follow: Good deeds contribute nothing to salvation. Our life does not follow us after death. After death we are saved by mercy alone because of our faith, no matter how we lived in the world. The most flagrant criminal is saved by faith in the final moments of life. Evil is wiped away instantly. These thoughts and conclusions and others like them rise out of that premise; they are links in a chain running from it. But if neighborly love and living a good life were the premise, the reality in each case would be seen to be totally different.

Because God said, symbolizes divine foresight. This can be seen from 8095
the symbolism of *God said,* when it predicts the future, as divine foresight, as also in §§5361, 6946.

Maybe the people will have regrets when they see war means that they 8096
will turn away from the truth when they come under attack. This is established by the symbolism of *having regrets* as turning away from the truth (discussed below) and from that of *war* as spiritual battles (discussed in §§1664, 1788, 2686) and therefore as attacks.

The reason having regrets means turning away from the truth is this: The exodus of the children of Israel from Egypt, their long stay in the wilderness, and their entry into the land of Canaan symbolize their being led constantly toward what was good and therefore toward heaven. Having regrets and returning to Egypt, then, mean departing from what is good and consequently turning away from truth. This is because Egypt (or Egyptians) symbolizes people whose faith is detached from neighborly love and who oppose the church's truth (§§6692, 7039, 7097, 7317, 7766, 7926).

[2] Regarding attacks by spirits who possess religious truth that lacks goodness, as symbolized by Philistines: In the other life these spirits harass the upright and constantly attack the goodness in religion (which is neighborly love). This is because they take with them to the next life the principles they seized on in the world. They hold on to those principles until they have undergone devastation—that is, until they have been stripped of all knowledge of religious concepts—and have been sent to hell.

Today such spirits exist in large numbers. They live out in front, off to the right, on a plane below the sole of the foot. The place where they live is a sort of city. I have been allowed to speak with spirits from there many times, listening to their arguments in favor of faith alone (which are penetrating) and their attacks on neighborly love (which are insolent).

This, then, is what is meant in an inner sense where the text says that they were not led by way of the land of the Philistines, and that if they had been, they might have had regrets when they saw war.

8097 *And return to Egypt* means descending into falsity that is totally opposed to the truth and goodness taught by faith. This can be seen from the symbolism of *Egypt* as that which opposes the truth and goodness taught by faith (§§6692, 7039, 7097, 7317, 7766, 7926). Obviously to *return* there means to descend into falsity.

8098 *And God led the people around by way of the wilderness* means that under divine protection they were led by their trials to reaffirm the truth and goodness in their faith, as the following shows: *God led* symbolizes providence, as above at §8093, or to put it another way, divine protection. And the *way of the wilderness* means for undergoing times of trial and accordingly for reaffirming the truth and goodness in their faith (since trials are the means by which that happens).

A wilderness means a place that is uninhabited and undeveloped, as discussed at §2708. In a spiritual sense it symbolizes a place where there is no goodness or truth, and also where truth has not yet united with goodness. So a wilderness symbolizes the state of people in whom truth and goodness need to unite. Since they are united only by times of trial, these too are symbolized, but only when the number forty is added, whether it is forty years or forty months or forty days. Forty symbolizes trials and their duration, however long that is (§§730, 862, 2272, 2273). The forty years the children of Israel wandered in the wilderness symbolize trials, and there are descriptions of the trials they actually underwent. From the following verses in Moses it is clear that they were led into the wilderness to undergo those trials and thereby fulfill a representative role:

> You shall remember all the path by which Jehovah your God has led you *these forty years in the wilderness,* to *afflict you, to test you,* to know what was in your heart. He fed you manna in the wilderness—which your ancestors did not recognize—to afflict you, *to test you,* in order to do good to you in your aftertime. (Deuteronomy 8:2, 16)

Because forty is a symbol for trials and the length of time they last, and the wilderness is a symbol for the state of people undergoing trial, the Lord went out into the wilderness when he was being tested and was there forty days (Matthew 4:1, 2, and following verses; Luke 4:1, 2 and following verses; Mark 1:12, 13).

To the Suph Sea symbolizes the damnation they first passed through. **8099**
This is clear from the symbolism of the *Suph Sea* as the hell inhabited by people who separate faith from neighborly love and live evil lives. Because the Suph Sea is hell, it is also damnation.

Here is why they first passed through damnation: As was described in previous chapters [§§6854, 6914, 7090, 7828, 7849, 7932], people who were part of the spiritual church were held till the Lord's Coming in an underground realm, where they were persecuted by spirits who championed a faith separated from neighborly love. When the spiritual were liberated from that realm, they were not taken right up into heaven but rather were first led into a second state, a state of purification, which is a state of trial. The truth and goodness in faith can be neither reaffirmed nor united together without trials, and until truth and goodness were reaffirmed and united, these people could not be raised into heaven. This situation was represented by the fact that the children of Israel were not led immediately into the land of Canaan but first into the wilderness, where they stayed for forty years, undergoing various kinds of trials described in the books of Moses.

[2] To expand on the statement that they first passed through the Suph Sea—symbolizing the hell inhabited by spirits with a detached faith and an evil life—and consequently through the midst of damnation: Let me say that this hell is out in front, deep down under the hells of adulterers,

and stretches a fair distance off to the left. It is separated from the hells of the adulterers by the waters of a kind of sea. To the right there but not as deep is the gathering place of spirits devoted to the truth but not the goodness that goes to make up faith, who are symbolized by Philistines (discussed just above at §8093). The underground realm where the victims of persecution live is under the sole of the foot, slightly out in front. Inhabitants who are delivered from this persecution are not conducted to the right, since that is where the spirits symbolized by the Philistines are, but are conducted to the left through the middle of the hell we are talking about here. They also emerge from that hell on the left, where there is a sort of wilderness.

Twice I have been allowed to observe that spirits being released from persecution pass along this route. As they go they are protected so carefully by the Lord that not a hint of evil, let alone of damnation, touches them, because they are surrounded by a pillar of angels among whom the Lord is present. This was represented by the passage of the children of Israel through the Suph Sea.

[3] The same thing is also meant by the following in Isaiah:

> Wake up, wake up! Put on strength, arm of Jehovah! Are you not what *drained the sea, the waters of the great abyss,* what made the *depths of the sea* a path for the redeemed to cross? (Isaiah 51:9, 10)

The arm of Jehovah is the Lord in his divine humanity. The waters of the great abyss and the depths of the sea are the hell inhabited by spirits who detach faith from neighborly love and live an evil life. The water of the kind of sea they live beneath is falsity, because in the other life, falsity looks like thick, dark clouds, and also like a flood of water (§§739, 4423, 7307). The redeemed who were to cross are the people the Lord delivered. [4] In the same author:

> Jehovah remembered the days of old, [remembered] Moses, [remembered] his own people. *Where is the one who brought them up from the sea* with the shepherd of his flock? Where is the one who put the spirit of his holiness in their midst? (Isaiah 63:11)

In this enigmatic saying, Moses means the Lord, who is also the shepherd of the flock. The people he brought up from the sea mean those he delivered from damnation. [5] In Jeremiah:

> The earth trembled with the sound of their fall. A cry! Their voice was heard *in the Suph Sea.* (Jeremiah 49:21)

The Suph Sea stands for hell. After all, this passage, which is about Edom and the damnation of it, says that its voice was heard coming from the Suph Sea, when in reality it was not Edomites but Egyptians who drowned in that sea. Plainly, then, the Suph Sea symbolizes hell and damnation. Edom in this verse symbolizes people who reject doctrinal truth and embrace falsity because of their evil rising out of self-love (§3322).

All this evidence now shows what the Suph Sea symbolizes in an inner, representative sense. It also shows what is symbolized by the passage of the children of Israel through that sea and the drowning of the Egyptians in it, as described in the next chapter.

And the children of Israel went up armed from the land of Egypt means **8100**
that they were released from the state of persecution and in the process underwent preparation to endure times of trial, as the following shows: Going up *armed* means that they were prepared. Here it means being prepared to endure times of trial, because they were going to be led through the Suph Sea into the wilderness, and a wilderness means a state in which one undergoes trials (see above at §8098). The *children of Israel* represent people of the spiritual church, as noted many times. And the *land of Egypt* symbolizes a state of persecution, as dealt with at §7278. *Going up from there* means being released or freed.

This shows that *the children of Israel went up armed from the land of Egypt* means that they were released from the state of persecution and in the process underwent preparation to endure trials. (For the difference between trials and persecution, see §7474.)

Exodus 13:19. *And Moses took Joseph's bones with him, because [Joseph]* **8101**
had put the children of Israel under a solemn oath, saying, "God will unfailingly visit you, and you must bring my bones up from this place with you."

And Moses took Joseph's bones with him symbolizes the representation of a religion among them. *Because [Joseph] had put the children of Israel under a solemn oath, saying,* symbolizes an obligation. *God will unfailingly visit you* means when the last and first days of the church arrive. *And you must bring my bones up from this place with you* again symbolizes the representation of a religion among them, as opposed to an *actual* religion, which is awake to the inner dimension as well [as the outer].

There is no need to explain these words further, since they were **8102**
already explained at Genesis 50:24, 25, where similar words occur; see §§6590–6592.

[2] Exodus 13:20, 21, 22. *And they traveled from Succoth and camped in Etham, on the edge of the wilderness. And Jehovah went before them by day*

in a pillar of cloud to lead them on the way and by night in a pillar of fire to give them light, for going by day and by night. The pillar of cloud did not go away by day or the pillar of fire by night [from] before the people.

And they traveled from Succoth and camped in Etham symbolizes a second state after their deliverance. *On the edge of the wilderness* symbolizes a first state of trials. *And Jehovah went before them* symbolizes the Lord's unceasing presence. *By day in a pillar of cloud* means that any state of enlightenment was softened by dim truth. *To lead them on the way* symbolizes divine protection. *And by night in a pillar of fire to give them light* means that any state of dimness was softened by enlightenment from goodness. *For going by day and by night* symbolizes life as it was therefore lived in both states. *The pillar of cloud did not go away by day or the pillar of fire by night [from] before the people* means that the Lord's presence was constant.

8103 *And they traveled from Succoth and camped in Etham* symbolizes a second state after their deliverance. This can be seen from the fact that the *travels* and *encampments* of the children of Israel after they left Egypt symbolize the spiritual states of the people the Lord delivered, as discussed above [§§8091–8100]. Changes in state are symbolized by journeys from one place to another and by stops made in those places. The trip here from Succoth to Etham symbolizes a second state because the trip from Rameses to Succoth symbolized a first state (§7972).

Moreover, travels also symbolize the states and customs of a life, in the Word's inner meaning (§§1293, 3335, 5605), and encampments symbolize different arrangements of truth and goodness (§4236), which have to do with one's life.

8104 *On the edge of the wilderness* symbolizes a first state of trials. This is evident from the symbolism of a *wilderness* as a state in which one undergoes trials, as discussed above at §8098. Because that state began at the edge of the wilderness, the edge of the wilderness symbolizes a first state.

8105 *And Jehovah went before them* symbolizes the Lord's unceasing presence, as needs no explanation. For *Jehovah* being the Lord, see §8046 above.

8106 *By day in a pillar of cloud* means that any state of enlightenment was softened by dim truth, as the following shows: *By day* means in a state of enlightenment, because the times of day, such as morning, afternoon, evening, and night, correspond to different kinds of enlightenment—different forms of understanding and wisdom—in the next life (§§5672, 5962, 6110). Daytime is therefore a state of enlightenment, or clear perception, and night is a state lacking in enlightenment, or a state of dim perception (§7680). And *cloud* symbolizes dim truth because clouds either dispel the sun's bright light or weaken it.

[2] The Word often says that Jehovah appeared in a cloud or was surrounded with cloud or that there was cloud under his feet. In those passages the cloud means dim truth, and specifically the literal sense of the Word, because compared to the inner sense the literal sense is a dim form of truth. (See the preface to Genesis 18 and §§4391, 5922, 6343, 6752.) The dimness of the literal sense was symbolized by cloud when the Lord appeared to Peter, James, and John in glory (Luke 9:34) and when he appeared on Mount Sinai to the people, and to Moses when Moses approached him there [in the cloud] (Exodus 19:9; 20:21; 24:15, 16, 17, 18; 34:5). It was also symbolized by the Lord's so often saying he would come in the clouds of heaven (Matthew 24:30; 26:63, 64; Mark 13:26; 14:61, 62; Luke 21:27).

[3] The literal meaning of the Word is called a cloud because the inner meaning, which is called glory, cannot be comprehended by a person on earth unless that person has been reborn and then receives light. If the Word's inner meaning—divine truth in its glory—presented itself to people unreborn, it would be like a darkness that prevented them from seeing anything whatever. It would blind them, meaning they would believe nothing.

From this discussion you can see what cloud by day symbolizes: dim truth, and where the text is about the Word, the literal meaning.

[4] The verse says "in a *pillar* of cloud and fire" because a pillar symbolizes a support that props something up, as in Jeremiah 1:18; Psalms 75:3; Revelation 3:12; Job 9:6. It relates to the earthly level, because the earthly level is a support or base for the spiritual level. After all, the spiritual level comes to a halt at the earthly level and rests on it. That is why the feet of the angel coming down from heaven looked like *pillars of fire* in Revelation 10:1, because feet symbolize the earthly level (§§2162, 3147, 3761, 3986, 4280, 4938–4952, 5328).

To lead them on the way symbolizes divine protection. This can be **8107**
seen from the symbolism of *leading someone on the way,* when done by Jehovah, as providence and divine protection, which is mentioned in §§8093, 8098.

And by night in a pillar of fire to give them light means that any state of **8108**
dimness was softened by enlightenment from goodness. This can be seen from the symbolism of *night* as a state of dimness (discussed in §§1712,

6000), from that of *fire* as a loving goodness (discussed in §§934, 4906, 5215, 6314, 6832, 6834, 6849, 7324, 7852), and from that of *giving light* as enlightenment.

The reason Jehovah (the Lord) appeared or went before them in a pillar of cloud by day and a pillar of fire by night was that this represented conditions in heaven. In heaven there are endless changes and variations of state, since angels are constantly being perfected, which simply could not happen without perpetual changes in state. In general these changes and variations resemble time cycles in the world: the yearly cycles of spring, summer, fall, winter, and spring again, and the daily cycles of morning, afternoon, evening, night, and morning again. When it is morning and afternoon in heaven, the angels' intellect receives light from the Lord, but at the same time, dim truth like a cloud softens the light. When it is evening and night in heaven, their intellect is in dimness, but the Lord uses a loving goodness like an illuminating fire to soften the dimness.

That is what is represented by the pillar of cloud by day and the pillar of fire by night among the children of Israel in the wilderness.

8109 *For going by day and by night* symbolizes life as it was [therefore] lived in both states, as the following shows: *Going* and traveling symbolize living, as discussed in §§3335, 3690, 4882, 5493, 5605. And *day* symbolizes a state of enlightenment, while *night* symbolizes a state of dimness, as discussed just above in §§8106, 8108; so they symbolize both states.

8110 *The pillar of cloud did not go away by day or the pillar of fire by night [from] before the people* means that the Lord's presence was constant, as can be seen from the explanation above [§§8105–8108]. This is what the people saw when angels with the Lord in their midst appeared to them.

The Spirits and Inhabitants of Jupiter (Continued)

8111 SPENDING a lot of time with spirits from the planet Jupiter gradually made it plain to me that they are more upright than the spirits of many other planets. Their arrival when they came, their stay, and their inflow was so gentle and agreeable that words cannot express it. In the other world, integrity manifests itself as a soft, pleasant quality. It was very easy to distinguish their pleasant softness from that of the good spirits of our own planet.

When any slight disagreement arises among them, they see a kind of thin white streak of light like a bolt of lightning, or else they see a ribbon with twinkling stars on it. These are signs of disagreement, but any rift between them is quickly healed. **8112**

When stars twinkle and wander around, the sign is not a good one, but twinkling stars that stand still *are* a good sign.

It was not only by the mild and agreeable way they had of approaching and flowing in that I could recognize the presence of Jupiter's spirits. It was also that they acted primarily on my face, molding it into a smile of good cheer that they maintained there the whole time they were present. I heard that they do the same with the faces of their planet's inhabitants, because they want to inspire peace and joy in their hearts. **8113**

When these spirits inspired the same peace and joy in me, it tangibly filled my heart and chest, displacing cravings and worries about the future that rob a person of peace and joy and stir up various kinds of agitation and upheaval in the psyche. From this I could see what the life of Jupiter's inhabitants was like.

They also told me they are not afraid of death, except for the mild fear they have over the loss of their spouse and children. The reason they are not afraid is their sure knowledge that physical death is a continuation of life and that they will become still happier after they die.

I could tell that they had an even deeper state of happiness and that they were capable of being given a state deeper yet. The way to tell is that an individual's inner depths are not closed off but rather are open to the Lord; the more open one's inner reaches are, the more capable one is of receiving divine goodness and divine happiness. **8114**

The situation is entirely different with people who do not live by the plan ordained for heaven. In them, the inner depths are closed off and the outer surface is open to hell. Hell's inflow brings contempt for others, hatred, vengefulness, and cruelty, which they enjoy unleashing on anyone not worshiping them or catering to their corrupt desires.

The spirits of Jupiter cannot be together with spirits from our planet, because the spirits of our planet have a completely different nature and do not love and appreciate tranquillity the way the spirits of Jupiter do. They were surprised to hear that when spirits from our planet become angels, their hearts change radically and they retain hardly anything resembling the state they were in as spirits. **8115**

To show them this was so, choruses of angels from our planet came from heaven, one after another. (A chorus is a large group thinking, speaking, and acting as one, in an unbroken series of thoughts, words, or deeds. It is usually in choruses that the heavens celebrate the Lord. To read about them, see §§1648, 1649, 2595, 2596, 3350, 5182.) These choruses delighted the spirits of Jupiter with me so thoroughly that it seemed to them as though they had been caught up to heaven.

The choruses' tribute lasted about an hour. The pleasure the spirits took in it was communicated to me, and I was allowed to experience it myself. They said they would tell their friends elsewhere about it.

8116 They reported that in the area of their planet in which they lived there was a large number of people, as many as the planet could sustain. It was fertile, they said, and everything was abundant. The inhabitants there did not crave anything beyond what they needed to live on. That was why there was able to be such a large population.

8117 They reported further that they are divided up into nations, clans, and households there, and that they all live apart, among their own. Most of the time they associate with relatives, they said. No one ever covets another's property, nor does it occur to them to claim any of it for themselves, let alone break in and loot—which they count as a violation of human nature, and horrifying. When I wanted to say that on our planet we see war, plunder, and murder, they turned their backs and refused to listen.

8118 The earliest people on our planet lived a similar way, angels told me: They were divided up into nations, clans, and households. They were all content with their own possessions. It was completely unheard of for anyone to grow rich off another's possessions or to rule over others. So the ancient times and especially the very earliest times were more pleasing to the Lord than the ages that have followed. Because these were the conditions then, innocence also reigned supreme, and wisdom along with it. Everyone did what was good at the inspiration of goodness and did what was right because it was right. No one knew what it meant to do what was good or right for the sake of personal prestige or monetary gain. They spoke nothing but the truth, and they did this at the inspiration not so much of truth as of goodness, that is, not from a detached intellect but with an integrated will.

That is what the ancient era was like, which is why angels could then interact with people. They could bring people's minds (virtually separated from their bodies) with them into heaven, lead the people around, and show them the magnificent, happy sights there. They could also share their happiness and pleasure with them.

The ancient writers knew about those times, which they called the Golden or Saturnian Age.

[2] The reason those days were so ideal was, again, that people lived divided into nations, the nations were divided into clans, the clans were divided into households, and each household lived by itself. It never occurred to anyone to steal someone else's inheritance in order to acquire wealth and power. Self-love and materialism were far from their minds. Everyone was sincerely happy with his or her share and no less delighted by the bounty the next person enjoyed.

[3] However, in the next era, when a lust for power and for taking the belongings of others usurped the lower mind, this scene changed into its opposite. To protect itself the human race then grouped together into kingdoms and empires. Since the laws of neighborly love and conscience inscribed on the heart had lapsed, it was necessary to lay down laws for curbing violence. Under these laws, rank and wealth were rewards, and punishment was the loss of such rewards.

When conditions changed in this way, heaven itself withdrew from humankind. It has withdrawn further and further right to the modern age, when no one knows any longer whether there is a heaven or consequently a hell, and in fact people deny that either exists.

The purpose of this description is to illustrate by analogy what the state of people on Jupiter is like and where their integrity comes from, not to mention their wisdom, which will be discussed more later.

The spirits and inhabitants of Jupiter will be treated of again at the end of the next chapter [§§8242–8251]. 8119

Exodus 14

Teachings on Neighborly Love

8120 PEOPLE think that charity toward one's neighbor consists in giving to the poor, helping the needy, and doing good to anyone and everyone. Genuine charity, though, consists in acting prudently so as to bring about a good result. If you help poor and needy people who do evil, you are hurting your neighbor through them. The help you give hardens them in their evil and supplies them with the means of doing harm. It is quite different if you supply good people with resources.

8121 Charity for one's neighbor reaches far beyond the poor and needy, though. Charity for one's neighbor consists in doing what is right in everything one does and fulfilling one's duty in every responsibility. Judges who ensure justice is done for its own sake are exercising charity toward their neighbor. In punishing the guilty and acquitting the innocent they are exercising charity toward their neighbor because they are seeing to the welfare of their fellow citizen, their country, and the Lord's kingdom. They look after the Lord's kingdom by ensuring justice is done for its own sake, their fellow citizen by acquitting the innocent, and their country by punishing the guilty. Priests who teach what is true and lead people to what is good, for the sake of truth and goodness, are exercising charity.

By contrast, people who act this way for the sake of themselves and their worldly advantages are not exercising charity, because they love themselves rather than their neighbor.

8122 The case is the same for all other kinds of people, whether they are working in an official capacity or not: for children in relation to their parents, and parents in relation to their children; for servants in relation to their masters, and masters in relation to their servants; for subjects in relation to their monarch, and monarchs in relation to their subjects. The ones who do their duty out of duty and do what is just because it is just are exercising charity.

8123 The reason all this constitutes charity for one's neighbor is that everyone is our neighbor, though in different ways (§6818); our community small or large is even more our neighbor (6819, 6820); our country still more (6819, 6821); the church still more (6819, 6822); the Lord's kingdom still more (6819, 6823); and the Lord above all (6819, 6824). In the broadest possible sense, goodness radiating from the Lord is our neighbor (6706, 6711), so that which is just and right is also our neighbor.

Consequently, to do good always for the sake of goodness and to do justice for the sake of justice is to love one's neighbor and exercise charity. People who behave this way are acting out of a love for what is good and a love for what is just, so they are acting out of a love for those in whom there is goodness and justice.

To do injustice for the sake of any kind of gain, though, is to hate one's neighbor.

When you show charity toward your neighbor because you are inwardly moved to do so, then everything you think and say, everything you will and do holds charity for your neighbor within. It is fair to say that a person, or angel, *is* charity on the inside when goodness is her or his neighbor. **8124**

That is how far charity for one's neighbor extends.

Exodus 14

1. And Jehovah spoke to Moses, saying,

2. "Speak to the children of Israel and have them go back and camp before Pi-hiroth, between Migdol and the sea, before Baal-zephon. Opposite it you shall camp, by the sea.

3. And Pharaoh will say of the children of Israel, 'They stand perplexed in the land; the wilderness has closed in on them.'

4. And I will harden Pharaoh's heart, and he will pursue after them, and I will gain glory in Pharaoh and in all his army. And the Egyptians will know that I am Jehovah." And [the children of Israel] did so.

5. And the king of Egypt was told that the people had fled. And the heart of Pharaoh and of his servants turned against the people, and they said, "What is this we have done, that we have sent Israel away from serving us?"

6. And he hitched up his chariot and took his people with him.

7. And he took six hundred choice chariots and all the chariots of Egypt. And there were tertiary officers over all his men.

8. And Jehovah hardened the heart of Pharaoh, king of Egypt, and he pursued after the children of Israel. And the children of Israel were leaving with a high hand.

9. And the Egyptians pursued after them and overtook them camping by the sea—all Pharaoh's chariot horses and his riders and his army, by Pi-hiroth, before Baal-zephon.

10. And Pharaoh drew near, and the children of Israel raised their eyes, and here were the Egyptians setting out after them! And they were greatly afraid, and the children of Israel cried out to Jehovah.

11. And they said to Moses, "Were there no graves in Egypt, [that] you have taken us to die in the wilderness? What is this you have done to us, to bring us out of Egypt?

12. Isn't this the word that we spoke to you in Egypt, saying, 'Leave us alone and let us serve the Egyptians, because it is better for us to serve the Egyptians than die in the wilderness'?"

13. And Moses said to the people, "Don't be afraid. Stand firm and see Jehovah's salvation, which he will perform for you today, because the Egyptians whom you see today you will no longer see, forever.

14. Jehovah will fight for you, and you yourselves are to keep silent."

15. And Jehovah said to Moses, "Why are you crying to me? Speak to the children of Israel and have them set out.

16. And you, lift your staff and stretch your hand out over the sea and divide it, and have the children of Israel come into the middle of the sea on dry ground.

17. And I—yes, I—am hardening the heart of the Egyptians, who will come after them, and I will gain glory in Pharaoh and in all his army, in his chariots, and in his riders.

18. And the Egyptians will know that I am Jehovah, in my gaining glory in Pharaoh, in his chariots, and in his riders."

19. And the angel of God set out, marching in front of the camp of Israel, and [then] went behind them, and the pillar of cloud set out from in front of them and stood behind them.

20. And it came between the camp of the Egyptians and the camp of Israel, and it was cloud and darkness, and it lit up the night, and the one [the Egyptian] did not come near the other [the Israelite] the whole night.

21. And Moses stretched his hand out over the sea, and Jehovah made the sea depart with a strong east wind the whole night, and he made the sea into dry land, and the waters were divided.

22. And the children of Israel came into the middle of the sea on dry ground. And the waters were a wall to them on their right and on their left.

23. And the Egyptians pursued; and all Pharaoh's horses, his chariots, and his riders came after them to the middle of the sea.

24. And it happened in the morning watch that Jehovah looked out at the camp of the Egyptians from within the pillar of fire and cloud and troubled the camp of the Egyptians.

25. And he took off the wheels of [Pharaoh's] chariots and made [the wheels] go heavily, and the Egyptian said, "I will flee before Israel, because Jehovah fights for them against the Egyptians."

26. And Jehovah said to Moses, "Stretch your hand out over the sea and have the waters come back over the Egyptians, over [Pharaoh's] chariots, and over his riders."

27. And Moses stretched his hand out over the sea, and as morning drew near, the sea came back to its full force, and the Egyptians were fleeing in its path, and Jehovah shook the Egyptians off into the middle of the sea.

28. And the waters came back and covered the chariots and riders, all the army of Pharaoh, coming after them, into the sea; not even one was left among them.

29. And the children of Israel went on dry ground into the middle of the sea, and the waters were a wall to them on their right and on their left.

30. And on that day Jehovah saved Israel from the hand of the Egyptians, and Israel saw the Egyptians dead on the shore of the sea.

31. And Israel saw the great hand, [the works] that Jehovah performed among the Egyptians, and the people feared Jehovah and believed in Jehovah and in Moses his servant.

Summary

THE inner meaning of this chapter is about the first critical challenge 8125
faced by people of the spiritual church and about their passage through the middle of hell while being protected by the Lord. It also deals with the way people who detached faith from neighborly love were plunged into hell, where falsity that grows out of evil is found. The people whose

religion was spiritual are represented by the children of Israel; those who detached faith from neighborly love, by the Egyptians. The first challenge is depicted in the complaints the children of Israel voiced when they saw Pharaoh's army. Hell is symbolized by the Suph Sea, which the children of Israel were safely led through and the Egyptians drowned in. Falsity growing out of evil is symbolized by the waters that covered the Egyptians.

Inner Meaning

8126 EXODUS 14:1, 2, 3, 4. *And Jehovah spoke to Moses, saying, "Speak to the children of Israel and have them go back and camp before Pi-hiroth, between Migdol and the sea, before Baal-zephon. Opposite it you shall camp, by the sea. And Pharaoh will say of the children of Israel, 'They stand perplexed in the land; the wilderness has closed in on them.' And I will harden Pharaoh's heart, and he will pursue after them, and I will gain glory in Pharaoh and in all his army. And the Egyptians will know that I am Jehovah." And [the children of Israel] did so.*

And Jehovah spoke to Moses, saying, symbolizes instruction delivered by the Divine through divine truth. *Speak to the children of Israel* symbolizes an inflow of divine truth into people in the spiritual church. *And have them go back* means that they were not ready yet. *And camp before Pi-hiroth, between Migdol and the sea, before Baal-zephon* symbolizes the beginning of a state for the undergoing of trials. *Opposite it you shall camp, by the sea* means that [hell] was where their trials poured in from. *And Pharaoh will say of the children of Israel* symbolizes the thinking of the damned about the state of people in the spiritual church. *They stand perplexed in the land* means that they are confused on religious matters. *The wilderness has closed in on them* means that a dimness has enveloped them. *And I will harden Pharaoh's heart* means that spirits dedicated to falsity from evil would continue their obstinate behavior. *And he will pursue after them* means that they would keep trying to subdue them. *And I will gain glory* means that they would see a divine accomplishment of the Lord's divine humanity when falsity was dispersed. *In Pharaoh and in all his army* means that spirits devoted to falsity from evil plunged into hell, where falsity engulfed them like water. *And the Egyptians will know that I am Jehovah* means this taught them that the Lord is the only God. *And [the children of Israel] did so* symbolizes obedience.

And Jehovah spoke to Moses, saying, symbolizes instruction delivered by the Divine through divine truth, as the following shows: *Jehovah spoke, saying,* symbolizes instruction by the Divine (when it concerns events that have yet to be done or happen), as in §§7186, 7241, 7267, 7304, 7380, 7517. And *Moses* represents the Lord as divine truth, as discussed in §§6723, 6752, 6771, 6827, 7010, 7014, 7089, 7382. The reason it means *through* divine truth is that Moses, who represents divine truth, spoke to the people. The Divine itself cannot teach and talk with us or even with angels directly, only indirectly through divine truth (§7796). That is what the Lord's words in John mean: **8127**

> God has never been seen by anyone; the only-born Son, who is in the Father's embrace, is the one who has revealed him. (John 1:18; 5:37)

"The only-born Son" means the Lord as divine truth. It is because of his divine truth that the Lord calls himself the Son of Humankind (§§2628, 2803, 2813, 3704). Moreover, the Lord was divine truth when he was in the world, but afterward, when he had been glorified, he became divine goodness, even in regard to his human side. After that it was from divine goodness that divine truth—the Spirit of Truth, or the Holy Spirit—emanated.

Speak to the children of Israel symbolizes an inflow of divine truth into people in the spiritual church. This can be seen from the symbolism of *speaking* as an inflow (as discussed in §§2951, 5481, 5797, 7270) and from the representation of the *children of Israel* as people of the spiritual church (discussed in §§6426, 6637, 6862, 6868, 7035, 7062, 7198, 7201, 7215, 7223). Speaking means an inflow because in an inner, representative sense, Moses is divine truth, and divine truth enters our perceptions and thoughts by flowing into them. Thought based on perception is inward speech, and outward speech corresponds to it, so in an inner sense, outward speech means inward speech. **8128**

And have them go back means that they were not ready yet. This can be seen from the symbolism of *going back*—back from traveling by way of the land of the Philistines, back to traveling by way of the wilderness to the Suph Sea [Exodus 13:17, 18]—as not being ready yet. What is meant is not being ready yet for admission to heaven, which is symbolized by their entry into the land of Canaan. **8129**

What was explained and shown at verse 18 of the previous chapter (§§8098, 8099) can clarify the situation here and the fact that returning means not being ready. The situation was that these people could not be taken to heaven until they had undergone times of trial and the Lord had used those trials to reaffirm and unite truth and goodness. That is what readiness means here.

8130 *And camp before Pi-hiroth, between Migdol and the sea, before Baal-zephon* symbolizes the beginning of a state for the undergoing of trials. This can be seen from the symbolism of *camping* as the arrangement of truth and goodness into a pattern (discussed in §§4236, 8103 at the end), which in this case was for the undergoing of trials. A state for undergoing trials is what the places they camped in symbolize. The fact that this state is symbolized is clear from what follows: Pharaoh and his army soon pitched their own camp there, and when the children of Israel saw them, it brought them deep distress. This distress is what is meant by a first state of trial. See below at verses 9, 10, 11, 12.

8131 *Opposite it you shall camp, by the sea* means that [hell] was where their trials poured in from, as the following shows: *Opposite it* means close enough to be within sight, or in an inner sense, close enough that this was where it poured in from. *Camping* symbolizes the arrangement of truth and goodness into a pattern for the undergoing of trials, as directly above at §8130. And the *Suph Sea* symbolizes hell, with the falsity-from-evil it holds, as discussed at §8099.

I need to explain briefly how to understand the idea that this was where their trials poured in from. The trials we experience are spiritual battles between evil spirits and good spirits. Past deeds and thoughts that are in our memory are the source and grounds of the conflict. Evil spirits blame and attack us, but good spirits excuse and defend us. The struggles seem to take place inside us, because whatever comes to us from the spiritual world presents itself not as coming from there but rather as existing right within us; see §§741, 751, 761, 1820, 3927, 4249, 4307, 4572, 5036, 6657, 6666. (Spirits have the same experience when they undergo times of trial.) When we face these challenges imminently, then, the Lord reorganizes our inner attributes, or the truth and goodness we possess. He brings these into a state that allows us, through a direct inflow from him and an indirect inflow through heaven, to resist the falsity and evil that come from the hells. In this way we can be protected while we are in crisis.

When we are being tested, we really are close to hell. We are especially near the hell symbolized by the Suph Sea, because that is the home of spirits who knew the truth [when they lived in the world] but led an evil life and therefore gave themselves over to falsity from evil. Anything that causes us distress during our ordeals flows in from the hells through spirits.

This shows what is meant by trials pouring in from hell, as symbolized by their camping opposite, by the Suph Sea.

And Pharaoh will say of the children of Israel symbolizes the thinking of 8132
the damned about the state of people in the spiritual church, as the following shows: *Saying* symbolizes thinking, as dealt with in §§7094, 7107, 7244, 7937. *Pharaoh* represents spirits who use falsity to inflict harassment, as dealt with in §§7107, 7110, 7126, 7142, 7220, 7228, 7317. Here he represents the damned, or spirits totally immersed in falsity from evil, because anyone totally immersed in falsity is under damnation. This state is symbolized by Pharaoh and the Egyptians after the firstborn there were killed, because the killing of the firstborn symbolizes damnation (§§7766, 7778). And the *children of Israel* represent people of the spiritual church, as mentioned just above at §8128.

They stand perplexed in the land means that they are confused on reli- 8133
gious matters. This is evident from the symbolism of *standing perplexed* as being tangled in confusion (discussed at §2831) and from that of the *land* as religious matters. For the idea that the land means the church, see §8011.

The wilderness has closed in on them means that a dimness has envel- 8134
oped them, as the following shows: *Closing in on them* means totally enveloping them, when the phrase has to do with the mental dimness symbolized by a wilderness. And a *wilderness* symbolizes dim faith, as explained in §7313.

And I will harden Pharaoh's heart means that spirits dedicated to falsity 8135
from evil would continue their obstinate behavior. This is established by the symbolism of *hardening* as being obstinate (noted in §§7272, 7300, 7305) and by the representation of *Pharaoh* as spirits immersed in falsity from evil—in other words, the damned (as above at §8132). Pharaoh's *heart* is mentioned because in a positive sense a heart symbolizes the goodness of heavenly love (§§3313, 3635, 3883–3896, 7542), so in a negative sense it symbolizes evil. Here it symbolizes evil in spirits who had a knowledge of faith but lived an evil life.

And he will pursue after them means that they would keep trying to 8136
subdue them. This can be seen from the symbolism of *pursuing after them* as trying to subdue them. [The Egyptians'] intent in pursuing [the children of Israel] was to force them back into a condition of servitude, and servitude connected with the Egyptians symbolizes an intent to subdue (§§6666, 6670, 6671).

8137 *And I will gain glory* means that they would see a divine accomplishment of the Lord's divine humanity when falsity was dispersed. This is clear from the symbolism of *gaining glory,* when it applies to Jehovah, or the Lord, as a divine accomplishment. Here it symbolizes a divine accomplishment of his divine humanity, because by coming into the world, taking on a human nature, and making it divine, the Lord threw all evil and falsity into hell, reduced the heavens to order, and delivered people of the spiritual church from damnation; see §§6854, 6914, 7091, 7828, 7932, 8018. That is the broad symbolism of gaining glory; but here it means that spirits who harassed the upright were thrown into hell, where they were submerged in falsity that resembled the waters of a sea. This was a divine accomplishment resulting from the Lord's mere presence.

[2] Further explanation is called for here. There are as many different hells as there are categories and subcategories of evil. Each hell is separated from the next by mists or clouds or water. In the next life, evil and falsity look to spirits' eyes like mists and clouds and also like water. Falsity-from-evil in people who once had a spiritual religion but lived an evil life looks like water, whereas falsity-from-evil in people who once had a heavenly religion looks like mists. These substances are what seem to surround the inhabitants of the hells, differing always in quantity and quality, thickness and thinness, darkness and obscurity, depending on the general and particular type of ill-intentioned falsity. The hell inhabited by believers in a faith detached from neighborly love who lived a life of evil is engulfed in what looks like seawater. Of course ill-intentioned falsity in the spirits living there does not look like water to them, only to people observing from outside.

Above this sea of theirs lie some hells populated by adulterers. The reason these hells are up there is that in an inner sense adultery stands for the adulteration of goodness and consequent twisting of truth, so it stands for evil that produces falsity opposed to religious truth and goodness (§§2466, 2729, 3399). This falsity is the same kind as that held by the inhabitants of the hell below, who lived contrary to the truth taught by their religion. They totally discounted the goodness urged by their religion as well, and because they did, they also adulterated and twisted everything the Word says about that goodness—in other words, about charity for one's neighbor and love for God.

[3] To say a little more about gaining glory in Pharaoh and in his army: As mentioned above, here it means being plunged into that hell and submerged in a kind of seawater at the mere presence of the Lord. Evil spirits flee the Lord's presence—that is, the presence of goodness and

truth from him. Goodness and truth have only to approach and these spirits suffer horror and torment. They also find themselves surrounded with their own evils and falsities, which burst out of them at such a time, forming a protective barrier around them to keep divinity from acting on them in a way that tortures them. This is the divine accomplishment symbolized by gaining glory in Pharaoh and in his army. The reason this is accomplished by the Lord's divine humanity is, again, that by coming into the world, taking on a human nature, and making it divine, the Lord threw all falsity and evil into hell, reduced truth and goodness in the heavens to order, and delivered people of the spiritual church from damnation.

In Pharaoh and in all his army means that spirits devoted to falsity 8138
from evil plunged into hell, where falsity engulfed them like water. This can be seen from the comments directly above at §8137 to the effect that *Pharaoh* symbolizes spirits thrown into hell, as does *his army.* Pharaoh symbolizes people devoted to falsity from evil, and his army, the falsity itself. For the meaning of an army as truth from goodness, see §§3448, 7236, 7988, and for its consequent meaning in an opposite sense as falsity from evil, see §3448.

I say that falsity engulfed them like water because in hell, falsity-from-evil of the kind held by religious people who had a detached faith and lived an evil life looks like water (§8137). That is why floods of water symbolize a stripping away of truth, and when they do, the water symbolizes falsity (§§705, 739, 756, 6346, 6853, 7307).

And the Egyptians will know that I am Jehovah means this taught them 8139
that the Lord is the only God. This is evident from the explanations at §§7401, 7444, 7544, 7598, 7636, where similar phrases occur.

And [the children of Israel] did so symbolizes obedience, as is evident 8140
without explanation.

Exodus 14:5, 6, 7, 8, 9. *And the king of Egypt was told that the people* 8141
had fled. And the heart of Pharaoh and of his servants turned against the people, and they said, "What is this we have done, that we have sent Israel away from serving us?" And he hitched up his chariot and took his people with him. And he took six hundred choice chariots and all the chariots of Egypt. And there were tertiary officers over all his men. And Jehovah hardened the heart of Pharaoh, king of Egypt, and he pursued after the children of Israel. And the children of Israel were leaving with a high hand. And the Egyptians pursued after them and overtook them camping by the sea—all Pharaoh's chariot horses and his riders and his army, by Pi-hiroth, before Baal-zephon.

And the king of Egypt was told that the people had fled means that adherents of utter falsity-from-evil thought that [members of the spiritual church] had been completely cut off from them. *And the heart of Pharaoh and of his servants turned against the people* means that the state existing among spirits dedicated to falsity that comes of evil changed into a state of evil. *And they said, "What is this we have done,"* symbolizes recrimination. *That we have sent Israel away from serving us?* means that they left those people alone rather than subduing them. *And he hitched up his chariot* symbolizes the distorted theology of a detached faith, in general. *And took his people with him* symbolizes each false idea individually, as well. *And he took six hundred choice chariots* symbolizes each and every false teaching of their detached faith, arranged in order. *And all the chariots of Egypt* symbolizes other false teachings that are subordinate to [the main teachings]. *And there were tertiary officers over all his men* means that they were reduced to order under general categories. *And Jehovah hardened the heart of Pharaoh, king of Egypt,* symbolizes obstinacy resulting from falsity that comes of evil. *And he pursued after the children of Israel* symbolizes an effort to subdue adherents of a faith united with neighborly love. *And the children of Israel were leaving with a high hand* means although they had been released by divine power from those spirits' attempts to subdue them. *And the Egyptians pursued after them* symbolizes the effect of the effort to subdue them made by spirits devoted to falsity that grows out of evil. *And overtook them camping by the sea* symbolizes communication throughout the area of hell in which falsity from evil had its home. *All Pharaoh's chariot horses and his riders and his army* symbolizes every manifestation of falsity rising out of a corrupted intellect. *By Pi-hiroth, before Baal-zephon* means where the communication and therefore the beginning of a state for the undergoing of trials came from.

8142 *And the king of Egypt was told that the people had fled* means that adherents of utter falsity-from-evil thought that [members of the spiritual church] had been completely cut off from them, as the following shows: *Being told* means thinking and reflecting, as mentioned in §§2862, 5508. Pharaoh represents adherents of falsity from evil, as mentioned above in §§8132, 8135. When he is called *king of Egypt,* he represents adherents of utter falsity (7220, 7228), because a monarch symbolizes truth (1672, 2015, 2069, 4575, 4581, 4966, 5044, 6148) and consequently, in a negative sense, falsity. And *fleeing* means being cut off.

8143 *And the heart of Pharaoh and of his servants turned against the people* means that the state existing among spirits dedicated to falsity that comes of evil changed into a state of evil, as the following shows: *Their heart turned* means that their state changed to one of evil. (Turning means a change, in this case a change of heart and therefore a change of state, as is obvious. For the idea that a heart stands for evil, see above at §8135.) *Pharaoh* represents those who are dedicated to falsity from evil, as mentioned above at §8132. *Servants* mean assistants of a lower class and therefore every last person dedicated to falsity from evil (§7396). And the children of Israel represent people of the spiritual church. Plainly, then, *the heart of Pharaoh and of his servants turned against the people* means that the state existing in all spirits dedicated to falsity that comes of evil changed to a state of evil directed against people of the spiritual church.

And they said, "What is this we have done," symbolizes recrimination— **8144**
self-recrimination—as is self-evident.

That we have sent Israel away from serving us? means that they left **8145**
those people alone rather than subduing them, as the following shows: *Sending away* means leaving alone. And when the Egyptians are talking about the children of Israel, *from serving us* means from assaulting them with false ideas and persecuting them (mentioned in §§7120, 7129) and in the process subduing them (§§6666, 6670, 6671).

And he hitched up his chariot symbolizes the distorted theology of a **8146**
detached faith, in general. This is evident from the symbolism of a *chariot* as a theology, which is discussed in §§2762, 5321, 5945. Here it symbolizes the distorted theology of a detached faith, because the chariot is Pharaoh's, and Pharaoh represents the falsity of a detached faith. People who separate faith from neighborly love and lead an evil life cannot help subscribing to falsity (§8094).

[2] The next part of the text is about a pooling together of all the falsity-from-evil held by the spirits who detached faith from neighborly love and lived an evil life. Earlier chapters [Exodus 7–12] were about the process of devastation that stripped away any religious truth they had until they were finally reduced to a state of utter falsity-from-evil and therefore of damnation. The current chapter now deals with their consignment to hell, because that is what follows damnation.

Here are the facts of the matter regarding this state of being cast into hell: When they are about to go to hell, all the hells with which they have communicated open up. This concentrates all the falsity they possess into one place, and the accumulated falsity is then poured into them, which means that falsity from evil condenses around them. To anyone observing from outside, the falsity looks like water (§§8137, 8138). It rises like steam from their way of life. When they are engulfed in this falsity, they are finally in hell.

What is accomplished when falsity from evil pools together and pours into them is that the consequences of the life they previously lived surround them and ever after stay with them. Their particular type of evil and consequent falsity marks them, and marks their hell, off from other hells.

[3] The fact that the theme here is the convergence of all their falsity-from-evil explains why the chapter mentions Pharaoh's chariot, his horses, riders, army, and people so many times: these things symbolize all the falsity they possessed. In the current verse, for instance, "He hitched up *his chariot* and took *his people* with him." Verse 7: "He took *six hundred* choice *chariots* and *all the chariots of Egypt."* Verse 9: "And the Egyptians pursued after them—all Pharaoh's *chariot horses* and *his riders* and *his army."* Verse 17: "I will gain glory in *Pharaoh,* in all his *army,* in his *chariots,* and in his *riders."* Verse 18 likewise. Verse 23: "And the Egyptians pursued, and *all Pharaoh's horses,* his *chariots,* and his *riders* came after them." Verse 25: "Jehovah removed the *wheels* of their *chariots."* Verse 26: "Have the waters come back over the Egyptians, over their *chariots,* and over their *riders."* Verse 28: "The waters came back and covered the *chariots* and *riders,* all the *army* of Pharaoh." These words are repeated as often as they are because they have to do with falsity from evil and the way it pooled and poured into these spirits. The various items are symbols for all aspects of falsity from evil: Pharaoh and the Egyptians, for the actual spirits who adopt such falsity; the chariots, for distorted teachings; the horses, for distorted information produced by a corrupted intellect; the riders, for the twisted reasoning that results; the army and people, for the falsity itself.

8147 *And took his people with him* symbolizes each false idea individually, as well. This is established by the symbolism of a *people* as truth and in a negative sense as falsity, which is discussed in §§1259, 1260, 3295, 3581. Here it symbolizes falsity from evil, which is represented by Pharaoh and the Egyptians.

When the text speaks of Pharaoh and his servants, or Pharaoh and his people, they symbolize every last person clinging to that falsity, and every last false idea (§7396).

8148 *And he took six hundred choice chariots* symbolizes each and every false teaching of their detached faith, arranged in order, as the following shows: *Six hundred* symbolizes all religious truth and goodness without exception, taken together, and therefore in the opposite sense all the falsity and evil belonging to a faith detached from neighborly love. This symbolism of six hundred can be seen from the explanation of the number six hundred thousand at §7973. And *chariots* symbolize religious teachings—in this case the teachings of a detached faith, as noted just above at §8146. *Choice* chariots symbolize the main teachings of that faith, on which all the other teachings hang. The teachings that hang on them, or are subservient to them, are symbolized by the "chariots of Egypt," discussed just below.

[2] It is important to know that the false notions symbolized here by Pharaoh, his army and people, and his chariots, horses, and riders belong mainly to people with a dogmatic faith. By this I mean people who convince themselves the teachings of their religion are true but live an evil life. A dogmatic faith can exist alongside an evil life; a saving faith cannot. A dogmatic faith is a conviction that everything the church teaches is true, but a conviction adopted not for truth's sake or for the sake of living a good life or even for the sake of salvation, since these people barely believe in salvation. No, what they seek is gain—in other words, to pile up honors and wealth and acquire prestige on that account. It is to obtain these advantages that they learn the teachings. Their goal, then, is to contribute not to religion or the salvation of souls but to serve themselves and their own. As a result it is all the same to them whether the teachings are true or false; they do not care, let alone ask the question. Truth for truth's sake does not touch their hearts in the least. Instead they find arguments to support the teachings no matter what those teachings are, and once they have done that, they persuade themselves the teachings are true. They do not stop to think that arguments can support falsity as easily as truth (§§4741, 5033, 6865, 7012, 7680, 7950). [3] This is the source of dogmatism. Its aim and focus is not one's neighbor or the good of one's neighbor or therefore the Lord but oneself and the worldly advantages of position and riches, so it unites with a life of evil, not a life of goodness. Faith united with a life of goodness brings salvation. This faith is given by the Lord, but dogmatic faith comes from a person himself or herself. The former lasts forever, but the latter dissolves in the next life. It dissolves in the world too for those who cannot profit from it. As long as it pays, they go to battle for it, as if they were battling for heaven itself. In reality, though, they are fighting not for that faith but for themselves. To them the teachings that constitute faith are the means of achieving a goal, and that goal is position and wealth.

In the world, it is hard to distinguish people subscribing to this faith from people whose faith is saving. They speak and preach with a passion resembling zeal for the teachings, although the passion actually rises out of self-love and materialism.

[4] It is these people especially who are symbolized by Pharaoh and the Egyptians. In the other world they are purged of that faith. Once purged, they dwell in utter falsity-from-evil, because falsity then bursts forth from their evil. All evil carries related falsity with it, because the two are closely connected. The falsity becomes visible when such people are left to the evil they have lived. The evil then resembles a fire, and the falsity resembles the glimmer of that fire.

This type of evil and resulting falsity is entirely different from other kinds. It is more despicable than the others, because it attacks the goodness and truth that go to make up faith. Such falsity accordingly harbors profanation. To engage in profanation is to acknowledge what is true and good but live contrary to it (§§593, 1008, 1010, 1059, 2051, 3398, 3898, 4289, 4601, 6959, 6963, 6971).

8149 *And all the chariots of Egypt* symbolizes other false teachings that are subordinate to [the main teachings]. This can be seen from the symbolism of Pharaoh's chariots as the main teachings embodying falsity, on which all the other teachings hang. As a consequence of this symbolism, the *chariots of Egypt* symbolize false teachings subordinate to the teachings mentioned directly above in §8148. The king and his chariots symbolize something primary; the people (the Egyptians) and their chariots, something secondary.

Religious teachings among people who lead evil lives are described here as false, even though they can be true to a greater or lesser extent. The reason I describe them as false is that truth is not true in people who lead a life of evil, so far as those people themselves are concerned. When they use teachings to do evil in their life, it sheds its trueness and takes on the character of falsity. This is because it then holds evil as its goal and unites with that evil. Truth cannot be united to evil without turning into falsity, and it turns into falsity when it is misinterpreted and in this way perverted. That is why I describe religious teachings among these people as false even if the teachings themselves are true. The rule is that truth is rendered false in people who lead evil lives, and falsity is rendered true in people who lead good lives. The reason falsity is turned into truth among the latter people is that they use it in such a way that it harmonizes with something good, which actually eliminates falsity's rough edges; see §8051.

And there were tertiary officers over all his men means that they were reduced to order under general categories. This can be seen from the symbolism of *tertiary officers* as general categories with their subcategories. The reason tertiary officers have this symbolism is that the word *tertiary* comes from *three,* and three symbolizes what is complete and whole (§§2788, 4495, 7715), while officers symbolize leading elements. The two words together stand for general categories. Under the general categories come all the different elements—in order—that need to form a series. Being arranged in order under general categories enables individual details to cohere, to take shape, and to develop a group character. (Regarding general categories, with their subcategories and the individual details under these, see §§920, 2384, 3739, 4325 at the end, 4329, 4345, 4383, 5208, 5339, 6115, 6146.) **8150**

And Jehovah hardened the heart of Pharaoh symbolizes obstinacy resulting from falsity that comes of evil. This can be seen from the symbolism of *hardening a heart* as being obstinate, as mentioned in §§7272, 7300, 7305, 7616. It says *Jehovah* hardened Pharaoh's heart, which on an inner level means that spirits intent on evil and falsity are actually the ones who harden themselves. So evil and falsity is actually what hardens itself. On this subject, see §§2447, 6071, 6991, 6997, 7533, 7643, 7877, 7926. **8151**

And he pursued after the children of Israel symbolizes an effort to subdue adherents of a faith united with neighborly love, as the following shows: *Pursuing* symbolizes an effort to subdue them, as at §8136. And the *children of Israel* represent people of the spiritual church, as noted many times, so they represent adherents of a faith united with neighborly love. After all, people of the spiritual church adhere to that faith in both their theology and their life. For people with a genuinely spiritual religion, the goodness taught by faith (meaning neighborly love) is the crucial element and therefore comes in first place. But the truth taught by faith (meaning faith itself) is the crucial, first-place element for people who detach faith from the goodness it teaches in both their theology and their life. They do not belong to the spiritual church, because the way a person lives is what constitutes religion. Theological teachings do not, except to the extent that they are incorporated into life. **8152**

The Lord's church, then, is plainly not here or there [Luke 17:21] but everywhere, both within kingdoms where the church exists and outside them, where people live by the commandments of neighborly love. That is why the Lord's church lies scattered throughout the globe and yet is one church. When religion consists in life, not in theology separated from life, the church is unified, but when religion consists in theology, there are many churches.

8153 *And the children of Israel were leaving with a high hand* means although they had been released by divine power from those spirits' attempts to subdue them, as the following shows: The *children of Israel* represent people of the spiritual church, or people with a faith united to neighborly love, as directly above at §8152. *Leaving* means being delivered, or being released from the effort to subdue them symbolized by "pursuing" (§8152). And a *high hand* symbolizes divine power. A *hand,* you see, symbolizes power (§§878, 3387, 4931–4937, 5327, 5328, 5544, 6292, 6947, 7011, 7188, 7189, 7518, 7673, 8050, 8069), and *high* means divine. The reason high means divine is that heights refer to heaven, where the Divine is. That is why the Word says that Jehovah (the Lord) dwells on high, and calls him the Highest One. In Isaiah, for instance:

> Jehovah has been *exalted,* because he inhabits the *heights.* (Isaiah 33:5)

In the same author:

> This is what the *High and Lofty One* dwelling to eternity has said, and he whose name is the Holy One: "In what is holy and *high* I dwell." (Isaiah 57:15)

In David:

> Jehovah sent *from on high* and carried me away. (Psalms 18:16)

Jehovah is therefore called the *Highest One* in Deuteronomy 32:8; Daniel 4:17, 24, 34; 7:18, 22, 25; Psalms 7:17; 9:2; 18:13; 46:4; 50:14; 57:2; 82:6.

[2] Since heights symbolized heaven and the divinity that fills it, people of the representative church established divine worship on mountains and high elevations. For the same reason, they built high places to worship on as well. Mention of these places is scattered through the narrative and prophetic parts of the Word, as in Ezekiel:

> You built a *high place* for yourself and made a *lofty spot* for yourself on every street. At the head of every road you built your *high place.* (Ezekiel 16:24, 25, 31)

The reason elevation symbolized divinity is that the sky symbolized heaven. People even believed heaven was located in the sky, although the wiser of them knew that heaven was not on high but existed where a loving goodness did, or inside a person, wherever that person was.

For the idea that "high" means inward, or that it means the goodness that lies within, see §§450, 1735, 2148, 4210, 4599.

And the Egyptians pursued after them symbolizes the effect of the effort to subdue them made by spirits devoted to falsity that grows out of evil, as the following shows: *Pursuing* symbolizes an effort to subdue, as above at §8152. Here it symbolizes the effect of that effort, since it is a repetition of the phrase. And the *Egyptians* symbolize spirits devoted to falsity that grows out of evil, as mentioned many times before. 8154

And overtook them camping by the sea symbolizes communication throughout the area of hell in which falsity from evil had its home, as the following shows: *Overtaking* symbolizes communication, because in a spiritual sense, overtaking or reaching someone means an inflow that communicates. In this instance it is a communication of the falsity-from-evil belonging to the spirits symbolized by the Egyptians, shared with the people symbolized by Israel. The fact that the communication took place in that area can be seen from the trial they first underwent there. The trial is discussed below [§§8158–8176]. All trials spring from an inflow of the hells and therefore from communication with them (8131). *Camping* symbolizes the Lord's rearrangement of truth and goodness into a pattern suited to the undergoing of trials (8103, 8130, 8131). And the *sea*—the Suph Sea, here—symbolizes the hell in which is found the falsity-from-evil belonging to spirits whose faith is detached from neighborly love and whose life is evil (8099, 8137, 8148). 8155

All Pharaoh's chariot horses and his riders and his army symbolizes every manifestation of falsity rising out of a corrupted intellect, as the following shows: *Horses* symbolize the intellect, as discussed in §§2761, 2762, 3217, 5321, 7024, 8029. Here they symbolize the corrupted intellect found in people devoted to evil and therefore to falsity. *Chariots* symbolize doctrinal teachings, as discussed in §§2762, 5321, 5945, 8146. *Riders* symbolize matters of the intellect, as discussed at §6534. In this case they symbolize distorted reasoning that comes from a corrupted intellect. And an *army* symbolizes falsity, as mentioned above at §8138. This makes it clear that *Pharaoh's chariot horses and his riders and his army* symbolize information, reasoning, and falsity rising out of a corrupted intellect, and consequently every manifestation of falsity. 8156

By Pi-hiroth, before Baal-zephon means where the communication and therefore the beginning of a state for the undergoing of trials came from. This can be seen from the remarks above at §8130. 8157

Exodus 14:10, 11, 12, 13, 14. *And Pharaoh drew near, and the children of Israel raised their eyes, and here were the Egyptians setting out after them!* 8158

And they were greatly afraid, and the children of Israel cried out to Jehovah. And they said to Moses, "Were there no graves in Egypt, [that] you have taken us to die in the wilderness? What is this you have done to us, to bring us out of Egypt? Isn't this the word that we spoke to you in Egypt, saying, 'Leave us alone and let us serve the Egyptians, because it is better for us to serve the Egyptians than die in the wilderness'?" And Moses said to the people, "Don't be afraid. Stand firm and see Jehovah's salvation, which he will perform for you today, because the Egyptians whom you see today you will no longer see, forever. Jehovah will fight for you, and you yourselves are to keep silent."

And Pharaoh drew near symbolizes a heavy inflow of ill-intentioned falsity from there. *And the children of Israel raised their eyes* symbolizes the intellectual side of the mind, and thought. *And here were the Egyptians setting out after them* symbolizes falsity becoming more and more severe all the time. *And they were greatly afraid* symbolizes horror. *And the children of Israel cried out to Jehovah* symbolizes a plea for help. *And they said to Moses* symbolizes the trial at its peak, when despair set in. *Were there no graves in Egypt, [that] you have taken us to die in the wilderness?* means that if they were to be damned, it was all the same whether damnation came through falsity inflicted by their persecutors or through a state of trials in which they would succumb. *What is this you have done to us, to bring us out of Egypt?* means that delivery from the onslaughts of falsity would be useless. *Isn't this the word that we spoke to you in Egypt, saying,* means that this was the kind of thing they thought when they were being persecuted by falsity. *Leave us alone and let us serve the Egyptians* means that they would not be held back from surrendering. *Because it is better for us to serve the Egyptians than die in the wilderness* means that being damned by the violence falsity inflicts in a state of persecution would be preferable to being damned by succumbing in times of trial. *And Moses said to the people* symbolizes being lifted out of the state of despair by divine truth. *Don't be afraid* means not to despair. *Stand firm and see Jehovah's salvation* symbolizes being saved by the Lord alone without contributing in any way. *Which he will perform today* means to eternity. *Because the Egyptians whom you see today you will no longer see, forever* means that once the falsity has been laid aside, it will remain out of sight to eternity. *Jehovah will fight for you* means that the Lord alone bears the weight of the battle in times of trial. *And you yourselves are to keep silent* means that they will accomplish nothing whatever by their own strength.

8159 *And Pharaoh drew near* symbolizes a heavy inflow of ill-intentioned falsity from there. This can be seen from the representation of *Pharaoh* as people devoted to falsity from evil (discussed in §§8132, 8135, 8146, 8148) and from the symbolism of *drawing near* as an inflow.

The subject of the inner meaning is the first critical challenge faced by people who have been delivered, and when we are tested, it is always through an inflow from the hells. Spirits from hell stir up in us every bad thing that we have done or thought and bring it out in the open. They use it to blame and condemn us, which wounds our conscience and inflicts mental distress. It is the inflow of the hells that accomplishes this—especially the hell represented by the Suph Sea. From these considerations you can see that on a spiritual level (when that level of meaning has to do with times of trial), drawing near symbolizes an inflow.

[2] Since the next verses deal with the first trial faced by people of the spiritual church, it needs to be known that they could not be tested until the Lord had glorified his human nature, or made it divine, and become present with them through it. Had they been tested earlier they would have succumbed, because people of the spiritual church were saved only by the Lord's divine humanity.

The following words in Malachi stand for trials that people of the spiritual church were to undergo after the Lord had come into the world and gained the capacity to fight the hells on their behalf, operating from his divine humanity:

> Suddenly to his Temple will come the Lord, whom you seek, and the Angel of the Covenant, whom you desire. "Watch: He is coming!" Jehovah Sabaoth has said. "Who will be able to endure the day of his coming, and who will stay standing when he appears? *For he is like a smelter's fire and like fullers' soap; he will sit smelting and purging silver and will purify the children of Levi and refine them like gold and like silver,* so that they may come bringing a minha to Jehovah in righteousness. Then the minha of Judah and Jerusalem will be sweet to Jehovah, as in the days of old and as in former years." (Malachi 3:1, 2, 3, 4)

This is obviously about the Lord's Coming. The children of Levi are people of the spiritual church, because Levi symbolizes neighborly love, or spiritual goodness (§§3875, 4497, 4502, 4503). The smelter's fire means trials that purify, and purging and refining the Levites like gold and silver stands for this purification. The minha they would bring to Jehovah is faith and neighborly love. The days of old and former years are the ancient churches and the state that then characterized worship of the Lord.

[3] As for times of trial, what happens during them (as I said above at §8131) is that the hells fight against us, and the Lord fights for us. Every

time the hells foist a false thought on us, the Divine responds. Falsity from the hells is introduced into our outer, earthly self and flows into it, but the response from the Divine works on our inner, spiritual self. The inflow from the Divine does not intrude as much on our awareness as hell's does, nor does it rouse specific thoughts, only general thoughts. It operates in such a way that we barely sense it except as a kind of hopefulness and resulting comfort, but the hope and comfort hold countless gifts to which we are oblivious. These gifts take a form that harmonizes with our passions or loves, especially our passion or love for the truth and goodness that form our conscience.

[4] The purpose of these remarks has been to make it known that the time the children of Israel spent in the wilderness depicts the series of trials undergone by people of the Lord's spiritual church who were delivered. The reason they were tested was to be further prepared for heaven. Trials are the only means for strengthening and uniting goodness and truth, and they are the means of integrating faith into neighborly love and neighborly love into faith.

The following words of the Lord in Matthew mean that people in the church will undergo trials:

> Any who do not *take up their cross* and follow after me are unworthy of me. (Matthew 10:38, 39; Mark 8:31–end)

In the same author:

> He said to his disciples, "If any want to come after me, they should deny themselves, *take up their cross,* and follow me." (Matthew 16:24, 25; Luke 9:23, 24)

In Luke:

> Any who *do not carry their cross* and come after me cannot be my disciples. (Luke 14:27)

In Mark:

> Jesus said to the rich man: "Come, follow me, *taking up the cross.*" (Mark 10:21)

And in Matthew:

> Don't suppose that I came to send peace onto the earth; *I came not to send peace but a sword.* (Matthew 10:34)

[5] It is important to know, though, that we ourselves do not do the fighting during our crises; the Lord alone fights for us, even though it

looks as though we are doing it. And when the Lord fights for us, we always win.

Few are put to the test these days because people do not live a life of religion, which means they do not have a conscience formed of truth. People who do not have a conscience formed of truth by living a good life succumb in their trials, which brings them into a worse state than before.

And the children of Israel raised their eyes symbolizes the intellectual **8160**
side of the mind, and thought. This can be seen from the symbolism of *eyes,* which stand for the intellectual side of the mind, as discussed in §§2701, 3820, 4403–4421, 4523–4534. *Raising* one's eyes therefore symbolizes insight, perception, and thought (§§2789, 2829, 3198, 3202, 4083, 4086, 4339).

And here were the Egyptians setting out after them symbolizes falsity **8161**
becoming more and more severe all the time. This can be seen from the symbolism of an *Egyptian* as someone devoted to falsity from evil and so as the falsity-from-evil itself (discussed in §§8132, 8135, 8146, 8148) and from that of *setting out after them* as an inflow and closer communication. "Pharaoh drew near" symbolized an inflow of ill-intentioned falsity (§8159), so "setting out after them" symbolizes an even more direct and therefore severe inflow. That is why falsity that becomes more severe all the time is being symbolized.

The next part of the text depicts a trial that comes about through an inflow of ill-intentioned falsity from the hells, which is why this verse depicts the approach of that falsity, or its growing severity.

And they were greatly afraid symbolizes horror. This can be seen from **8162**
the symbolism of *being afraid,* when it applies to spiritual trials, as dread or horror.

The reason fear means horror is that when a spiritual crisis looms, falsity and evil pummel our conscience and therefore our inner self (since conscience is a function of the inner self). The result is dread, which consists in aversion combined with fear of spiritual death. The mere inflow of falsity and evil arouses dread in the conscientious. After all, conscience is a product of religious truth and goodness, meaning that it is a product of what composes our spiritual life. Falsity and evil are destroyers of that life, so they are would-be bringers of death, in the sense of damnation. That is what causes horror.

And the children of Israel cried out to Jehovah symbolizes a plea for **8163**
help, which needs no explanation.

And they said to Moses symbolizes the trial at its peak, and despair. **8164**
This can be seen from the words that follow, which *they said* includes.

The next words are obviously words spoken when the trial has reached its peak and despair has set in. I speak of despair because it usually is the end (or comes near the end) of spiritual trials (§§1787, 2694, 5279, 5280, 7147, 7155, 7166).

Not many today undergo spiritual trials, with the result that few know much about them, so let me say a little more.

There are spiritual trials and earthly trials. Spiritual trials test the inner self; earthly trials, the outer self. Spiritual trials can happen in either the absence or the presence of earthly trials. In earthly trials it is our body, status, financial situation—in short, our earthly life—that suffers, as for instance when we experience sickness, misfortune, persecution, unjust punishment, and so on. The distress that then arises is what is meant by earthly trials. These challenges contribute nothing whatever to our spiritual life, nor can they be called trials, only afflictions. They arise out of wounds sustained by our earthly life, a life of self-love and materialism. Even criminals go through these vexations from time to time, and the degree of pain and distress they feel depends on the degree to which they themselves and their worldly advantages are what they love and what bring them alive.

[2] Spiritual trials, however, test our inner self and attack our spiritual life. In spiritual trials we do not worry about any loss of earthly life but of faith and charity and consequently of salvation. These struggles are often triggered by earthly struggles, because during them, in sickness or pain or the loss of wealth, prestige, and so on, we might wonder about the help the Lord offers or about his providence and about the situation—the fact that the wicked are boasting and gloating when the good are in agony and are suffering various types of pain and loss. If we do wonder about these things, spiritual trial then combines with earthly trial.

This was true of the Lord's final trial—in Gethsemane and during the Crucifixion—which was the worst of all.

These remarks clarify the difference between earthly and spiritual trial.

There is also a third type, depressive anxiety, which usually traces its cause to a diseased condition of body or mind. It can have either a certain measure of spiritual trial in it or no spiritual trial at all.

8165 *Were there no graves in Egypt, [that] you have taken us to die in the wilderness?* means that if they were to be damned, it was all the same whether damnation came through falsity inflicted by their persecutors or through a state of trials in which they would succumb, as the following shows: *Graves* symbolize damnation, as discussed in §§2916, 5832. *Egypt* symbolizes persecution, as discussed at §7278, because the Egyptians and

Pharaoh represent inhabitants of the other world who use falsity to inflict harassment (7097, 7107, 7110, 7126, 7142, 7317). *Dying* also symbolizes damnation, as discussed in §§5407, 6119, 7494. And a *wilderness* symbolizes a state for undergoing trials (8098). So dying in the wilderness means succumbing in times of trial and being damned. From this you can see that *were there no graves in Egypt, [that] you have taken us to die in the wilderness?* means that if they were to be damned, it was all the same whether damnation came through falsity inflicted by their persecutors (their previous state) or through trials in which they would succumb (the state they later came into).

[2] These words are plainly words of despair. People in despair, the final stage of trial, actually think like this, and they are then heading downhill or sliding into hell, metaphorically speaking. Such thinking at such a time does no harm, though, and angels pay no attention to it, because everyone has limited strength. When a crisis reaches the utmost limit of our strength, we can bear it no further and we sink. At that point, however, when we are sliding downhill to a fall, the Lord lifts us up, freeing us from despair. Most of the time we are then brought into a state of hope, which leads to sunny consolation and to bliss.

I speak of damnation through a state of trials in which they would succumb because people who succumb in times of trial come into a state of damnation. The point of these ordeals is to strengthen truth and goodness and unite them, so as to produce faith and neighborly love. When we win in our trials we gain this outcome, but when we succumb, we reject truth and goodness and strengthen falsity and evil. That is what brings us a state of damnation.

What is this you have done to us, to bring us out of Egypt? means that delivery from the onslaughts of falsity would be useless, as the following shows: *What is this you have done to us?* means that it would be useless. Being *brought out* means being delivered. And *Egypt* symbolizes the inflicting of persecution, as mentioned directly above at §8165. **8166**

Isn't this the word that we spoke to you in Egypt, saying, means that this was the kind of thing they thought when they were being persecuted by falsity, as the following shows: *Isn't this the word that we spoke?* means that this was the kind of thing they thought because *this word* means this matter and consequently this kind of thing, and *speaking* means thinking. (For the symbolism of speaking as an inflow and its reception, see §§5797, 7270, 8128. For its consequent symbolism as thought too, §§2271, 2287, 2619.) And *Egypt* symbolizes persecution by falsity, as above at §8165. **8167**

8168 *Leave us alone and let us serve the Egyptians* means that they would not be held back from surrendering, as the following shows: *Leaving us alone,* when spoken of in relation to attacks by the persecutors, means not stopping them or holding them back. And *serving the Egyptians* means surrendering in defeat to the spirits attacking with falsity, so ["let us serve them"] means not holding them back from surrendering.

Here is why *leaving us alone* means not stopping them or holding them back, when the phrase has to do with an inflow of divine truth (represented by Moses) during a state of attack and a state of trial: Two forces or powers act on us. One is caused by falsity the hells bring into our outer self, the other by truth the Lord instills into our inner self (§8159). These two forces combat one another. The falsity the hells introduce takes its force and power from the love we have for ourselves and our worldly advantages, [2] but the truth the Lord instills takes its force and power from love for our neighbor and for the Lord. When we conquer, the inner force and power gains the permanent upper hand, because it is divine. It keeps the force or power of falsity from growing beyond the point where it can be repelled. When the two forces act, then, the inner force from the Lord constantly holds us back and stops falsity from dragging us down to the point where we would succumb. When two opposing forces act, it is common for one to pull and the other to pull in the opposite direction. The individual emotions that go to make up love are the forces of the spiritual world, and the means by which they operate are truths or, in a negative sense, falsities.

8169 *Because it is better for us to serve the Egyptians than die in the wilderness* means that being damned by the violence falsity inflicts in a state of persecution would be preferable to being damned by succumbing in times of trial, as the following shows: *Being better than something* means being preferable. *Serving the Egyptians* symbolizes succumbing to the false thinking of the persecuting spirits, because serving means being subdued (§§6666, 6670, 6671) and therefore succumbing—here, to the false thinking of the persecutors. *Dying* symbolizes damnation, as above at §8165. And the *wilderness* symbolizes a state of undergoing trials, as discussed at §8098. Clearly, then, *it is better for us to serve the Egyptians than die in the wilderness* means that succumbing to falsity under attack would be preferable to succumbing in times of trial.

As a matter of fact it is true that succumbing in the former state is better than succumbing in the latter. Succumbing in times of trial means committing oneself to falsity and evil that oppose religious truth and goodness.

Succumbing under a state of siege also means committing oneself to falsity and evil, but not in direct opposition to religious truth and goodness. Succumbing in times of trial, then, obviously involves blaspheming and sometimes even profaning what is true and good; and being damned for profanation is the greatest, most horrific damnation of all.

And Moses said to the people symbolizes being lifted out of the state of despair by divine truth. This is evident from the subsequent words Moses said, which involve the idea of being lifted out of a state of despair. **8170**

I speak of divine truth as the agent because it is the only means by which we are lifted up in a state of trial. In an inner, representative sense, *Moses* means divine truth; see §§6752, 7010, 7014, 7089.

Don't be afraid means not to despair. This is established by the symbolism of *being afraid* as being horrified, which is discussed above at §8162. Here it means to despair, because at the beginning of our trials, spiritual fear is horror, but at the end it is despair. Spiritual fear is the fear of damnation. **8171**

Stand firm and see Jehovah's salvation symbolizes being saved by the Lord alone without contributing in any way, as the following shows: *Standing firm and seeing* means believing. For the symbolism of seeing as understanding, acknowledging, and believing, see §§897, 2150, 2325, 2807, 3863, 3869, 4403–4421, 5400. And *Jehovah's salvation* symbolizes being saved by the Lord. Here, where the theme is deliverance from times of trial, it symbolizes being saved by the Lord alone without contributing in any way. For *Jehovah* in the Word being the Lord, see §§1343, 1736, 2921, 3023, 3035, 5041, 5663, 6281, 6303, 6905, 6945, 6956. **8172**

The people are being told here to believe that they are saved by the Lord alone without contributing at all because this is the main requirement for faith during times of crisis. If we believe we can resist by our own strength when we are being tested, we succumb. This is because we are laboring under a delusion. The delusion leads us to claim the credit as our own and therefore to demand that we be saved by ourselves, which shuts out any inflow from the Divine. People who believe the Lord alone resists in times of crisis are the ones who overcome, because they have truth on their side. They give credit to the Lord and can tell they are saved by the Lord alone. People with the faith that comes of neighborly love attribute all salvation to the Lord and none to themselves.

Which he will perform today means to eternity. This is clear from the discussion in §§2838, 3998, 4304, 6165, 6984 of the symbolism of *today* as eternity. **8173**

8174 *Because the Egyptians whom you see [today] you will no longer see, forever* means that once the falsity has been laid aside, it will remain out of sight to eternity, as the following shows: *Egyptians* symbolize people devoted to falsity from evil (discussed in §§8132, 8135, 8146, 8148) and therefore falsity-from-evil itself. And *no longer seeing,* when the phrase has to do with falsity, means being laid aside, because the falsity in us is not expelled but rather is laid aside. The Lord withholds us from evil and the resulting falsity and keeps us on a good path (§§1581, 2256, 2269, 2406, 4564). And *forever* means to eternity.

8175 *Jehovah will fight for you* means that the Lord alone bears the weight of the battle in times of trial. This can be seen from the symbolism of *fighting for you,* when it has to do with Jehovah's role in times of trial, as bearing by himself the weight of the battles we then have. For the idea that Jehovah is the Lord, see just above at §8172.

The reason the Lord alone endures the battles we face during our trials and is victorious in them is that only the Divine can overcome the hells. If the Divine did not counteract the hells, they would flood in on us like an immense ocean, one hell after another. Our strength would be completely inadequate to resist them, especially since on our own we are nothing but evil and consequently nothing but hell—from which the Lord extricates us at that time and withholds us afterward. See the discussion at §§1581, 1661, 1692, 6574.

8176 *And you yourselves are to keep silent* means that they will accomplish nothing [whatever] by their own strength. This is evident from the symbolism of *keeping silent* as being still, and—since the subject is times of trial—as not thinking or believing they accomplish anything by their own strength. On this topic, see the discussion and explanation above at §§8172, 8175.

Nonetheless they should not take this as an excuse to let their hands hang loose, waiting for direct inspiration. No, they must fight as if on their own, all the while acknowledging and believing it is the Lord who acts. See §§1712, 1937, 1947, 2882, 2883, 2891.

8177 Exodus 14:15, 16, 17, 18. *And Jehovah said to Moses, "Why are you crying to me? Speak to the children of Israel and have them set out. And you, lift your staff and stretch your hand out over the sea and divide it, and have the children of Israel come into the middle of the sea on dry ground. And I—yes, I—am hardening the heart of the Egyptians, who will come after them, and I will gain glory in Pharaoh and in all his army, in his chariots, and in his riders. And the Egyptians will know that I am Jehovah, in my gaining glory in Pharaoh, in his chariots, and in his riders."*

And Jehovah said to Moses symbolizes an urgent message. *Why are you crying to me?* means that there is no need for intervention. *Speak to the children of Israel* symbolizes an inflow and a perception. *And have them set out* symbolizes continuing developments, lasting until the people's preparation is complete. *And you, lift your staff* symbolizes the power of divine truth. *Stretch your hand out over the sea* symbolizes a wielding of power in the area of the hell where falsity from evil is found. *Divide it* symbolizes dispersal of the falsity there. *And have the children of Israel come into the middle of the sea on dry ground* means so that people of the spiritual church can pass through in safety, free from an inflow of falsity. *And I—yes, I—am hardening the heart of the Egyptians* symbolizes the obstinacy of falsity from evil. *Who will come after them* symbolizes an effort to inflict violence by pouring on falsity-from-evil. *And I will gain glory in Pharaoh and in all his army, in his chariots, and in his riders* means that they will see the divine goodness of the Lord's divine humanity bring about the dispersal of falsity and twisted reasoning. *And the Egyptians will know that I am Jehovah* means so as to reveal that the Lord alone is God and that there is no other god besides him. *In my gaining glory in Pharaoh, in his chariots, and in his riders* means—as above, and as a result—that they will see the Lord on his own bring about the dispersal of falsity, false teachings, and twisted reasoning.

And Jehovah said to Moses symbolizes an urgent message. This is estab- **8178**
lished by the symbolism of *Jehovah said*—when the focus is on being raised up out of trials and delivered from them—as an urgent message, as in §§7033, 7090.

Why are you crying to me? means that there is no need for intervention. **8179**
This is clear from the symbolism of *crying to Jehovah* as intervening—intervening to deliver them from their trial. In consequence of this symbolism the question, *Why are you crying to me?* means, "Why are you intervening when there is no need for intervention?" The next words are therefore "Speak to the children of Israel and have them set out," which means that they will have help but the trial will still continue until their preparation is complete.

[2] Let me explain about the lack of need for intervention. People who are being tested often slacken their hands, resorting exclusively to prayers, which they pour forth ardently. They do not realize that prayer

does no good then and that they need instead to fight the falsity and evil the hells introduce. The weapons for the battle are religious truths, which do help, because they strengthen goodness and truth in its opposition to falsity and evil. What is more, we must fight as if we were on our own during our struggles and trials, while still acknowledging and believing that it is the Lord who acts (see above at §8176). If we do not fight as if we were on our own, we do not adopt as our own the goodness and truth that flow in from the Lord through heaven. If we do fight as if we were on our own, believing nonetheless that it is the Lord who acts, we do make goodness and truth our own. This provides us with a new selfhood, called heavenly autonomy, which is a new will.

[3] Besides, people who engage in no other definite activity than prayer when they are being tried do not know that they would not be ready for heaven—and consequently could not be saved—if their crisis were interrupted before being brought all the way to its conclusion. This is another reason the prayers of people under trial are not much listened to. The Lord seeks the final goal, which is our salvation. He alone knows what the end is; we do not; and he does not act on prayers rebelling against the salvation he has in view.

For people who conquer in times of trial, the truth of this is reinforced. People who do not conquer, having been unheard, entertain doubts about divine aid and divine power, and sometimes, having slackened their hands, partially succumb.

These comments show what it means to say there is no need for intervention: that we are not to rely on prayer. When prayer has a divine origin, it always contains the thought and belief that the Lord alone knows whether the object of the prayer is useful or not. The person praying therefore submits the hearing of the prayer to the Lord and immediately adds the plea, "Lord, let your will be done, not mine," in keeping with the Lord's words during his heaviest trial, in Gethsemane (Matthew 26:39, 42, 44).

8180 *Speak to the children of Israel* symbolizes an inflow and a perception. This can be seen from the symbolism of *speaking.* When divine truth (represented by Moses) is said to speak to people in the spiritual church (the children of Israel), it symbolizes an inflow and a resulting perception, as also in §§2951, 5481, 5797, 7270, 8128.

8181 *And have them set out* symbolizes continuing developments, lasting until the people's preparation is complete. This is evident from the symbolism of *setting out* as further developments and continuation (discussed in §§4375, 4554, 4585, 5996). After all, the message is that they must not cry out, or plead, but continue their journey to the Suph Sea and through it to the wilderness beyond. So the meaning is that they will continue on through hell—crossing it in safety—to a constant series of trials until their preparation is complete. (For the symbolism of the Suph Sea as hell, see §§8099, 8137, 8148, and for that of the wilderness as a state of undergoing trials, see §8098.)

And you, lift your staff symbolizes the power of divine truth. This can 8182
be seen from the symbolism of a *staff* as power (discussed in §§4013, 4015, 4876, 4936, 6947, 7011, 7026) and from the representation of Moses, the one told to lift his staff, as divine truth (mentioned many times before).

Stretch your hand out over the sea symbolizes a wielding of power in 8183
the area of the hell where falsity from evil is found. This can be seen from the symbolism of *stretching a hand out* as a wielding of power (discussed at §7673) and from that of the *sea,* which in this case is the Suph Sea, as the hell in which is found the ill-intentioned falsity adopted by people who were once part of the church (discussed in §§8099, 8137, 8148). More will be said about this hell at the end of the final chapters of Exodus, where the hells will be described from experience, the Lord in his divine mercy willing.

Divide it symbolizes dispersal of the falsity there. This can be seen from 8184
the symbolism of *dividing that sea* as dispersing the falsity-from-evil in that hell. Falsity looks like water there, as the explanation above in §§8099, 8137, 8148 indicates. When a pillar of angels in which the Lord is present passes through that hell, falsity ebbs away and the water there, which is falsity, accordingly disappears. This shows that *dividing the sea* symbolizes a dispersal of the falsity in the hell represented by the Suph Sea.

And have the children of Israel come into the middle of the sea on dry 8185
ground means so that people of the spiritual church can pass through in safety, free from an inflow of falsity. This can be seen from the symbolism of *coming* or entering through the *middle* as passing through, from the representation of the *children of Israel* as people of the spiritual church (mentioned many times), and from the symbolism of *on dry ground,* which means in safety, free from an inflow of falsity. The waters of that sea symbolize falsity from evil (§§8137, 8138), so dry ground means being free of falsity. Dry ground and drying up have the same symbolism in David:

> You shattered the heads of Leviathan; you *divided spring and river;* you *dried up strong rivers.* (Psalms 74:14, 15)

Drying up strong rivers stands for dispersing more powerful types of falsity. [2] In Zechariah:

> I will gather them, because I will redeem them; I will *bring them back from the land of Egypt,* and from Assyria I will gather them. And to the land of Gilead and Lebanon I will bring them. *[Israel] will cross through the sea of distress.* But he will *strike the waves in the sea* and *dry up all the depths of its current.* And the pride of Assyria will be thrown down, and the staff of Egypt will withdraw. And I will make them mighty in Jehovah. (Zechariah 10:8–end)

This is about people who rely on themselves and their own wisdom in spiritual matters and about the dispersal of falsity achieved through times of trial. The land of Egypt stands for knowledge; Assyria, for reasoning based on knowledge. Crossing [through] the sea of distress stands for trials. Striking the waves in the sea and drying up the depths of its current stand for dispersing the falsity involved. "The pride of Assyria will be thrown down, and the staff of Egypt will withdraw" means that they will no longer rely on their own wisdom. Instead they will rely on wisdom from the Lord, which is symbolized by "I will make them mighty in Jehovah." [3] Likewise in Isaiah:

> He is saying to Jerusalem, "You will be inhabited," and to the cities of Judah, "You will be rebuilt (and its wastelands I will raise up)"; he is saying to the abyss, "*Drain away,* and *your rivers I will dry up.*" (Isaiah 44:26, 27)

Saying to the abyss, "Drain away," and drying up its rivers stands for scattering evil and falsity.

When water symbolizes truth, however, dryness symbolizes a state of nontruth, or a state devoid of truth, as in Isaiah:

> I will pour *water* out on thirsty land, and *brooklets on dry ground.* (Isaiah 44:3)

The water and brooklets stand for truth, the dry ground for a place where there is no truth. [4] In Jeremiah:

> O sword against the Chaldeans and against the inhabitants of Babylon! O sword against its horses and against its chariots! *Drought on its waters, so that they dry up!* (Jeremiah 50:35, 37, 38)

Chaldeans stand for people who profane what is true, and inhabitants of Babylon for people who profane what is good (§§1182, 1283, 1295, 1304, 1306, 1307, 1308, 1321, 1322, 1326). A sword stands for truth fighting falsity, and for falsity fighting truth, so it stands for devastation (2799, 4499, 6353, 7102). Horses stand for what is intellectual (2761, 2762, 3217, 5321, 6125, 6534). Chariots stand for doctrinal teachings (5321, 8146, 8148). Drought on its waters so that they dry up stands for a vitality missing from truth because it has been rendered false.

On the other hand, when the Word ascribes dryness or desiccation to other items, such as trees, grass, a harvest, or bones, it reverses the usual symbolism of these items. In addition, land itself is called dry in relation to the sea, and in that case dry land relates to goodness, and the sea, to truth.

And I—yes, I—am hardening the heart of the Egyptians symbolizes the obstinacy of falsity from evil. This can be seen from the symbolism of *hardening a heart* as obstinacy (dealt with in §§7272, 7300, 7305, 7616) and from the representation of the *Egyptians* as people committed to falsity from evil (dealt with in §§8132, 8135, 8148). **8186**

When the Word says Jehovah hardens hearts or causes something bad, then in the inner sense, where real truth is laid bare, the meaning is that people immersed in falsity and evil harden their own hearts or bring their own evil on themselves. See §§2447, 6071, 6991, 6997, 7533, 7632, 7877, 7926.

Who will come after them symbolizes an effort to inflict violence by pouring on falsity-from-evil. This is established by the symbolism of *coming after them* as an inflow of falsity-from-evil as well as an effort to subdue and (accordingly) inflict violence on them. After all, drawing near them symbolizes an inflow (§8159), setting out after them symbolizes an inflow and a closer communication (§8161), and pursuing after them symbolizes an effort to subdue them (§§8136, 8152, 8154). Coming after them therefore symbolizes an effort to inflict violence on them by pouring on falsity-from-evil. **8187**

And I will gain glory in Pharaoh and in all his army, in his chariots, and in his riders means that they will see the divine goodness of the Lord's divine humanity bring about the dispersal of falsity and twisted reasoning, as the following shows: *Gaining glory in Pharaoh and in his army* symbolizes the way people who revel in ill-intentioned falsity plunge into hell—where falsity engulfs them like water—at the mere presence of the Lord's **8188** divine humanity, as discussed above at §8137. *Pharaoh* represents people who revel in ill-intentioned falsity; the *army* symbolizes falsity itself; *his chariots,* false teachings; and *his riders,* twisted reasoning. These are discussed above at §§8146, 8148.

8189 *And the Egyptians will know that I am Jehovah* means so as to reveal that the Lord alone is God and that there is no other god besides him. This can be seen from the explanations in §§7401, 7444, 7544, 7598, 7636, where similar words occur.

8190 *In my gaining glory in Pharaoh, in his chariots, and in his riders* means that they will see the Lord on his own bring about the dispersal of falsity and of false teachings and reasoning, as just above at §8188.

8191 Exodus 14:19, 20, 21, 22. *And the angel of God set out, marching in front of the camp of Israel, and [then] went behind them, and the pillar of cloud set out from in front of them and stood behind them. And it came between the camp of the Egyptians and the camp of Israel, and it was cloud and darkness, and it lit up the night, and the one [the Egyptian] did not come near the other [the Israelite] the whole night. And Moses stretched his hand out over the sea, and Jehovah made the sea depart with a strong east wind the whole night, and he made the sea into dry land, and the waters were divided. And the children of Israel came into the middle of the sea on dry ground. And the waters were a wall to them on their right and on their left.*

And the angel of God set out symbolizes an orderly arrangement imposed by divine truth. *Marching in front of the camp of Israel* means with respect to truth and goodness in the church. *And [then] went behind them* symbolizes protection against an inflow of ill-intentioned falsity into the will. *And the pillar of cloud set out from in front of them and stood behind them* symbolizes the Lord's presence guarding the will, as it had previously guarded the intellect. *And it came between the camp of the Egyptians and the camp of Israel* means between falsity-from-evil on one side and truth-from-goodness on the other. *And it was cloud and darkness* symbolizes the thickening of ill-intentioned falsity on one side. *And it lit up the night* symbolizes enlightenment from well-intentioned truth on the other. *And the one [the Egyptian] did not come near the other [the Israelite]* means that there was consequently no communication between them. *The whole night* means in a dim state. *And Moses stretched [his] hand out over the sea* symbolizes the power of divine truth wielded over hell. *And Jehovah made the sea depart with a strong east wind* symbolizes the means by which falsity was dispersed. *The whole night* means in a dim state. *And he made the sea into dry land* symbolizes the dispersal of falsity. *And the waters were divided* symbolizes being separated and isolated from truth. *And the children of Israel came into the middle of the sea on dry ground* symbolizes safe entry into and passage through hell, free from an inflow of falsity, by people of the spiritual church. *And the waters were a wall to them on their right and on their left* means that they were kept from falsity on every side.

And the angel of God set out symbolizes an orderly arrangement imposed 8192
by divine truth, as the following shows: In this verse, *setting out* symbolizes the creation of an orderly arrangement. The reason it has this symbolism is that the pillar of cloud, which was a band of angels that had previously marched in front of the children of Israel, now inserted itself between the camp of the Egyptians and the camp of Israel. In doing so it brought darkness to the Egyptians and light to the children of Israel. The Lord arranged for this to result when the angel of God (the pillar) set out, moving to a position between the camps, which is why setting out symbolizes the creation of an orderly arrangement here. The *angel of God* symbolizes divine truth. *God* by itself also symbolizes divine truth, because where the Word is talking about truth, the name God is used, but where it is talking about goodness, the name Jehovah is used (§§2586, 2769, 2807, 2822, 3921, 4402, 7010, 7268, 7873).

[2] Regarding angels, be aware that in the Word they stand for the Lord (§§1925, 3039, 4085), so that the Lord is actually called an angel (§§6280, 6831). Angels consequently symbolize divine truth, because divine truth radiating from the Lord makes heaven and therefore shapes the angels who constitute heaven. The more they accept the divine truth coming from the Lord, the more angelic they are. This can be seen from angels' resistance and even hostility to having any truth or goodness attributed to them, because all of it is the Lord's in them. That is why the Lord is called the all-in-all of heaven, and why heaven's inhabitants are said to be in the Lord. What is more, because of the divine truth angels accept from the Lord, the Word calls them gods (§§4295, 7268). For the same reason the term for God in the original language is plural.

[3] Be aware also that the Word speaks of a single angel even when it is many angels who are meant. One example is this verse, which talks about the angel of God when it means the pillar, made up of many angels, that marched in front of the children of Israel.

The Word also refers to angels by such names as Michael, Raphael, and so on. People who do not know the Word's inner meaning believe that Michael or Raphael is an individual angel who is supreme among the angels with him, but these names in the Word do not designate an individual angel. Instead they mean the angelic role itself and therefore the Lord's divine nature in regard to that role.

8193 *Marching in front of the camp of Israel* means with respect to truth and goodness in the church. This can be seen from the symbolism of the *camp* as truth and goodness. The camp means the whole congregation of Israel, and the congregation of Israel symbolizes all goodness and truth in their entirety (§§7830, 7843). For this reason an encampment symbolizes an arrangement determined by truth and goodness (§§8103 at the end, 8130, 8131, 8155). The identification of *Israel* with the spiritual church has been demonstrated many times.

8194 *And [then] went behind them* symbolizes protection against an inflow of ill-intentioned falsity into the will. This is evident from the meaning of *going behind* the children of Israel as protecting them against assault by the Egyptians, or, in an inner sense, against an inflow of the falsity-from-evil symbolized by the Egyptians (§§8132, 8135, 8148). The reason it means against an inflow into the will is that in the universal human (that is, the spiritual world), anything connected with the will appears behind the back; anything connected with the intellect, before the face.

In respect to an inflow into our will and into our intellect, the important thing to know is that the Lord takes the greatest possible care not to let hellish spirits affect our will. If they acted on our will after our rebirth (after we had become a church), we would be doomed, because our will is nothing but evil. That is why, in people whose religion is spiritual, the Lord regenerates the intellectual side of the mind and forms a new will there that is totally separate from the will they inherit. On this subject, see §§863, 875, 927, 1023, 1043, 1044, 2256, 4328, 4493, 5113.

From this you can now see why *went behind them* symbolizes protection against an inflow of ill-intentioned falsity into the will.

8195 *And the pillar of cloud set out from in front of them and stood behind them* symbolizes the Lord's presence guarding the will, as it had previously guarded the intellect, as the following shows: The *pillar of cloud* symbolizes the Lord's presence, as noted at §8110. (The pillar of cloud was a band of angels that had the Lord in its midst.) *In front of them* symbolizes the intellect, and *behind them* symbolizes the will, as discussed directly above at §8194. The fact that protection is meant is obvious.

8196 *And it came between the camp of the Egyptians and the camp of Israel* means between falsity-from-evil on one side and goodness marked by truth on the other. This can be seen from the symbolism of a *camp* as goodness and truth in their entirety (mentioned just above at §8193) and therefore, in a negative sense, as evil and falsity in their entirety. The camp of the *Egyptians* accordingly means falsity from evil, because the Egyptians themselves symbolize falsity that comes of what is evil (§§8132, 8135, 8148), and the camp of *Israel,* goodness marked by truth, because Israel symbolizes truth that comes of what is good (§7957). *Coming between them* obviously means preventing ill-intentioned falsity from flowing in.

And it was cloud and darkness symbolizes the thickening of ill-intentioned falsity on one side. *And it lit up the night* symbolizes illumination from well-intentioned truth on the other. This can be seen from the following: *Cloud and darkness* symbolize a thickening of ill-intentioned falsity. (On the point that *cloud* symbolizes falsity, see §§1043, 1047, 8137, 8138; and that *darkness,* [or shadow,] does too, §§1839, 1860, 4418, 4531, 7688, 7711.) *Lighting up the night* symbolizes illumination from well-intentioned truth. (On the point that a pillar of fire by night means that a state of dim truth was softened by enlightenment from goodness, see §8108.) **8197**

[2] Why did the pillar bring darkness to the Egyptians and light to the children of Israel? The Lord's presence (symbolized here by the pillar) is heavenly light itself. That is the source from which heaven receives its light, which is a thousand times brighter than the noonday light in the world. The same light turns into darkness among the evil, though, even if they are standing right in it. The denser the ill-intentioned falsity among them, the darker the light turns. The reason is that divine truth radiating from the Lord looks like light to angels' eyes, but to anyone devoted to ill-intentioned falsity it can only look like darkness, not light. Falsity opposes truth and snuffs it out. That is why the pillar—which was the Lord's presence—brought cloud and darkness on the Egyptians (symbolizing people devoted to falsity from evil) and lit up the night for the children of Israel (symbolizing people devoted to truth from goodness). On the point that the Lord appears to each of us according to our nature, see §§1861 at the end, 6832.

And the one [the Egyptian] did not come near the other [the Israelite] means that there was consequently no communication between them. This is established by the symbolism of *coming near* as an inflow and communication, as mentioned at §8159. **8198**

The whole night means in a dim state. This is established by the symbolism of *night* as a state of dimness regarding religious truth and goodness, as discussed in §§1712, 6000. In this verse, night symbolizes the dimness that comes right after trials. People who have been delivered from trials enter **8199** a dim phase first before they reach clarity, because the falsity and evil the hells introduced cling for a while. Only gradually do they dissipate.

8200 *And Moses stretched his hand out over the sea* symbolizes the power of divine truth wielded over hell. This can be seen from the symbolism of stretching a hand out as a wielding of power (discussed in §§7673, 8183), from the representation of *Moses* as divine truth (mentioned many times), and from the symbolism of the *sea*—here, the Suph Sea—as hell (discussed in §§8099, 8137, 8138).

I speak of wielding the power of divine truth because all divine power comes through truth emanating from the Lord. This truth has created everything, as stated in John:

> Everything was made by the Word, and nothing that was made was made without him. (John 1:3)

The Word is the Lord in respect to divine truth. Through this truth he brings order to everything in heaven and in hell. It is also the source of all order on earth. It accomplished all the miracles. In short, divine truth contains all power, so that in fact it is power itself.

In the other life there are some who possess more truth than others. This gives them so much power that they can go anywhere in the hells without danger. At their presence the inhabitants of the hells flee in every direction. There are also some who use truth from the Divine to exercise magical powers. Both groups will be described at the end of various chapters, where the hells will be discussed, by the Lord's divine mercy.

People who regard the causes of things from a shallow, earthly viewpoint cannot help perceiving truth from the Divine as a mere object of thought, with no essential reality. But actually it is reality itself, from which everything in both the spiritual and physical worlds takes its reality.

8201 *And Jehovah made the sea depart with a strong east wind* symbolizes the means by which falsity was dispersed, as the following shows: *Making something depart* means dispersing it. A *sea* symbolizes falsity. Here the sea means its water, which stands for falsity; see §§8137, 8138. And an *east wind* symbolizes a means of destruction, as discussed at §7679. Here it symbolizes the means by which falsity was destroyed and therefore by which it was dispersed.

8202 *The whole night* means in a dim state, as above at §8199.

8203 *And he made the sea into dry land* symbolizes the dispersal of falsity. This can be seen from the symbolism of a *sea* as falsity (as just above at §8201) and from the meaning of *making something into dry land* as dispersing it. Crossing on dry land or ground means in safety, free from an inflow of falsity, when the phrase is used to describe the way the seawater was moved aside; see above at §8185.

And the waters were divided symbolizes being separated and isolated from truth. This can be seen from the symbolism of the *waters' dividing* as the dispersal and disappearance of falsity, as explained above at §8184. Because it symbolizes this, it symbolizes separation and isolation [of falsity] from truth. **8204**

And the children of Israel came into the middle of the sea on dry ground symbolizes safe entry into and passage through hell, free from an inflow of falsity, by people of the spiritual church. This can be seen from the explanation above at §8185, where similar words appear. **8205**

And the waters were a wall to them on their right and on their left means that they were kept from falsity on every side. This can be seen from the symbolism of *waters*—the waters of this sea—as falsity from evil (discussed in §§8137, 8138), from that of *being a wall to them* as being kept from falsity (discussed below), and from that of *on their right and on their left* as on every side. **8206**

The fact that *being a wall to them* means being kept from falsity—when it is water (symbolizing falsity) that is the wall—is due to the way things work in human beings. When the Lord holds us in what is good and true, falsity and evil move to the sides and stand there like a wall, because they are incapable of entering an environment that contains goodness and truth. The reason they cannot enter is that the Lord is present in goodness and truth, and the Lord's presence forces evil and falsity back on all sides. Goodness and truth are completely opposed to evil and falsity, so the two parties cannot occupy the same space without destroying one another. [2] It is goodness accompanied by truth that destroys (or at least shoves aside) evil accompanied by falsity. That is because goodness with its truth is divine, so it has all power; evil with its falsity is hellish, so it has no power. Goodness works from inside, evil from outside. When the evil in us together with the falsity in us stands at the side like a wall, as described, it looms all around us. It is always trying to crash in on us but cannot because the Lord's presence in goodness and truth prevents it.

This is what is symbolized by the fact that the waters were like a wall to them on the left and on the right.

For the idea that the Lord keeps us from evil and falsity by holding us in goodness and truth, see §§1581, 2406, 4564. No one can be kept from what is evil and held in what is good, though, without having received that capacity by exercising neighborly love in the world. A life of goodness, or a life in keeping with religious truth, gives us the capacity, so a desire or love for what is good does so. People whose way of life led them to love what is good and to desire it can live in an environment of goodness and truth, but people whose way of life led them to put on an evil nature cannot.

8207 Exodus 14:23, 24, 25. *And the Egyptians pursued; and all Pharaoh's horses, his chariots, and his riders came after them to the middle of the sea. And it happened in the morning watch that Jehovah looked out at the camp of the Egyptians from within the pillar of fire and cloud and troubled the camp of the Egyptians. And he took off the wheels of [Pharaoh's] chariots and made [the wheels] go heavily, and the Egyptian said, "I will flee before Israel, because Jehovah fights for them against the Egyptians."*

And the Egyptians pursued symbolizes an effort made by falsity from evil to inflict violence. *And came after them* symbolizes an attempted inflow. *All Pharaoh's horses, his chariots, and his riders, into the middle of the sea* means that hell was filled with information produced by a corrupted intellect, with false doctrinal teachings, and with twisted reasoning. *And it happened in the morning watch* symbolizes a state of darkness and ruin for people devoted to falsity from evil, and a state of light and salvation for people devoted to truth [from] goodness. *That Jehovah looked out at the camp of the Egyptians* symbolizes a divine inflow reaching out from there to the people trying to inflict violence through falsity. *From within the pillar of fire and cloud* symbolizes the resulting presence of divine goodness and truth there. *And troubled the camp of the Egyptians* means that the falsity and evil projected by these people consequently rebounded on them. *And he took off the wheels of [Pharaoh's] chariots* means that the power to introduce falsity was taken away. *And made [the wheels] go heavily* symbolizes resistance and powerlessness. *And the Egyptian said,* symbolizes a thought at that time. *I will flee before Israel* means that they would separate from people dedicated to goodness from truth and truth from goodness. *Because Jehovah fights for them against the Egyptians* means that the Lord alone bears the weight of the battle against falsity and evil.

8208 *And the Egyptians pursued* symbolizes an effort made by falsity from evil to inflict violence. This is established by the symbolism of *pursuing,* when it is the Egyptians who pursue, as an effort to subjugate (mentioned in §§8136, 8152, 8154) and therefore to inflict violence, and by the representation of the *Egyptians* as people devoted to falsity from evil (discussed in §§8132, 8135, 8146, 8148) and therefore also as falsity-from-evil itself.

And came after them symbolizes an attempted inflow. This can be seen from the symbolism of *coming after someone*—when the ones who do so are people involved in falsity from evil—as an attempt to inflict violence through an inflow of such falsity, as dealt with at §8187. The reason it symbolizes an attempt is that the demons and spirits of hell cannot hurt good people but keep trying anyway. There is an aura given off by the hells that can be called an aura of efforts to do evil. I have even been allowed to perceive it a number of times. The efforts it makes are unceasing, and at the least opportunity the efforts explode into action. This aura, though, is held in check by an aura of heavenly efforts from the Lord to do good. Because it comes from the Divine, it holds all power. **8209**

[2] Despite the power imbalance, an equilibrium is maintained between these diametrically opposed efforts. The purpose of the equilibrium is to leave us in freedom and therefore with the power to choose, and to enable us to reform. All reformation takes place in freedom; without freedom there is no reformation.

Spiritual effort is the same as the power of will. While we are being reformed, we are kept in equilibrium (or freedom) between willing what is good and willing what is evil. The more we then lean toward willing what is good, the more we lean toward heaven and distance ourselves from hell. To the same extent, the new will we now receive from the Lord prevails over the self-will we received by inheritance from our parents and by the daily acts of our life ever after. So when we have reformed enough to will what is good and to desire it, the goodness pushes the evil away. This is because the Lord is present in goodness, since goodness comes from him, is therefore his, and is in fact him.

From this you can see how matters stand with the attempts made on us by various types of inflow.

All Pharaoh's horses, his chariots, and his riders, into the middle of the sea means that hell was filled with information produced by a corrupted intellect, with false doctrinal teachings, and with twisted reasoning, as the following shows: *Pharaoh's horses* symbolize information produced by a corrupted intellect, *Pharaoh's chariots* symbolize false doctrinal teachings, and *Pharaoh's riders* symbolize the twisted reasoning that results, all of which are discussed above in §§8146, 8148. And *into the middle of the sea* means filling hell. **8210**

[2] The reason these three parts of Pharaoh's army—his horses, chariots, and riders—are mentioned again here is that the final stage of devastation was at hand for people in the church who detached faith from

neighborly love and lived a life of evil. The final stage is a stage of being thrown into hell, and being thrown into hell means being thickly surrounded by falsity from evil. When the evil have been purged of everything true and good, you see, and have been left to the wickedness and distorted thinking belonging to their way of life, the hells they communicated with through that wickedness open up. All the evil they adopted as their own rushes in on them from those hells. Falsity welling up out of the evil then creates around them an aura that looks like a thick cloud, or like water. The conclusion of this process finds them in hell, because they are then shut off from all communication with heaven. They are also separated from other hells. This is what is referred to as being cast into hell.

[3] That is why the horses, chariots, and riders are mentioned at this point, when they were going into the middle of the sea. As has been mentioned, the Suph Sea symbolizes hell, and the horses, chariots, and riders symbolize all falsity and everything that comes of falsity-from-evil, which was now unleashed on them, with the result that they were isolated from the other hells by each individual type of falsity from evil. That is the specific theme of the next verses: 24, 25, 26, 27, 28.

8211 *And it happened in the morning watch* symbolizes a state of darkness and ruin for people devoted to falsity from evil, and a state of light and salvation for people devoted to truth from goodness. This can be seen from the symbolism of the *morning watch* as a state of enlightenment and salvation, and in a negative sense, as a state of darkness and ruin. The reason the morning watch has this symbolism is that in the other world, states of faith and love resemble and therefore correspond to the times of day in the world: morning, afternoon, evening, and night (§§2788, 5672, 5962, 6110). States also change in about the same way the times of day change. The end and beginning of these changes is the early morning, particularly at half-light, because that is when night ends and day begins. In the state that corresponds to morning, good people start to gain light in matters of faith, and warmth in matters of neighborly love. The reverse is also true, because the evil start to be clouded with falsity and chilled by evil. Morning is therefore a state of darkness and ruin for the evil and of light and salvation for the good.

[2] These states in heaven give rise to states on earth of light and warmth, darkness and cold, which alternate yearly and daily. Anything that arises in the physical world traces its origin and cause to the things that arise in the spiritual world. After all, the whole of nature is actually a theater representing the Lord's kingdom (§§3483, 4939, 5173, 5962). That is where correspondence comes from. Admittedly, variations on earth of light and

shadow, heat and cold are due to differences in the height of the sun, yearly and daily and by geographic region. But these are the direct causes existing in the physical world. They were created to reflect the same phenomena in the spiritual world, which are their prior causes and which bring about the causes seen in the physical world. Nothing orderly exists anywhere on the earthly plane that does not trace its cause and origin to the spiritual plane—that is, through the spiritual plane to the Divine.

[3] The text here is explained by the fact that morning in relation to good people symbolizes the start of enlightenment and salvation, and in relation to evil people, the start of darkness and ruin. That is why Jehovah is said to have looked out at the camp of the Egyptians in the morning watch, troubled it, taken off the wheels of their chariots, and shaken them off into the middle of the sea, while saving the children of Israel.

These remarks now show what the following Scripture passages mean in a spiritual sense. In Isaiah:

> *In the daytime* you will cause your sapling to grow, and *in the morning, your seed to bloom.* (Isaiah 17:11)

In the same author:

> Around the *time of evening,* terror! *Before morning* there is *none.* (Isaiah 17:14)

In the same author:

> Jehovah, be their arm *every morning,* our salvation also at a time of distress. (Isaiah 33:2)

In Ezekiel:

> This is what the Lord Jehovih has said: "Evil! Watch: an evil is coming, an end comes, here comes the end! *Morning is coming upon you,* inhabitant of the land; the day of upheaval is near." (Ezekiel 7:5, 6, 7)

In Hosea:

> This is what he has said to you, Bethel, because of your extreme wickedness: "*In the morning the monarch of Israel will assuredly be cut off.*" (Hosea 10:15)

In David:

> Make me hear your mercy *in the morning.* Deliver me from my foes, Jehovah! (Psalms 143:8, 9)

Then there is the fact that it was *when dawn rose* that the Lord saved Lot and rained sulfur and fire onto Sodom and Gomorrah (Genesis 19:15 and following verses).

[4] Because morning symbolizes a state of light and salvation for the good and a state of darkness and ruin for the evil, it also symbolizes the era of the Last Judgment, when people intent on goodness are to be saved and people intent on evil are to perish. As a consequence, it symbolizes the end of the previous church and the start of a new church, which are what the Last Judgment in the Word means (§§900, 931, 1850, 2117–2133, 3353, 4057, 4535). This is what morning symbolizes in Daniel:

> He said to me, "Up till evening [and] *morning* two thousand three hundred times, and then the Holy Place will be set right." (Daniel 8:14)

And in Zephaniah:

> *In the morning, in the morning* Jehovah will *offer judgment as a light* and will not fail. I will cut off nations, and their corners will be laid waste. (Zephaniah 3:5, 6)

And in Isaiah too:

> One is shouting to me from Seir, "*Guard, what is [left] of the night? Guard, what is [left] of the night?*" The guard said, "*Morning comes, and also night.* If you are seeking, then seek, return, come!" (Isaiah 21:11, 12)

In these passages the morning stands for the Lord's Coming and for enlightenment and salvation at that time, so it is about a new religion. The night stands for the state in which the individual and the church then dwell, which is one of utter falsity-from-evil.

[5] The text speaks of a morning *watch* because the night was divided into watches, and the last watch in the night and the first in the day was the morning watch. The guards of the watch stood on the walls looking for approaching enemies and shouting news of what they saw. In an inner, representative sense these guardians mean the Lord, and a watch means his constant presence and protection (§7989), as in David:

> *Your guardian* will not slumber; indeed, the *guardian of Israel—Jehovah your guardian*—will not slumber or sleep. Jehovah is your shade on your right hand; by day the sun will not strike you, or the moon in the night. *Jehovah will guard you* from every evil; he will guard your soul. (Psalms 121:3, 4, 5, 6, 7)

Guards also mean the prophets and priests and consequently the Word, in Isaiah:

> *On your walls,* Jerusalem, *I have set up guards; all day* and *all night* they will not keep silent, making mention of Jehovah. (Isaiah 62:6)

And in Jeremiah:

> There is a day when *guards will shout* on Mount Ephraim, "Rise, so that we can go up [to] Zion to Jehovah our God!" (Jeremiah 31:6)

That Jehovah looked out at the camp of the Egyptians symbolizes a divine inflow reaching out from there to the people trying to inflict violence through falsity, as the following shows: When Jehovah is said to *look out* into the distance, it symbolizes his inflow reaching out. Clearly his inflow is meant by his looking out at someone, because when he gazes at people, he is presenting himself in person; and to those guided by his truth-from-goodness, he gives a perception of what is good and true. These things he accomplishes by his inflow. That is why angels pour the emotion that drives their life into anyone they look on. And the *camp of the Egyptians* symbolizes falsity from evil, as discussed in §§8193, 8196. Because spirits dedicated to falsity from evil were then pursuing the children of Israel, an effort to inflict violence through falsity is also symbolized (§8208). **8212**

From within the pillar of fire and cloud symbolizes the presence of divine goodness and truth there. This can be seen from the symbolism of the *pillar of fire and cloud* as the presence of the Lord (noted at §8110) and therefore of divine goodness and truth, because goodness and truth are present wherever the Lord is. For more detail on the symbolism of the pillar of fire and cloud, see §§8106, 8108. **8213**

And troubled the camp of the Egyptians means that the falsity-from-evil projected by these people consequently rebounded on them. This is evident from the symbolism of *troubling the camp of the Egyptians* as the turning back of ill-intentioned falsity on spirits who were trying to inflict that falsity on people devoted to truth and goodness. The reason for this symbolism is that it describes the effect the Lord's presence has on evil people. The evil, who want to inflict violence on the good by introducing falsity and evil, incur the penalty of retaliation, in which the falsity and evil they intend to inflict rebound on them. This punishment, which is called a punishment in retaliation, comes from the following law ordained for heaven: **8214**

> Everything whatever that you want people to do to you, also do to them yourselves. This is the Law and the Prophets. (Matthew 7:12)

So people who do good from good motivations, or from the heart, receive goodness from others, while people who do evil from evil motivations, or from the heart, receive evil from others. That is why every good deed carries its reward with it and every evil deed carries its punishment (§§696, 967, 1857, 6559).

From this you can now see that *Jehovah troubled the camp of the Egyptians* means that the ill-intentioned falsity projected by these people rebounded on them to trouble them. On the point that this is what happens among the evil as a result of the Lord's presence, see §7989.

8215 *And he took off the wheels of [Pharaoh's] chariots* means that the power to introduce falsity was taken away. This is clear from the symbolism of *taking off* as taking away, from that of a *wheel* as the power to move forward (discussed below), and from that of Pharaoh's *chariots* as distorted doctrinal teachings (dealt with in §§8146, 8148) and therefore as falsity.

The symbolism of a *wheel* in a positive sense can be seen from that of a chariot, [or carriage]. These vehicles were of two kinds: those used for hauling goods and those used in battle. The carriages used for hauling goods symbolized true doctrinal teachings, and in a negative sense, false teachings. The chariots used in battle also symbolized doctrinal teachings, in both senses, but militant ones. So they symbolized truth itself and falsity itself equipped for battle. This shows what a *chariot wheel* means: the power of moving forward. Here it means the power to introduce falsity and fight truth. Such a power belongs to the intellectual side of a person's mind, so a wheel also symbolizes the intellect in regard to theological issues.

[2] In the other life one often sees carriages of different shapes and sizes loaded with various kinds of merchandise. When a carriage appears, it symbolizes the full range of truth, or doctrinal teachings, which are in effect containers of truth. The merchandise symbolizes religious knowledge used for various purposes. Carriages appear when angels in heaven are discussing theology. Since spirits lower down cannot comprehend what the angels are saying, the conversation is displayed representationally. Again, the dialog appears to some people as a carriage, which presents every single word in a perfectly visible form, enabling the viewer to see and understand the verbal content instantly. Some of the content is visible from the shape of the carriage, some from its construction, some from its color, some from its wheels, some from the horses pulling it, some from the goods it carries. It is because of these representations that chariots in the Word symbolize doctrinal teachings.

[3] This helps somewhat to show that the wheels of chariots symbolize the power of the intellect. After all, just as a chariot depends on wheels for its motion and progress, the truth embodied in doctrinal teachings depends on the intellect for its advancement. That is what the wheels in Isaiah symbolize:

> . . . whose arrows are sharp, and all his bows bent. The hooves of his horses are considered to be like rock; his *wheels, like a windstorm.* (Isaiah 5:28)

This is about one who destroys truth. The arrows are false ideas, and the bows are a distorted theology (§§2686, 2709). The horses' hooves are items of information on the level of the senses, produced by a corrupted intellect (§7729). The wheels are the power to corrupt and destroy truth, as a windstorm would. [4] In Ezekiel:

> I saw the living creatures, *when look! One wheel on the earth* among the living creatures for the four faces of each. The *appearance of the wheels, and their wheelworks,* were like the form of a tarshish, and the likeness was the same for the four of them. Moreover, their appearance and their wheelworks *were like a wheel in the middle of a wheel.* On all four of their sides, wherever they went, they went; they did not turn in any direction as they went. As for their rims, these had both height and fearsomeness. Moreover, *their rims were full of eyes all around* for the four of them. So when the living creatures went, *the wheels went with them. The spirit of the living creature was in the wheels.* (Ezekiel 1:15–21 and 10:9–14)

The four living creatures, which were guardian beings, symbolize the Lord's providence (§308). The wheels symbolize divine understanding, or foresight, which is why the text says that the wheels went when the living creatures did, that their rims were full of eyes, and that the spirit of the living creature (truth that comes of wisdom) was in them. [5] In Daniel:

> I was looking, until thrones were overturned, and the Ancient One sat. His clothing was like white snow, the hair of his head like clean wool; his throne was fiery flames, *his wheels a burning fire.* (Daniel 7:9)

The Ancient One is the Lord in respect to his divine goodness. The overturned thrones are falsities. His clothing is divine truth as it appears on the surface; the hair of his head is divine goodness as it appears on the surface. His throne is heaven and the church. The wheels are components of wisdom and understanding and are therefore divine truths. The burning fire is the whole dimension of love and charity. In addition, under the ten washbowls around Solomon's temple there were *wheels of bronze:*

> *The work of the wheels was like the work of a chariot wheel;* their *hands* and their *backs* and their *treads* and their *spokes* were all cast work. (1 Kings 7:30, 31, 32, 33)

The washbowls with their stands symbolized containers for truth, truth being what purifies and regenerates a person. The wheels symbolized powers of the intellect, which are the means of making progress.

8216 *And made [the wheels] go heavily* symbolizes resistance and powerlessness. This can be seen from the symbolism of a wheel, which means the power to introduce falsity, as discussed directly above at §8215. So *making [the wheels] go heavily* means hindering them by resisting them and therefore means powerlessness.

8217 *And the Egyptian said,* symbolizes a thought—a thought in the mind of people immersed in falsity from evil. This can be seen from the symbolism of *saying,* when evil is looming, as a thought (as in §§7094, 7107, 7244, 7937), and from that of an *Egyptian* as a person intent on falsity from evil (discussed in §§8132, 8135, 8146, 8148).

8218 *I will flee before Israel* means that they would separate from people dedicated to goodness from truth and truth from goodness. This is evident from the symbolism of *fleeing* as separating (mentioned in §§4113, 4114, 4120) and from the representation of *Israel* as people in the spiritual church—in other words, people dedicated to goodness from truth and truth from goodness (discussed at §7957).

8219 *Because Jehovah fights for them against the Egyptians* means that the Lord alone bears the weight of the battle against falsity and evil. This is evident from the explanation above at §8175, where similar words appear.

8220 Exodus 14:26, 27, 28. *And Jehovah said to Moses, "Stretch your hand out over the sea and have the waters come back over the Egyptians, over [Pharaoh's] chariots, and over his riders." And Moses stretched his hand out over the sea, and as morning drew near, the sea came back to its full force, and the Egyptians were fleeing in its path, and Jehovah shook the Egyptians off into the middle of the sea. And the waters came back and covered the chariots and riders, all the army of Pharaoh, coming after them, into the sea; not even one was left among them.*

And Jehovah said to Moses symbolizes an inflow. *Stretch your hand out over the sea* symbolizes the power of divine truth wielded over hell. *And have the waters come back over the Egyptians* means that falsity would rebound onto and engulf people devoted to falsity-from-evil. *Over [Pharaoh's] chariots, [and] over his riders* symbolizes distorted doctrinal teachings and reasoning produced by a corrupted intellect. *And Moses stretched his hand out over the sea* once again symbolizes divine power wielded over hell. *And as morning drew near, the sea came back to its full force* symbolizes the rebounding of ill-intentioned falsity onto them because of the Lord's presence. *And the Egyptians were fleeing in its path* means that they drowned themselves in falsity-from-evil on their own. *And Jehovah shook the Egyptians off into the middle of the sea* means that as a result they consigned themselves to hell—the abode of falsity from evil—on their own. *And the waters came back* symbolizes the rebounding of falsity on them. *And covered the chariots and riders and all the army of Pharaoh* means that their falsities buried them. *Coming after them, into the sea* means that the falsity took possession of them. *Not even one was left among them* symbolizes each and every one of them.

And Jehovah said to Moses symbolizes an inflow. This can be seen from the symbolism of *Jehovah said* as an inflow when the phrase has to do with the wielding of power through the divine truth represented by Moses, as also in §§7291, 7381. **8221**

Stretch your hand out over the sea symbolizes the power of divine truth wielded over hell. This is clear from the explanation above at §8200, where similar words occur. **8222**

And have the waters come back over the Egyptians means that falsity from evil would rebound onto and engulf people devoted to that falsity, as the following shows: *Waters* symbolize falsity, as discussed in §§6346, 7307, 8137, 8138. *Have the waters come back,* then, symbolizes a rebounding or turning back of falsity. In this context it also symbolizes being engulfed, because the agent is the waters of the Suph Sea, which stand for the falsity-from-evil adopted by members of the church who lived a life of detached faith and of evil. And *Egyptians* symbolize people devoted to falsity from evil, as mentioned many times. **8223**

To learn about the rebounding or turning back of falsity on those who were intending to pour falsity out over people devoted to truth and goodness (represented by the children of Israel), see §8214 above. What is said there is that the evil intended toward others rebounds on oneself and that this effect originates in the law of the divine plan, "*Do nothing to another but what you want others to do to you*" (Matthew 7:12). To this law, never changing and never-ending in the spiritual world, the laws of retaliation laid down in the representative church trace their origin. They consist of the following in Moses:

> If harm is done, you shall give soul for soul, eye for eye, tooth for tooth, hand for hand, foot for foot, burn for burn, wound for wound, blow for blow. (Exodus 21:23, 24, 25)

In the same author:

> *If a man deals damage to his neighbor, as he has done, so it shall be done to him,* break for break, eye for eye, tooth for tooth. *As he dealt damage to another, so it shall be dealt to him.* (Leviticus 24:19, 20)

In the same author:

> If a witness answers with a lie against his or her fellow, you shall *do to the witness as the witness thought to do to his or her fellow.* (Deuteronomy 19:18, 19)

The above quotations demonstrate plainly that these laws trace their origin to the universal law, never changing and never-ending in the spiritual world, that you should not do to others except as you want others to do to you. It is perfectly clear, then, how to understand the idea that the falsity-from-evil one intends to inflict on others rebounds or turns back onto oneself.

[2] Here is more about the operation of this law in the other world: In the case of a response in kind or retaliation for evil, the evil are the ones who inflict it, never the good; it comes from the hells, never from the heavens. After all, the hells and their wicked inhabitants never stop itching to hurt others. It is the core pleasure of their life, so as soon as they receive permission, they make bad things happen, not caring who the victim is, whether evil or good, friend or foe. Since by law of the divine plan evil is to rebound on one who intends evil, therefore when the law permits, the evil inhabitants of the hells pounce. It is they who do so, never the good inhabitants of the heavens. The latter never stop desiring to do good to others. It is the central pleasure of their life, so as soon as they have the opportunity, they do good, to enemies as well as friends. They do not even resist evil, because all that is good and true is defended and protected by the laws of the divine plan. That is why the Lord says:

> You have heard that it was said, "Eye for eye and tooth for tooth." But I tell you, don't resist evil. You have heard that it was said, "You shall love

your neighbor and hate your enemy." But I tell you, love your enemies, bless those who curse you, do good to those who hate you, so that you may be the children of your Father in the heavens. (Matthew 5:38, 39, 43, 44, 45)

[3] In the other world, when the evil want to hurt the good, often they are punished severely and find the harm they intend to others recoiling on themselves. When this happens, it looks like revenge by the good, but it is not revenge, and it is not at the hand of good people but of evil people who are then given that opportunity by the law of the divine plan. The good do not have ill wishes even toward the evil, but they cannot take away the sting of punishment, because they are focused on a good outcome. It is exactly the same as a judge seeing an evildoer punished, or as parents seeing their child disciplined by a teacher. Evil disciplinarians punish others from a lust for hurting them, but good disciplinarians, from a desire to help.

This shows what is meant by the Lord's words above from Matthew about loving one's enemy, and about the law of retaliation, which he did not abolish but explained. What he disclosed was that people who love in a heavenly way should not take pleasure in retaliation, or revenge, but in benefitting others, and that the law of the divine plan that protects what is good does so spontaneously, by means of evil people.

Over [Pharaoh's] chariots, and over his riders symbolizes distorted doctrinal teachings and reasoning produced by a corrupted intellect. This can be seen from the symbolism of Pharaoh's *chariots* as distorted doctrinal teachings (discussed in §§8146, 8148, 8215) and from that of *riders* as reasoning produced by a corrupted intellect (discussed in §§8146, 8148). **8224**

And Moses stretched his hand out over the sea symbolizes divine power wielded over hell, as above in §§8200, 8222. **8225**

And as morning drew near, the sea came back to its full force symbolizes the rebounding of ill-intentioned falsity onto them because of the Lord's presence, as the following shows: *Coming back,* when it is the ill-intentioned falsity symbolized by the waters of the Suph Sea that are said to do it, symbolizes the rebounding or turning back onto them, as discussed just above at §8223. The *sea*—in this case its water—symbolizes the falsity-from-evil found in hell, as discussed in §§6346, 7307, 8137. The *drawing near of morning* symbolizes the Lord's presence, as discussed below. And *to its full force* means in keeping with the overall state and orderly design of hell. Even in the hells there is order, as much as in **8226** the heavens. In the hells, the inhabitants are grouped by evil, just as the inhabitants in the heavens are grouped by goodness. In the hells, though, they associate like gangs of thieves.

The meaning of the *drawing near of morning* as the presence of the Lord can be seen from the remarks above at §8211 showing that morning is a state of darkness and ruin for the evil and of light and salvation for the good. These states result from the mere presence of the Lord (§§7989, 8137, 8138, 8188) and of his divine humanity (§8159).

[2] The same thing said here about the Egyptians is said about Babylon in Jeremiah:

> He is the one who forms everything, especially the staff of his inheritance. Jehovah Sabaoth is his name. You are a hammer to me, the weapons of war, and through you I will scatter nations and through you I will destroy kingdoms and through you I will scatter the *horse* and its *chariot* and through you I will scatter the *chariot* and *its rider.* I will *repay* to Babylon and to all the residents of Chaldea all their evil that they did in Zion before your eyes. (Jeremiah 51:19, 20, 21, 24)

In this passage Babylon symbolizes people who were part of the church but profaned what was good. Chaldea symbolizes those who profaned what was true. Here too the content of their intellect and therefore their teachings and twisted reasoning are symbolized by the horse, the chariot, and its rider; and the ruination of these things, by their dispersal. The Lord in his divine humanity, whose presence scatters them, is meant by the words "He is the one who forms everything, especially the staff of his inheritance. Jehovah Sabaoth is his name. You are a hammer to me, the weapons of war. Through you I will scatter nations and through you I will destroy kingdoms." The nations stand for what is evil and the kingdoms for what is false. This passage too shows that the evil they do to others rebounds or turns back on them, because it says they will be repaid for their evil. Other passages throughout also say that on the day of punishment, revenge or retribution will be exacted.

8227 *And the Egyptians were fleeing in its path* means that they drowned themselves in falsity-from-evil on their own. This is plain from the symbolism of *fleeing in the path of* the sea as drowning themselves on their own in the falsity-from-evil symbolized by the waters of that sea (§8226).

Here is the situation: People who do not know the causes behind things cannot help believing that the evils befalling the wicked—punishment, devastation, damnation, and in the end, consignment to hell—come from the Divine. After all, that is exactly how it looks, because such experiences are precipitated by his presence (§§8137, 8138, 8188). However, no such outcome results at the hand of the Divine, only at the hand of the wicked themselves. The one goal of the Divine and his presence is the protection and salvation of the good. When he is present with the good, guarding them against the evil, the evil blaze still more hotly against them and even more hotly than that against the Divine himself, whom they hate intensely. People who hate the good hate the Divine most of all. They therefore attack, and the more they attack, the more they hurl themselves (by the law of the divine design) into punishment, devastation, damnation, and finally hell. This makes it clear that the Divine, or the Lord, does nothing but good and does evil to no one. Rather, people who are intent on evil invite such consequences on themselves.

That is what *the Egyptians fled in the path of the sea* means: that they drowned themselves in falsity-from-evil on their own.

[2] On this subject something further should be noted: Another reason people believe evils come from the Divine is that he tolerates them and does not take them away. Anyone who tolerates something and does not take it away when possible seems to will it and therefore to cause it. But the Divine tolerates evils because he cannot prevent them or take them away. After all, he wills nothing but goodness, so if he prevented or took away the evils of punishment, devastation, persecution, trials, and so on, he would in effect will evil, because then the wicked could not be corrected. Evil would grow till it overwhelmed goodness.

The situation is like that of a monarch who pardons the guilty. Such a monarch is responsible for any wrong these culprits then do in her or his kingdom and also for giving others free rein, not to mention the fact that the wicked become hardened in their evil. A monarch who is just and good, then, theoretically could rescind punishment but is actually unable to, because to do so would be to do evil, not good. It is important to know that in the other life, all punishments (and all trials) have the doing of good as their goal.

And Jehovah shook the Egyptians off into the middle of the sea means **8228**
that as a result they consigned themselves to hell—the abode of falsity from evil—on their own. This can be seen from the symbolism of *shaking someone off into the sea* as consigning someone to falsity-from-evil, since the waters of this sea symbolize such falsity (§§6346, 7307, 8137, 8138). For the idea that the evils the Word attributes to Jehovah (or the Lord) in its literal sense come from the very people devoted to evil, not at all from

the Lord, and that the Word is to be understood this way in its inner sense, see §§2447, 6071, 6991, 6997, 7533, 7632, 7643, 7679, 7710, 7877, 7926, 8227.

8229 *And the waters came back* symbolizes the rebounding of falsity on them. This is established by the explanation above in §§8223, 8226.

8230 *And covered the chariots and riders and all the army of Pharaoh* means that their falsities buried them. This can be seen from the symbolism of *covering* as blanketing and therefore burying, and from that of the *chariots and riders of Pharaoh* as distorted doctrinal teachings and twisted reasoning that combat truth and goodness, or in general, as falsity-from-evil itself. For the meaning of chariots as distorted teachings and of riders as the reasoning a corrupted intellect produces, see §§8146, 8148, and for their combativeness toward truth and goodness, see §8215.

8231 *Coming after them, into the sea* means that the falsity took possession of them. This can be seen from the symbolism of *coming after them* as taking possession of them, when it describes the waters of the *sea* as doing so, symbolizing falsity from evil.

8232 *Not even one was left among them* symbolizes each and every one of them, as is self-evident.

This verse has told how people who had subscribed to falsity from evil were plunged into hell, or consigned to it. Few, however, know what it means to be plunged into hell or consigned to it. Most think it means being thrown down into a specific location where the Devil and the Devil's crew live and being tortured by them there. But that is not the case. When these people are consigned to hell, it actually means they are totally surrounded by the ill-intentioned falsity they adopted in the world. Once surrounded, they are in hell.

The evil and falsity that then forms their environment is what actually tortures them. However, the torment comes not from grief over the evil they have done but from the fact that they *cannot* do evil, since doing evil is the highest pleasure of their life. There, when they wrong others, the people they wrong punish and abuse *them.* The main motivation the inhabitants have in mistreating each other is a lust for absolute power and also, to achieve that goal, a lust for dominating others. If the victims of such a spirit do not allow themselves to be dominated, the spirit acquires the power by punishing and torturing them in a thousand different ways. In hell, though, the dominance they constantly struggle for switches back and forth, so that the individuals who once punished and tortured others are then punished and tortured in turn. This continues as long as it takes for the ambition to finally fade, out of fear of punishment.

This now shows where hell comes from and what it is. Hellfire is actually the cravings of self-love, which inflame and torment the hellish (§§6314, 7324, 7575).

Exodus 14:29, 30, 31. *And the children of Israel went on dry ground into the middle of the sea, and the waters were a wall to them on their right and on their left. And on that day Jehovah saved Israel from the hand of the Egyptians, and Israel saw the Egyptians dead on the shore of the sea. And Israel saw the great hand, [the works] that Jehovah performed among the Egyptians, and the people feared Jehovah and believed in Jehovah and in Moses his servant.* **8233**

And the children of Israel went on dry ground into the middle of the sea means that people intent on goodness from truth and truth from goodness passed through that hell in safety, free of harassment. *And the waters were a wall to them on their right and on their left* means that they were kept from falsity on every side. *And on that day Jehovah saved Israel from the hand of the Egyptians* means that in this state the Lord protected people of the spiritual church from any violence inflicted by falsity from evil. *And Israel saw the Egyptians dead on the shore of the sea* symbolizes a view of the damned as they scattered in all directions. *And Israel saw the great hand, [the works] that Jehovah performed among the Egyptians,* symbolizes acknowledgment of the Lord's omnipotence. *And the people feared Jehovah* symbolizes adoration. *And believed* symbolizes faith and trust. *In Jehovah and in Moses his servant* symbolizes the Lord in regard to his divine goodness and in regard to the divine truth emanating from him and ministering.

And the children of Israel went on dry ground into the middle of the sea **8234**
means that people intent on goodness from truth and truth from goodness passed through that hell in safety, free of harassment. This can be seen from the explanation above at §8185, where similar words appear.

I speak of people intent on goodness from truth and on truth from goodness, by which I mean the spiritual church. People whose religion is spiritual start with goodness-from-truth and move to truth-from-goodness. At first they do good because truth orders them to, so they act out of obedience, but then they do good because they want to. At that point they are looking at truth from the viewpoint of goodness, and they are acting on it, also out of goodness. Plainly, then, until people of a spiritual religion receive a new will from the Lord—until they have been reborn—they act on truth out of obedience, but after they have been reborn, they act on truth because they want to. Truth then turns into goodness, in their case, because it enters their will. To act from obedience is to act on the intellect; to act on desire is to act from the will.

So in addition, people who act on the truth from obedience have an outer religion, whereas people who act on truth from desire have an inner religion.

This shows that people of the spiritual church are meant by those described as devoted to goodness from truth and truth from goodness.

8235 *And the waters were a wall to them on their right and on their left* means that they were kept from falsity on every side. This can be seen from the explanation above at §8206, where the same words appear.

8236 *And on that day Jehovah saved Israel from the hand of the Egyptians* means that in this state the Lord protected people of the spiritual church from any violence inflicted by falsity from evil. This is evident from the symbolism of *saving* as protecting, from the meaning of *on that day* as in this state (for the symbolism of a day as a state, see §§23, 487, 488, 493, 893, 2788, 3462, 3785, 4850), from the representation of *Israel* as people of the spiritual church (mentioned frequently), and from that of the *Egyptians* as spirits devoted to falsity from evil (also mentioned frequently). From this it is plain that saving someone from their hand means protecting someone from violence inflicted by spirits devoted to falsity from evil.

8237 *And Israel saw the Egyptians dead on the shore of the sea* symbolizes a view of the damned as they scattered in all directions. This can be seen from the symbolism of *seeing* as the view or regarding of something; from the representation of the *Egyptians* as spirits devoted to falsity from evil; from the symbolism of the *dead* as the damned (discussed in §§5407, 6119, 7494); and from the meaning of *on the shore of the sea* as around the edges of hell. Obviously shores are the edges, and the symbolism of the sea as hell has been shown before [§§8099, 8137, 8138]. This is why seeing them dead on the shore of the sea symbolizes a view of the damned as they scattered in all directions.

Since I mention a view of the damned, I should explain how this matter stands. The inhabitants of the hells are not visible to those in another hell, not even to those in the next hell, because they are completely segregated. They do appear to the inhabitants of heaven, though, whenever it pleases the Lord. The Lord governs the hells with the help of angels, whom he enables to stay where they are and still see everything that happens down there. This he does for the sake of maintaining order even in hell and of preventing its inhabitants from abusing each other any more than permissible. This regulatory function is given to angels, and with it, power over the hells.

Good spirits too are sometimes allowed to look into the hells and see what is happening there, because the divine plan allows what lies below to be seen from above, but not what lies above to be seen from below. The inhabitants of heaven, then, can see the hells and the people in them, but not the reverse. (That is why goodness can see evil but evil cannot see goodness, since goodness is higher and evil lower.)

And Israel saw the great hand, [the works] that Jehovah performed among **8238**
the Egyptians, symbolizes acknowledgment of the Lord's omnipotence, as the following shows: *Seeing* symbolizes understanding, acknowledging, and believing, as discussed in §§897, 2150, 2325, 2807, 3796, 3863, 3869, 4403–4421, 5400, 6805. A *great* or mighty or strong or high *hand* attributed to *Jehovah,* or the Lord, symbolizes omnipotence, as discussed in §§878, 7188, 7189, 7518, 8050, 8069, 8153. And the *Egyptians* represent people under damnation, or at this point, residents of hell.

And the people feared Jehovah symbolizes adoration. This is clear from **8239**
the symbolism of *fearing Jehovah* as worship grounded in love or in faith or in fear (discussed at §2826) and therefore as adoration.

And believed symbolizes faith and trust. This is evident from the sym- **8240**
bolism of *believing* as having faith and also trust, because anyone with faith has trust. Trust comes of love, through faith, so trust in Jehovah (the Lord) exists only in people who are loving—loving of the Lord and of their neighbor—because only they possess faith.

In Jehovah and in Moses his servant symbolizes the Lord in regard to **8241**
his divine goodness and in regard to the divine truth emanating from him and ministering, as the following shows: In the Word, *Jehovah* means the Lord (see §§1343, 1736, 2921, 3023, 3035, 5663, 6281, 6303, 6945, 6956) and specifically the Lord's divine goodness (§§2586, 2769, 2807, 2822, 4402, 6905). *Moses* represents the divine truth emanating from the Lord, as discussed in §§6752, 7010, 7014, 7089, 7382. I speak of the Lord in regard to divine goodness and divine truth because divine goodness is in the Lord and divine truth comes from him. The relationship of divine goodness to divine truth is like the relationship of the sun's fire to the radiating light; the light is not in the sun but comes from it. And a *servant* symbolizes something that ministers. "Servant" is the name for someone who serves and therefore for someone who assists (see §7143). So in the Word, the

Lord in respect to the divine humanity he had when he was in the world is called a servant (§3441), because he then served, as he even says:

> Anyone among you who wants to become great will have to be your attendant, and anyone who wants to be first will have to be your slave. Just as *the Son of Humankind did not come to be served but to serve others.* (Matthew 20:26, 27, 28; Mark 10:43, 44, 45)

The Spirits and Inhabitants of Jupiter (Continued)

8242 WHAT kind of face the inhabitants of Jupiter have was also shown to me. It was not the actual inhabitants I saw but spirits with the same face they had when they were living on their planet.

First, though, one of their angels appeared behind a white cloud and gave permission, and that is when two faces were shown. They resembled the faces of people on our own planet, glowing, but more beautiful. From them shone sincerity and modesty.

8243 Whenever the spirits of Jupiter were with me, the faces of our own planet's inhabitants looked smaller than usual to me. The reason they looked smaller was that an idea those spirits had that their faces were larger than ours was flowing in. While they are living as humans on their planet, they believe that after death their faces will be bigger, and round. Because the notion has been imprinted on them, it lasts, and when they become spirits, they appear to themselves to have a larger face.

The reason they believe their faces will be larger is that they say the face is not part of the body. This is because they use it for speaking and expressing their thoughts, so that the mind is essentially visible through the face. As a consequence, they think of the face as the mind in a tangible form. Since they know they will grow wiser when their life in the world ends, they believe the tangible form of their mind—their face—will increase in size.

8244 While in the world they also believe that after death they will feel fire warming their face. They draw this conclusion because the wiser ones of them know that the fire of the spiritual world is love, and that this fire is the fire of life, which gives warmth to angels. Moreover, any of them that lived lives of heavenly love achieve their desire [after death] and feel their face grow warm with something like fire. When they do, it is not heat but love that ignites the inner depths of their mind.

For this reason they also wash and clean their face often, and carefully protect it from the hot sun. They have a covering made of a bluish bark that they wrap around their head to shield their face. They do not care much about their body, though. 8245

About the faces of people on our planet they said these were not good-looking. Surprised to find that the faces of some had warts and pimples and other flaws, they said such a thing is never seen among them. Some faces made them smile, though. These were the ones that were cheerful and smiling and that jutted out around the lips. 8246

The reason they smiled at smiling, cheerful faces was that this is how almost all the faces of people on their own planet look, which in turn is because they do not worry about the future or have many worldly cares. Worry and care are what induce depression and anxiety on one's spirits and consequently on one's face. If the faces of people who are not good exhibit hilarity and smiles, the effect goes only skin deep, not down into the muscles within. It is different with the inhabitants of Jupiter. 8247

The reason they smiled at faces that jutted out around the lips was that they speak mainly through their face, especially through the area around their lips. Besides, they never dissemble, or speak differently than they think, so they do not control their face but relax it. The case is different with people who have learned since childhood to pretend. They pinch their face from within to keep the least thought from gleaming out. Even on the outside they do not relax it but rather keep it ready to relax or contract as cunning prompts.

Observation of the muscles around the lips can reveal the truth of this situation, because there are multiple interwoven, interlaced series of muscle fibers there created not just for chewing and for saying words but also for expressing the thoughts of the mind and heart.

I was also shown how they use their face to present their thoughts. The different emotions that love inspires in them are displayed through facial expressions and changes in those expressions. The thoughts the emotions hold within them are displayed through changes in deeper-lying structures. I cannot describe it any more fully. 8248

The inhabitants of Jupiter do have verbal speech, but the volume is lower than with ours. Each of the two kinds of speech helps the other, and the facial speech infuses the verbal speech with life.

8249 From angels I learned that the very first way people on every planet talked was with their face and that this primal speech had two starting points: the lips and the eyes. The reason this type of speech came first is that the face is perfectly formed for presenting an image of our thoughts and desires. That is why the face is called the visible form and indicator of the mind. Another reason this was the first type of speech is that sincerity existed in the first or earliest times (§8118). People did not have thoughts, and did not want to have thoughts, that they were unwilling to show in their face. So the feelings in their heart and the thoughts in their mind could be presented in full and living form. The feelings and thoughts were visible to the eye, virtually taking shape before it, great numbers of them in each expression. This kind of speech was therefore as superior to verbal speech as seeing is to listening—that is, as observing a scene is to hearing it described. The angels added that this sort of speech is compatible with the speech of angels and that people actually communicated with angels in those days. What is more, speech of the face, or rather speech of the mind through the face, is angelic speech as it exists in a person, in its lowest, most physical form; it is the presence of one individual's inner vision, or thought, in another individual's thoughts. This is not true of words uttered by the mouth.

For the idea that the earliest people on this planet spoke the same way, see §§607, 608, 1118, 1120, 7361.

Anyone can see that the earliest people could not have spoken in words, because words were not directly instilled into the tongue. They had to be invented and applied to the things being talked about, which could not have happened except over time.

8250 This kind of speech lasted just as long as sincerity and straightforwardness existed among humankind, but eventually the mind started to think one thing and say another, which happened when people started to love themselves rather than their neighbor. As soon as thought and speech parted ways, verbal speech began to take over, and the face either turned mute or joined the mouth in lying. That caused the inner structure of the face to change, pinch, harden, and become almost devoid of life, but the outer structure, aflame with the fire of self-love, to seem full of life. The underlying lifelessness, which serves as an inner basis [for this dishonesty], is not visible to the human eye, only to the eyes of angels, since they see inwardly.

Such are the faces of people who think one way and speak another. The pretense, hypocrisy, cunning, and deceit that constitute modern wisdom cause these effects.

[2] The situation is quite different in the other life, though. No one there is allowed to speak and think two different ways. Any discrepancy is perceived clearly in every word and in every sound articulated. When it is perceived, the spirit exhibiting the discrepancy is banished from society and subjected to corporal punishment. The spirit is then forced by various means to match speech to thought and thought to will, until that spirit has a single, undivided mind. If good, the spirit has to wish well and to think and speak truth from goodness. If evil, the spirit has to wish ill and to think and speak falsity from evil. Until that has been accomplished, a good spirit cannot be lifted up to heaven and an evil spirit cannot be thrown into hell. Nothing but evil is to be found in hell, and the falsity there is to be from evil. Nothing but goodness is to be found in heaven, and the truth there is to be from goodness.

More will be said about the spirits and inhabitants of Jupiter at the  8251
end of the next chapter [§§8371–8386].

Exodus 15

Teachings on Neighborly Love

8252 A person in the church must have a life of religious devotion and a life of neighborly love; the two must be brought together. A life of religious devotion without a life of neighborly love is of no use, but the one combined with the other is of every use.

8253 A life of religious devotion is to think devoutly and speak devoutly, make plenty of time for prayer, behave humbly when praying, go to church, listen carefully and reverently to the preaching, take Holy Supper every year, and faithfully carry out all the other acts of worship prescribed by the church.

A life of neighborly love, on the other hand, is to wish well and do well to one's neighbor and to apply justice and fairness, goodness and truth to every deed and to every responsibility. To put it briefly, a life of love consists in being useful.

8254 The most genuine way of worshiping the Lord consists in a life of neighborly love, not a life of religious devotion without a life of neighborly love. Living a devout life and not a charitable life means wanting to take care of oneself alone, not one's neighbor. Living a devout life and at the same time a charitable life means wanting to take care of oneself for the sake of one's neighbor. The former type of life is based on love for oneself; the latter on love for one's neighbor.

8255 The Lord's words in Matthew make it plain that to do good is to worship the Lord:

> *Everyone who hears my words and does them I will compare to a prudent man. But everyone hearing my words and not doing them will be compared to a stupid man.* (Matthew 7:24, 26)

8256 Besides, it is the quality of the neighborly love we practice that determines our character, not the quality of the religious devotion we practice apart from the love we show. So it is our life of neighborly love that remains with us forever, not our life of piety, except to the extent that it harmonizes with our life of love. The fact that our life of neighborly love remains with us forever is plain from the Lord's words in Matthew:

> *The Son of Humankind will come in the glory of his Father, with his angels. And then he will repay every person according to that person's deeds.* (Matthew 16:27)

And in John:

> *Those who have done good deeds will emerge into a resurrection filled with life, but those who have done evil deeds, into a resurrection filled with judgment.* (John 5:29)

This is also clear from the words of Matthew 25:31–end.

When I speak of that life by which we mainly worship the Lord, I **8257**
mean living by his commandments in the Word, which teach us what faith and neighborly love are. This kind of life is a Christian life and is called a spiritual life. In contrast, living by the laws of justice and honor but not by the Lord's commandments is a civic, moral life. A civic, moral life makes us citizens of the world, but a spiritual life makes us citizens of heaven.

Exodus 15

1. Then Moses and the children of Israel sang this song to Jehovah and said, saying, "[I will sing] to Jehovah, because he has risen very high! The horse and its rider he has cast into the sea.

2. My strength and song is Jah, and he has become my salvation. This is my God, and I will set up a dwelling place for him; my father's God, and I will exalt him.

3. Jehovah is a man of war; Jehovah is his name.

4. The chariots of Pharaoh and his army he has cast into the sea, and the choicest of the tertiary officers have been drowned in the Suph Sea.

5. The abysses covered them; they went down into the depths like a stone.

6. Your right hand, Jehovah, is imposing in its strength. By your right hand, Jehovah, you shatter your foe.

7. And in the vastness of your magnificence you destroy those rising up against you; you send forth your wrath, it devours them like stubble.

8. And by the wind from your nostrils the waters were heaped up, the streams stood like a mound, the abysses congealed in the heart of the sea.

9. Our foe said, 'I will pursue, overtake, divide the plunder; my soul will be filled with them. I will draw my sword; my hand will drive them off.'

10. You blew with your wind, the sea covered them; they sought the depths like lead in vast waters.

11. Who is like you among the gods, Jehovah? Who is like you, majestic in holiness, to be venerated with praises, doing a wonder?

12. You stretched out your right hand: the earth swallowed them.

13. In your mercy you led this people, you redeemed them; [in] your might you guided them to your holy dwelling.

14. The peoples heard; they trembled. Agony seized the inhabitants of Philistia.

15. Then panic beset the commanders of Edom, the powerful of Moab; terror seized them. All the inhabitants of Canaan collapsed.

16. Horror and dread fell on them; in the greatness of your arm they are cut off like a stone until your people crosses over, Jehovah, until [this] people [of whom] you took possession crosses over.

17. You will bring them in, you will plant them on the mountain of your inheritance, in the place where you were to dwell. You performed your work, Jehovah; your sanctuary, Lord, your hands prepared.

18. Jehovah will reign to eternity and forever,

19. because Pharaoh's horse with his chariot and with his riders came into the sea, and Jehovah brought back over them the waters of the sea. And the children of Israel went on dry ground through the middle of the sea."

20. And Miriam the prophetess, the sister of Aaron, took the tambourine in her hand, and all the women went out after her with tambourines and with dances.

21. And Miriam answered them, "Sing to Jehovah, because he has risen very high; the horse and its rider he has cast into the sea."

22. And Moses caused Israel to set out from the Suph Sea, and they went away to the wilderness of Shur and went three days in the wilderness and did not find water.

23. And they came to Marah and could not drink the water for bitterness, because it was bitter, so he called its name Marah.

24. And the people murmured against Moses, saying, "What shall we drink?"

25. And he cried out to Jehovah, and Jehovah showed him a piece of wood, and he threw it [into] the water, and the water became sweet. There he set them a statute and a judgment, and there he tested them.

26. And he said, "If you listen intently to the voice of Jehovah your God and do what is right in his eyes and heed his commandments and keep all his statutes, I will not lay on you any disease that I laid on the Egyptians, because I am Jehovah your healer."

27. And they came to Elim, and there were twelve springs of water there and seventy palm trees. And they camped [there] next to the waters.

Summary

THE inner meaning of the current chapter celebrates the Lord and **8258**
the way he dealt with the evil and the good after he glorified his human side. The evil who were persecuting the good in the other life he cast into the hells, and the good who were being persecuted he took up to heaven. That is what the inner meaning of this mystical song contains.

Next that meaning deals with the second challenge faced by people **8259**
of the spiritual church, as depicted in the people's murmurs at Marah, where the water was bitter. Then it deals with the comfort given them, which is symbolized by the encampment at Elim, with its twelve springs and seventy palm trees.

Inner Meaning

EXODUS 15:1, 2. *Then Moses and the children of Israel sang this song* **8260**
to Jehovah and said, saying, "I will sing to Jehovah, because he has risen very high! The horse and its rider he has cast into the sea. My strength and song is Jah, and he has become my salvation. This is my God, and I will set up a dwelling place for him; my father's God, and I will exalt him."

Then Moses and the children of Israel sang this song to Jehovah symbolizes glory given to the Lord by people of the spiritual church for their deliverance. *And said, saying,* means that this came about from a spiritual inflow. *I will sing to Jehovah* means that the glory is the Lord's alone. *Because he has risen very high* means that he revealed his divinity within his humanity. *The horse and its rider he has cast into the sea* means through this: that as a result of his mere presence, falsity from evil was condemned and thrown into hell. *My strength* means that all power comes from him. *And song is Jah* means that all faith and all the glory it imparts originate in the divine truth emanating from him. *And he has become my salvation* symbolizes being saved as a result. *And I will set up a dwelling place for him* means that when he is present in the goodness that comes from himself, he will in effect be in his heaven. *My father's God* means that there was no other Divine acknowledged by the ancient churches. *And I will exalt him* means that even today he is worshiped as divine.

8261 *Then Moses and the children of Israel sang this song to Jehovah* symbolizes glory given to the Lord by people of the spiritual church for their deliverance, as the following shows: *Singing a song* symbolizes giving glory, as discussed below. The reason it is glory given to the Lord is that in the Word, *Jehovah* means the Lord (§§1343, 1736, 2921, 3023, 3035, 5041, 5663, 6280, 6281, 6905, 6945, 6956). And *Moses and the children of Israel* represent people of the spiritual church, because Moses together with the people represents that church, Moses representing its head (since he also represents divine truth), and the people (the children of Israel), the church itself. For the meaning of the children of Israel as people of the spiritual church, see §§6426, 6637, 6862, 7035, 7062, 7198, 7201, 7215, 7223. The fact that the glory they give the Lord is for their deliverance is plain from explanations in the previous chapter. As shown there, people of the spiritual church were saved only by the Lord's coming into the world. Till then they were kept in an underground realm, where they were persecuted by spirits intent on falsity-from-evil. They were delivered by the Lord after he made the human nature in himself divine. On the fact that people of the spiritual church were saved only by the Lord's coming into the world, see §§2661, 2716, 2833, 2834, 6372. On the fact that they were kept in an underground realm till then and were delivered by the Lord when he made the human nature in himself divine, see §§6854, 6914, 7035, 7091 at the end, 7828, 7932, 8018, 8054.

[2] The reason *singing a song* means giving glory—and a *song* is therefore the glory given—is that songs in the ancient church and in the Jewish church that followed it were prophetic. They told about the Lord, saying in particular that he would come into the world to destroy the

mob of devils that would be more predatory than ever at that time, and to deliver the faithful from its assaults. Since these messages were contained in the inner meaning of the prophecies delivered in the songs, the songs themselves symbolize glory given to the Lord or celebration of him from heartfelt gladness. One of the main ways a glad heart expresses itself is with song, because in a song, happiness spontaneously bursts into sound.

It is because of this prophetic message that the songs refer to Jehovah (the Lord) as a hero, a man of war, God of the legions, a conqueror, one's strength, a fortress, a shield, and one's salvation. For the same reason, they refer to the Devil's crew after its destruction as a foe that has been struck, swallowed up, drowned, and thrown into hell.

[3] Even in former times there were people ignorant of any inner meaning who believed the songs were referring to phenomena of the physical world, such as the earthly enemies, battles, victories, disasters, and drownings described in the outer meaning. However, there were also people who knew that all prophecies held something heavenly and divine inside and that this content was represented in the literal images. These people knew the songs were saying that the faithless would be damned and the faithful saved by the Lord when he came into the world. People who knew this, who thought about it and were touched by the thought, felt a deep happiness, whereas the first group felt only a superficial happiness. At the same time, the angels present with them were giving glory to the Lord. So both the singers and their listeners felt an awe and bliss flowing in from heaven that inspired them with heavenly gladness, making them feel as though they had been lifted up to heaven.

That is the effect religious songs had on the ancients, and that is the effect they have today too, because spiritual angels are especially moved by songs about the Lord, his kingdom, and the church.

The songs had this effect because of the way they stirred heartfelt gladness that burst from inside all the way to the outermost fibers of the body, causing these fibers to vibrate with happiness and also with holy awe. But the effect was due also to the fact that when the heavens give glory to the Lord, they do so in choruses and therefore in the blended harmony of many voices. For that reason, the speech of angels is musical and marked by rhythmic cadences. (On choruses, see §§2595, 2596, 3350, 5182, 8115. On angelic speech and its rhythmic cadences, see §§1648, 1649, 7191 at the end.) That is why the ancients who were part of the church used songs, psalms, and musical instruments of various kinds to give glory to the Lord. What brought joy above all other joys to the ancient people who were part of the church, you see, was to remember that the Lord was going to come and save the human race.

[4] It is plain from songs in the Word that prophetic songs gave glory to the Lord in their inner meaning. In Isaiah, for example:

> I, Jehovah, have called you in righteousness and will hold your hand; I myself will guard you *and give you as a pact for the people, as a light for the nations,* to open blind eyes, *to lead the prisoner out from prison, those sitting in darkness out of the jailhouse. Sing Jehovah a new song;* his praise, you farthest part of the earth! Let the wilderness and its cities lift up their voice. Let those who live on the rock *sing; let them give glory to Jehovah.* Jehovah will go forth as a *hero;* as a *man of wars* he will stir up his zeal. He will be stronger than *his enemies.* (Isaiah 42:6, 7, 8, 9, [10, 11, 12, 13])

This is obviously about the Lord, who was coming to deliver people suffering spiritual captivity. That is why it says, "Sing Jehovah a new song" and "Let those who live on the rock sing." Likewise in the same author:

> *I gave you as a pact with the people,* to restore the earth, to distribute devastated inheritances, *to say to prisoners, "Go out!";* to those in darkness, "Show yourselves!" On paths they will graze, and on all the slopes will be their pasture. *Sing, you heavens,* and *rejoice,* earth, and *break into song, you mountains,* because Jehovah has comforted his people and will have mercy on his afflicted ones. (Isaiah 49:8, 9, 10, 13, and following)

This too is about the Lord's Coming and the deliverance of prisoners. [5] In David:

> *Sing Jehovah a new song,* bless his name, recount his *glory* among the nations! All the gods of the peoples are worthless. But Jehovah made the heavens; *glory* and *honor* stand before him, strength and beauty are in his sanctuary. Give Jehovah *glory* and *strength;* give *Jehovah the glory due his name.* Say among the nations, "Jehovah reigns"; indeed the world is made firm and is not dislodged. *Jehovah has come, has come to judge the earth!* (Psalms 96:1–end)

In the same author:

> Jehovah brought me up *out of the pit of devastation,* out of the muddy clay, and set my feet on a rock *and put into my mouth a new song* [of] praise to our God. Many will see and trust. (Psalms 40:2, 3)

These passages also show that a song is the glory one gives to the Lord for one's deliverance. What the songs hold within them is gladness of heart and exaltation of the Lord—gladness of heart over the Lord's Coming and the salvation it would bring, and exaltation because of his victory over one's spiritual enemies. And that is what giving glory to him means: gladness of heart combined with exaltation of him.

[6] The fact that songs symbolized gladness of heart is evident in David:

> Give thanks to Jehovah on a harp; on a ten-string lute make music to him. *Sing him a new song,* play skillfully with a loud sound, because he *gathers the waters of the sea like a heap,* he puts abysses in his treasures. (Psalms 33:2–7)

In Isaiah:

> The joy of tambourines will cease; the commotion of revelers will cease; the joy of a harp will cease. *They will not drink wine with a song.* (Isaiah 24:8, 9)

And in Amos:

> I will turn your feasts into mourning *and all your songs* into a lament. (Amos 8:10)

The use of songs to exalt Jehovah, or the Lord, can be seen in David:

> David is Jehovah's servant, *and he spoke to Jehovah the words of this song:* Jehovah is my strength; Jehovah is my rock and my fortress and my rescuer, my God, my towering rock in which I trust, my shield and the horn of my salvation, my refuge. Him who is praised I will call on: Jehovah. Then I will be preserved from my foes. (Psalms 18: heading, 1, 2, 3, and following verses)

In the same author:

> Jehovah is my strength and my shield, *so with song I will acclaim him.* Jehovah is strength to them, and the strength of his anointed one's acts of salvation. (Psalms 28:7, 8)

In the same author:

> Your salvation, God, will lead me on high; *I will praise the name of God with a song* and *exalt him* with acclamation. (Psalms 69:29, 30)

[7] It can be seen in John as well that songs had to do with the Lord:

> The twenty-four elders *sang a new song,* saying: "You are worthy to take the book and open its seals, because you were killed and redeemed us for God with your blood." (Revelation 5:9, 10)

And in the same author:

> I saw seven angels *who were singing the song of Moses, the servant of God,* and the *song of the Lamb,* saying, "Great and marvelous are your deeds, Lord God Almighty; just and true are your ways, you monarch of the saints. Who would not fear you, Lord, and would not *give glory to your name?"* (Revelation 15:[1,] 2, 3, [4])

The song of Moses and the Lamb is the song in Exodus 15. It is called the song of the Lamb because it talks about giving glory to the Lord.

8262 *And said, saying,* means that this came about from a spiritual inflow. This can be seen from the symbolism of *saying* as an inflow, when the subject is glory given to the Lord in song. On the point that an inflow is one of the meanings of "saying," see §§5743, 6152, 6291, 7291, 7381, 8221.

8263 *I will sing to Jehovah* means that the glory is the Lord's alone. This is clear from the symbolism of *singing to Jehovah* as giving glory to the Lord (discussed just above at §8261) and consequently as the fact that the glory is his. It is his alone because the Lord is the one whom the Word calls Jehovah (§8261) and is therefore the only God.

The Word is constantly saying that glory and honor must be given to God alone. Anyone who does not know the Word's inner depths is likely to believe that the Lord desires and loves glory the way a person in the world does, partly because the Lord deserves glory more than anyone else in the universe. It is not for his own benefit, though, that the Lord wants glory, but rather for the benefit of the person offering it. People who honor the Lord do so in reverent awe of him as supreme and in humility over their own comparative nothingness. So the glory we give the Lord contains both awe and humility, which means that when giving glory, we are in a state in which we accept an inflow of goodness from the Lord. We therefore accept love for him as well. That is why he wants us to honor him. See §§4347, 4593, 5957. For the idea that a humble heart is what accepts an inflow of goodness from the Lord, see §§3994, 7478.

8264 *Because he has risen very high* means that he revealed his divinity within his humanity. This can be seen from the symbolism of *rising high,* when said of the Lord, as revealing the divinity within his humanity. The reason rising very high has this symbolism is that what is divine is highest, or supreme, and when the Lord was in the world, he made the human nature in himself divine. That is how he "rose very high." For the scriptural meaning of "high" as divine, see §8153. The verse says that he rose very high—symbolizing a revelation of the divinity within his humanity—because the song tells how the Lord, after he had made his human side divine, threw the evil into the hells and took the good up to heaven (§8258) by his mere presence (§7989). After all, to cast the evil into the hells and take the good up to heaven by one's mere presence requires divinity.

The horse and [its] rider he has cast into the sea means that as a result **8265**
of his mere presence, falsity from evil was condemned and thrown into hell, as the following shows: A *horse* here symbolizes the falsity produced by a corrupted intellect. A horse generally stands for the intellect; see §§2761, 2762, 3217, 5321. In a negative sense it stands for a corrupted intellect, which is no intellect at all, so in this sense it symbolizes falsity, and a horse of Pharaoh's symbolizes falsity in the form of knowledge (§§6125, 8146, 8148). A *rider* symbolizes the twisted reasoning that results, as dealt with in §§8146, 8148. And *casting into the sea* means damning and throwing into hell. The *sea*—the Suph Sea, here—is the hell in which is found the falsity-from-evil promoted by people in the church who had a detached faith and lived an evil life; see §§8099, 8137, 8148. That is why the falsity is described as being from evil.

The previous chapter [§§8137, 8214, 8226–8227] showed that this falsity was damned and thrown into hell by the Lord's mere presence. The evil cannot begin to bear or endure the divine presence, because it distresses and tortures them and almost kills them, so to speak; they behave as though they are in the throes of death. This is because divinity contains all power. It destroys and extinguishes what opposes it, so it snuffs out falsity and evil. People who cling to falsity and evil consequently struggle to survive in the divine presence and sense more or less of hell inside themselves, depending on how close that presence is. To keep them from being tormented and totally destroyed, though, they are cloaked in their own falsity and evil. These resemble clouds that naturally break up the inflow from the Divine or repel or smother it, just as earthly clouds or mists do to sunrays.

[2] That is the meaning of the following words in John:

> They will say to the mountains and rocks, "Collapse on us and hide us from the face of the one sitting on the throne and from the anger of the

> Lamb! Because the great day of his anger has come; who, then, can stay standing?" (Revelation 6:16, 17)

The mountains and rocks that they will tell to collapse on them and hide them symbolize evil and falsity; the anger of the Lamb symbolizes torment. It looks as though the Divine in his anger inflicts torment, when in reality it is falsity and evil itself that does so. The same is true of Isaiah 2:10; Hosea 10:8; Luke 23:30. The fact that damnation results from the Lord's presence alone is also symbolized by the following words later on in this song:

> You send forth your wrath, it devours them like stubble. And by the wind from your nostrils the waters were heaped up, the streams stood like a mound. You blew with your wind, the sea covered them; they sought the depths. You stretched out your right hand: the earth swallowed them. (Exodus 15:7, 8, 10, 12)

Likewise in many other passages in the Word.

8266 *My strength* means that all power comes from him. This is clear from the symbolism of *strength* as might and power, and since it says *my* strength and is ascribed to Jehovah (the Lord), the meaning is that all power comes from him.

8267 *And song is Jah* means that all faith and all the glory it imparts originate in the divine truth emanating from him. This can be seen from the symbolism of a *song,* when ascribed to Jehovah, as glory given to the Lord, which is discussed above at §8261. When it is ascribed to a person, though, as it is here, it symbolizes glory radiating from faith and accordingly faith that radiates glory. All the glory we possess comes from our faith in the Lord, because faith that really is faith is from him. As a result the Lord is within our faith, meaning that glory itself is there too.

Another reason any glory we have comes from faith is that to the eyes of angels, divine truth—the source and conduit of faith—appears as a light and as the glow and radiance of that light. This radiance, together with magnificent effects the light produces in heaven, is called glory. So glory is actually divine truth and is therefore faith.

[2] *Jah* means divine truth emanating from the Lord's divine humanity because the name comes from "Jehovah." It is called Jah because it is not the essential reality but rather is the manifestation of that reality. Divine truth is an emerging presence, while divine goodness is the essential reality itself; see §6880. That too is why the text says, "My song is Jah": because a song symbolizes faith, which relates to divine truth.

Jah symbolizes divine truth in David as well:

> *Sing to God;* praise his name! Extol the one riding on the clouds *by his name, Jah,* and rejoice before him. (Psalms 68:4)

To praise and extol God by his name, Jah, is to praise and extol him with divine truth. Again, in the same author:

> In tight-bound anguish I called on *Jah; Jah* answered me with a broad place. Jehovah helped me; my strength and *song* is *Jah.* Let me not die but live, and I will proclaim the deeds of *Jah!* I will enter through the gates of righteousness and acclaim *Jah.* (Psalms 118)

In this passage, Jah is the Lord as divine truth. The same applies to the *Jah* in *hallelu-Jah* [Praise the Lord!] (Psalms 105:45; 106:1, 48; 111:1; 112:1; 113:1, 9; 115:17, 18; 116:19).

And he has become my salvation symbolizes being saved as a result, **8268**
which is clear without explanation.

And I will set up a dwelling place for him means that when he is pres- **8269**
ent in the goodness that comes from himself, he will in effect be in his heaven. This can be seen from the symbolism of a *dwelling place* said to be Jehovah's (the Lord's) as goodness. The Lord's dwelling place is goodness because everything good is from him. So goodness is the Lord's to such an extent that it can be said that goodness *is* the Lord. When the Lord dwells in goodness, he dwells in his divinity, and he cannot dwell anywhere else, in keeping with his words in John:

> Jesus said, "If any love me, they keep my word, and my Father loves them, *and we will come to them and make a home in them."* (John 14:23)

Goodness from the Divine is depicted here as loving the Lord and keeping his word, because goodness is a matter of love. It is with a person doing this that the text says they will make a home—that is, with the goodness in such a person.

I say he will in effect be in his heaven because heaven is called God's dwelling place on account of the goodness from the Lord that exists in heaven and composes it. The Lord is in effect in his heaven in every individual too when he is in the goodness there, because our heaven is goodness, and goodness puts us among the angels in heaven.

This now shows that *I will set up a dwelling place for him* means that when he is present in the goodness that comes from himself, he will in effect be in his heaven.

8270 *My father's God* means that there was no other Divine acknowledged by the ancient churches. This is established by the symbolism of a *father* as the ancient church, which is discussed in §§6050, 6075, 7649, 8055. The *God* of his father therefore means the Divine acknowledged by the ancient churches. Their Divine was the Lord (see §§6846, 6876, 6884), and they understood Jehovah to be no one but the Lord (§§1343, 5663).

8271 *And I will exalt him* means that even today he is worshiped as divine. This can be seen from the symbolism of *exalting* as worship, when the text is saying that a person will exalt Jehovah. Worshiping the Lord as divine obviously consists in exalting him above oneself, which happens in proportion to the depth of one's humility before him. Humility is essential to the worship of God. When we possess this essential quality, we are in a state in which we accept from the Lord the truth taught by faith and the goodness urged by neighborly love. So we are in a state in which we worship him. If we exalt ourselves before the Lord, on the other hand, we close off the inner depths of our mind to the acceptance of goodness and truth from him.

For the meaning of exalting oneself, [or rising high,] when the Lord is said to do it, see above at §8264.

8272 Exodus 15:3, 4, 5. *"Jehovah is a man of war; Jehovah is his name. The chariots of Pharaoh and his army he has cast into the sea, and the choicest of the tertiary officers have been drowned in the Suph Sea. The abysses covered them; they went down into the depths like a stone."*

Jehovah is a man of war means that the Lord protects against all evil and falsity from the hells. *Jehovah is his name* means that everything comes from him alone. *The chariots of Pharaoh and his army he has cast into the sea* means that ill-intentioned falsities threw themselves into the hells at the Lord's presence—the ill-intentioned falsities in particular and in general of people who were part of the church and whose life was evil. *And the choicest of the tertiary officers* symbolizes all [those falsities] and each of them individually. *Have been drowned in the Suph Sea* means that these people closed themselves in with falsity from evil. *The abysses covered them* means that falsity from evil cravings blanketed them. *They went down into the depths like a stone* means that they sank to the nether regions like weights.

8273 *Jehovah is a man of war* means that the Lord protects against all evil and falsity from the hells. This is evident from the symbolism of a *man of war* as the one who fights and conquers falsity and evil—in other words, fights and conquers the hells. Here it symbolizes the one who protects us from them. When the hells attack (as already shown [§§8159, 8172, 8175, 8219, 8236]), the Lord alone fights on our behalf and protects us, and does so unremittingly, especially during our times of trial, which are spiritual battles.

The first reason the Lord is called a man of war is that when he was in the world he worked alone, by himself, to fight the hells, most of which yawned open at that time, their inhabitants attacking all new arrivals to the other world in an effort to crush them. And why was the Devil's gang—the hells—then especially predatory? Evil and falsity had grown so far beyond measure that they were too strong to be opposed by the divine quality passing through heaven (which constituted the Lord's divine humanity before his Coming). Divinity itself was therefore pleased to do three things simultaneously: It took on a human nature, which it made divine. It allowed itself to be subjected to battles, through which it cast that mob of devils into hell, locked them up there, and put them under heaven's power. And it reduced the heavens themselves to order. These battles are the reason the Lord was first called a man of war. Later, when he had conquered the hells as described and had become righteousness, he was called this because he protects us with divine power, constantly, especially when we face the struggles of spiritual trial.

[2] The fact that the Lord alone, by himself, fought the hells and conquered them is expressed this way in Isaiah:

> *Judgment has been driven back, and justice has stood far off, since truthfulness stumbled in the street, and uprightness cannot approach. Meanwhile truthfulness has gone missing, and anyone departing from evil is insane. Jehovah saw—and it was evil in his eyes—that there was no judgment, and he saw that there was no man and was astounded that no one was interceding. Therefore his arm achieved salvation for him, and his righteousness supported him. So he put righteousness on like a coat of armor, and a helmet of salvation on his head.* (Isaiah 59:14, 15, 16, 17)

This depicts the conditions of the day in both worlds and shows that the Lord by himself, alone, restored the deteriorating state of affairs. Likewise in another place in the same author:

> *Who is this who comes from Edom, spattered in his clothes, from Bozrah? [Who is] this one, honorable in his apparel, marching in the abundance of his strength? "It is I who speak in righteousness, impressive at salvation. The winepress I have trodden alone, and from among the peoples not a man was with me, so my victory over them was spattered on my clothes. The day*

> *of revenge was in my heart, and the year of my redeemed had come. I had looked around, but no one was helping, and I was astounded, but no one was supporting me, so my arm achieved salvation for me."* (Isaiah 63:1, 2, 3, 4, 5)

This passage shows that in the world the Lord fought the hells all alone and conquered them.

[3] To say something about struggling with the hells and overcoming them: Anyone who conquers the hells once conquers them permanently, because in winning, we gain power over them. To that extent we strengthen ourselves in the goodness that comes from love and the truth that leads to faith and make them our own. From then on, the hells do not dare any attempt on the goodness and truth we possess. When the Lord was in the world, he allowed all the hells to inflict spiritual crises and struggles on him, through which he made the humanity in himself divine, while at the same time reducing the hells to obedience forever; see §§1663, 1668, 1690, 1692, 1737, 1813, 1820, 2776, 2786, 2795, 2813, 2814, 2816, 4287. That is why the Lord alone has eternal power over the hells, and he uses his divine power to fight on our behalf.

This is why the Lord is called a *man of war* and a hero, which occurs in Isaiah too:

> Jehovah will go forth as a *hero;* as a *man of wars* he will stir up his zeal. He will be stronger than his enemies. (Isaiah 42:13)

And in David:

> Who is this glorious monarch? Jehovah, *mighty* and a *hero;* Jehovah, a *war hero.* Who is this glorious monarch? *Jehovah Sabaoth* [Jehovah of the Legions]. (Psalms 24:8, 10)

[4] Where the Word mentions war, in an inner sense it means spiritual war, which is a war on falsity and evil, or to put it another way, on the Devil, or the hells (§§1664, 2686). The Lord's battles or struggles against the hells are dealt with in the inner meaning of both the narrative and the prophetic books of the Word. So are his battles and struggles *for* humankind.

Those ancients who had the Lord's church among them also had a Word, no longer extant, that contained both narrative and prophecy. The narrative part was called *The Book of the Wars of Jehovah,* and the prophetic part, *The Utterances.* This Word is mentioned in Moses, Numbers 21:14, 27. The fact that the term used [for "utterances"] in Numbers 21:27 means prophecies is plain from its meaning in Numbers 23:7, 18; 24:3, 15. The term *The Wars of Jehovah* there [in Numbers 21:14] was intended to mean the Lord's battles and victories against the hells when he was in the world and his battles and victories for humankind, the church, and his kingdom ever after. The hells are always trying to rise up, their sole aim in life being to dominate others, but the Lord and the Lord alone pushes them back down. Their efforts to break out are like something suddenly boiling over and splashing toward our back. Whenever they try this, though, large numbers of them are thrust farther down into hell.

Jehovah is his name means that everything comes from him alone. **8274**
This is evident from the symbolism of *Jehovah's name* as all the faith and love, or all the truth and goodness, collectively, with which the Lord is worshiped (discussed in §§2724, 3006, 6674), and in the highest sense as the Lord's divine humanity (§§2628, 6887), from which all the faith, love, truth, and goodness come. Because of this, and because Jehovah is reality itself and is therefore the core reality of everything, *Jehovah is his name* clearly means that everything comes from the Lord alone.

The chariots of Pharaoh and his army he has cast into the sea means **8275**
that ill-intentioned falsities threw themselves into the hells at the Lord's presence—the ill-intentioned falsities in particular and in general of people who were part of the church and whose life was evil—as the following shows: *Chariots* symbolize falsity, as discussed in §§8146, 8148, 8215. Here they symbolize particular falsities, because the verse also mentions the *army,* which symbolizes falsity in general. For the symbolism of an army as falsity, see §§3448, 8138, 8146, 8148. *Pharaoh* and the Egyptians represent people in the church who had a detached faith and an evil life and were therefore devoted to utter falsity-from-evil, as discussed in §§7926, 8132, 8135, 8138, 8148. The *sea*—the Suph Sea, here—symbolizes hell, where people devoted to that falsity live, as discussed in §§8099, 8137, 8148. *He has cast them into the sea,* then, means that he threw them into hell, and in an inner sense, that they actually threw themselves there at the Lord's mere presence; see §8265. These remarks show that *the chariots of Pharaoh and his army he has cast into the sea* means that ill-intentioned falsities threw themselves into the hells at the Lord's presence—the ill-intentioned falsities in particular and in general of people who were part of the church and whose life was evil.

And the choicest of the tertiary officers symbolizes all [those falsities] and **8276**
each of them individually. This can be seen from the symbolism of *tertiary officers* as general categories with their series of subcategories (discussed at

§8150) and therefore as all of them as a whole and each individually. To speak of general categories is to include the subcategories that form them and in addition the individual elements that come under the subcategories and form *them.* Without the individual elements, a general category is nonexistent. After all, it is described as general on account of these elements, because it is a complex of many elements. That is why tertiary officers symbolize all [those falsities] and each individually.

Their being described as *choicest* means that they are the leading ones—the leading falsities—under which the others come.

8277 *Have been drowned in the Suph Sea* means that these people closed themselves in with falsity from evil. This can be seen from the symbolism of *being drowned*—here, drowned in the waters of the *Suph Sea*—as closing oneself in with falsity from evil. The waters of that sea symbolize falsity (§§8137, 8138), and being drowned means being closed in. This is because falsity closes in on the inhabitants of the hells and surrounds them the same way water closes in on and surrounds people who are drowning. For the idea that they plunge themselves into falsity, or close themselves in with it, see §§7926, 8227, 8228.

8278 *The abysses covered them* means that falsity from evil cravings blanketed them. This is clear from the symbolism of *abysses* as falsity from evil cravings. Abysses in the Word mean water, large quantities of water in deep places. Water in a good sense symbolizes truth, while in the opposite sense it symbolizes falsity (§§739, 790, 2702, 3058, 3424, 4976, 5668), and the depths symbolize the hells. That is why abysses stand for falsity from evil cravings and also for the hells.

The meaning of abysses in the Word as water in deep places and as water in large quantities can be seen in Ezekiel:

> The water made the cedar grow, *the abyss made it tall,* so that with its rivers [the abyss] went around its planting-place and sent out channels of water to all the trees of the field. (Ezekiel 31:4)

In David:

> He split rocks in the wilderness and *gave the people great abysses to drink from;* he brought streams out of the rock and sent water down like streams. (Psalms 78:15, 16)

In Moses:

> A good land, a land of rivers of water, springs, and abysses issuing from the valley and from the mountain. (Deuteronomy 8:7)

In these passages abysses stand for copious amounts of water; and water in copious amounts—abysses—in turn stands for religious truth in abundance. "He gave them great abysses to drink from out of the rock" stands for giving them religious truth to drink that would not run out, because a rock is faith from the Lord and consequently the Lord in regard to faith. Abysses issuing from the valley and from the mountain stand for religious truth arising from love. That is why Joseph's blessings included "*Blessings of the abyss lying below*" (Genesis 49:25; Deuteronomy 33:13).

[2] The meaning of abysses as falsity from evil cravings and so as the hells can be seen in Isaiah:

> Wake up, as in the days of old, [as in] the generations of eternity! Is it not you who drains the sea, the *waters of the great abyss,* and makes the *depths of the sea* into a path for the redeemed to cross? (Isaiah 51:9, 10, 11)

In the same author:

> Jehovah, who split the waters before them, *who led them through the abysses!* Like a horse in the wilderness, they did not stumble. (Isaiah 63:12, 13)

In Ezekiel:

> This is what the Lord Jehovih has said: "When I turn you into a ruined city, like cities that are not inhabited; *when I bring up against you the abyss,* and *many waters cover you . . .*" (Ezekiel 26:19)

In John:

> I saw a star from the sky fallen to the earth, which was given the *key to the pit of the abyss* and *opened the pit of the abyss.* (Revelation 9:1, 2, 11)

In the same author:

> The beast that came up *out of the abyss* made war with them. (Revelation 11:7)

Again in the same author:

> The beast that you saw was and [now] is not *and is about to come up out of the abyss* and go to destruction. (Revelation 17:8)

In these passages the abysses stand for the hells and accordingly for falsity from evil cravings as well, since this falsity exists in the hells and makes them what they are.

[3] Since this is the symbolism of abysses, they also symbolize times of trial, because falsity and evil introduced by the hells are what bring about trials. The word is used in this sense in Jonah:

> Water surrounded me right to my soul; *the abyss circled me.* (Jonah 2:5)

In David:

> *Abyss is shouting to abyss* at the sound of your songs; all your breakers and your waves have passed over me. (Psalms 42:7)

In the same author:

> You who showed me distresses numerous and evil: turn and revive me, and *cause me to turn and come up out of the abysses of the earth.* (Psalms 71:20)

8279 *They went down into the depths like a stone* means that they sank to the nether regions like weights, as the following shows: *Going down*—going down to lower regions like weights—means sinking. The *depths* symbolize the nether regions where the hells are, as discussed below. And *like a stone* means like a weight. Comparison is made to a stone because a stone in a positive sense symbolizes truth (discussed in §§643, 1298, 3720, 3769, 3771, 3773, 3789, 3798, 6426) and in a negative sense, then, falsity. What is more, falsity-from-evil by its very nature sinks to the bottom, as a heavy object does in the world. In contrast, truth-from-goodness by its very nature rises to the top, as a light object does in the world. That is why the evil are found in the area above the hells as long as they have not yet been purged in respect to truth. As soon as they have been stripped of truth, it is as if wings have been cut off them, and they drop like weights. The worse their ill-intentioned falsity, the farther down they go. So it is that depths, like abysses, symbolize the hells. Depths symbolize evil in hell, and abysses, the falsity-from-evil there. In Jeremiah, for example:

> Run away! They turned their backs; *they took themselves down into the depths to live.* (Jeremiah 49:8, 30)

In David:

> The waters have come right to my soul; I have sunk *in the clay of the deep* and cannot stand. I have come into the *depths of the waters,* and a wave has overwhelmed me. Rescue me from the clay so that I do not sink! May I be rescued from those who hate me and *from the depths of*

> *the waters;* may a wave of waters not overwhelm me, *nor the deep swallow me,* nor the pit close its mouth over me. (Psalms 69:1, 2, 14, 15)

In Micah:

> He will cast all my sins *into the depth of the sea.* (Micah 7:19)

The reason *deep* means hell and the wickedness there is that it is the opposite of *high,* which symbolizes heaven and has to do with goodness (§8153).

Evil also corresponds to a heavy object on earth, which falls of its own weight, and therefore to the heaviness of a stone, when a stone symbolizes falsity.

Exodus 15:6, 7, 8, 9, 10. *"Your right hand, Jehovah, is imposing in its strength. By your right hand, Jehovah, you shatter your foe. And in the vastness of your magnificence you destroy those rising up against you; you send forth your wrath, it devours them like stubble. And by the wind from your nostrils the waters were heaped up, the streams stood like a mound, the abysses [congealed] in the heart of the sea. Our foe said, 'I will pursue, overtake, divide the plunder; my soul will be filled with them. I will draw my sword; my hand will drive them off.' You blew with your wind, the sea covered them; they sought the depths like lead in vast waters."* **8280**

Your right hand, Jehovah, is imposing in its strength means that the Lord's omnipotence was demonstrated. *By your right hand, Jehovah, you shatter your foe* symbolizes the effect omnipotence has on evil and its related falsity, whose power is annihilated. *And in the vastness of your magnificence you destroy those rising up against you* means that the Divine rejects opposing forces as insignificant. *You send forth your wrath* symbolizes a fury of passion in the evil and their effort to do violence. *It devours them like stubble* symbolizes the resulting devastation and damnation, which are self-inflicted. *And by the wind from your nostrils the waters were heaped up* symbolizes falsity gathered into a single place through the presence of heaven. *The streams stood like a mound* means that persistent would-be evildoers could not harass their victims at all. *The abysses congealed in the heart of the sea* means that utter falsity from cravings springing from self-love was completely unable to escape. *Our foe said,* symbolizes the thinking of people before the Coming of the Lord who were committed to evil and its related falsity. *I will pursue* symbolizes persecution. *Overtake* symbolizes domination. *Divide the plunder* symbolizes enslavement. *My soul will be filled* symbolizes pleasure. *I will draw the sword* symbolizes continuous fighting on the part of falsity from evil.

My hand will drive them off means that in their power they will destroy heaven. *You blew with your wind* symbolizes the presence of the Lord and his angels. *The sea covered them* means that all the falsity they had adopted engulfed them. *They sought the depths like lead* means that evil dragged them down to lower realms the way heavy weights would in the world. *In vast waters* symbolizes immersion in huge amounts of falsity.

8281 *Your right hand, Jehovah, is imposing in its strength* means that the Lord's omnipotence was demonstrated. This is evident from the symbolism of *Jehovah's right hand* as omnipotence (discussed below) and from that of *imposing in its strength* as a demonstration of omnipotence, because the strength that makes divine power imposing demonstrates that power.

Jehovah's right hand means omnipotence because a hand in the Word symbolizes power, and therefore a right hand symbolizes extraordinary power. When Jehovah is spoken of as having a hand or a right hand, then, it means divine power, which is omnipotence. (For the meaning of a hand and a right hand as power, see §§878, 4931–4937, 6292, 6947, 7188, 7189, 7518; and when the hand is said to be Jehovah's, as omnipotence, §§3387, 7518, 7673, 8050, 8069, 8153.)

[2] The meaning of Jehovah's right hand as divine power, or omnipotence, can also be seen from the following passages in the Word. In Matthew:

> Jesus said, "*From now on you will see the Son of Humankind sitting on the right [hand] of power* and coming in the clouds of heaven." (Matthew 26:64; Mark 14:62)

In Luke:

> *From this time now, the Son of Humankind will be sitting on the right [hand] of God's strength.* (Luke 22:69)

And in David:

> Jehovah said to my Lord, "*Sit at my right [hand]* till I have made your enemies your footstool. You are a priest forever after the manner of Melchizedek." *The Lord at your right* has struck the kings on the day of anger. (Psalms 110:1, 4, 5; Matthew 22:43, 44)

If you do not know that when a right hand is said to be Jehovah's it symbolizes omnipotence, there is only one idea you can take from these words of the Lord's: that the Lord will sit at his Father's right [hand] and exercise dominion like one who sits at the right of an earthly monarch. The inner sense, though, teaches us what sitting at his right [hand] means in these passages, namely, divine omnipotence. That is why the phrases "sit on the right [hand] *of power*" and "on the right [hand] *of God's strength*" are used.

[3] The Lord is plainly the possessor of the omnipotence, because these passages are about the Lord, and "the Lord" in David and "the Son of Humankind" in the Gospels mean the Lord as divine truth. Divine truth is what receives omnipotence from divine goodness. (For the idea that omnipotence belongs to divine truth, see §§6948, 8200. That more generally speaking, power belongs to truth-from-goodness, 3091, 3563, 4932, 6344, 6423. That a hand is therefore associated with truth, 3091, 4932. And that the Son of Humankind is divine truth radiating from the Lord, 2159, 2803, 2813, 3704.)

[4] The right hand symbolizes divine power, or omnipotence, in the following passages in David too:

> Now I know that Jehovah saves his anointed one; [let him] answer him in heaven *through the saving powers of his right hand.* (Psalms 20:6)

In the same author:

> Jehovah, observe from the heavens and see, and visit this grapevine and the cutting that *your right hand* planted; [look] on the Son you strengthened for yourself. (Psalms 80:14, 15, [17])

In the same author:

> You have an *arm* with strength; mighty is *your hand; your right hand* will be lifted high. (Psalms 89:13)

In the same author:

> My strength and song is Jah; he has become my salvation. The voice of a glad shout and of salvation in the tents of the righteous: "*Jehovah's right hand has done a mighty deed, Jehovah's right hand* is high, *Jehovah's right hand has done a mighty deed!*" (Psalms 118:14, 15, 16)

[5] In these passages Jehovah's right hand stands for omnipotence, and in the highest sense, for the Lord as divine truth. This is even clearer elsewhere in David:

> Let *your hand,* Jehovah, be favorable to the *man of your right hand,* to the Son of Humankind you strengthened for yourself. (Psalms 80:17)

The man of Jehovah's right hand and the Son of Humankind stand for the Lord as divine truth. In the same author:

> You yourself *by your hand* drove away the nations; it was not by their own sword that they took possession of the land, and it was not their *arm* that saved them but *your right hand* and *your arm* and the light of your face. (Psalms 44:2, 3)

The light of Jehovah's face is divine truth radiating from divine goodness, so his right hand and arm are also that truth. And in Isaiah:

> God has sworn by *his right hand* and by *his arm of strength.* (Isaiah 62:8)

Here too God's right hand and his arm of strength stand for the Lord as divine truth. After all, Jehovah, or the Lord, swears by no one but himself (§2842) and therefore by divine truth, which is himself, since it comes from him.

[6] That is why the Lord from time to time in the Word is called not only the right hand of Jehovah and his arm but also the strength by which he shatters foes, and a hammer, as in Jeremiah 51:19, 20, 21, and following verses.

In addition, the Lord came into the world and became divine truth, and then divine goodness with divine truth radiating from it, for three reasons: to shut all evil and falsity up in the hells, to gather goodness and truth into the heavens, and to arrange it into divine order there.

This discussion now shows that in the Word, Jehovah's right hand symbolizes the omnipotence the Divine has by means of divine truth.

The meaning of the right hand as extraordinary power traces its origin to the universal human, or heaven. The individuals there who relate to the shoulders, arms, and hands are those with a power that comes from truth arising out of goodness—in other words, from faith arising out of love (§§4931–4937, 7518).

8282 *By your right hand, Jehovah, you shatter your foe* symbolizes the effect omnipotence has on evil and its related falsity, whose power is annihilated. This can be seen from the symbolism of *Jehovah's right hand* as the Lord's omnipotence (discussed directly above at §8281), from that of *shattering* as annihilating, and from that of a *foe* as evil and falsity—since that is exactly what foes, enemies, and haters mean in the Word's spiritual sense.

Foes, enemies, and haters are so called not because the Lord is their foe or hates them but because they oppose the Divine with hatred and hostility. When they bring about their own devastation and hurl themselves into damnation and into hell, it looks to them as though these experiences come from the Divine.

This appearance or illusion brings to mind people who see the sun revolving daily around our planet and believe that the sun is therefore what moves, when it is really the earth. It also brings to mind people transgressing the law who are judged for their transgression by a monarch or a judge and receive a punishment they believe comes from the monarch or judge when it really comes from the transgressors themselves. Again, it brings to mind people who have thrown themselves into water or fire, or against a drawn sword or an enemy troop, and of course believe those things have hurt them when it is really they who have harmed themselves. The situation is the same for people with evil in their heart who brashly challenge the Divine and hurl themselves into the middle of [hell].

And in the vastness of your magnificence you destroy those rising up against 8283
you means that the Divine rejects opposing forces as insignificant. This can be seen from the symbolism of *vast magnificence* as the power the Divine has over that which opposes him, from the symbolism of *destroying* as rejecting as insignificant, and from the symbolism of *those rising up against one* as opponents and therefore as opposing forces.

You send forth your wrath symbolizes a fury of passion in the evil, and 8284
their effort to do violence. This can be seen from the symbolism of *wrath* attributed to Jehovah, or the Lord, as the destruction and punishment of efforts made by opponents of the Divine who want to do violence to the people under his protection. This looks like anger and wrath coming from the Divine, but they themselves are actually responsible (see §§5798, 6071, 6997). Not only anger and wrath but everything evil that happens is attributed to the Divine when it really comes from them (§§2447, 6071, 6991, 6997, 7533, 7632, 7643, 7679, 7710, 7877, 7926, 8223, 8227, 8228). An aura of efforts to do evil wafts continually from the hells, but an aura of efforts to do good wafts continually from the heavens (§8209).

It devours them like stubble symbolizes the resulting devastation and 8285
damnation, which are self-inflicted. This can be seen from the symbolism of *devouring* as consuming and in a spiritual sense as devastating and damning. The consuming of people immersed in evil consists in devastation and damnation, because at this stage they are without any true ideas and are consumed instead with utter falsity-from-evil, which means they no longer have any spiritual life. The text says "like stubble" because this symbolizes a thorough stripping away, which is the same as devastation.

8286 *And by the wind from your nostrils the waters were heaped up* symbolizes falsity gathered into a single place through the presence of heaven. This can be seen from the symbolism of the *wind from [Jehovah's] nostrils* as heaven (discussed below), from that of *being heaped up* as being gathered into a single place, and from that of *waters* as falsity (dealt with in §§7307, 8137, 8138). Being damned and thrown into hell means being engulfed in falsity from evil once it has all been gathered together (see §§8146, 8210, 8232), which results from the Lord's mere presence (§8265).

The *wind from Jehovah's* (the Lord's) *nostrils* stands for heaven because it means the breath of life and therefore divine life. Divine life constitutes the life force of heaven, so the wind from Jehovah's nostrils symbolizes heaven. That is why the same word in the original language means both wind and spirit, [or breath].

[2] The symbolism of the wind (or breath) from Jehovah as the life force of heaven and of a person in heaven (a person reborn) can be seen in David:

> By Jehovah's word were the heavens made, and *by the spirit* [wind] *of his mouth,* the whole army of them. (Psalms 33:6)

In the same author:

> You gather *their spirit,* they breathe their last and return to their dust; *you send out your spirit* [wind], they continue to be created. (Psalms 104:29, 30)

In Ezekiel:

> Jehovah said to me, "Will these bones live?" Then he said, "Prophesy *over the spirit;* prophesy, son of humankind, and *say to the wind,* 'This is what the Lord Jehovih has said: "*From the four winds, come, spirit,* and *breathe* into these slain so that they may live."'" And *the spirit came into them* and they came back to life. (Ezekiel 37:3, 9, 10)

In John:

> I saw four angels standing on the four corners of the earth *holding back the four winds of the earth* so that *the wind would not blow on the earth* or on the sea or on any tree. (Revelation 7:1)

Here the wind stands for the life force of heaven, that is, divine life, as it also does in Job:

> The *spirit of God* made me, and the *breath of Shaddai gave me life.* (Job 33:4)

[3] Since the wind symbolized life, the Lord in teaching about a person's rebirth also says:

> The *spirit* [wind] *blows where it wishes,* and you hear its voice but do not know where it is coming from or where it is going; *this is the way with everyone who is born of the spirit.* (John 3:8)

And since the wind or breath from Jehovah symbolized life from the Divine, where the text is talking about the new life in Adam it says:

> Jehovah *breathed into his nostrils the breath of lives,* and the human was made into a living soul. (Genesis 2:7)

This verse speaks of nostrils because it is through our nostrils that we breathe, and through breathing that we have life, as in Isaiah:

> Keep away from humans, *whose breath is in their nose.* (Isaiah 2:22)

In Jeremiah:

> The *spirit of our nostrils*—Jehovah's anointed—was caught in their snares, he of whom we had said, "In his shadow we will live among the nations." (Lamentations 4:20)

"Jehovah's anointed" stands for the Lord; the "spirit of our nostrils" for life from him. In Job:

> As long as my soul is in me *and the wind of God is in my nose,* . . . (Job 27:3)

[4] So the wind from Jehovah's nostrils symbolizes life from the Lord and consequently, in the broadest sense, heaven. Because of this, and because the mere presence of the Lord—or the presence of heaven, where the Lord is—throws evil and falsity into hell (§8265), that outcome is also symbolized by the wind from Jehovah's nostrils, as in David:

> The channels of the sea showed, the foundations of the world were exposed, because of Jehovah's rebuke, *from the breath of the spirit of his nose.* (Psalms 18:8, 15; 2 Samuel 22:16)

In Isaiah:

> *Jehovah's breath* like a sulfurous fire kindles it. (Isaiah 30:33)

In the same author:

> No, they are not planted; no, they are not sown; no, their trunk does not take root in the earth; *and yes, he breathes on them,* and they wither, so that a windstorm can take them away like stubble. (Isaiah 40:24)

And in David:

> *He sends his wind* and melts them. *He makes his wind blow;* the waters flow. (Psalms 147:17, 18)

This is why the *nose,* when it is said to be Jehovah's, or the Lord's, can symbolize wrath and therefore the punishment, devastation, and damnation of people committed to evil and falsity. Examples may be found in Numbers 25:4; Deuteronomy 7:4; Judges 2:14; Isaiah 9:12; Jeremiah 4:8; Hosea 14:4; Psalms 6:1; 86:15; 103:8; 145:8; and many other places. And *blowing through the nostrils* or *breathing* means growing angry in Deuteronomy 4:21; Isaiah 12:1; Psalms 2:12; 60:1; 79:5; 85:5.

8287 *The streams stood like a mound* means that persistent would-be evildoers could not harass their victims at all, as the following shows: *Standing like a mound,* when it describes falsity from evil, means persistently attempting evil, because when streams stand like a mound, they loom ready to fall but are held back by a stronger force. And *streams* symbolize falsity from evil, as water also does (§§7307, 8137, 8138), but the falsity is referred to as *streams* because of the stream of harassment with which the spirits tried to flood their victims.

8288 *The abysses congealed in the heart of the sea* means that utter falsity from cravings springing from self-love was completely unable to escape, as the following shows: *Congealing,* in reference to the inhabitants of the hells, symbolizes not being able to escape. *Abysses* symbolize falsity from evil cravings and also the hells, as discussed above at §§8278, 8279. And the *heart of the sea* symbolizes evil that embodies self-love, and falsity growing out of that evil. In a positive sense a heart symbolizes heavenly goodness, which is goodness embodying love for the Lord (discussed in §§3635, 3883–3896, 7542), so in a negative sense it symbolizes the evil that embodies self-love. This evil is the opposite of the goodness that embodies love for the Lord, while the evil that embodies a love of worldly advantages is the opposite of spiritual goodness, which is goodness embodying love for one's neighbor. From this you can see that *the abysses congealed in the heart of the sea* means that utter falsity from cravings springing from self-love was completely unable to escape.

Here is the reason for saying it cannot escape: Abysses and the heart of the sea symbolize the hells, which are the home of falsity from cravings, or falsity from evil. Because the inhabitants are engulfed in their own falsity-from-evil there, they can no longer work their way out, since the Lord's divine nature stands in the way of the falsity there.

Our foe said, symbolizes the thinking of people before the Coming of the Lord who were committed to evil and its related falsity. This can be seen from the symbolism of *he said* as thoughts, as in §§3395, 7244, 7937, and from that of a *foe* as people committed to evil and falsity, since that is precisely who the enemy is in a spiritual sense (§8282). 8289

The thinking of people before the Coming of the Lord is symbolized because in those days a hellish mob prowled around with almost complete freedom, persecuting all the spirits there and trying to overpower them all. The thinking of the hellish people at that time is depicted in this verse by "I will pursue, overtake, divide the plunder; my soul will be filled. I will draw my sword; my hand will drive them off." However, this boast of theirs turned into a lament when the Lord came into the world. The next verse depicts this reversal with the words "You blew with your wind, the sea covered them; they sought the depths like lead in vast waters." Concerning the change of state that the Lord's Coming brought on these people, see §§6854, 6914, 7091, 7828, 7932, 8018, 8054.

I will pursue symbolizes persecution. This is clear from the symbolism of *pursuing*—when people intent on evil promise to do it to people intent on what is good—as persecuting them and trying to dominate them. 8290

Overtake symbolizes domination. This is clear from the symbolism of *overtaking*—when people intent on evil promise to do it to people intent on what is good—as dominating them. 8291

Divide the plunder symbolizes enslavement. This is clear from the symbolism of *plunder* as the people dominated. *Dividing* the plunder, then, means reducing others to slaves whom they share out among themselves, so it stands for enslavement. 8292

My soul will be filled symbolizes pleasure, as is self-evident. 8293

The text says *my soul will be filled* because the highest pleasure of hell's inhabitants is to hurt others. Some in hell do this for no reason, just because they enjoy it. Others do it in order to reduce people to slaves, whom they then intend to abuse.

Hardly anyone would believe that people who live evil lives enjoy this kind of pleasure in the other life. Not even the evildoers themselves would believe it, because as long as they are in the world, they are held in check by fear—fear that the law will punish them and fear that they will lose their position, wealth, reputation, or even life. Such fears keep them from outward wrongdoing, so they imagine they are not that type. In the other world, though, reflection on the loss of their life, wealth, position, and reputation is taken from them and they are left to their wickedness.

Under those circumstances, the delight in wrongdoing that previously lay hidden in their will, surfacing whenever they could allay their fears, reveals itself. By then the delight makes up the substance of their life, which is the life of hell.

8294 *I will draw the sword* symbolizes continuous fighting on the part of falsity from evil, as the following shows: A *sword* symbolizes truth battling falsity and evil, and in the opposite sense, falsity battling truth and goodness, as discussed in §§2799, 4499. And *drawing* or baring it symbolizes fighting that continues till one's enemy has been defeated.

A sword unsheathed or drawn symbolizes continuous fighting elsewhere too. In Moses:

> You yourselves I will scatter among the nations, and I will *draw the sword after you.* (Leviticus 26:33)

In Ezekiel:

> His whole company I will scatter to every wind, and I will *draw the sword after them.* (Ezekiel 12:14)

In the same author:

> This is what Jehovah has said: "Here, now, I am against you; I will *draw my sword out of its sheath* and cut off from you the righteous person and the ungodly person. *My sword will come out of its sheath* against all flesh from south to north, so that all flesh may know that I Jehovah have *drawn the sword out of its sheath and it shall no longer return."* (Ezekiel 21:3, 4, 5)

Unsheathing or drawing the sword stands for not giving up the fight until one's enemies have been defeated, so it stands for continuous fighting.

Continuous fighting against evil and falsity is also symbolized by the *unsheathed sword* of the *leader of Jehovah's army* seen by Joshua when he came into the land of Canaan (Joshua 5:13). The meaning was that they were to fight the nations there and destroy them. The nations that then possessed the land of Canaan symbolize spirits before the Lord's Coming who occupied an area of heaven later given to members of the Lord's spiritual kingdom (§§6914, 8054).

8295 *My hand will drive them off* means that in their power they will destroy heaven. This is established by the symbolism of *driving off* as overthrowing and thus destroying and by that of a *hand* as power (discussed in §§878, 4931–4937, 6292, 6947, 7188, 7189, 7518). Heaven is symbolized because the text says the enemy will drive them off, meaning from heaven; when the reins on evil spirits are loosened, they have the audacity and impudence to imagine they can destroy heaven itself. All the spirits in the hells oppose heaven, because they oppose goodness and truth, so they constantly itch to destroy it. So far as they are allowed to attempt it, they do (§8273 at the end).

[2] The desire to destroy heaven or to overthrow its inhabitants is not put into action through an aggressive invasion, as it would be on earth, because this kind of invasion or battle is not possible in the other life. No, the way it is accomplished is through the destruction of the truth that leads to faith and of the goodness that comes from love, because faith's truth and love's goodness are heaven. This destruction is what battles and wars in the other world consist in, and at the ends of the chapters, where I deal with the hells—the Lord in his divine mercy willing—I will describe how dreadful and ferocious those struggles are.

This is the only way to understand the war depicted in John:

> There was *war* in heaven: Michael and his angels *fought* against the dragon; the dragon in turn *fought,* as did his angels, but they did not prevail. (Revelation 12:7, 8)

You blew with your wind symbolizes the presence of the Lord and his **8296**
angels. This is plain from the explanation above at §8286.

The sea covered them means that all the falsity they had adopted engulfed **8297**
them. This can be seen from the symbolism of *covering* as engulfing and from that of the *sea*—here, the waters of the Suph Sea—as falsity from evil. The Suph Sea also symbolizes hell. (These meanings of the sea are discussed in §§8099, 8137, 8138, 8148; the fact that the inhabitants are engulfed in falsity from evil is discussed in §§8210, 8232.)

They sought the depths like lead means that evil dragged them down to **8298**
lower realms the way heavy weights would in the world. This can be seen from the symbolism of the *depths,* which are the lower realms and the hells, and the evil there, as discussed at §8279. *Seeking* the depths, then, means being dragged there by evil. For the idea that the wicked, because of their evil, sink to the nethermost regions the way heavy weights would in the world, see §8279.

It says *like lead* because lead symbolizes evil. Verse 5 above said, "They went down into the depths of the sea like a stone," because the stone there symbolizes falsity. Both falsity and evil are heavy, so both sink, but it is still evil that makes a thing spiritually heavy and causes it to drop under its own weight, so to speak. This is not so for falsity in itself, but it happens because of the evil it contains; falsity has no weight on its own but it has weight on account of the evil, causing it to plummet.

[2] Keep in mind that all metals symbolize goodness or truth, and in an opposite sense, evil or falsity. Lead is less prized than the other metals, so it symbolizes the lowest kind of evil, which is what evil on the outer earthly level is. In a positive sense it symbolizes goodness on that same level. In Jeremiah, for example:

> They are all flagrant rebels, slanderers, *bronze* and *iron*, all of them dealers of destruction. The bellows grew hot; *the lead was consumed by the fire.* In vain did he thoroughly refine them, since the wicked were not pried off. *Spurned silver* they will call them, because Jehovah has spurned them. (Jeremiah 6:28, 29, 30)

And in Ezekiel:

> Son of humankind, the house of Israel has become dross to me. They are all *bronze* and *tin* and *iron* and *lead* in the middle of a furnace; the *dross of silver* they have become. (Ezekiel 22:18)

8299 *In vast waters* symbolizes immersion in huge amounts of falsity. This is evident from the symbolism of *waters* as falsity from evil, which is mentioned just above at §8297. *Vast* waters, then, are huge amounts of falsity. For the idea that [the inhabitants of the hells] are immersed in falsity, or engulfed by it, see §§8210, 8232.

8300 Exodus 15:11, 12, 13. *"Who is like you among the gods, Jehovah? Who is like you, majestic in holiness, to be venerated with praises, doing a wonder? You stretched out your right hand: the earth swallowed them. In your mercy you led this people, you redeemed them; in your might you guided them to your holy dwelling."*

Who is like you among the gods, Jehovah? means that all truth-from-goodness radiates from divine humanity. *Who is like you, [majestic] in holiness?* means that everything holy comes from him. *To be venerated with praises* means that glory and thanks are his alone. *Doing a wonder* means that he provides all the means of exercising power. *You stretched out your right hand* means that the power he wielded over all things was revealed by [the following]. *The earth swallowed them* means that his mere presence brought about damnation and hell for them. *In your mercy you led this people* symbolizes a divine inflow into those who had abstained from evil and had therefore received goodness. *You redeemed them* means whom he delivered from hell. *In your might you guided them to your holy dwelling* means that the Lord's divine power lifted them to heaven, to what is divine there.

Who is like you among the gods, Jehovah? means that all truth-from-goodness radiates from the Lord's divine humanity. This is clear from the symbolism of *gods* as truth, which is discussed in §§4402, 7268, 7873. Here they symbolize truth from goodness, because they are being compared to Jehovah, seeing that the verse says, "Who is like you among the gods, Jehovah?" On the point that *Jehovah* in the Word is the Lord, see §§1343, 1736, 2921, 3023, 3035, 5041, 5663, 6280, 6281, 6303, 6905, 6945, 6956. The reason divine humanity is meant by Jehovah here is that this song is about the way people in the spiritual church were saved by the Lord's coming into the world and then by the divine humanity; see §§2661, 2716, 2833, 2834, 6372, 6854, 6914, 7035, 7091 at the end, 7828, 7932, 8018, 8054. **8301**

The reason these words mean that all truth-from-goodness radiates from the Lord's divine humanity is that truth can come from anyone, but truth that is good can come only from the Lord and consequently from people whom the Lord endows with goodness. Truth separated from goodness, on the other hand, can also be found in the thoughts and on the lips of people who have a dogmatic faith but live an evil life, and also of many other people in the church. Such truth is not good, though, so it does not come from the Lord, it comes from the people themselves.

[2] You can see that truth from goodness originates in the Lord by considering that the Lord is goodness itself, because he is love itself. From love comes truth, like light from the blazing sun. Truth that comes from goodness resembles the light of spring and summer, which holds warmth inside it and brings everything on earth to life. Truth that does not come from goodness, however, resembles the light of winter, when everything on earth dies off.

The reason gods stand for truth from goodness is that in a positive sense they mean angels, who are called gods because they are substances or forms designed to receive truth that contains goodness from the Lord. [3] In the following passages as well, gods mean angels and consequently truth-from-goodness radiating from the Lord. In David:

> God stands *in the assembly of God; in the midst of the gods* he will pass judgment. I have said, "*You are gods,* and you are all children of the Highest One." (Psalms 82:1, 6)

It can be seen that the gods here mean truth radiating from the Lord, since the passage first speaks of the assembly of *God* in the singular and then says "in the midst of the *gods.*" The term *God* is used in the Word when the subject is truth (see §§2769, 2807, 2822, 3921, 4287, 4402, 7010), and in the highest sense it stands for divine truth coming from the Lord (§7268). In the same author:

> I will acclaim you with my whole heart; *in the presence of the gods I will make music to you.* (Psalms 138:1)

In the same author:

> *There is none like you among the gods, Lord.* (Psalms 86:8)

In the same author:

> A great God is Jehovah, and a *great monarch over all gods.* (Psalms 95:3)

In the same author:

> You, Jehovah, are over all the earth; *you are greatly exalted above all gods.* (Psalms 97:9)

In the same author:

> I know that Jehovah is great, and *our Lord,* [greater] *than all gods.* (Psalms 135:5)

For the same reason, Jehovah is called Lord of the lords and *God of the gods* in Deuteronomy 10:17; Joshua 22:22; Psalms 136:2.

[4] The reason for saying so many times that Jehovah was above all gods and that he was God of the gods was that in those days people worshiped many gods. Nations were distinguished from each other by the gods they worshiped, and each nation believed its own god was supreme. The result was that polytheism was fixed in everyone's mind, and people argued about which of the gods was greatest. (Many passages in the Word's narratives make this quite clear.) It was more firmly fixed in the minds of Jews than others. All this explains why the Word so often repeats that Jehovah was greater than all gods and was the King and God of the gods.

The fact that Jews had a polytheistic viewpoint more firmly fixed in their minds than other nations is plain enough from their frequent defection to the worship of other gods. Their apostasy is described in many places in the Word's narrative books, such as Judges 2:10–13, 17, 19; 3:5, 6, 7; 8:27, 33; 10:6, 10, 13; 18:14, 17, 18, 20, 24, 31; 1 Samuel 7:3, 4; 8:8; 1 Kings 14:23, 24; 16:31, 32, 33; 18:20 and following verses; 21:26;

22:53; 2 Kings 16:10 and following verses; 17:7, 15, 16, 17; 21:3–7, 21; 23:4, 5, 7, 8, 10, 11, 12, 13; and other places.

[5] The mind of the people of that nation was so unsound that they acclaimed Jehovah alone with their lips but acknowledged other gods at heart. This is obvious from their behavior even after they witnessed so many miracles in Egypt and so many afterward. They saw the sea divided before them and Pharaoh's army drowned, a pillar of cloud and fire constantly in view, manna raining down from the sky daily, and the very presence of Jehovah displayed in such an impressive and terrifying way on Mount Sinai [Exodus 13, 14, 16, 19, 20]. Yet after they had offered up an acclamation of Jehovah as the only God, what happened a few weeks later? Just because Moses was delayed, they demanded molded gods for themselves to worship, and when Aaron had created them, the people honored them with divine worship through feasting, burnt offerings and sacrifices, and dance [Exodus 32:1–6, 19]. This shows that the worship of many gods remained fixed in their hearts.

It can also be seen in Jeremiah that that nation was more polytheistic than any other nation in the whole world:

> *Has a nation changed its gods? And [yet] my people has exchanged its glory for that which is of no use. Be shocked over this, you heavens, and shudder; tremble greatly. According to the number of your cities were your gods, Judah.* (Jeremiah 2:11, 12, 28)

[6] What is more, the character of that nation is such that its people worship outward forms—and therefore idols—more than any other nation does, not wanting to know anything whatever about the inner dimension. They are the greediest nation of all, and the type of greed they have is to love gold and silver for the sake of gold and silver, not for the sake of any use to which it can be put. Such an attitude is extremely degraded. It drags the mind right down into the body, immersing it there, and closes up the inner reaches so tightly that not a bit of faith or love from heaven can penetrate.

This demonstrates how big a mistake people make in believing that that nation will again be chosen, or that the Lord's church will again pass into its hands and all other nations will be rejected. The reality is that you will sooner convert stones than the people of that nation to belief in the Lord.

The belief that the church will again pass into the hands of that nation came about because many passages in the prophetic parts of the Word say its people are going to return. Believers in this idea fail to realize, though, that in such passages, Judah, Jacob, and Israel refer not to that nation but to people in whom the church exists.

8302 *Who is like you, [majestic] in holiness?* means that everything holy comes from him. This can be seen from the symbolism of *who is like you, [majestic] in holiness?* which means that no one is as holy, or, in an inner sense, that everything holy comes from him, since he is holiness itself.

By "everything holy" I mean divine truth issuing from the Lord. This truth is called holy and is also meant by the Holy Spirit, so the Holy Spirit is therefore called the Spirit of Truth (John 14:16, 17; 15:26, 27; 16:13), and it is said that the Holy Spirit would be sent by the Lord (John 15:26, 27) and that it would take its proclamations from him (John 16:15). Because holiness is a quality of divine truth issuing from the Lord, angels who accept that truth are called holy (Matthew 25:31; Mark 8:38; Luke 9:26), as are the prophets, and above all the Word, which is divine truth itself.

Furthermore, it is on account of divine truth—which is the Lord because it comes from the Lord—that he is called the Holy One of Israel, the Holy One of Jacob, and the Sanctuary of God.

8303 *To be venerated with praises* means that glory and thanks are his alone. This can be seen from the symbolism of *being venerated with praises,* which, when it describes Jehovah, means that he is to be celebrated and worshiped and therefore that glory and thanks are his alone.

8304 *Doing a wonder* means that he provides all the means of exercising power. This can be seen from the symbolism of *wonders* and miracles as the means of divine power, which is discussed at §6910.

The reason wonders are means of divine power is that they led people to believe that Jehovah was the supreme God, that in fact there was no God but him, and consequently that he alone was to be worshiped. People who knew this was true were then introduced to truth associated with the worship of him. Such truth is the means of power, because all power in a spiritual sense resides in truth from the Divine (§§3091, 6344, 6423, 6948, 8200). Power in a spiritual sense is to set the mob from hell to flight and cast it out of oneself, which is accomplished only through truth.

These remarks now explain why *doing a wonder* means that the Lord provides all the means of exercising power.

Wonders symbolize the means of divine power in David too:

> Sing to Jehovah, make music to him, *meditate on all his wonders,* glory in his holy name! Seek Jehovah and his strength, seek his face constantly;

recall his wonders, his portents, *and the judgments of his mouth.* (Psalms 105:1–5)

The Lord's words to Peter make it plain that all power resides in the truth that belongs to faith from the Lord:

> I say to you: you are Peter, and *on this rock* I will build my church, and the gates of hell will not prevail over it, and I will give you the keys to the kingdom of the heavens. (Matthew 16:18, 19)

Peter represents faith here, and in the Word a rock symbolizes faith, while a key means power; see the preface to Genesis 22 and §§4738 at the end, 6344 at the end.

You stretched out your right hand means that the power he wielded over all things was revealed by [the following]. This is established by the symbolism of *stretching out* as a word used for the wielding of power, and when Jehovah is said to do it, for omnipotence (discussed in §7673); and by the symbolism of a *right hand* as divine power (discussed above at §8281). The idea that the power he wielded over all things was revealed by [the following] can be seen from the next clause: "the earth swallowed them," meaning that the Lord's mere presence brought them damnation, or hell. **8305**

The earth swallowed them means that his mere presence brought about damnation and hell for them. This is evident from the symbolism of *being swallowed by the earth* as damnation and hell. After all, being swallowed by the earth means falling into hell, or being thrown down there. Hell truly is deep below, too, since it is as far as possible from the sun of heaven, which is the Lord. The heavenly sun is the highest point. Distance from it is determined by the type and amount of evil and of falsity from evil, which is why heaven appears above and hell beneath. Moreover, the place populated by spirits immersed in falsity from evil and consequently by the damned looks like wilderness land, which is called cursed ground. Spirits being thrown into hell are cast down below that place (§7418). This happens as a result of the Lord's mere presence (see §8265). That is why *the earth swallowed them* symbolizes damnation and hell. This symbolism can be seen in Moses: **8306**

> Concerning Korah, Dathan, and Abiram, Moses said to the congregation, "If Jehovah creates a new creation, and *the earth opens its mouth* and *swallows them* and everything they have, *so that they go down into hell alive,* you will know that these men have angered Jehovah." And the

earth that was under them *split open, and the earth opened its mouth* and *swallowed them,* and they *went down into hell alive,* they and all they had. (Numbers 16:30, 31, 32, 33)

8307 *In your mercy you led this people* symbolizes a divine inflow into those who had abstained from evil and had therefore received goodness. This can be seen from the symbolism of *leading in mercy* as receiving what is divine. Since the individuals who receive what is divine are those who abstain from evil, they are the people whose experience of divine inflow is being symbolized.

Here is how mercy from the Lord works: The Lord's mercy rests on every person all the time, because the Lord wants to save all of us without exception, but this mercy does not affect us until the evil in us is moved aside. Evil and the falsity that grows out of it block and hinder the inflow of mercy. As soon as evil is moved aside, in flows mercy. That is, in flows the goodness brought by mercy from the Lord, which consists in neighborly love and faith. Clearly, then, the Lord's mercy is universal, or directed toward everyone, but it is also directed in a particular way toward people who refrain from evil.

Refraining from evil is something we can do on our own, but receiving goodness is not. The reason we can refrain from evil on our own is that the Lord is constantly flooding our will with the urge to do so. By this means he puts it within our reach to freely stop doing wrong and make an effort to do right.

The Lord also gives us the ability to understand what is true. If we do not understand, it is because we do not want to, and that is because of wickedness in our life. Falsity defends evil, and truth condemns it. That is why we cannot be endowed with spiritual goodness by the Lord and therefore cannot be led in mercy unless we desist from evil.

8308 *You redeemed them* means whom he delivered from hell. This is established by the symbolism of *redeeming* as delivering from hell, which is mentioned in §§7205, 7445.

8309 *In your might you guided them to your holy dwelling* means that the Lord's divine power lifted them to heaven, to what is divine there, as the following shows: *Guiding in might,* when the phrase has to do with being lifted to heaven by the Lord, means being lifted with divine power. The fact that *might* means power is obvious. And the *holy dwelling* symbolizes heaven, where the Divine is found. After all, holiness is predicated of divine truth radiating from the Lord (§8302), and this divine truth makes heaven.

[2] The *dwelling* place of Jehovah, or the Lord, is heaven, and also goodness, since goodness holds heaven within it. This can be seen from the following passages. In Moses:

> *Look back from your holy dwelling, from heaven,* and bless the people of Israel. (Deuteronomy 26:15)

In Isaiah:

> *Look out from heaven* and observe *from* your *holy* and beautiful *dwelling place.* (Isaiah 63:15)

In David:

> ". . . if I give sleep to my eyes, until I find a spot for Jehovah, the *dwelling places* of mighty Jacob!" Look, we heard of him in Ephrata; we found him in forest fields. *We will enter his dwelling places.* (Psalms 132:4, 5, 6, 7)

[3] The fact that the dwelling place of Jehovah (the Lord) is found in goodness can be seen in Zechariah:

> Rejoice and be glad, daughter of Zion! Watch: I myself am coming *to dwell in your midst.* Many nations will cling to Jehovah on that day and will become my people, *for I will dwell in you.* (Zechariah 2:10, 11)

And in Ezekiel:

> I will put my sanctuary in their midst forever; *so will my dwelling place be among them.* (Ezekiel 37:26, 27)

The sanctuary is the place for divine truth that holds divine goodness.

Exodus 15:14, 15, 16. *"The peoples heard; they trembled. Agony seized the inhabitants of Philistia. Then panic beset the commanders of Edom, the powerful of Moab; terror seized them. All the inhabitants of Canaan collapsed. Horror and dread fell on them; in the greatness of your arm they are cut off like a stone until your people crosses over, Jehovah, until this people [of whom] you took possession crosses over."* **8310**

The peoples heard symbolizes everyone everywhere who was intent on falsity from evil. *They trembled* symbolizes terror. *Agony seized the inhabitants of Philistia* means that people whose faith was detached from anything good despaired of widening their sphere of control. *Then panic beset the commanders of Edom* symbolizes the same despair in people who lived a life of self-centered evil. *The powerful of Moab* symbolizes people who lived a life of self-centered distortions. *Terror seized them* means that they dared nothing. *All the inhabitants of Canaan collapsed* symbolizes the same effect in people who were part of the church and who adulterated what was good and distorted what was true. *Horror and [dread] fell on them* means that they had no hope of dominating others. *In the greatness of your arm* means with omnipotence. *They will be cut off like a stone* symbolizes sinking like a weight. *Until your people crosses over* means that everyone with the ability to accept truth-from-goodness and goodness-from-truth would therefore be saved, without any danger of being persecuted. *Until this people crosses over* means that those in the church who were committed to truth and goodness would therefore be saved. *[Of whom] you took possession* means who had therefore become the Lord's.

8311 *The peoples heard* symbolizes everyone everywhere who was intent on falsity from evil. This can be seen from the symbolism of *peoples* as anyone intent on truth from goodness, and in a negative sense, on falsity from evil, as discussed in §§1259, 1260, 3295, 3581, 4619.

I speak of such individuals as intent on falsity from evil in order to distinguish them from people intent on falsity but also on goodness. Within the church, those who accept heresies but live a good life are the ones focused on falsity and at the same time on what is good. Outside the church, everyone with goodness is part of this group. False thinking in people outside the church does not damn them, unless it is the kind of thinking that opposes what is good and undermines an actual life of goodness. Falsity that does not oppose what is good is still false, strictly speaking, but in the face of a well-lived life—which it does not oppose—it nearly divests itself of its distorted nature, by connecting itself with goodness. This type of falsity, you see, can adapt to what is good and to what is evil. If it adapts to something good, it turns gentle. If it adapts to something evil, it turns harsh. For it is just as easy to use falsity for a good purpose as to use truth for an evil purpose. Consider that all kinds of true ideas are rendered false when they are used for something evil.

Take the idea that faith alone saves us. In itself this idea is false, especially in an evil person who uses it to dismiss the goodness urged by neighborly love, saying, for instance, that doing such good contributes nothing at all to salvation. However, this false idea softens in people who live a good life. They connect it with something good, saying that faith alone saves us but that faith is not faith unless it is accompanied by its fruit, and accordingly that faith is not faith except where there is goodness. Likewise for all other falsities.

[2] The next parts of the text are about everyone who was attached to the falsity that grows out of evil and to the evil that grows out of falsity and was thrown into hell when the Lord came into the world. There are many kinds of evil, so there are also many kinds of falsity, because every kind of evil has its falsity connected to it. Falsity is a product of evil and is evil that has been given form. In exactly the same way, our intellect is the form of our will. Through our intellect our will brings itself out into the light, shapes and forms itself, and presents itself in mental images, presents the mental images in ideas, and presents the ideas in words.

These remarks are intended to show that there are many types of evil and therefore of falsity. At first they were depicted as Egyptians, but now, in these verses, they are depicted as the inhabitants of Philistia, the commanders of Edom, the powerful of Moab, and the inhabitants of Canaan, about whom it says that panic and terror took hold of them. This was because they had heard that spirits whose faith was detached from neighborly love and who lived an evil life—symbolized by the Egyptians—had been thrown into hell, and that they themselves were likewise to be cast down there. The purpose of this relocation was to enable spirits with truth and goodness to pass through safe and unscathed and be led on to heaven, as symbolized by these words in verses 16 and 17 below: "Horror and dread fell on them; in the greatness of your arm they are cut off like a stone until your people crosses over, Jehovah, until this people [of whom] you took possession crosses over. You will bring them in and plant them on the mountain of your inheritance, in the place where you were to dwell."

They trembled symbolizes terror, as is self-explanatory. **8312**

Agony seized the inhabitants of Philistia means that people whose faith **8313**
was detached from anything good despaired of widening their sphere of control. This is clear from the symbolism of *agony* as despair over their inability to widen their sphere of control any further (discussed below) and from that of the *inhabitants of Philistia* as believers in faith alone, detached from any charitable goodness (discussed in §§1197, 1198, 3412, 3413, 8093, 8096, 8099). What distinguishes Philistines from Egyptians is the fact that Philistines discount neighborly love and the goodness it urges, believing that we are saved without it, by faith. This theological principle of theirs gives birth to many errors: that mercy saves us no matter how we lived; that faith washes away all sin and evil; that when we have been washed, we walk about absolved; that we can be saved instantaneously, even in the final hour of death, by relying on our faith; and as

a consequence, that the ability to cherish heavenly love is not what makes heaven in us. People of this mindset are Philistines and are described as foreskinned because of the evil in which their life consists, which is the kind that rises out of self-love and materialism.

[2] The reason *agony* means despair here is that it is referring to the most intense pain, like that of childbirth. In fact, the word in the original language is used for labor pains. Despair, or the worst pain, is depicted in the Word as the agony of a woman in labor, as in David:

> The monarchs assembled; terror clutched them—*agony like that of one in labor.* (Psalms 48:4, 6)

In Jeremiah:

> You who reside in Lebanon, nesting in the cedars, how much grace will you find when pains come on you, *agony like that of one in labor?* (Jeremiah 22:23)

In the same author:

> The king of Babylon has heard their report, so his hands have gone limp; *distress has seized him, agony like that of one in labor.* (Jeremiah 50:43)

In Isaiah:

> The day of Jehovah is near, like devastation from Shaddai, therefore all hands go limp, and every human heart dissolves, and they are terrified. *Wrenching pains and agonies seize them; they go into labor like one giving birth.* (Isaiah 13:6, 7, 8)

[3] In Jeremiah:

> Look: a people is coming from the land of the north, and a large nation will be stirred up from the flanks of the land. Bow and spear they grasp. It is a cruel [people], and they have no mercy. Their voice booms like the sea, and they ride on horses. [Each] is prepared as a man for war against you, daughter of Zion. We heard the report of it; our hands went limp. *Distress seized us; agony like that of one in labor.* (Jeremiah 6:22, 23, 24)

This passage is about the stripping away of truth in individuals devoted to evil. A people from the land of the north stands for those devoted to falsity from evil. A large nation from the flanks of the land stands for those devoted to the kind of evil that stands diametrically opposed to what is good. "Bow and spear they grasp" means that they use distorted religious teachings as weapons. "Their voice booms like the sea" stands for rationalizations based on those teachings. "They ride on horses" stands for arguments that pretend to be intelligent. A man prepared for war stands for an obsessive desire to attack truth. The daughter of Zion stands for a church in which goodness exists. "Distress seized us" stands for grief that truth had been assaulted. Agony like that of one in labor stands for despair that what was good had been wounded. This explanation shows that the agony here symbolizes despair over the wounding of goodness.

[4] Why does *agony seized the inhabitants of Philistia* symbolize despair or hopelessness, specifically about widening their sphere of control? In the other life, the constant effort of Philistines—people who posit that salvation results from faith alone, without neighborly kindness—is to dominate others, which they do by fighting those others. This they continue as long as they have not yet had their knowledge of religious concepts stripped from them.

All in the other life keep the religious principles they had had during bodily life, and no one changes those principles into something true except people who lived a good life. Goodness longs for truth and accepts it willingly, because goodness and truth share the same nature. People who lived an evil life do not change. They are rigid, they reject truth, and they are so deeply in the dark that they cannot even see truth. All they see is confirmation of their own principles, and they are totally blind to anything contradicting those principles.

People like this still consider themselves the most discerning of all, but they do not know how to do anything except reason from assumptions they have made. So they are the main attackers of neighborly love and therefore the main seekers of control over others. Consider that people with neighborly love are humble; they want to be lowly servants to everyone else. People who believe in faith without neighborly love, on the other hand, are arrogant; they want to be supreme masters served by everyone else. As a result they also equate heaven with the glory of ruling others, and since they consider themselves more discerning than anyone else, they imagine they will be archangels with large numbers of servants. They also believe that, as it says in Daniel:

> Those who understand will shine like the radiance of the expanse, and those who cause many to be righteous [will shine] like stars to eternity and forever. (Daniel 12:3)

But instead of radiance, darkness is their lot.

8314 *Then panic beset the commanders of Edom* symbolizes the same despair in people who lived a life of self-centered evil, as the following shows: *Commanders* symbolize the leading people in a group and therefore everyone, as discussed below. And *Edom* represents people whose self-centered evil motivates them to seize on falsity and reject truth. In an abstract sense it represents self-centered evil that connects with falsity and rejects truth, so it also represents people who live a life of that kind of evil—self-centered evil.

As for *commanders,* they symbolize the leading people in a group, and in an abstract sense, leading elements. So they symbolize every element, because when commanders are mentioned by name, everyone under them is also meant. It is like the use of a monarch's name to mean everyone in the kingdom; the figurative use of the name is due to the monarch's greater power. Where the Word mentions commanders by name, they symbolize general (leading) elements that are categories for all the other elements, just as tertiary officers do (§§8150, 8276). The term is used in connection with goodness, and in a negative sense with evil. Chiefs also symbolize general (main) elements that are categories for all the other elements (§§1482, 2089, 5044), but they are mentioned in connection with truth.

[2] It is important to know that the Word contains terms belonging to the spiritual category and terms belonging to the heavenly category. That is, it contains terms that express concepts involving truth, or faith, and terms that express concepts involving goodness, or love. There are also terms that are used for both. If you know all this, then the moment you look at or read the Word (especially in its original language), you can tell where the inner meaning is dealing with concepts involving truth or with concepts involving goodness.

That is how matters stand with the symbolism of chiefs and commanders: chiefs symbolize main elements and relate to the truth a person believes, but commanders symbolize leading elements and relate to the goodness a person loves. In a negative sense chiefs relate to the falsity a person believes, and commanders to the evil a person loves.

[3] So it is that the rulers in Edom were called commanders, as is evident from Genesis 36:15, 16, 17, 18, 19, 21, 29, 30, 40, 41, 42, 43. The reason for this term is that Edom symbolized goodness that comes from heavenly love, and in a negative sense, evil that comes from self-love. Among the offspring of Ishmael, though, the people in charge were called chiefs rather than commanders (Genesis 25:16), because Ishmael symbolized people in possession of truth (§§3263, 3268, 4747).

For the same reason, the people in charge in Israel were also called chiefs (Numbers 7:2, 10, 18, 24, 30, 36, 42, 48, 54), because Israel represented people with the truth and goodness that belong to faith. The people in charge in Judah, on the other hand, were called commanders, because Judah represented people with the goodness that belongs to love, as in Zechariah:

> Let that one be like a *commander in Judah.* (Zechariah 9:7)

And in the same author:

> *Judah's commanders will say* in their heart, "For my sake I will strengthen the residents of Jerusalem in Jehovah Sabaoth their God." On that day I will make *Judah's commanders* like a fiery furnace among the sticks. (Zechariah 12:5, 6)

The powerful of Moab symbolizes people who lived a life of self-centered distortions, as the following shows: The *powerful* symbolize that which reigns supreme and predominates. And *Moab* represents people of worldly goodness who readily allow themselves to be led astray, as discussed in §2468, so it represents people who live a life of distorted thinking. People with worldly goodness rather than goodness based on religious truth—who lack spiritual goodness—let themselves be lured into believing all kinds of falsity and consequently into living by it. Their main inducement to abandon truth for falsity is arguments pandering to their desires. These are the people meant by Moab. People involved in worldly goodness and not in spiritual goodness can never be guided by any inflow from heaven; see §§3470, 3471, 3518, 4988, 4992, 5032, 6208, 7197, 8002. **8315**

The word for "the powerful" in the original language applies to people who are devoted to truth because they are devoted to what is good, and in a negative sense to people who are devoted to falsity because they are devoted to evil. The word is used in this sense in Ezekiel 31:11; 2 Kings 24:15.

Terror seized them means that they dared nothing. This can be seen from the symbolism of being *seized with terror* as daring nothing. When people are terror-stricken, their blood runs cold, floods into their veins, and comes to a standstill, which makes their muscles become weak and their strength fail, so that they dare nothing. **8316**

All the inhabitants of Canaan collapsed symbolizes the same effect in people who were part of the church and who adulterated what was good and distorted what was true. This is established by the symbolism of the **8317** *inhabitants of Canaan* as people in the church and particularly as the people there who adulterated what was good and distorted what was true. The inhabitants of Canaan symbolize people in the church because the Lord's church had existed in the land of Canaan since the very earliest times; see §§3686, 4447, 4454, 4516, 4517, 5136, 6516. They also symbolize people who adulterated what was good and distorted what was true because the nations there that the children of Israel were to drive out represent evils and falsities associated with the faith; see §8054. This is because they had once been part of the church.

8318 *Horror and dread fell on them* means that they had no hope of dominating others. This is clear from the symbolism of *horror and dread.* When these words apply to people involved in self-love and in self-centered falsity and evil—the people symbolized by the commanders of Edom and the powerful of Moab—it means that they have no hope of dominating others. People given to self-centered evil crave power over others at all times, but when terror of a victorious enemy falls on them, they cease hoping for dominance.

[2] It needs to be known that evil has two sources: self-love and love of worldly advantages. People obsessed with the evil rising out of self-love have love for themselves alone. They despise everyone except those who make common cause with them, and when they love those people it is not those people they love but themselves, because they see themselves in them. Evil from this origin is the worst of all, because it causes people not only to despise all others in comparison with themselves but also to rail against them, hate them for the slightest reason, and seek to ruin them. So vengefulness and cruelty become the highest pleasure of their life. Spirits with this kind of evil live in hell at a depth determined by the nature and amount of their self-love.

[3] People obsessed with the evil rising out of love of worldly advantages also disdain their neighbor, valuing fellow humans only for their wealth and therefore prizing the wealth, not the person. They long to take everything their neighbor has for their own, and when this greed is active in them, they are totally devoid of charity and mercy. Depriving others of their possessions is the highest pleasure in life for them, especially for the filthy misers among them—the ones who love gold and silver for the sake of the gold and silver, not for any use they can make of it.

Spirits in whom this evil predominates also live in hell, but not as far down as spirits committed to the evil rising out of self-love.

[4] There is a third source of evil in addition to these two, which is to do wrong in following the principles of a misguided religion. People under the sway of self-love and love of worldly advantages consider this kind of wrong to be evil, but people who love their neighbor and their God do not, because the intention is good, and the intent qualifies everything else; see §8311.

In the greatness of your arm means with omnipotence. This is clear from the symbolism of an *arm* as power (discussed in §§878, 4931–4937), and when ascribed to the Divine, as omnipotence. 8319

They will be cut off like a stone symbolizes sinking like a weight. This is clear from the explanations above in §§8279, 8298. 8320

Until your people crosses over means that everyone with the ability to accept truth-from-goodness and goodness-from-truth would therefore be saved, without any danger of being persecuted. This can be seen from the symbolism of *crossing over* as being saved, without any danger of being persecuted. Once those spirits devoted to falsity from evil who inflicted the persecution have been thrust out of the way, into hell, there is no one left to put up obstacles; there is no one left to introduce falsity and evil that block the reception of goodness and truth from the Lord. That is what crossing over symbolizes here. 8321

Until those evil spirits had been thrown into hell, hardly anyone could cross over—be saved—because while the spirits were at large they were constantly stirring up evil and falsity among new arrivals to the other world. This drew the newcomers away from what was good and true. So in order to deliver people with goodness and truth from those spirits, the Lord came into the world and, while here, allowed himself to be tested over and over. By always winning in these tests he subdued all such spirits, and then by his presence he caused them to be thrown into hell, where they will be held captive forever, besieged by their own evil and falsity.

[2] The *people* here means individuals with the ability to accept truth-from-goodness and goodness-from-truth, because in a general way, a people symbolizes anyone supplied with the truth and goodness taught by faith (§§1259, 1260, 3295, 3581, 4619). Here it refers to Israel—that is, people in the spiritual church, people with truth from goodness and goodness from truth (§§7957, 8234).

The ability to accept truth-from-goodness and goodness-from-truth is attributed to them because no spirit has that ability except one who lived a life of neighborly love. A life of love gives us the ability. Anyone who believes faith without neighborly love can grant us that quality is greatly mistaken. Faith without love is hard and resistant and rejects all inflow from the Lord, but love combined with faith is yielding and soft and accepts his inflow. That is why charity gives us the ability but faith without charity does not. And since charity gives us the ability, charity is also what saves us. People who are saved are saved not by neighborly love they themselves generate but by love the Lord gives them for their neighbor, so they are saved by the ability to receive that love.

8322 *Until this people crosses over* means that those in the church who were committed to truth and goodness would therefore be saved. This can be seen from the explanation directly above.

8323 *[Of whom] you took possession* means who had therefore become the Lord's. This can be seen from the symbolism of *taking possession* as being his. Since people with truth and goodness—people whom the Lord came into the world to save—are the ones under discussion here, they are the ones symbolized as being the Lord's. Elsewhere they are called the redeemed, as in Isaiah:

> Are you not what drained the sea, the waters of the great abyss, what made the depths of the sea a path *for the redeemed to cross?* Thus may *those redeemed by Jehovah* return. (Isaiah 51:10, 11)

8324 Exodus 15:17, 18, 19. *"You will bring them in, you will plant them on the mountain of your inheritance, in the place where you were to dwell. You performed your work, Jehovah; your sanctuary, Lord, your hands prepared. Jehovah will reign to eternity and forever, because Pharaoh's horse with his chariot and with his riders came into the sea, and Jehovah brought back over them the waters of the sea. And the children of Israel went on dry ground through the middle of the sea."*

You will bring them in symbolizes being lifted up. *And plant them* symbolizes being continually regenerated. *On the mountain of your inheritance* symbolizes the heaven where there is charitable goodness. *In the place where you were to dwell* means where the Lord is. *You performed your work, Jehovah* means that it is from the Lord alone. *Your sanctuary, Lord, your hands prepared* symbolizes the heaven inhabited by people who have accepted religious truth from the Lord. *Jehovah will reign to eternity and forever* means that the Lord alone is Lord of heaven and earth. *Because Pharaoh's horse with his chariot and with his riders* symbolizes all the falsity produced by a corrupted intellect in people with a detached faith and an evil life. *Came into the sea* symbolizes damnation. *And Jehovah brought back over them the waters of the sea* means that the falsity-from-evil they intended to inflict on good people rebounded on themselves at the Lord's presence among the good. *And the children of Israel went on dry ground through the middle of the sea* means that people with goodness from truth and truth from goodness passed safely through that area of hell.

You will bring them in symbolizes being lifted up. This can be seen 8325
from the symbolism of *bringing someone in*—into heaven—as lifting the person up. It is described as an upward motion because in the external sight of spirits, heaven is on high. To eyes that see inwardly, as angels' eyes do, heaven is within. In the other life, everything inward is represented visually as being above, and everything outward as being below, so heaven appears above and hell below (§§2148, 3084, 4599, 5146). It is states of truth and goodness (and in a negative sense, states of falsity and evil) that are represented in the other life as heights and depths and, in short, as distances and places (see §§2625, 2837, 3356, 3387, 4321, 4882, 5605, 7381).

[2] From this experience alone you can form a conclusion about the difficulty that physically oriented people have trying to grasp spiritual phenomena and consequently to grasp the way things work in heaven. Which of them can understand that space and time do not exist in heaven? Or that these are replaced by states? Space is replaced by states of goodness, or states of being, and time by states of truth, or states of emergence, but who among them can comprehend this? Surely people who focus all their attention on the earthly plane have to believe that where time and space are absent there is an absolute void and vacuum. So if they decide privately that they should not believe anything they cannot grasp, they obviously plunge into gross error. On many other points too the situation is the same as with space and time. For example, physically oriented people cannot help falling into fanciful ideas about the Divine when, thinking in temporal terms, they wonder what the Divine did before creating the world, from eternity up to that point. They cannot be extricated from this knot until notions of time and space have been put aside. When angels think about this aspect of eternity, they do not think at all in terms of time but in terms of state.

[3] In the other world are seen two statues, partly flesh and partly stone, located at the outer bounds of the created universe, out in front and toward the left. I hear that they swallow up people who ruminate on what the Divine did from eternity before creating the world. The swallowing up represents the fact that because we humans cannot help thinking in terms of space and time, we cannot extricate ourselves from the

quandary on our own, only by the power of the Divine. This is accomplished either by putting the rumination itself to flight or by removing the notion of time.

8326 *And plant them* symbolizes being continually regenerated. This is evident from the symbolism of *planting* as regenerating, because regeneration resembles a plant. When a tree is planted, it branches out, comes into leaf, and produces fruit. From the seeds of the fruit it grows into new trees and repeats the cycle again and again. The process of rebirth in us is similar, so the Word compares us to a tree and a person reborn to a garden or paradise. The religious truth we know is compared to the leaves, and the neighborly good we do to the fruit. The seeds from which new trees grow are compared to truth born of goodness, or what is the same, to faith born of neighborly love.

I describe rebirth as continual because we start regenerating but never stop. We are constantly being perfected not only while we live in the world but also in the other life forever. Yet we can never arrive at such perfection that we can be compared to the Divine.

8327 *On the mountain of your inheritance* symbolizes the heaven where there is charitable goodness. This can be seen from the symbolism of an *inherited mountain* as heaven. A mountain symbolizes a loving goodness (§§795, 796, 2722, 4210, 6435). An inheritance symbolizes the living energy from another—here, the living energy of the Lord and therefore a life of goodness and truth received from the Lord, because people who live this kind of life are called heirs of the kingdom and children of the kingdom (§§2658, 2851, 3672, 7212). As an inherited mountain symbolizes these things, it also symbolizes heaven, because heaven is heaven on account of the loving goodness there, and it is the inheritance of people who are the Lord's.

8328 *In the place where you were to dwell* means where the Lord is. This can be seen from the symbolism of a *place* as a state (mentioned just above at §8325)—here, a state of goodness from the Divine, since heaven is meant—and from the meaning of Jehovah's dwelling place, or *where you were to dwell,* as where the Lord is. For the connection of dwelling with goodness, see §§2712, 3613, and for the idea that Jehovah's dwelling place is goodness and is therefore heaven, see §§8269, 8309. For the fact that the Lord is the one the Word refers to as Jehovah, see above at §8261.

The Lord often mentions the *Father who is in the heavens,* and where he does, it means the Divine in heaven. So it means the goodness that constitutes heaven. Divinity regarded in itself is above the heavens, but the divine presence *in* the heavens is goodness in the truth that radiates from the Divine. That is what is meant by the Father in the heavens in Matthew:

> . . . so that you may be the children of the *Father who is in the heavens;* so that you may be perfect, as *your Father who is in the heavens* is perfect. (Matthew 5:45, 48; 6:1)
>
> *Our Father who is in the heavens,* may your name be held sacred! (Matthew 6:9)
>
> . . . the one doing the will of the *Father who is in the heavens.* (Matthew 7:21)

Other passages are Matthew 10:32, 33; 16:17; 18:10, 14, 19. [2] The divine presence in the heavens is goodness in the divine truth that radiates from the Lord, but the divinity that exists above the heavens is divine goodness itself. *The place where you were to dwell* symbolizes heaven, where divine truth radiating from the Lord is found, since this constitutes heaven.

How is it that divine truth radiating from the Lord can be the goodness that exists in heaven? Comparison with the sun and the light that comes from it can illustrate. In the sun there is fire, but what comes from the sun is light. The light holds warmth that makes gardens grow and become like Eden. The sun's actual fire does not travel to earth, because it would scorch and consume everything; only light containing warmth from the sun's fire passes across. This light in a spiritual sense is divine truth. The warmth is the goodness within truth radiating from divine goodness. The paradise it generates is heaven.

You performed your work, Jehovah means that it is from the Lord alone. **8329**
This can be seen from the symbolism of *performing one's work,* which, when it has to do with regeneration and with heaven, means that it is from the Lord alone, since all of regeneration and all of heaven is from him.

Your sanctuary, Lord, your hands prepared symbolizes the heaven inhab- **8330**
ited by people who have accepted religious truth from the Lord. This can be seen from the symbolism of the *sanctuary* as the heaven where religious truth is found (discussed below), and from that of *your hands prepared,* which means that it comes from the Lord.

The reason the text says of the sanctuary that *your hands prepared* it is that hands, like the sanctuary, are mentioned in connection with truth, and symbolize power. (For the connection of hands with truth, see

§§3091, 8281, and for their symbolism as power, 878, 3387, 4931–4937, 5327, 5328, 6292, 6947, 7011, 7188, 7189, 7518, 7673, 8050, 8069, 8153, 8281. For the connection of the sanctuary with truth, see §8302.) The preceding phrases—"the place where you were to dwell" and "you performed your work, Jehovah"—are mentioned in connection with goodness, because they refer back to the inherited mountain, which symbolizes the heaven where there is charitable goodness (8327). (For the idea that some words in Scripture relate to goodness and some to truth, see §8314.)

[2] Let me briefly identify the heaven where there is charitable goodness (symbolized by the inherited mountain) and the heaven where there is religious truth (symbolized by the sanctuary). The heaven that holds charitable goodness is inhabited by the more internal citizens of the Lord's spiritual kingdom, while the heaven that holds religious truth is inhabited by the more external citizens of that kingdom. The internal ones have true love for their neighbor and consequently faith. The external ones are the ones with faith but not yet with neighborly love. The latter do good out of obedience; the former, out of genuine desire. This clarifies what I mean by the heaven where there is charitable goodness and the heaven where there is religious truth.

[3] As for the *sanctuary,* in the highest sense it means religious truth from the Lord. In a representative sense it means the Lord's spiritual kingdom, the spiritual church, and therefore a person in that church who has been reborn. In an abstract sense it means the truth of which faith is composed and accordingly faith itself. For a discussion of what holiness is, see above at §8302.

Therefore heaven is called a sanctuary because of the religious truth it has from the Lord, as in David:

> May Jehovah answer you in the day of distress; *may he send you help from his sanctuary* and support you from Zion. (Psalms 20:1, 2)

The sanctuary stands for the heaven where there is religious truth; Zion, for the heaven where there is a loving goodness. [4] In the same author:

> They saw your strides, God, the strides of my God, my King, *in the sanctuary.* God is fearsome; the God of Israel, *from his sanctuaries.* (Psalms 68:24, 35)

The sanctuary stands for the heaven where there is religious truth, so the passage speaks of God rather than Jehovah, and refers to him as the King. This is because "God" is used where the subject is truth, and "Jehovah" where it is goodness (§§2586, 2769, 2807, 2822, 3921 at the end, 4402, 7010, 7268), and because a king means truth (§§1672, 1728, 2015, 2069, 3009, 4575, 4581, 4966, 5044, 5068, 6148). [5] In the same author:

> They will praise Jah because he looked out from the *height of his sanctuary;* Jehovah looked back *from the heavens* to the earth to hear the prisoner's groan, to open up for the children of death. (Psalms 102:18, 19, 20)

Once again the sanctuary stands for the religious truth in heaven. In the same author:

> *Praise God in his sanctuary;* praise him in the expanse his strength created! (Psalms 150:1)

Praising God in his sanctuary means being moved to appreciation by religious truth from the Lord. Praising him in the expanse his strength created means being moved to appreciation by charitable goodness from the Lord.

Jehovah will reign to eternity and forever means that the Lord alone is Lord of heaven and earth, as the following shows: Of *Jehovah,* or the Lord, we can say that he *will reign to eternity and forever.* Of angels too we can say that they will reign, it is true, but only under the Lord's power, so that it is still the Lord alone who reigns through them. **8331**

Among those ancients who were part of the church it was customary to say "God reigns" and "God will reign forever," which meant that all would be well with the church, because there would then be goodness and truth from the Divine in it. The general meaning was that Jehovah alone was God. [Among people] who had been taught about the Lord's Coming, it meant that the Lord is the only Lord of heaven and earth.

As it was customary for the ancients in the church to say "God will reign," several of David's psalms are marked *Jehovah will reign;* see Psalms 93:1; 97:1; 99:1. And in the same author:

> *Jehovah will reign forever; your God,* Zion, for generation after generation. Alleluia! (Psalms 146:10)

In Isaiah:

> How gratifying on the mountains are the feet of the one who brings good news, who says to Zion, "*Your God will reign!*" (Isaiah 52:7)

This is about the Lord. In John:

> *The kingdoms of the world have come to belong to our Lord* and his Christ, and he will *reign forever and ever.* (Revelation 11:15)

And in the same author:

> I heard the voice of one saying, "Alleluia, *because the Lord God reigns!"* (Revelation 19:6)

These passages show also that the phrases were expressions of joy. That is the reason for shouting "Alleluia!" and for saying, "How gratifying are the feet of the one who brings good news, who says, 'Your God [will] reign!'"

It is plain in Matthew that the Lord is Lord of heaven and earth:

> Jesus said to the disciples, "All power in heaven and on earth has been given to me." (Matthew 28:18)

8332 *Because Pharaoh's horse with his chariot and with his riders* symbolizes all the falsity produced by a corrupted intellect in people with a detached faith and an evil life. This can be seen from the symbolism of *Pharaoh's horse* and *his chariot* and *his riders* as all the falsity produced by a corrupted intellect (discussed in §§8146, 8148) and from the representation of Pharaoh and the Egyptians as people who detached faith from neighborly love and lived an evil life (discussed in §§7926, 8148).

8333 *Came into the sea* symbolizes damnation. This can be seen from the symbolism of the *Suph Sea* as hell (dealt with in §§8099, 8137, 8138). Here it symbolizes damnation, because it says that they came into the sea and then that Jehovah brought back over them the waters of the sea, meaning that they sank into hell. Damnation comes before hell.

8334 *And Jehovah brought back over them the waters of the sea* means that the falsity-from-evil they intended to inflict on good people rebounded on themselves at the Lord's presence among the good. This can be seen from the symbolism of *Jehovah brought back over them the waters of the sea* as the rebounding onto them of the falsity-from-evil they intended to inflict on good people.

Falsity from evil pools together, pours into spirits intent on evil, and surrounds them (see §8146). The falsity-from-evil they intend for others rebounds on them, by a law of the divine plan (8214, 8223, 8226). To be engulfed by falsity from evil is to be thrown into hell (8210, 8232). This is accomplished by the Lord's mere presence with the good when he is protecting them and giving them the gift of heaven and heavenly joy (8137 at the end, 8265).

And the children of Israel went on dry ground through the middle of the sea means that people with goodness from truth and truth from goodness passed safely through that area of hell. This is evident from the explanations in §§8099 and 8185. 8335

Exodus 15:20, 21. *And Miriam the prophetess, the sister of Aaron, took the tambourine in her hand, and all the women went out after her with tambourines and [with] dances. And Miriam answered them, "Sing to Jehovah, because he has risen very high; the horse and its rider he has cast into the sea."* 8336

And Miriam the prophetess, the sister of Aaron, took the tambourine in her hand symbolizes glory given to the Lord from good actions inspired by faith. *And all the women went out after her* symbolizes every type of goodness that is associated with truth. *With tambourines and with dances* symbolizes celebration offered with joy and gladness. *And Miriam answered them* symbolizes a response. *Sing to Jehovah* means that the glory is the Lord's alone. *Because he has risen very high* means that he revealed his divinity within his humanity. *The horse and its rider he has cast into the sea* means through the fact that as a result of his mere presence, falsity in the spirits' faith and evil in their way of life plunged into hell.

And Miriam the prophetess, the sister of Aaron, took the tambourine in her hand symbolizes glory given to the Lord from good actions inspired by faith, as the following shows: *Miriam* represents good actions inspired by faith. After all, Moses represents true ideas of faith that emanate directly from the Lord and therefore inner truth, while Aaron represents true ideas of faith that emanate indirectly from the Lord and therefore outer truth (§§7009, 7089, 7382). So Miriam is good actions inspired by faith that emanate indirectly from the Lord, because when men represent truth, the women associated with them represent goodness (6014). Since Miriam along with the women represents an outer kind of goodness, she is also called the *sister of Aaron* but not the sister of Moses. In addition, goodness and truth resemble a sister and brother (3160). However, it needs to be realized that women represent goodness and men represent truth where the text is dealing with a spiritual religion. Where it is dealing with a heavenly religion, women represent truth, and men goodness (4823). A *prophetess* symbolizes someone who teaches doctrine, as discussed in §§2534, 7269. Here it symbolizes someone who praises the Lord in chorus—in other words, gives glory to him from good actions inspired by faith—because 8337

Miriam sang to Jehovah just as Moses and the men of Israel did. For the meaning of singing as giving glory, see §§8261, 8263, 8267. And *taking the tambourine in her hand* means giving glory from good actions inspired by faith. A tambourine is mentioned in connection with spiritual goodness, which is the same as faith-based goodness (4138).

[2] Many types of musical instruments were used in worship of God in past times but with many differences in that use. To speak generally, wind instruments were used to express various desires for goodness, and stringed instruments, desires for truth. This was due to the correspondence of the two methods of producing sound with those kinds of desires.

People recognize that certain types of instruments express one kind of earthly emotion and other types another, and that when suitable music meets up with the appropriate instrument, it actually arouses those emotions. Professional musicians know this and put the knowledge to good use. The reason for the phenomenon springs from the actual nature of the sounds and their compatibility with those emotions. Humankind first learned about it not from science and art but from listening with a sensitive ear. Quite plainly, then, the connection between music and emotion comes from an origin not in the physical but in the spiritual world, and from correspondence at that—the correspondence between qualities in the physical world that result from the divine design, and qualities in the spiritual world. All the different musical sounds correspond to states of joy and gladness in the spiritual world, and states of joy and gladness there rise out of desires, which in that world are desires for goodness and truth.

This discussion now shows that musical instruments correspond to pleasures and delights connected with spiritual and heavenly desires and that some musical instruments correspond to spiritual desires, others to heavenly desires. See what has been said and shown on this subject before in §§418, 419, 420, 4138.

[3] As for *tambourines* specifically, they correspond to spiritual goodness, or a truth-oriented goodness. One reason for the correspondence is that a tambourine is neither a stringed nor a wind instrument, but because it is made of leather, it is sort of like a string instrument with one very wide string. Another reason is that it is lower pitched than strings and louder. This meaning is also clear in the Word where it mentions a tambourine, as in Isaiah:

> *The joy of tambourines will cease;* the commotion of revelers will cease; the joy of a harp will cease. (Isaiah 24:8)

The joy of tambourines stands for the pleasures yielded by desires for good actions that are inspired by faith; the joy of a harp, for the pleasure yielded by a desire for true insights of faith. In Jeremiah:

> I will build you anew that you may be rebuilt, virgin of Israel; *you will decorate your tambourines anew* and go out *into the dance* of the merry. (Jeremiah 31:4)

Decorating tambourines stands for giving glory to God out of spiritual goodness, since the verse is about the spiritual church (the "virgin of Israel"). [4] Likewise in Ezekiel:

> You were in Eden, the garden of God. The *workmanship of your tambourines* and your pipes was prepared in you on the day when you were created. (Ezekiel 28:13)

This is about Tyre, which symbolizes a knowledge of goodness and a knowledge of truth. The tambourines and pipes symbolize the desires associated with the first kind of knowledge and the joys associated with the second kind. In David:

> They saw your strides, God, the strides of my God in the sanctuary. The singers went in front, the strummers came after, *in the middle of the young women playing tambourines.* (Psalms 68:24, 25)

In the same author:

> Shout to the God of Jacob; lift a song and *give [voice to] the tambourine,* the pleasing harp with the lute. (Psalms 81:1, 2)

In the same author:

> Sing Jehovah a new song. Let them praise his name in dance; *with tambourine* and harp they will make music to him. (Psalms 149:1, 3)

Praising Jehovah with a tambourine stands for giving him glory with the pleasure of desiring the goodness taught by faith. Praising him with a harp stands for giving him glory with the delight of desiring the truth taught by faith. [5] In the same author:

> *Praise God with tambourine* and with dance; praise him with strings and organ; praise him with sounding cymbals; praise him with clamoring cymbals. (Psalms 150:3, 4, 5)

Praising God with tambourine and with dance stands for praising him from the good desires and true insights of faith. Praising him with strings and organ stands for doing so from truth and from a goodness growing out of truth.

Since all instruments correspond to and once symbolized pleasures and delights connected with spiritual and heavenly desires, many of David's psalms were marked to indicate how they were to be played: on the *neginoth,* on the *nechiloth,* on the octave, *shiggaion, gittith, muth-labben, sheminith, shoshannim,* and *machalath.*

8338 *And all the women went out after her* symbolizes every type of goodness that is associated with truth. This can be seen from the symbolism of *women,* who stand for desires for goodness when men stand for desires for truth, as noted directly above at §8337.

8339 *With tambourines and with dances* symbolizes celebration offered with joy and gladness, as the following symbolism shows: A *tambourine* is mentioned in connection with a desire for spiritual goodness, or a truth-oriented goodness, and it symbolizes pleasure or joy in that desire, as discussed just above at §8337. A *dance* is mentioned in connection with a desire for spiritual truth, and it symbolizes delight or gladness in that desire, as discussed below.

In ancient times people showed heartfelt gladness not only through musical instruments and song but also through *dance.* The joy in their heart, the joy deep in their body, burst spontaneously into various activities such as singing and dancing.

The kinds of gladness that outstripped all others in ancient times were spiritual ones, or gladness in the feelings that are produced by spiritual types of love—gladness stirred by desires for goodness and truth. This is why people at that time felt inspired to combine dance with song and with musical harmony and use this as a way to give evidence of their joy.

That is why the Word mentions dancing, which symbolizes gladness in desires for truth (or faith) that comes from goodness (or neighborly love). In Jeremiah, for instance:

> You will decorate your tambourines anew *and go out into the dances of the merry.* Their soul will become like a watered garden, and they will not grieve anymore; *then the young woman will rejoice in dance,* as will the young men and the old together. (Jeremiah 31:4, 12, 13)

In the same author:

> The joy of our heart will end; *our dance has turned into mourning.* (Lamentations 5:15)

In David:

> *You have turned my mourning into a dance for my sake.* (Psalms 30:11)

In the same author:

> *Let them praise his name in dance;* with tambourine and harp they will make music to him. (Psalms 149:3; 150:4)

People outside the church also worshiped God with playing and dancing, as can be seen in Exodus 32:6, 19.

[2] I speak of joy and gladness because in the Word, joy has to do with goodness, and gladness with truth. As a consequence, the Word often mentions both joy and gladness simultaneously, as in Isaiah:

> Indeed, it is *joy* and *gladness* to kill an ox. (Isaiah 22:13)

In the same author:

> *Joy* and *gladness* will overtake them, and sorrow and groaning will flee. (Isaiah 35:10)

In the same author:

> *Joy* and *gladness* will be found in Zion; acclamation and the voice of song. (Isaiah 51:3, 11)

In Jeremiah:

> The *voice of joy* and the *voice of gladness,* and the voice of the bridegroom and the voice of the bride. (Jeremiah 33:11)

In Zechariah:

> To the house of Judah, the fast of the tenth [month] will serve for *joy* and *gladness.* (Zechariah 8:19)

In David:

> You will make me hear *joy* and *gladness.* (Psalms 51:8)

In these passages, joy relates to goodness, and gladness to truth, so both are mentioned. Otherwise one term would have sufficed. That is the nature of the Word's sacred phrasing, whose purpose is to bring into every detail of the Word the heavenly marriage of goodness and truth (§§683, 793, 801, 2173, 2516, 2712, 4137, 5138, 5502, 7945).

And Miriam answered them symbolizes a response. This can be seen from the symbolism of *answering* as a response, when the focus is on 8340 giving glory to the Lord in song. In the ancients' sacred worship it was customary to have choral singing, to which one singer or several would answer. This represented the kind of response and answer that the church receives from heaven and that heaven receives from the Lord. That is what is symbolized in Hosea:

> I will *answer* and sing to [Ephraim]. (Hosea 14:8)

And in Moses:

> Then Israel sang this song: "Gush up, you spring! *Give answer concerning it!*" (Numbers 21:17)

8341 *Sing to Jehovah* means that the glory is the Lord's alone. This can be seen from the explanation above at §8263, where similar words appear.

8342 *Because he has risen very high* means that he revealed his divinity within his humanity. This can be seen from the explanation above at §8264, where the same words appear.

8343 *The horse and its rider he has cast into the sea* means that as a result of his mere presence, falsity in the spirits' faith and evil in their way of life plunged into hell. This can be seen from the symbolism of a *horse and rider* as falsity from evil (dealt with in §§8146, 8148) and from the symbolism of *casting something into the sea* as casting it into hell (dealt with in §§8099, 8137, 8138). For the fact that the mere presence of the Lord brought this about, see §§8137 at the end, 8265.

The reason I say falsity and evil plunged into hell is that falsity and evil themselves are what are cast into hell, dragging along with them anyone to whom they cling. When people live evil lives, they come to embody falsity from evil, so when evil with its falsity is sent below, these embodiments to which it clings are drawn down with it. Falsity and evil are exhalations from the hells that flow into people whose evil way of life has shaped their inner depths into something receptive of that inflow. Everything we think or want flows into us—from heaven if it is good, from hell if it is evil; see §§2886, 2887, 2888, 4151, 4249, 5846, 6189, 6191, 6193, 6203, 6206, 6213, 6324, 6325, 7147, 7343. This is the reason for saying that falsity in the spirits' faith and evil in their way of life plunged into hell.

When angels think and speak about the hells, then, they think and speak about falsity and evil in the abstract, separate from hell's inhabitants. Angels always set aside any thought of the person, staying with the thought of the thing itself (§§5225, 5287, 5434).

Exodus 15:22, 23, 24, 25, 26. *And Moses caused Israel to set out from the Suph Sea, and they went away to the wilderness of Shur and went three days in the wilderness and did not find water. And they came to Marah and could not drink the water for bitterness, because it was bitter, so he called its name Marah. And the people murmured against Moses, saying, "What shall we drink?" And he cried out to Jehovah, and Jehovah showed him a piece of wood, and he threw it [into] the water, and the water became sweet. There he set them a statute and a judgment, and there he tested them. And he said, "If you listen intently to the voice of Jehovah your God and do what is right in his eyes and heed his commandments and keep all his statutes, I will not lay on you any disease that I laid on the Egyptians, because I am Jehovah your healer."* **8344**

And Moses caused Israel to set out from the Suph Sea symbolizes what came next in the pattern laid out by divine truth, after they had crossed that area of hell. *And they went away to the wilderness of Shur* symbolizes the state of trial they were then brought into. *And went three days in the wilderness and did not find water* symbolizes a shortage and in the end a complete absence of truth. *And they came to Marah* symbolizes the state of trial. *And could not drink the water for bitterness, because it was bitter* means that the truth seemed unpleasant to them, because they had no desire for goodness. *So he called [its] name Marah* symbolizes the state of trial and the nature of the trial. *And the people murmured against Moses* symbolizes grief because of the harshness of the trial. *Saying, "What shall we drink?"* means that they could not bear the truth, which was unpleasant to them because they had no desire for it. *And he cried out to Jehovah* symbolizes pleading with the Lord out of grief. *And Jehovah showed him a piece of wood* means that the Lord inspired goodness. *And he threw it into the water* means that he touched the truth with it. *And the water became sweet* means that the truth turned pleasant as a result. *There he set them a statute and a judgment* symbolizes a revelation at that point of truth describing the divine design. *And there he tested them* means for times of trial in general. *And he said,* symbolizes instruction. *If you listen intently to the voice of Jehovah your God* symbolizes belief in the Lord's commandments. *And do what is right in his eyes* symbolizes a life in keeping with them. *And heed his commandments* symbolizes obeying and living by the goodness taught by faith, which is religion's inner dimension. *And keep all his statutes* symbolizes living by the truth taught by faith, which is religion's outer dimension. *I will not lay on you any disease that I laid on the Egyptians* means that they were to be withheld from the evil indulged in by people with a detached faith and an evil life. *Because I am Jehovah your healer* means that the Lord alone preserves us from evil.

8345 *And Moses caused Israel to set out from the Suph Sea* symbolizes what came next in the pattern laid out by divine truth, after they had crossed that area of hell, as the following shows: *Setting out* symbolizes the next developments in the pattern of life and a continuation of that pattern, as discussed in §§4375, 4554, 4585, 5996, 8181. *Moses* represents divine truth, as mentioned in §§7010, 7014, 7382. So *Moses caused them to set out* symbolizes what came next in the pattern laid out by divine truth. *Israel* represents people of the spiritual church who were kept in the underground realm until the Lord's Coming, when they were delivered, as discussed in §§6854, 6914, 7828, 7932, 8018, 8321. And the *Suph Sea* symbolizes the hell inhabited by spirits who had been part of the church but detached faith from neighborly love and lived an evil life, as discussed in §§8099, 8137, 8148. On the point that when [the inhabitants of the underground realm] were delivered they were led through the hell symbolized by the Suph Sea, consult §8099.

8346 *And they went away to the wilderness of Shur* symbolizes the state of trial they were then brought into. This is clear from the symbolism of *going away* as being brought into, and from that of the *wilderness of Shur* as a state of trial. A wilderness stands for a state in which one undergoes trial (see §§6828, 8098), and Shur stands for religious information that has not yet come alive (§1928), so it means the kind of information that will be brought to life through times of trial. Spiritual life is acquired through challenging experiences—spiritual battles, or battles against evil and falsity—and through victory in those battles. (For the idea that people in the spiritual church underwent trials after the Lord came into the world and could not undergo them any earlier, see §8159.)

8347 *And went three days in the wilderness and did not find water* symbolizes a shortage and in the end a complete absence of truth. This is evident from the symbolism of *three days* as something complete (discussed in §§2788, 4495, 7715), from that of a *wilderness* as a state in which one undergoes times of trial (mentioned directly above at §8346), and from that of *water* as religious truth (discussed in §§2702, 3058, 3424, 4976, 5668), so that *not finding* water means a shortage of truth. Its complete absence is symbolized by *going three days.*

It says "in the wilderness" because that is where they were tested, as is reported below [§§8348–8352].

8348 *And they came to Marah* symbolizes the state of trial. This can be seen from the fact that they were tested there, which is said below in these words: "There he set them a statute and judgment, *and there he tested them*" (verse 25).

8349 *And could not drink the water for bitterness, because it was bitter* means that the truth seemed unpleasant to them, because they had no desire for goodness. This can be seen from the symbolism of *drinking* water as accepting truth and applying it under the supervision of goodness (discussed in §§3069, 5709), from that of *water* as truth (noted just above at §8347), and from that of *bitter* as unpleasant (discussed at §7854). Plainly, then, *they could not drink the water for bitterness, because it was bitter* means that the truth seemed unpleasant to them. This was due to their lack of desire for goodness because all the pleasure truth provides springs from goodness. A desire for truth traces its origin to goodness because goodness loves truth, and truth loves goodness. The two are essentially joined in a marriage.

It is recognized that we all want to learn about the things we love and hold as our goal. People who love what is good—who wish with all their heart to worship God and help their neighbor—love to learn what leads to that end, so they love to learn truth. This shows that all desire for truth comes from goodness.

[2] To be sure, there are people who live evil lives and still want to learn truth, but they have no desire for truth, only a desire to reinforce the teachings of the church so that they can win themselves glory, that is, reputation, prestige, and riches. A genuine desire for truth is a longing to know what is true for the sake of life in the world and for the sake of life eternal.

People with this genuine desire come into crisis when they start to run out of truth, even more so when the truth they know looks unpleasant. This crisis originates in broken-off contact with anything good. Their communication with goodness is interrupted as soon as they become involved in themselves, because self-involvement causes them to slide into self-centered and materialistic evil. The moment they sink to that level, they begin to sense truth as unpleasant; but as soon as they emerge from the state, truth turns delightful.

This is meant below [§§8354–8356] by the curing of the bitter water when the piece of wood was thrown in, because wood symbolizes that which is good.

8350 *So he called [its] name Marah* symbolizes the state of trial and the nature of the trial. This is evident from the fact that the names given to things discussed in the Word embrace the nature and state of the topic under discussion (§§2643, 3422, 4298, 4442). In the current passage, then, *Marah* symbolizes the nature and state of the trial these verses deal with. Besides, "Marah" means "bitter."

8351 *And the people murmured against Moses* symbolizes grief because of the harshness of the trial. This can be seen from the symbolism of *murmuring* as complaints of the type people make when they are being tested and therefore grief due to the harshness of a trial.

The murmurings of the children of Israel in the wilderness depict the trials that people in the Lord's spiritual church underwent after they were delivered from persecution, and also the trials people of that church will undergo in the future. Since spiritual trials are usually drawn out to a point of despair (§§1787, 2694, 5279, 5280, 7147, 7166, 8165), murmuring symbolizes complaints rising out of the grief experienced in times of trial, as in Exodus 16:2, 3; 17:3; Numbers 14:27, 29, 36; 16:11. The text says the murmuring was *against Moses* because it was against the Divine, and Moses represents divine truth (§§6723, 6752, 6771, 6827, 7010, 7014, 7089, 7382).

[2] In regard to the trials that people in the spiritual church underwent and will undergo in the future, it needs to be known that faith—and therefore neighborly love—can never be planted in people of that church except through trials. This is because during our troubles we are in a fight against falsity and evil. Falsity and evil flow into our outer self from the hells, but goodness and truth flow in through our inner self from the Lord, and the result is a battle between our inner and outer selves, which is called a trial. To the extent that this compels our outer self to obey our inner self, we have faith and neighborly love planted in us. After all, our outer, earthly plane is a container designed to receive truth and goodness from our inner plane. If the container is incompatible, it does not accept anything coming from inside but rather rejects it or snuffs it out or smothers it, and then there is no rebirth.

That is why times of trial are necessary if we are to be reborn, which is accomplished by our having faith and neighborly love planted in us, and a new will and new intellect accordingly formed in us. For this reason the Lord's church is called the church militant. See earlier remarks and evidence concerning this in §§3928, 4249, 4341, 4572, 5356, 6574, 6611, 6657, 7090 at the end, 7122, 8159, 8168, 8179, 8273.

Saying, "What shall we drink?" means that they could not bear the truth, which was unpleasant to them because they had no desire for it. This can be seen from the symbolism of *drinking* as learning truth, accepting it, desiring it, and consequently adopting it, as discussed in §§3069, 3168, 3772, 4017, 4018. Here it means being unable to bear the truth, which was unpleasant to them because they had no desire for goodness, as symbolized by the bitterness of the water, as explained above at §8349. **8352**

Let me describe the current trial: They are grieving and complaining that truth, which had pleased them before and was therefore the substance of their spiritual life, or the life of heaven for them, now seems unpleasant, so unpleasant they can hardly stand it.

[2] A physically oriented person would not believe an issue of this type could stir any grief. Such a person thinks, "What do I care whether truth is pleasant or unpleasant? If it is unpleasant, away with it!" Spiritual people feel entirely differently, though. The highest pleasure of their life is to be taught truth and gain light on matters pertaining to their soul and consequently to spiritual life. When truth is lacking, then, their spiritual life suffers and struggles, which causes them grief and distress. This is because a desire for goodness is always flowing in from the Lord through the inner self, stirring up whatever is compatible in the outer self. Previously these compatible elements aroused a pleasure in the desire for truth, but they are attacked by self-centered and materialistic evil, which the person also used to sense as delightful. That brings the two kinds of pleasure or desire into conflict, which sparks distress, which in turn triggers grief and fretfulness.

[3] I need to explain briefly about trials that arise out of a shortage of truth. Goodness and truth nourish our spiritual life just as food and drink nourish our physical life. If goodness is lacking, that is like having too little to eat, and if truth is lacking, that is like having too little to drink. The resulting grief resembles the grief caused by hunger and thirst.

This comparison grows out of correspondence. Food corresponds to that which is good, and drink to that which is true. Since the two pairs correspond, food and drink provide us with better, more fitting nourishment when we sup or dine while enjoying a conversation with others on our favorite topics than when we sit at the table alone, without companionship. In the latter case the vessels that absorb the food are constricted, but in the former case the same vessels are open. Such is the effect of the correspondence between spiritual food and physical food.

I speak of enjoying conversation with others on favorite topics because everything we love relates to goodness and truth. There is nothing in the world that does not relate to one or the other. What we love comes under the category of goodness (as it seems to us), and what teaches us about goodness (and thus unites with goodness) comes under the category of truth.

8353 *And he cried out to Jehovah* symbolizes pleading with the Lord out of grief. This is established by the symbolism of *crying out* as entreaty (mentioned at §6801) and as inner mourning (§7782) and therefore as pleading in grief, too. (In the Word, *Jehovah* is the Lord; see §8261.)

8354 *And Jehovah showed him a piece of wood* means that the Lord inspired goodness, as the following shows: *Showing,* when Jehovah (the Lord) does it, symbolizes giving someone a perception, which he accomplishes by an inflow, so it symbolizes inspiration. And a *piece of wood* symbolizes goodness, as discussed in §§643, 2784, 2812, 3720.

8355 *And he threw it into the water* means that he touched the truth with it. This can be seen from the symbolism of *throwing* (wood) *into the water* as touching truth with goodness, since wood means goodness and water means truth. (For the meaning of wood as goodness, see directly above at §8354, and for that of water as truth, §§2702, 3058, 3424, 4976, 5668, 8349.)

8356 *And the water became sweet* means that the truth turned pleasant as a result. This can be seen from the symbolism of *sweet* as pleasing—because sweetness in a spiritual sense is the sweet part of life, which is the same as pleasure—and from that of *water* as truth (mentioned directly above at §8355).

Here is the situation: It is out of goodness that we desire truth, because goodness and truth unite in a kind of marriage and consequently love each other as spouse loves spouse. For the same reason the Word compares the bond between goodness and truth to a marriage and refers to the truth and goodness born of that union as sons and daughters.

This shows that the pleasure associated with a desire for truth traces its cause purely and simply to goodness. The same thing is plain from experience, since people who live a good life—who love God and their neighbor—also love faith and its truth. In consequence, as long as goodness flows in and they accept it, truth seems pleasing. However, as soon as the inflow of goodness stops, that is, as soon as evil starts to predominate and to prevent goodness from flowing in, they immediately feel a displeasure for truth. Truth and evil mutually loathe and reject each other.

From this you can now see why the order was given to throw a piece of wood into the bitter water and why it turned the water sweet. The Divine would never have commanded it had it not had this kind of symbolism, because the Divine could sweeten the water without wood.

There he set them a statute and a judgment symbolizes a revelation at that point of truth describing the divine design. This can be seen from the symbolism of a *statute* as outer truth for the church and from that of a *judgment* as inner truth for the church. *Setting* someone a statute and a judgment, then, means arranging matters to reflect the truth, so it means revealing the truth. The reason a statute means outer truth describing the divine design is that every outward practice of the church was called a statute, while all inner truth of this kind was called a judgment. **8357**

And there he tested them means for times of trial in general. This is evident from the verses above and below. The verses above treat of the people's first trial in the wilderness. The verses below deal with instructions on how they would have to live in order not to succumb in times of trial. **8358**

And he said, symbolizes instruction. This is established by the symbolism of *saying* as instruction, when Jehovah is doing it and the subject is truth that describes the divine plan for times of trial. The symbolism is the same in §§6879, 6881, 6883, 6891, 7186, 7267, 7304, 7380, 7517, 8127. **8359**

If you listen intently to the voice of Jehovah your God symbolizes belief in the Lord's commandments. This can be seen from the symbolism of *listening* as perception and faith (discussed in §§3921, 5017, 7216) and from that of *Jehovah's voice* as a pronouncement from the Word and therefore as a commandment of the Lord's (discussed at §6971). **8360**

And do what is right in his eyes symbolizes a life in keeping with them, as the following shows: *Doing what is right* means living by the dictates of truth. And *in Jehovah's eyes* means before the Lord and therefore in keeping with his commandments, because the Lord is in his commandments when we live by them. Besides, people who believe in the Lord are said to be in his eyes. **8361**

To go back to the word *listening,* [or hearing,] strictly speaking it symbolizes obedience (§§2542, 3869, 5017), but when the word *doing* is also used, as it is here, then listening symbolizes faith and doing symbolizes life. This can be seen in the Lord's words in Matthew:

> Everyone *who hears my words* and *does them* I will compare to a prudent man, but everyone *hearing my words and yet not doing them* will be compared to a stupid man. (Matthew 7:24, 26)

In Luke:

> Everyone who comes to me and *listens to my sayings and does them*—I will show you whom that person is like. (Luke 6:47)

In the same author:

> The seed in the good earth—these are the ones who with a heart uncomplicated and good *hear the word,* hold on to it, and *bear fruit* in patience. (Luke 8:15)

In the same author:

> Jesus said, "My mother and my siblings are those *who hear the word of God and do it."* (Luke 8:21)

In these passages, to listen, [or hear,] means to perceive, understand, and believe, while to do means to live by that which one perceives, understands, and believes.

On the other hand, where hearing is mentioned and doing is not, hearing symbolizes faith in our will and in our actions and therefore obedience. This is because anything we hear with our ears crosses over into our inner vision, the vision of our intellect, where it is taken up by our will and completes the circle by passing into action. The word *hear,* then, naturally means obedience as well, as in "listening to" or "heeding" someone; see §§4652–4660.

8362 *And heed his commandments* symbolizes obeying and living by the goodness taught by faith, which is religion's inner dimension. This can be seen from the symbolism of *heeding* as obeying and living by, and from that of *commandments* as the Word's inner truth (discussed at §3382) and therefore as the truth taught by faith that constitutes religion's inner dimension. I refer to this truth as the *goodness* taught by faith because it is willed.

8363 *And keep all his statutes* symbolizes living by the truth taught by faith, which is religion's outer dimension. This can be seen from the symbolism of *keeping* too as living, and from that of *statutes* as the Word's outer truth (discussed in §§3382, 8357) and therefore the truth taught by faith that constitutes religion's outer dimension.

Many passages in the Word refer to statutes and commandments, and when the one is mentioned alongside the other, a statute symbolizes the outer part of the church and a commandment the inner part.

8364 *I will not lay on you any disease that I laid on the Egyptians* means that they were to be withheld from the evil indulged in by people with a detached faith and an evil life, as the following shows: A *disease* symbolizes evil, as discussed below. The *Egyptians* represent people with a detached faith and an evil life, as discussed in §§7097, 7317, 7926, 8148. And *not laying it on you*—when this refers to a disease, which symbolizes evil—means that they were to be withheld from evil. Jehovah, or the Lord, does not remove evil but rather holds us back from it and keeps us on a good path (§§929, 1581, 2256, 2406, 4564, 8206). That is why not laying a disease on them means that they were to be withheld from evil.

[2] A *disease* stands for evil because what is symbolized in the inner meaning is the kinds of things that affect our spiritual life. The diseases that affect our spiritual life are different kinds of evil, which are called cravings and obsessions.

Faith and neighborly love constitute our spiritual life. This life falls ill when falsity replaces the true ideas of faith and evil replaces the good desires of neighborly love. Falsity and evil send our spiritual life to a death that is called spiritual death and is the same as damnation, just as disease sends our earthly life to its death. That is why disease symbolizes evil in an inner sense. The diseases of the Egyptians symbolize the evil into which people with a detached faith and an evil life threw themselves and which they used for harassing the upright. This evil is discussed earlier, where the plagues in Egypt are explained.

[3] Diseases mean evil in other Scripture passages as well, as for instance in Moses:

> If you keep the *commandments* and *statutes* and *judgments* that I am commanding you today, Jehovah will *remove* from you *every disease;* and he will *not lay on you any of the bad sicknesses of Egypt* that you know of, but will put them on those who hate you. (Deuteronomy 7:11, 15)

In the same author:

> If you do not obey the voice of Jehovah your God, watching to do *all his commandments* and *his statutes,* Jehovah will send onto you the curse, the confusion, and the rebuke, every time you send out your hand, until you are destroyed. Because of the wickedness of your deeds, with which you abandoned me, Jehovah will *make the contagion cling to you* until he has consumed you off the earth. Jehovah will *strike you with consumption* and *with warm fever* and *with burning fever* and *with hot fever* and *with dehydration* and *with blight* and *with mildew,* which will dog you until you perish. Jehovah *will strike you with the sores of Egypt* and *with*

> *hemorrhoids* and *with rash* and *with itching,* so that you cannot be healed. Jehovah will *strike you with madness* and *with blindness* and *with a shock to the heart.* You will go *mad* from the glance of your eyes. Jehovah will *strike you with bad sores on your knees* and *on your thighs* from which you cannot be healed, from the sole of your foot right to the crown of your head. He will *fling back onto you all the sickness of Egypt,* also *every disease* and *every plague* that is not written in the book of this law. Jehovah will *give you a quivering heart, a wasting of the eyes,* and an *ache in your soul.* (Deuteronomy 28:15, 20, 21, 22, 27, 28, 34, 35, 60, 61, 65)

All the diseases named here symbolize spiritual diseases. Spiritual disease is evil destructive of the vital energy in a will that seeks goodness, and falsity destructive of the vital energy in an intellect that comprehends truth—destructive, in short, of the vital spiritual energy in faith and neighborly love. Physical illness even corresponds to this evil and falsity, because all illness in the human race rises out of evil and falsity, since it rises out of sin (§§5712, 5726). Every ailment corresponds to its own form of evil, too. This is because all of our life comes from the spiritual world. If our spiritual life sickens, then, evil is channeled off into our earthly life, where it turns into disease. See what I have to say from experience about the correspondence of disease with evil in §§5711–5727.

[4] Disease has the same kind of symbolism elsewhere, as for example in Moses:

> You shall worship Jehovah your God, so that he can bless your bread and your water and that I can *remove disease from your midst.* (Exodus 23:25)

In the same author:

> If you spurn *my statutes* and if your soul disdains my judgments, so that you do not do all *my commandments,* while you render my pact void, I will order *terror* upon you, along with *consumption* and *with burning fever, which will waste your eyes* and *torture your soul.* (Leviticus 26:15, 16)

Consumption stands for a decrease in truth and an increase in falsity. A burning fever stands for a craving for evil. In Isaiah too:

> Why do you withdraw even farther? The *whole head has taken on disease* and the *whole heart is faint.* From the sole of the foot right to the head, there is no soundness in it; *wound* and *scar* and *recent injury,* not pressed out and not bandaged and not softened with oil. (Isaiah 1:5, 6)

It escapes no one that the disease, wound, scar, and injury mean sin. Likewise in Ezekiel:

> Doom to the shepherds of Israel! The *weak sheep* you do not strengthen, the *sick sheep you do not heal,* and the sheep with a fracture you do not bandage. (Ezekiel 34:[2,] 4)

In David:

> My iniquities have passed over my head. *My wounds have turned foul-smelling, have festered,* because of my stupidity. *My intestines are full of burning, and there is no soundness in my flesh.* (Psalms 38:4, 5, 7)

[5] Since disease symbolizes flaws and evil in people's spiritual life, different types of disease symbolize different types of flaws and evil in that life. Contagion symbolizes a stripping away of what is good and true (see §§7102, 7505), and leprosy, the profanation of what is true (§6963).

The general symbolism of disease as sin can also be seen in Isaiah:

> *He was a man in pain* and *one who knew disease.* We therefore in effect hid our faces from him; he was despised, so that we did not value him. Nevertheless *our diseases he bore* and *our pain he shouldered,* and *through his wounds* health has been given to us. (Isaiah 53:3, 4, 5)

This is about the Lord.

[6] As disease represented iniquity and evil in people's spiritual life, the diseases the Lord healed symbolize deliverance from various kinds of evil and falsity that were plaguing the church and the human race and would have brought spiritual death. This is because what makes divine miracles different from other miracles is the fact that states of the church and of the heavenly kingdom are wrapped up in them and are their focus. For this reason the Lord's miracles consisted mainly in the healing of diseases. That is the meaning of the Lord's message to the disciples whom John [the Baptist] sent:

> Report to John what you are hearing and seeing: *The blind see* and *the lame walk, the leprous are cleansed* and *the deaf hear, the dead rise again* and the poor hear the gospel. (Matthew 11:4, 5)

That is why it is so often said that the Lord *healed every disease* and *sickness* (Matthew 4:23; 9:35; 14:14, 35, 36; Luke 4:40; 5:15; 6:17; 7:21; Mark 1:32, 33, 34; 3:10).

8365 *Because I am Jehovah your healer* means that the Lord alone preserves us from evil. This can be seen from the symbolism of *healing* as curing people of evil and preserving them from it. Since disease symbolizes evil, healing symbolizes a curing of it and preservation from it. This is the case in many other places in the Word too, such as in Moses:

> I kill and bring to life, I strike a blow and *heal.* (Deuteronomy 32:39)

In Jeremiah:

> *Heal me, Jehovah, that I may be healed; save me that I may be saved!* (Jeremiah 17:14)

In the same author:

> *I will improve your health* and *heal you of the blows dealt you.* (Jeremiah 30:17)

In David:

> Their whole bed you have transformed *in their illness.* I said, "Jehovah, have mercy on me! *Heal my soul, for I have sinned against you."* (Psalms 41:3, 4)

There are many other passages besides, such as Isaiah 6:10; 53:5; 57:18, 19; Jeremiah 3:22; 17:14; Hosea 6:1; 7:1; 11:3; 14:4; Zechariah 11:16; Psalms 30:2; and elsewhere. Since healing had this symbolism, the Lord also calls himself a doctor:

> The well do not need a doctor, only the ill. I did not come to call the righteous but sinners to repentance. (Matthew 9:12, 13; Mark 2:17; Luke 5:31, 32)

8366 Exodus 15:27. *And they came to Elim, and there were twelve springs of water there and seventy palm trees. And they camped there next to the waters.*

And they came to Elim symbolizes a state in which they were enlightened and touched and therefore in which they were comforted after their trial. *And there were twelve springs of water there* symbolizes abundant quantities of truth for them there. *And seventy palm trees* means the same for truth-based goodness. *And they camped there next to the waters* means that after their trial, religious truth was rearranged by a loving goodness.

8367 *And they came to Elim* symbolizes a state in which they were enlightened and touched and therefore in which they were comforted after their trial. This can be seen from the symbolism of *Elim,* in that it implies and symbolizes the state and nature of the attribute under discussion—as do all the other places the children of Israel went (see §§2643, 3422, 4298, 4442). Here it symbolizes the state after a trial, which is a state of being enlightened and touched and therefore comforted. After any spiritual trial comes a shedding of light and a touching of the heart and consequently delight and pleasure; delight comes when light is shed by truth, and pleasure comes when the heart is touched by goodness. (For the idea that comfort follows times of trial, see §§4572, 5246, 5628, 6829.) [2] That is because through spiritual struggle, truth and goodness are planted in us and yoked together. This leads our spirit farther up into heaven, to communities there that we had never before been a part of. When the trial is over, there opens up a channel of communication with heaven that had previously been partly closed. This contact enlightens and touches us and accordingly brings us delight and pleasure, because the angels with whom we are allowed to communicate then flow in by means of truth and goodness.

Being enlightened by truth and feeling delight as a result is symbolized by the twelve springs of water, because springs symbolize truth. Being touched by truth-based goodness and feeling pleasure as a result is symbolized by the seventy palm trees, as discussed below [§8369].

And there were twelve springs of water there symbolizes abundant quantities of truth for them there. This can be seen from the symbolism of *twelve* as everything taken together (discussed in §§2089, 2129 at the end, 2130 at the end, 3272, 3858, 3913, 7973) and therefore as abundant quantities, and from that of *springs* as religious truth (discussed in §§2702, 3096, 3424, 4861). This shows that *twelve springs of water* symbolize abundant quantities of truth. 8368

It follows that this clause also symbolizes enlightenment and the delight it yields. Anyone with abundant quantities of truth receives enlightenment too, and anyone with enlightenment (and a sincere desire for truth) feels delight.

And seventy palm trees means the same for truth-based goodness—that is, abundant quantities of it, as the following shows: *Seventy* symbolizes everything taken together, much as twelve does (discussed at §7973). And *palm trees* symbolize goodness in a spiritual religion, which is truth-based goodness. Since palms symbolize goodness, they also symbolize a desire for goodness and the pleasure that results, because all pleasure results from a desire for goodness. 8369

Since this was the symbolism of palms, they were used for religious celebrations, such as the Feast of Booths, in keeping with these words in Moses:

> On the first day you shall take yourselves the fruit of a noble tree, *palm fronds,* and the branch of a dense tree, and river willows. And you are to *be glad before Jehovah* your God for seven days. (Leviticus 23:40)

The fruit of a noble tree symbolizes heavenly goodness; palms, spiritual goodness, or goodness that comes of truth; the branch of a dense tree, truth in the form of knowledge; and river willows, truth on the lowest level of the earthly plane. These four, then, symbolize all varieties of goodness and truth in their order.

[2] The following words in John also indicate that palms symbolized sacred celebration inspired by goodness:

> When a numerous crowd that had come to the feast heard that Jesus had come into Jerusalem, *they took up branches of palm trees* and went to meet him and shouted, "Hosanna! A blessing on the one who comes in the Lord's name, the King of Israel!" (John 12:12, 13)

And in the same author, in the Book of Revelation:

> I looked, when there! a numerous crowd standing before the throne and before the Lamb, dressed in white robes, and *palms in their hands.* (Revelation 7:9)

In Joel:

> The grapevine has dried up, and the fig tree droops, the pomegranate tree *and also the palm tree; all joy has dried up* from among the children of humankind. (Joel 1:12)

In David:

> *The upright will flourish like a palm tree;* they will grow like a cedar in Lebanon. (Psalms 92:12)

The palm tree stands for goodness and the cedar for truth.

[3] Because a palm tree symbolizes goodness, it also symbolizes wisdom, since wisdom is a function of goodness. Wisdom is what was symbolized by the palm trees carved onto the walls of the Temple along with guardian beings and flowers. The Temple, you see, symbolized the Lord himself, and in a representative sense, heaven (§§2777, 3720). The guardian beings,

palm trees, and flowers on the walls symbolized providence, wisdom, and understanding received from the Lord and therefore everything that goes to make up heaven.

The fact that these were carved onto the walls of the Temple can be seen in 1 Kings:

> All the walls of the House, all around, Solomon *carved with open carvings of guardian beings* and *palm trees* and *open flowers.* And on the two doors made of olive wood he *carved carvings of guardian beings* and *palm trees* and *open flowers* and overlaid them with gold, so that he spread gold *on the guardian beings* and *on the palm trees.* (1 Kings 6:29, 32)

[4] The carvings represented a heavenly state. The guardian beings represented the Lord's providence and consequently the fact that everything comes from him. (For the meaning of the guardian beings as providence, see §308.) The palm trees represented wisdom, which comes of goodness from the Lord, and the flowers represented understanding, which comes of truth from the Lord. The gold with which the guardian beings and palm trees were overlaid symbolized a loving goodness, which is the dominant trait throughout the heavens. (For the meaning of gold as a loving goodness, see §§113, 1551, 1552, 5658.)

For the same reason, Ezekiel, in describing the new temple (which symbolizes the Lord's heaven), says that *guardian beings* and *palm trees* were everywhere on the walls (Ezekiel 41:17, 18, 20, 25, 26).

And they camped there next to the waters means that after their trial, **8370**
religious truth was rearranged by a loving goodness. This is evident from the symbolism of *camping* as the arrangement of truth and goodness into a pattern (dealt with in §§8103 at the end, 8130, 8131, 8155) and from that of *waters* as religious truth (dealt with in §§2702, 3058, 3424, 4976, 5668). The reason *they camped there next to the waters* means that religious truth was rearranged by a loving goodness is this: A camp symbolizes truth and goodness (§§8193, 8196), camping symbolizes the orderly arrangement of truth and goodness, and *next to the waters* means in keeping with truth imparted by the Divine.

I say it was rearranged by a loving goodness because a loving goodness does all the work of reorganizing truth. Truth applies itself in subordination to goodness and at its direction, and combines with goodness to form a single body (so to speak) in the image of the person in whom they both exist. I say "in the image of the person in whom they exist" because a person's spirit is the actual person (it is the person's inner self), and its image matches perfectly the pattern in which truth is arranged by goodness in that person. That is why it happens that when angels appear in person, an aura of loving goodness pours from them, touching the hearts of those present, and faith with its truth gleams from their faces. In the spiritual world such attributes are seen and perceived clearly.

I say that the rearrangement comes after times of trial because although goodness and truth are planted in us through trials, they are not reorganized till afterward. Conditions during a crisis are chaotic; afterward they are calm. It is when they are calm that things fall into place. So times of trial are actually followed by delight in being enlightened by truth, and pleasure in being touched by goodness, as discussed just above at §8367.

The Spirits and Inhabitants of Jupiter (Continued)

8371 SPIRITS from that planet also informed me about various practices among the inhabitants there, such as their manner of walking, their diet, their homes, and so on.

In regard to their manner of walking, they do not go upright like the inhabitants of our planet and many other planets, nor do they crawl the way animals do. Instead, as they walk they help themselves along with their hands, rising halfway up on their feet from time to time. Another thing they do in walking is to turn their face to the side and back every third step, bowing slightly, in a single quick motion. This is because they consider it improper for others to look at them from any angle except face-on.

8372 As they walk along this way, they keep their face pointing forward, looking out in front, never down at the ground. To face down they call damnable. Only the most contemptible among them do that, and they are banished from society if they do not learn to look out front.

8373 When they sit, they look like the people on our planet, with the upper part of their body erect, but they sit cross-legged.

They are very careful not only when walking but also when sitting to be seen face-on, not from the back. They are willing and happy for others to see their face, because in it their mind is visible. They never display a face at odds with their thoughts and are not even capable of doing so. From it bystanders can also plainly tell a person's feelings about them, which the person does not hide. In particular they can tell whether a person's apparent friendliness is sincere or pretended.

All this was shown to me by their spirits and confirmed by their angels. **8374**
For this reason too they do not seem to walk upright like others but to help themselves forward with their hands (almost like swimmers in the water) and to look around from time to time.

Inhabitants who live in the warm zones go naked except for a loin- **8375**
cloth. They are not ashamed of their nudity, because they have chaste minds, love only their spouses, and abhor adultery.

They were shocked to find that when spirits from our planet saw the way they walked and their nakedness, they laughed at them and had obscene thoughts. Our spirits paid no attention whatever to the heavenly way they live, only to details like these. Their spirits said it was a sign that our spirits are more interested in bodily and worldly matters than heavenly ones and that filth monopolizes our thinking.

I told them that nakedness is not shameful or scandalous to people who live chastely, in a state of innocence, but only to those who live lecherous, shameless lives.

When the inhabitants of that planet lie in bed, they face out into the **8376**
bedroom, not back toward the wall. Their spirits told me this and said it is because they believe that they are facing the Lord when they do so and that they are turning away from him if they face backward.

Something like this had occurred to me a number of times when I myself was in bed, but the reason for it I had not known before.

They enjoy leisurely dining, not so much for the pleasure of the food **8377**
as for the pleasure of the conversation then. When they sit at the table, they sit not on chairs, benches, raised grassy banks, or the grass itself but on the leaves of a certain tree. They were reluctant to say what tree the leaves came from, but I made a number of guesses, and when I finally mentioned fig leaves, they said yes.

They went on to say that they prepared their food with an eye not **8378**
to its flavor but mainly to its usefulness. Useful food, they added, tastes good to them.

Some spirits discussed the issue and said that the practice is a good idea, because to follow it is to take to heart the concept of a healthy mind in a healthy body. For people with whom flavor rules, quite the opposite: the body sickens, or at least weakens internally, so the mind does too. That is because the welfare of the mind matches conditions in the parts of the body receiving [its inflow], just as the quality of vision matches the condition of the eye. Putting appetite in charge leads to the insanity of equating all the pleasure in life and the so-called highest good with luxury and self-indulgence. It also leads to cleverness in matters focusing on the body and the world but stupidity in matters requiring thought and judgment. This causes a person to resemble a brute animal, to which such individuals also compare themselves—not inappropriately.

8379 Their dwellings were also shown to me. They are low, made of wood, lined with a pale blue bark, and dotted with tiny stars all around and overhead to resemble the sky. They like to make the interiors of their houses look like the visible heavens, with all their constellations. This is because they believe the angels have their homes there.

They also have tents, domed and oblong, again sprinkled inside with little stars on a blue field. In these they gather during the day to keep the hot sun from damaging their face. (They protect their face as much as possible, since they do not consider it part of the body.) One of their major concerns is to assemble these tents of theirs and keep them clean. They eat in them too.

8380 They do not care much about worldly interests, because they live by themselves in clans, seeking nothing more than nourishment and a place to live. Anything beyond that they do not count as a necessity, so they do not account it useful. Their greatest concern is the rearing of their children, whom they love most tenderly.

8381 Whenever spirits from Jupiter observed the horses of our planet, the horses looked smaller than usual to me, even though they were reasonably sturdy and tall. The effect was produced by the image of their own horses in the minds of that planet's spirits. They said that they had the same creatures, though much bigger, but that theirs are wild, living in the woods. The sight of these horses terrifies them, they said, even though the animals are harmless, and they added that they have a natural, inborn fear of them. This gave me occasion to ponder the reason for their fear. In the spiritual world a horse represents an intellect formed of knowledge (§§2761, 2762, 6534), and since the idea of using knowledge to cultivate the intellect frightens them, a horse triggers a wave of fear. In what follows you will see that they are uninterested in the knowledge of which human learning consists [§8627].

Spirits from Jupiter placed emissaries (or delegates) with me a number of times to facilitate communication, and they stayed quite a while. 8382
The experience allowed me to see what their character was, that they were totally different from the spirits of our planet. While they were with me, spirits from our planet often harassed them, but they did not care. They just reported it to the company of spirits from Jupiter that had delegated them. When reporting, they pulled away from me a little.

Some evil spirits from our planet were once allowed to exercise their 8383
evil skills and harass the spirits from Jupiter with me. The spirits of Jupiter put up with them for quite a while but finally confessed they could no longer stand it. "We don't think there are any worse people," they said. "They warp our imagination and our thinking so badly that we feel as though we are tied up with ropes we cannot escape from without divine help."

Once, when I read something in the Word about our Savior's suffering [on the cross], certain European spirits dragged in some appalling obstacles to belief with the intention of leading Jupiter's spirits astray. Someone asked who these spirits were and what they had been in the world. It was discovered that some of them had been preachers, not unlike those who call themselves members of the Society of the Lord, or Jesuits, and that they had then been able to move the crowd to tears with their sermons about the Lord's suffering. "This is because in the world they thought one way and spoke another," I told the spirits of Jupiter; "they carried one thing in their hearts and bore another on their lips. Now they are not allowed to speak so deceptively, because when they become spirits, they are forced to speak exactly as they think."

The spirits of Jupiter were absolutely dumbfounded to think that such a big discrepancy could exist between a person's interiors and exteriors—the discrepancy of speaking and thinking in completely different ways. For them it would be impossible.

The spirits of Jupiter have a gentle, agreeable way of approaching 8384
people and a careful way of talking; they weigh their words. This characteristic they draw from their life in the world, where others use various methods of forcing them to repent if they do or say anything out of line. For the obstinate the method is punishment.

They observed that I was thinking I wanted to publish this informa- 8385
tion in our world. They did not want me to publish it, because they are

forbidden to disseminate what their spirits tell them. They were surprised to hear that such information could be shared widely just by the written word. So I told them about the printing press, the Word, and religious teachings in our world and said that the press brings the Word and the teachings out into the public, where people learn about them.

8386 There will be more about the spirits and inhabitants of the planet Jupiter at the end of the next chapter [§§8541–8547].

[CONTINUED IN VOLUME 12]

Biographical Note

EMANUEL SWEDENBORG (1688–1772) was born Emanuel Swedberg (or Svedberg) in Stockholm, Sweden, on January 29, 1688 (Julian calendar). He was the third of the nine children of Jesper Swedberg (1653–1735) and Sara Behm (1666–1696). At the age of eight he lost his mother. After the death of his only older brother ten days later, he became the oldest living son. In 1697 his father married Sara Bergia (1666–1720), who developed great affection for Emanuel and left him a significant inheritance. His father, a Lutheran clergyman, later became a celebrated and controversial bishop, whose diocese included the Swedish churches in Pennsylvania and in London, England.

After studying at the University of Uppsala (1699–1709), Emanuel journeyed to England, the Netherlands, France, and Germany (1710–1715) to study and work with leading scientists in western Europe. Upon his return he apprenticed as an engineer under the brilliant Swedish inventor Christopher Polhem (1661–1751). He gained favor with Sweden's King Charles XII (1682–1718), who gave him a salaried position as an overseer of Sweden's mining industry (1716–1747). Although Emanuel was engaged, he never married.

After the death of Charles XII, Emanuel was ennobled by Queen Ulrika Eleonora (1688–1741), and his last name was changed to Swedenborg (or Svedenborg). This change in status gave him a seat in the Swedish House of Nobles, where he remained an active participant in the Swedish government throughout his life.

A member of the Royal Swedish Academy of Sciences, he devoted himself to studies that culminated in a number of publications, most notably a comprehensive three-volume work on natural philosophy and metallurgy (1734) that brought him recognition across Europe as a scientist. After 1734 he redirected his research and publishing to a study of anatomy in search of the interface between the soul and body, making several significant discoveries in physiology.

From 1743 to 1745 he entered a transitional phase that resulted in a shift of his main focus from science to theology. Throughout the rest of his life he maintained that this shift was brought about by Jesus Christ, who appeared to him, called him to a new mission, and opened his perception to a permanent dual consciousness of this life and the life after death.

He devoted the last decades of his life to studying Scripture and publishing eighteen theological titles that draw on the Bible, reasoning, and his own spiritual experiences. These works present a Christian theology with unique perspectives on the nature of God, the spiritual world, the Bible, the human mind, and the path to salvation.

Swedenborg died in London on March 29, 1772 (Gregorian calendar), at the age of eighty-four.

The Swedenborg Foundation

is a nonprofit organization supported by the contributions of individuals and foundations. All the books we publish are made possible by the generous support of our donors. Connect with us at www.swedenborg.com to support this and other publishing projects, learn about membership opportunities, and purchase or freely access Swedenborg's writings.